S0-AZG-470

TRUSTEE FOR A CITY:
RALPH LOWELL OF BOSTON

TRUSTEE

MARK I. GELFAND

FOR A CITY

RALPH LOWELL OF BOSTON

NORTHEASTERN UNIVERSITY PRESS • Boston

Northeastern University Press

Copyright 1998 by Mark I. Gelfand

Library of Congress Cataloging-in-Publication Data
Gelfand, Mark I.
Trustee for a city : Ralph Lowell of Boston / Mark I. Gelfand.
p.   cm.
ISBN 1-55553-369-8 (cloth : alk. paper)
1. Lowell, Ralph, 1890–1978.   2. Boston (Mass.)—Biography.
3. Elite (Social sciences)—Massachusetts—Boston—Biography.
4. Bankers—Massachusetts—Boston—Biography.   5. Boston (Mass.)—
Social life and customs.   6. Lowell family.   I. Title.
F73.54.L69G45   1998
974.4'6104'092—dc21
[b]   98-22252

Designed by Janice Wheeler

Composed in Dante by G&S Typesetters, Austin, Texas.
Printed and bound by Maple Press, York, Pennsylvania.
The paper is Maple Eggshell, an acid-free sheet.

MANUFACTURED IN THE UNITED STATES OF AMERICA
02   01   00   99   98   5   4   3   2   1

In loving appreciation of
AMELIE RUSSELL GELFAND
ETHAN RUSSELL GELFAND

In loving memory of
ADAM RUSSELL GELFAND
(April 20, 1981–February 6, 1992)
Our Sun

CONTENTS

ILLUSTRATIONS

PREFACE

This is a biography of a man and his city. "Other cities have their histories," observed *Fortune* magazine in 1933. "The history of Boston is biography. And the Bostonian is by all odds the city's most striking characteristic." Although each of America's major metropolises can assemble a colorful cast of notable individuals to flesh out its past, only Boston's heritage is presented in terms of a specific class. "A Bostonian, as all the world understands the epithet," *Fortune* continued, "is a member of one of the old Yankee families. . . . A Bostonian, that is to say, is a Cabot or a Lowell." Six decades later, the "Cold Roast Boston" or "Brahmin Boston" that *Fortune* referred to, and which Ralph Lowell (1890–1978) grew up in, has faded away, replaced by a "New Boston," which Ralph Lowell helped to create. What follows is an attempt to use biography to examine change and continuity in one of this nation's most fascinating cities.

Two books published during Ralph Lowell's lifetime amplified *Fortune's* description of "a Bostonian." *The Proper Bostonians* (1947) by Cleveland Amory, himself a scion of a Boston "First Family," is an anecdotal description of the important traits, and especially the eccentricities, of this august group. From their having "Grandfather on the Brain" to their "Belles and Grandes Dames," from their generous charitable giving to their penny-pinching on themselves, from their lack of manners to their exclusive clubs, Boston's elite in the nineteenth and twentieth centuries is both pilloried and celebrated in Amory's volume. Ralph Lowell is mentioned just once—as the fourth-generation trustee of his family's educational trust. But his ancestors and relatives are well represented, particularly his paternal grandfather, Judge John Lowell. Amory tells of the morning the maid burned the last of the oatmeal in the judge's household. For Mrs. Lowell, "this is no minor domestic tragedy. To the best of his wife's knowledge Judge John Lowell has up until this morning had oatmeal every single day of his life. The silence is nerve-racking. Slowly the paper is lowered and the face of the judge appears. Then the reply: 'Frankly, my dear, I never did care for it.'" For Amory the significance of the story is that "in Boston the tradition of the ceremonial breakfast lives on"—he notes that "Mrs. Ralph Lowell . . . serves oatmeal every morning." By the 1960s, however, Ralph Lowell was no longer eating oatmeal.

A decade before Amory supplied Boston's Brahmins with a new label, novelist John P. Marquand personalized the type in his Pulitzer Prize–winning novel, *The Late George Apley* (1937). With his archaic and parochial values, his snobbery, and his inability to move beyond his environment, George Apley (1866–1933) became the symbol of a caste totally out of touch with the times. Ralph Lowell, making his way through life a generation after the fictional Apley, was born into many of the same constraints, but was able to break free of more of them. "For better or worse," George Apley advised his son, "we are what we are. Don't try to be different." Lowell would not be too much "different," but neither would he follow only along the "narrow groove" Apley had found carved out for him by his family. The Boston of Lowell's era was open to greater change than the city Apley knew, and Lowell adjusted—although not always willingly—to his new surroundings.

Lowell generally felt uncomfortable about being associated with Marquand's protagonist. (A journalist meeting him for the first time in 1962 described Lowell in his notes as "an amiable man of 72 with a white mustache and a quick smile who is the personification of that stock cartoon character, the Old Grad.") However, he fully subscribed to one aspect of the Apley credo. George's father told him that it was his "obligation . . . to try to make your life worth while with the advantages God has given you," and George told his son that one should "think of one's self as a steward who owes the community a definite debt." Apley tried to live according to these beliefs, but approached death convinced that "everything I have done has amounted almost to nothing." Lowell, exposed to the same values as a youth and conveying them to his own children, left a remarkable legacy of achievement.

Marquand, who subtitled his book "A Novel in the Form of a Memoir," advanced his narrative largely through the device of the "collected letters" of George Apley. Although some of Ralph Lowell's correspondence has been preserved, the most important source of information about his life is his diaries. The first entries are those of a teenager; the last find him in his eighties. The record is broken by large gaps; except for some short periods, there is nothing for the years 1914–1938. Since Lowell's conscious intent in keeping diaries was not to record history—he thought his children might find them of interest—there are important omissions even where he kept a faithful accounting of his activities. People and issues often are not fully identified; a pending matter may be discussed at some length and its resolution days or weeks later not mentioned at all. Nonetheless, the diaries offer a rare opportunity to trace the career of an individual who operated largely outside the public realm, but whose accomplishments served the public weal.

Although less well known than his distant cousin the poet Robert Lowell (1917–1977), Ralph Lowell is equally worthy of biographical attention. The only place Robert and Ralph came close to crossing paths regularly was at McLean Hospital, in suburban Boston, where the former went for psychiatric help and the latter was chairman of the trustees' committee. Ralph Lowell was neither as creative nor as disturbed as Robert. But he led an incredibly rich life that offers fascinating insights into a social milieu that has all but disappeared. His story exemplifies the efforts of a pivotal generation to come to grips with a world quite different from the one into which they were born.

ACKNOWLEDGMENTS

This project has taken quite a while and I have incurred many personal debts in completing it. I owe the most, perhaps, to an individual I did not have the opportunity to meet. Charlotte Loring Lowell died in 1984, a few years before I began my study of her husband's career, but it was her strong commitment to and pride in Ralph's civic activities that made this biography possible. By compiling scrapbooks documenting his busy schedule and, more important, by making sure that Ralph's diaries and other papers found a welcome home in the Massachusetts Historical Society (of which he had been a member since 1945), Mrs. Lowell has provided students of twentieth-century Boston with valuable resources. Carrying on the tradition, her children have welcomed me into their homes and offices to share memories of their parents.

Two other Lowell relatives were also particularly supportive. Ralph's nephew John Lowell Thorndike, the family's unofficial historian of his generation, and his wife, Dorothy, allowed me to hunt through their attic for documents and pictures. They also offered perceptive insights that only people close to a situation but not personally involved in it can supply. Mr. Thorndike's nephew Will, although too young to offer firsthand information about his great-uncle and learning of the biography only in its later stages, took a keen interest in the endeavor and played an indispensable role in seeing it through to publication.

One of the advantages of doing recent history is the chance to have contact (if only by mail) with many of the people who figure in your chronicle, and I wish to thank those individuals (only some of whose names appear in the endnotes) who helped me better understand Ralph Lowell's Boston: the late David W. Bailey; Richard E. Bennink; the late William Bentinck-Smith; Gerald W. Blakeley; Francis H. Burr; the late Harold Clancy; the late John F. Collins; Lawrence Creshkoff; Robert T. H. Davidson; David M. Davis; H. Bruce Ehrmann; the late Byron K. Elliott; David Farrell; Lawrence H. Fuchs; G. H. Griffiths; Edward J. Hanify; William Harley; Francis W. Hatch; the late Robert Haydock Jr.; David O. Ives; Ernest W. Jennes; Edward J. Logue; Francis de Marneffe; David A. Mittell; Ruth Perkins; George Putnam; Perry Rathbone; James T. Robertson; E. G. Sherburne Jr.; Richard Norton Smith; Roger P. Sonnabend; Davis Taylor; W. Nicholas Thorndike; Richard J. Whalen; Donald J. White; and William W. Wolbach. Two individuals were especially helpful. Although we never had an opportunity to talk face-to-face, Parker Wheatley, through many telephone conversations and lengthy correspondence, provided me with his side of the enormously productive yet awkward relationship he had with the Trustee of the Lowell Institute. If Mr. Wheatley could not overcome the barriers "Cold Roast Boston" placed before outsiders, David C. Crockett was the consummate insider, and in several interviews—conducted at the Massachusetts General Hospital and the Tavern Club—he allowed me to get around some of those hurdles, as I sought to comprehend a society far different from the one with which I was familiar.

Skilled professionals at several libraries and archives facilitated my use of their collections. At the Massachusetts Historical Society, where I spent much of my time, Virginia Smith and Peter Drummey made me feel at home as I worked my way through Mr. Lowell's diaries and Mrs. Lowell's papers; and Chris Steele assisted in the reproduction of photographs. When I first approached WGBH/Channel 2 about using its archives, I was met by puzzled looks—the station did not have any organized set of records—but since then, under the able direction of Mary Ide, this leader in educational broadcasting has put its historical house in order. Harley P. Holden, Curator of the Harvard University Archives, speedily processed my requests for permission to examine closed materials. The Museum of Fine Arts' Maureen Melton was most cooperative in making the papers in her domain available. Aaron Schmidt of the Print Department of the Boston Public Library helped me use the photograph files of the *Boston Herald*; at the *Boston Globe*, Timothy Leland, Peter Southwick, and Lisa Tuite were most cooperative. Margo McDonough and her staff at the Interlibrary Loan Department at O'Neill Library of Boston College were indefatigable in tracking down my requests for odd items, while John Atte-bury and Ron Patkus of the College's Burns Library assisted me in us-ing their special collections. Robert Bruns, the O'Neill Library's history specialist, was an expert source of information about both new and old publications.

I am grateful to John Weingartner at Northeastern University Press for his faith in this project and his excellent ideas for making it better. Thanks are also due Martha Yager for her deft copy editing and Ann Twombly for her patience and skill in guiding the book into print.

Several colleagues in the Boston College History Department were generous in sharing their encyclopedic knowledge of Boston, as well as their common sense. Andrew Bunie, Thomas H. O'Connor (who also in-troduced me to Northeastern University Press), and Alan Lawson read se-lected chapters—if this material has not been improved as a consequence, the fault is mine, not theirs. In her own quiet way, Lois Bilsky was most help-ful, and Jim Cronin was most thoughtful in a time of need. Connie Burns and Rick Gentile were graduate students when I came to B.C. nearly a quar-ter century ago, and they have never ceased educating this New Yorker about the wonders and subtleties of their native city. I hope that they will be able to recognize their contributions, along with those of the late Allen M. Wakstein (a Bostonian through and through), to this biography.

The family of any biographer must feel that they have had an uninvited visitor thrust into their midst, and my wife Amelie and son Ethan have more reason than most to resent that intrusion—for Ralph Lowell, once allowed into our household, has stayed for a very long time. But neither has ever expressed a negative thought or even a discouraging word. They have put up with a great deal, but have always remained supportive. I rec-ognize that it could not have been done without them and want them to see this book as I do: a joint enterprise.

I wish I could stop here, with expressions of heartfelt gratitude to so many, but the years of preparing this study of one individual's rich life have also been filled with death and tragedy. Only weeks after I began, my father passed away. No books will be written about Samuel Gelfand, but he deserves at least part of a paragraph. He had arrived in this country as a young boy fleeing czarist Russia, when Ralph Lowell was an undergrad-uate at Harvard, and while he would not have a formal education beyond the eighth grade, my father became a model American success story. Very much at home in the business climate of Manhattan's Lower East Side, he rose into the middle class and, with my mother, raised four sons, sent them off to college, and saw them become professionals and start families of their own. When he died, in great pain, a day after his eighty-third birthday, we who knew and loved him could both mourn our loss and celebrate a life fully lived.

Several years later my wife lost her father. Martin Russell had ancestral roots in New England as deep as those of Ralph Lowell, but by the early twentieth century his family had relocated to New York. A teenager during the Great Depression, he served in the army in Europe, married a girl from Brooklyn and had three children, earned a Master's degree in geology, and eventually became an editor of technical publications. An uncommonly generous person, he volunteered to edit my chapters as I composed them; unfortunately, much was still unwritten when he died suddenly of a heart attack. Although he enjoyed pointing out the foibles of modern life, he got the most out of life of anyone I have known; he had just finished one of his favorite pastimes—picking wild blueberries—when his heart gave out.

I doubt I would have offered either of these brief profiles of private lives if there had not been a third and, by any manner of reckoning, unnatural death. Our older son, Adam, was just a few weeks short of his ninth birthday when he was diagnosed with an inoperable brain tumor, and only two months short of his eleventh birthday when he died. Lacking the objectivity (that I hope is present in the pages that follow) necessary to capture Adam's essence in my own words, I will rely on a portion of the remarks his Grandma Julia Gelfand delivered at his funeral: "I could say he was a special child, but every child is special. But I do think he had a special quality. Kind, generous, gentle, so loving and caring. And so unassuming, considering what a brilliant mind that child had. Sometimes I think he was a special gift, given to us just for a little time. But in those few years he made such an impact on so many people, that he has left an indelible mark on all those who were privileged to know and love him."

The Lowells of Boston: A Genealogy

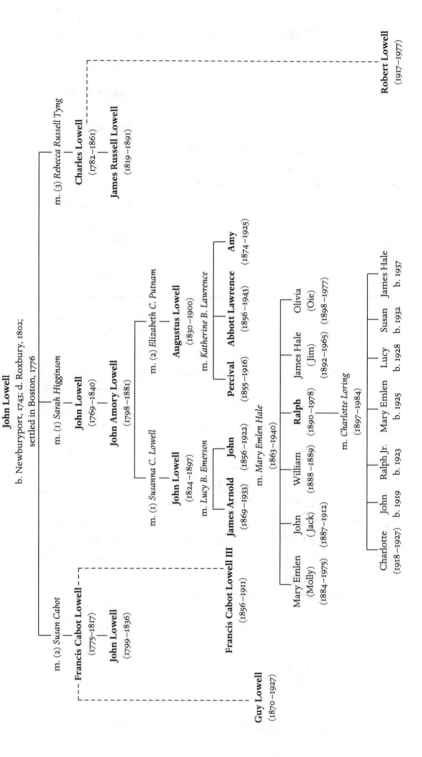

TO BE BORN A LOWELL,
1890-1940

Life magazine typically employed eye-catching cover photographs to spur newsstand sales, and the March 18, 1957, issue was no exception: it featured a color photo of veteran vaudeville star Beatrice Lillie with scantily clad (for the 1950s) showgirls from the New Ziegfeld Follies. In the top right-hand corner, however, the attention of potential buyers was directed to an article of a different sort. "One of America's Great Families — The Lowells of Massachusetts," proclaimed the bold type, and inside, readers found a ten-page spread describing how "the descendants of a famous family carry on their great tradition." Pictured at the beginning was sixty-six-year-old Ralph Lowell in a three-piece suit sitting in his suburban Boston home, his Phi Beta Kappa key hanging from his vest pocket, his honorary degree from Harvard clearly visible on the wall behind him. "Though [the Lowells] have been ambitious as anyone else," the text noted, "long tradition has taught them to measure success in useful citizenship rather than wealth. Centuries of dedication to their community has made them one of America's first families." [1]

Life had broached the idea for the article with Ralph Lowell the preceding fall. The Boston correspondent informed him in a letter that the magazine was planning a series on "America's great families" and expected over the next two years to profile an undetermined number of such families from different regions of the country. "No family in New England, or indeed the entire nation," the *Life* man wrote, "is more deserving of the label of 'great' than the Lowells. This I say not as an offering of flattery—it is simply a fact." *Life* promised to do nothing that might "detract from the dignity" of the family and to take special care to "avoid embarrassment." Lowell would have veto power over every picture and "every bit of written material" before the article went to press.[2]

Believing the focus of the project would be historical, Ralph gave his blessing, just as he had a decade earlier when he assisted in the preparation of a book detailing the Lowells' place in American society through ten generations.[3] That volume had stopped with his parents' generation; as research for the *Life* article began to center increasingly on Ralph he sought to back out, not wanting the magazine to "blow my horn." He exploded when he heard that *Life* photographers would be at Thanksgiving dinner (Mrs. Lowell had given her consent). "The day belongs to the family," he wrote in his diary, "and pictures of it for publication is a cheapening of the day and [an] invasion of the privacy of the family." Ralph told *Life* he had "no desire to be 'exploited'" and said the article should be canceled "to save both our time and our tempers." To appease him, *Life* reaffirmed his veto power; after discussing the matter with his wife and younger brother, he agreed to allow a Thanksgiving Day group photograph of himself and Charlotte Lowell, five of their children (along with four spouses), and eleven of their grandchildren. (Not present were a daughter, son-in-law, and one grandchild.) A follow-up plea from the number-two man in the Time-Life hierarchy, who served with Lowell on the Harvard Board of Overseers, brought a renewal of Ralph's full cooperation.[4]

In January, Lowell was presented with galleys of the *Life* piece and gave his approval. "I don't think the article will do much harm,"

he noted in his diary. The March publication date also pleased him—
it meant that when the magazine came out, he and Charlotte would
be on a cruise ship in the Atlantic off the coast of Africa. By the time
he returned to Boston in April, that issue of *Life* would have faded
from view.[5]

While paying homage to the "remarkable impression" left on
America by earlier generations of Lowells—two notable poets, four
federal judges, a famous college president, a key player in the birth
of industrial New England, an astronomer who discovered a planet
he never saw, and several who helped run Harvard and M.I.T.—the
article focused on the contemporary crop of Lowells. Those pictured were Ralph's brother and two sisters, and five close and distant
cousins; among the latter was poet Robert Lowell, who had won the
Pulitzer Prize at age thirty a decade earlier. But the dominant figure
was Ralph, whom the article described as "a Republican, Mason,
clubman, and reasonably wealthy banker, . . . a man of culture, humor, and deep interest in his community." Citing his membership
on the boards of sixty-five organizations, among them six hospitals
and twelve welfare organizations, *Life* observed that "to accomplish
his monumental daily schedule he lives quietly, entertains rarely, in-
sists on punctuality." Photographs showed Ralph at the bank where
he was president and chairman of the board; at the Museum of Fine
Arts, where he was president; at Harvard's Peabody Museum, in his
capacity as chairman of the Overseers' Committee to Visit the Department of Anthropology; at M.I.T., where he was a Life Member
of the Corporation; and at the studios of WGBH-TV, whose very
existence was the product of his activities as Trustee of the Lowell
Institute. The article's coda was the Thanksgiving Day portrait of
Ralph and his family.*

---

* *Life* profiled two other families, the du Ponts of Wilmington, Delaware, and the Evanses of
Denver, in a similar fashion over the next two years; in neither instance, however, did an indi-

Several years later, recounting for an interviewer the story of the *Life* profile, Ralph insisted on drawing a distinction between publicity for the Lowell family—which he believed appropriate—and publicity for himself. "[H]ell, I don't want them to treat me," he declared, "because I'm just a product of the Lowell family. If it wasn't for what the Lowell family had done in the past, they wouldn't be picking on me, you see. So, they shouldn't put me up as the top thing." When the interviewer pressed him further, asking if he felt the uniqueness of belonging to such a family, Ralph interjected: "No, what I mean is that I'm trying to carry on the traditions of the Lowell family, and if the Lowell family were different, I'd feel the same way about being a member of that family. It just happens that there have been quite a number of distinguished Lowells, that's all." But being one of the Lowells, given what they were, meant a lot to Ralph.[6]

---

vidual living member of the family receive the attention accorded Ralph Lowell. *Life*, August 19, 1957, pp. 99–111; June 15, 1959, pp. 103–111.

1

"Where the Lowells speak to the Cabots . . ."

GROWING UP IN
BRAHMIN BOSTON

A t every stage of his life, Ralph Lowell viewed the world—and perhaps more important, the world viewed him—through a lens shaped by his family name. Opportunities were offered and setbacks cushioned by the fact that Ralph belonged to one of the most prominent families in Boston and New England. Being born a Lowell imposed significant burdens in terms of other people's expectations and Ralph's sense of obligation to meet the standards established by his ancestors. But it also gave Ralph a substantial head start in making his life a full and rich one.

OF LOWELLS NAMED JOHN AND OTHERWISE

Lowells had been making their mark in Massachusetts for slightly more than a century before Ralph was born in 1890, but it was during the first forty years of his life that the clan's fame reached its peak. Although the death in 1891 of James Russell Lowell at the age of seventy-two closed a much heralded literary career that had helped make nineteenth-century Boston the "Athens of America," younger Lowells soon made their own reputations. Francis Cabot Lowell III, great-grandson and namesake of the man who brought the industrial revolution to America in the 1810s, was first a federal district court judge and then a circuit court judge, duplicating the careers of two earlier Lowells who had been appointed to the bench by Presidents Washington and Lincoln, respectively. Stepping into a fresh field, Francis Cabot Lowell's first cousin Guy Lowell became a successful architect; among his designs were three buildings at Harvard, the new home of Boston's Museum of Fine Arts, and a hexagon-shaped county courthouse in Manhattan, which was built after he won a national competition.

A trio of Lowell siblings from another branch of the family attained wider notoriety. Percival, bearing the name of the first Lowell to settle in America in 1639, earned recognition initially as an expert on Japanese culture, then turned to astronomy, building an observatory in Arizona in 1894. His "discovery" of a network of canals on Mars and his suggestion that it indicated the presence of intelligent life created a sensation. Percival's later work in calculating the perturbations in Neptune's orbit proved to be more substantial; it pointed the way toward the detection, fourteen years after his death in 1916, of a ninth planet, Pluto, whose name incorporates this Lowell's initials.

Closer to home, Percival's sister Amy developed into an iconoclast. None of the previous generations of Lowell women had been anything but dutiful and conventional daughters and wives, but Amy, inheriting considerable wealth at the age of twenty-six and never marrying, soaked up the insurgent spirit of the Progressive Era. From her cigar smoking, to her speaking out on local educational controversies, to her avant-garde poetry, for which she won recognition in literary circles, she made good newspaper copy.

And then there was Percival and Amy's brother, Abbott Lawrence, usually referred to in print as A. Lawrence, and known within the family as Lawrence. Named for his maternal grandfather, a towering figure in the history of New England's textile industry, Lawrence practiced law in partnership with his cousin Francis Cabot Lowell III for almost twenty years. Lawrence, however, found a legal career unsatisfying and, not dependent on the earnings it produced, he devoted much of his time to writing articles and books on government. In 1897 Lawrence's scholarship prompted an invitation from Harvard to teach; his course, Government 10, became so popular that three years later he was made a professor. Immersing himself in educational issues, Lawrence set his sights on the presidency of Harvard and in 1909 achieved his goal. Holding that position for almost the next quarter century, Lowell sat at the apex of Boston's social and cultural pyramid like few before him and none after.[1]

Percival, Amy, and Lawrence were first cousins of Ralph Lowell's father, but while they made headlines, John Lowell (1856–1922) lived his life in obscurity. Not that this life was without accomplishment: John enjoyed the respect of his peers in the legal profession and he gave liberally of his time to several community organizations. If he was overshadowed by his more creative and adventurous cousins, he bequeathed a legacy none of them did: children.

John was the sixth in a direct line of Lowells to be given that name. The first was a Congregationalist minister. The next two chose the law for a career; both were active politically, their involvement spanning the Revolutionary and Early National periods. The next John Lowell (who also used his middle name, Amory) followed his uncle, the first Francis Cabot Lowell, into textile manufacturing. John Amory Lowell's younger son, Augustus (the father of Percival, Amy, and Lawrence), maintained the Lowells' conspicuous position in New England's textile industry through the remainder of the nineteenth century, while his older son, John (Ralph's grandfather), opted to practice law.

Although Ralph's soft-spoken grandfather (1824–1897) eschewed the partisan brand of politics in which the two previous generations of Lowell lawyers had reveled, he matched or exceeded them in the number of his presidential appointments. John became a federal judge in 1865—he was one of the last of President Lincoln's nominees—because of his expertise in bankruptcy law and his family's influence. On the bench Lowell was known among members of the bar as a "wayward judge, independent to the verge of willfulness in establishing justice." It was said that he "loved justice more than he did law." In 1884, when he resigned his circuit court judgeship (to which he had been elevated in 1878), the Boston Merchants Association honored him with a dinner at the Hotel Vendôme attended by more than two hundred of the city's economic elite.[2]

Familial financial concerns were behind the decision to leave the bench. Public service entailed a sacrifice of income, a loss magnified by the wealth John's half-brother Augustus had accumulated as their father's business associate. John Amory Lowell generously supplemented his older son's judicial salary, but not enough to match the benefits that Augustus received from his textile interests. Moreover, Augustus had married a daughter of the wealthy Lawrence family; their combined wealth placed them among the very richest couples in Boston society. John's choice of a spouse left him further behind. Lucy Buckminster Emerson was the daughter of George B. Emerson, principal of one of the first private schools for young ladies and a botanist of some note. The Emersons were most respectable socially and quite comfortable economically, but not in the same category as the Lawrences. John and Lucy's children would always have the best that Boston had to offer, but Augustus's children were the beneficiaries of large trusts that allowed them to pursue their interests without regard to earning a living. The sons of John and Lucy had to find gainful employment.[3]

In the early 1880s the judge's oldest son, John, was struggling to establish a legal practice. He and his cousin Lawrence, who was seven months younger, had been classmates at Harvard College (class of 1877) and Harvard Law School, but their paths diverged. Lawrence regarded his years as an attorney as little more than a holding action while he developed his taste for scholarship and educational politics. For John, law was both a highly honored profession and a source of income, and it was to promote the latter benefit that his father removed his black robes and became John's partner. Drawing upon the older man's prestige and contacts, the firm of Lowell & Lowell prospered.

Employer liability law became the partnership's specialty. In 1887, the Massachusetts legislature stripped away many of the legal defenses that judges had constructed over the previous four decades to shield employers from damage suits filed by workers injured on the job. Confronted with a more level playing field in the courts, employers recognized the necessity of insuring themselves. The London-based Employers' Liability Assurance Company, the first firm to write such policies in the United States, located its American headquarters in Boston. To ease its entry into this new market, the company sought out local leaders for key positions; it appointed former judge John Lowell as general counsel.[4]

The general counsel not only advised the company on corporate matters but also supervised its extensive litigation practice. Policyholders looked to the company to defend them against employee suits, and this task the general counsel assigned to his son. The younger Lowell took to courtroom advocacy in a way his father never had, trying an average of 150 cases a year. Typically these cases were heard by a jury, but because juries were likely to be more sympathetic to the worker than to the employer or its insurer, Lowell became especially skillful in persuading judges to take cases away from the jury and decide them alone. Lowell was also adept at laying a basis for appeals, and he argued many of the cases that the Massachusetts Supreme Judicial Court heard in its attempts to clear up the ambiguities of the 1887 statute.[5]

After his father's death in 1897, Lowell succeeded him as general counsel, and through the first decade of the new century Employers' Liability's affairs remained the mainstay of his law firm's business. However, there was growing unhappiness in Massachusetts and elsewhere in the nation about the way industrial accidents were being handled in the legal system. Neither social reformers, who wanted greater security for workers, nor employers and insurance companies, which opposed the escalating costs of litigation and jury awards, found the uncertainties of the existing system acceptable. Following the lead of other states, Massachusetts passed the Workmen's Compensation Act of 1911, which replaced courtroom battles with administratively determined payments to injured workers. Lowell's highly technical game of legal maneuver was no longer useful; while the change did not wipe out Lowell's practice, it put a severe dent in it.[6]*

John had a longstanding interest in raising the ethics of the legal profession, and he spent much of the decade before his death in 1922 fighting for that cause. In an article that was published posthumously in the *American Bar Association Journal*, of which he had been an associate editor, Lowell pointed out how the passage of laws establishing new crimes had created additional opportunities for dishonest lawyers:

> Members of the bar are generally aware that for many years there has been a class of attorneys who devote themselves almost entirely to the criminal law. . . . The first essential function of the so-called criminal attorney is not to try cases to the end that justice may be done. He is, on the contrary, a broker in crime, . . . [and] conditions in the criminal law today offer him a profitable market.

Problems clearly existed in the criminal justice system—Lowell's article was sparked by the Massachusetts Supreme Judicial Court's removal of a district attorney from his office because he had solicited and accepted bribes in exchange for going easy on criminal suspects. But there was a distinct social dimension to the Brahmin attorney's harsh tone. Few lawyers practicing in the criminal courts shared Lowell's family background or education, and in keeping with the class consciousness of the times, the elite members of the bar viewed those who lacked such backgrounds and edu-

---

* John's younger brother and law partner, James Arnold Lowell, a state representative, shepherded the measure through the legislature.

cation as black marks on the profession, whether they practiced criminal law or not.[7]

Like his father, John steered clear of overt political action, but his legal career reflected century-old family attitudes on socioeconomic issues. Lowells had been Federalists when Jeffersonians championed republicanism, and they had been Whigs when Jacksonians advocated the rights of the common man. John Lowell's defense of employers in the courtroom and his campaign to keep pettifoggers out demonstrated a lack of sympathy for society's underdogs at a time when the baneful effects of Lowell-inspired industrialization and urbanization were reaching a crisis point. John passed on his conservative outlook to his children, for whom it remained a basic point of reference as they moved through their own tumultuous era.

MARY EMLEN HALE LOWELL

Through marriage the Lowells were linked to almost every prominent Boston family; through his mother, Ralph was also tied to the loftiest social circles in Philadelphia. Mary Emlen Hale carried the names of two of that city's finest Quaker families and was related to still another. A mid-nineteenth-century chronicler of distinguished Philadelphians described the Emlens as "one of the oldest and most respectable families of Friends." On her mother's side, Mary was descended from the Norris family, whose original forebear in North America had been designated by William Penn in his will as a trustee for the Holy Commonwealth that Penn had carved out along the Delaware River. Although not quite on the same level as the Emlens, the Hales had demonstrated their skills in the countinghouse and their commitment to good works. Mary was the only child of Sarah Emlen and James C. Hale. Ralph and his siblings never knew their maternal grandfather; he died in a carriage accident when Mary was just three. She was raised by her mother in Rittenhouse Square in a house they shared with Sarah's uncle.[8]

Mary was two months past her twentieth birthday when she married John Lowell, then twenty-seven, at Philadelphia's Saint James Episcopal Church in October 1883. The details of their meeting and courtship are unknown; the sole surviving piece of correspondence is a letter John wrote his younger brother when the engagement was announced in December 1882. "I am afraid," John noted, alluding to one of his great interests, "we shall have to convert her to base-ball, as she is very fond of cricket and goes to almost all the matches." Perhaps in exchange for this conversion, John left Unitarianism, which three preceding generations of Lowells had practiced, to join the Episcopalian communion of his bride. By the latter part of the nineteenth century, many of Philadelphia's leading Quaker families had adopted Episcopalianism, prodded by their female members who were attracted to the elaborate rites of that faith. Since several of Boston's finest families, including the Lawrences, had done likewise, the switch did no harm to the Lowells' social standing.[9]

John and Mary set up housekeeping in residences provided by his parents. During the 1850s John and Lucy Lowell had given up their house on Beacon Hill to settle in the Chestnut Hill district of Newton, five miles west of the State House. This area had been farmed since colonial times, but with the construction of a railroad line in the mid-nineteenth century, new uses for the land became practical. Francis L. Lee, the elder John's Harvard classmate and cousin, whose family had owned property there for three decades, decided to transform Chestnut Hill into a residential hamlet for Boston's wealthy. He enlisted the support of relatives—other Lees, a Saltonstall, and John Lowell—who agreed to purchase land and move their families there. By the 1880s they had created what one contemporary guidebook called a "charming semi-English suburb."

The Lowell estate of nearly 150 acres included Hammond's Pond and the woods that surrounded it to the east, north, and west. Except for the infrequent disturbance caused by a passing railroad train, the area was filled only with the sounds of nature. "[R]ank and luxuriant lowland glades alternated with rocky hills," making these woods "one of the most interesting and beautiful forests in New England, rich in every variety of ferns and lichens and abounding in rare plants and brilliant flowers." Raised in such surroundings, Ralph developed a love for nature that would stay with him until the day he died.[10]

When John and Lucy bought the property it was occupied by an eighteenth-century farmhouse, which they enlarged and remodeled extensively. It became the home of Ralph's parents after their marriage, and he was born there. John and Lucy moved into what once had been a barn but was now transformed into a striking Shingle-style house. Both homes were quite pleasant, but they were humble in comparison with the spacious mansion that merchant Ralph H. White constructed at the crest of Chestnut Hill in 1886 and the twenty-five-room, gray stone mansion that Christian Science founder Mary Baker Eddy purchased nearby in 1907.

John and Mary called Chestnut Hill home from spring until autumn. The remainder of the year they lived in the fashionable Back Bay, at a hotel for the first few years of their marriage and then in the townhouse at 24 Commonwealth Avenue, purchased by John's parents. This relocation afforded the adult Lowells of both generations a greater opportunity to participate in Boston's active social season, and gave Ralph and his siblings easier access to the city's private schools. Although the odd-numbered houses on the north side of Commonwealth Avenue usually were considered more desirable because they received sunlight in the front, number 24 had considerable social cachet because it was on the first block of Commonwealth, between Arlington and Berkeley Streets, just steps from the Public Garden. Like the dwellings in Chestnut Hill, the five-story building offered ample space for the Lowells and their staff of servants.[11]

Whether in Chestnut Hill or the Back Bay, Mary made for John "the sort of home the Lowell men had always loved, always had." Lowell men, observed John's cousin, "were never practical in home affairs, not even to the care of their own clothes, whether they put on an overcoat, had their gloves, carfare." With many Lowell relatives and friends living nearby, the Lowell residences saw a constant stream of visitors. "Everyone knew everything about everyone else every day down to the latest baby's last rash or tooth." [12]

To this big extended family John and Mary made their own substantial contribution. Their first child, Mary Emlen, was born in July 1884. Slightly less than three years later they had a son, John, and on Christmas Day of 1888 they had a second son, William Emlen, named after his mother's maternal grandfather. William died before reaching his first birthday. Two more sons followed: Ralph Emerson (as listed in the public records) in July 1890 and James Hale in May 1892. The family was completed in 1898 with the birth of Olivia, named for her father's deceased older sister.

In the naming of the children, Ralph was set somewhat apart. The parents apparently alternated between their families in searching for names, and Ralph was the only child with a name not easily recognizable as a Lowell, an Emlen, or a Hale. Instead, he was named in memory of his Grandmother Lucy's cousin, the Transcendentalist philosopher Ralph Waldo

Emerson, who had died in 1882. Before this not one of the Boston Lowells had been named Ralph.[13] As a youngster, Ralph did not appreciate his parents' decision. "Ralph," he observed decades later, "is not a nice name to give a little boy for, search history as one will, there is no great 'Ralph' for a daydreaming boy to make a hero of nor to emulate in his daily play. The nearest is Sir Ralph the Rover and he is not exactly a big-league hero that one could be proud of. But Ralph it is, a meaningless name in a family that abounds with names of men who have been a credit to society."[14]

By the time he went to college, and perhaps much earlier, Ralph had stopped using his middle name. Furthermore, unlike his siblings, Ralph had no nickname. Whereas Mary Emlen was Molly, John was Jack, James Hale was Jim, and Olivia was Oie, Ralph was almost always Ralph. Some of his childhood and college friends occasionally called him Rafe, but to his family and the rest of the world he was the much more formal Ralph.

A CHILDHOOD IN THE BACK BAY AND CHESTNUT HILL

His given name aside, Ralph enjoyed a childhood that was "a really free and good time."[15] Nurses, maids, cooks, and other servants were on hand to satisfy virtually every need and demand. Beyond the homes in Chestnut Hill and Back Bay, there were long summer vacations in Maine and New Hampshire. Sundays meant religious school, church services, and singing in the choir, but it was usually possible to duck out before the minister launched into his sermon. There were many good friends to play with (including Leverett Saltonstall, a future governor of Massachusetts and U.S. senator) and festive family gatherings at holidays. Young Ralph had difficulty controlling his temper, a problem that would continue to plague him as an adult, though it was not serious enough to interfere with his social development.

Physical ailments did, however, cause some alarm. In the winter of 1902, when he was eleven years old, Ralph complained of pains in his lower right side, and his family's physician, determining that the appendix was perforated, performed an emergency appendectomy on the Lowells' kitchen table. For the next five weeks, Ralph was confined to bed with drains in his side, and at the end of this period he had to "learn to walk all over again." It would be more than a year before he returned to school; in the meantime he was tutored at home. This medical crisis, coming after an earlier diagnosis of "a heart that would not stand physical exercise like that of other boys," led the doctor to tell Ralph's parents that he "would probably not grow very much" and, indeed, "would not live long." Relating the story to a grandson nearly seventy years later, Ralph, who had long fought a losing battle to keep his weight under two hundred pounds, concluded: "All of this is to prove that doctors can be wrong." [16]

Such questioning of authority, unusual for Ralph in his adult years, was even rarer in his childhood. He played his share of pranks at home and school and skipped church more often than his mother thought wise, but he was a dutiful and affectionate son. John and Mary were devoted parents, who both provided the amenities of an upper-class lifestyle and established moral parameters for their children. Mary, of course, had day-to-day responsibility for running the household, but John was always available for advice and guidance. Indicative of John's relaxed style was the letter he wrote to Ralph when he was a sophomore at Harvard:

> I thought you seemed disturbed at the probability of your not getting as high marks in your exams as you hoped for. We realize how hard it is to study in New London [where Ralph was assisting the rowing team] and shall not be disappointed whatever your marks are. Take it as easy as you can, have a good time, and don't smoke more than is good for you.

The parents' religious lessons took hold. When Ralph was seventeen and attending a boarding school in the Southwest, his baseball team had a game scheduled for December 25. Like his father, Ralph loved playing baseball, but not this day. "Brought up to consider Christmas Day as a kind of Sunday," Ralph knew that "his family would not like him" to participate. He explained this to his teammates and was the only one to sit out the game.[17]

John and Mary's problems with three of Ralph's siblings drew Ralph and his parents closer together. Molly, the eldest child, believed that her tradition-bound mother, having wanted her firstborn to be a son, never got over the disappointment of her daughter's arrival. Upon hearing of the birth of yet another brother, the not quite eight-year-old Molly ran away from home, to be found twelve hours later several miles way, asleep in a delivery wagon. Molly's rebelliousness continued through adolescence and prefigured an unsuccessful attempt at a painting career, an unhappy first marriage ending in divorce, and late in her life, conversion to Catholicism. The following letter from Ralph to his mother may have been prompted by her reporting one of the periodic crises in Molly's life while he was halfway around the globe:

> Surely, dear mother, I am the one that you should unburden your heart to, and I am glad to get such letters, for I know they make you feel better. I would be a pissant of a son, if I could only enjoy the things you and Father give me without also sharing your troubles, and I shall be very happy if you continue to "blow off" to me whenever you feel like it.

In the face of Molly's unconventionality, Ralph stood as a pillar of stability and solace for his parents.[18]

John, the oldest son and carrier of the most revered name in the family line, presented another type of challenge to his mother and father. He suffered from epilepsy, an illness whose social consequences were at least as severe as the physical difficulties it caused. Early twentieth-century society associated epilepsy with madness, criminality, and imbecility, and while Jack exhibited none of these traits, his "terrible disease," as Ralph called it in his diary, "made him an outcast" in Boston. Given the family's reluctance to use the malady's name even in the privacy of a diary entry, the details of its onset and its severity remain unknown. The first seizures (for which the treatment, doctors conceded, was "oftentimes no more rational than was given in the dark ages") may have occurred while Jack was at Harvard (1904–1908), probably sometime during the last two years. After graduation he soon left for Arizona. Ralph wrote in 1912 that Jack was "happy in the West, happy in his ranch [where he grew oranges], happy in his prospects, and happy in the fact that everyone who knew him loved him and respected him as one respects a silent hero who is fighting, with a smile on his face, terrible odds." Jack died in June 1912, a few hours after undergoing a gallbladder operation. His remains were returned to Boston and interred in the Lowell family plot.[19]

The problems of Ralph's younger brother, Jim, were of a far different order, but distressing nonetheless. Although an excellent student in preparatory school, Jim developed a great fondness for alcohol while at Harvard and came perilously close to flunking out in his sophomore year. He survived the immediate crisis, but drinking remained a hazard until he saw action in France during World War I. Military service made him a teetotaler, but it also inflicted some severe psychological scars, stripping him of the ambition that had been characteristic of most Lowell men. He earned a law degree and established a practice, but without distinction. In the fiftieth anniversary report of his 1914 Harvard class, Jim referred to "the curtain of obscurity that has hidden my mediocrity."*

Along with the pain caused by Jack's illness and the concerns generated by Molly's and Jim's failure to conform to familial expectations, John and Mary Lowell had to contend with a significant financial loss. When Ralph was eleven, a trusted adviser to the late Judge John Lowell embezzled a sizable part of the judge's estate, as well as a good portion of Lucy Emerson Lowell's inheritance from her father. The crime hardly left Ralph's grandmother or parents destitute, but it was enough to prompt this offer to Ralph's father from Henry Lee Higginson, one of Boston's richest men and a distant relation: "May I send in a couple of thousand dollars yearly to help fill the gap? You'd do it if you could in another case. We are cousins and fellow men—and it can only do some good—and you no harm. Be a philosopher and say it is the natural and right thing to agree with me. Else what twaddle we all talk."

Whether John accepted the gift is not known, but finances thenceforth became a source of worry. John and Mary did not appreciably change their lifestyle—they kept their two residences and the servants who maintained them, continued the boys' enrollment in private school, and gave "coming out" parties for Molly not only in Boston but in New York and Philadelphia as well. Nevertheless, more than most of their friends, the Lowell children were required to be conscious of the constraints on their parents' spending. Except for one period during the 1920s, when Ralph's association with Lee, Higginson & Co. seemed to promise brighter business prospects, his anxieties about money would persist until the 1950s.[20]

PREPARING FOR COLLEGE

One area in which John and Mary certainly would not scrimp was getting their sons ready for college, that is, Harvard. Boston's Brahmins had long relied on tutors or the Boston Latin School, which was public, to provide the necessary instruction, but by the close of the nineteenth century, pri-

---

* In the twenty-fifth anniversary report (1939), he wrote: "This morning I left my house, in which I was born and have lived all my life, to have my picture taken for [this] report, wearing the same suit and necktie worn when our senior class picture was taken. Surely Jimmy Lowell ain't changed much" (p. 494).

vate preparatory schools were the preferred choice. Some of these, like Phillips Exeter in New Hampshire and Groton in central Massachusetts, were boarding institutions, but most were day schools clustered in Boston's Beacon Hill and Back Bay. In the fall of 1900, Ralph entered the Volkmann School, just as his older brother John had done and his younger brother Jim would do in time.

Founded in 1895 by Arthur L. K. Volkmann, a native of Germany who had arrived in the United States in 1872 as a teenager, the school ranked among the most socially prestigious in Boston. It enrolled about one hundred boys in seven grades. Students were encouraged to fulfill Volkmann's credo: "Be a scholar if you can. If you can't be a scholar, be an athlete. If you can't be either a scholar or an athlete, be a gentleman." Ralph did well, if not spectacularly, as a scholar but was pretty much of a washout athletically. At various times he tried out for the hockey, baseball, and track teams but did not last long at any of them. In his diary he described himself as "absolutely hopeless" (hockey), "the worst one on the squad" (baseball), and "the laughing stock of the whole squad" (track). He fared better with the crew team. Given his comparatively low weight—less than a hundred pounds—Ralph had possibilities as a coxswain, but it was not a position he took to naturally. "I cannot steer to save my neck," he admitted in his diary. There was another drawback: "I don't know as I like the job of coxswain very well because you get all the blame." In the 1904–1905 school year, he was "chucked" from the team, but he came back in 1905–1906 and won the coxswain's spot on the first four-oar crew. However, in the big race of the season against rival schools, his team finished last in the semifinals, while Volkmann's second crew won its race in the fastest time achieved by any boat on the river. Ralph did not go out for crew in his final year.[21]

In June 1907, Ralph took the last of the Harvard entrance examinations for which he had been groomed during the past seven years. He took twelve in all, receiving three B's, four C's, four D's, and a failure in advanced French. This performance did not mark him as a scholar, but it was more than enough to get him admitted.[22]

With his parents' encouragement, Ralph delayed entering Harvard until the fall of 1908. Most freshmen came in at the age of eighteen, and John and Mary felt that Ralph, who had turned seventeen the month after his graduation from Volkmann's, could use another year of maturing. In a similar situation, Jack had spent his year between Volkmann's and Harvard at the Evans School in the Salt River valley of south-central Arizona, and Ralph did the same.

El Rancho Bonito (the school's formal name) was founded in 1902 by H. David Evans, an Englishman, who wanted to give boys on the verge of manhood the opportunity to develop the qualities of "self-reliance, independence and initiative." Life in the West, he wrote, "with its vision, distance and colour, could kindle a boy's imagination, and leave him with that ethereal spark which might at any time burst into flame." The Evans School and others like it touched a responsive chord in the psyche of the country's urban elite, which was distressed by its separation from nature and seeking ways to restore "strength to the fibre of the effete East." Among the students who spent a year at the Evans School during its three decades of operation were members of the Cabot, du Pont, Heinz, Pulitzer, Roosevelt, Saltonstall, and Vanderbilt families. In its first year the school had only three students, but by 1907 a dozen students were enrolled—about all that it could accommodate.

Ralph encountered living conditions far different from those he had known at home. Each boy had his own tent, spartanly furnished with a canvas cot, table, chair, bookshelf, and small stove. There were no servants to look after the boys, so they had to keep things neat and prepare their own meals, which included milking the cows. Evans imposed few rules, but a key requirement was that each student take care of the horse to which he had been assigned. Every morning Ralph would begin his day by watering, feeding, and cleaning his animal.[23]

Ralph had done little horseback riding in the East, and his first encounter with the western variety of horse did not go well. The day after he arrived, one of the staff tried to use Ralph's horse, Reddy, for a demonstration of how to mount. "[A]s soon as [the man] struck the saddle the horse reared and wheeled, and I nearly died of fright," Ralph reported in his diary. "So they brought out Pumps, a horse 28 years old. On this valiant steed I went to town." The next day Ralph tried Reddy for himself and "was run away with twice. Phew but that nag flew and all I did was to give it its head and hold onto the saddle." After a few more rides, Ralph and Reddy were getting along just fine and he decided to buy the horse. Five months later, after noting that he had been riding Reddy bareback with a shovel in one hand and a noose around the horse's nose, Ralph declared, "The Ralph Lowell of a year ago would have walked ten miles before he got on a horse."[24]

Although the primary aim of El Rancho Bonito was to develop character and physical strength, it was more than an eight-month summer camp for teenagers—it had an academic component as well. For several hours each weekday, the boys met with the teaching staff and worked on assignments. Ralph and his father had agreed that he would use this time to improve his French, German, and English, but soon after arriving in Arizona Ralph decided to add algebra to his studies. The course work proved more onerous than Ralph had anticipated and became the subject of one of his daily English compositions: "Is it Wise for a Minor to Disobey his Parents?" Parents do know best, he declared, and a child should follow their guidance:

> If your parents wish you to study, study. If they wish you to play, play. If they tell you how much to study, do not try to increase your study by doing more than they wish. If they send you to a place to gain health, and to lead an outdoor life, they don't expect you to retard yourself by too much study. All this, therefore, goes to prove that I am disobeying my parents in taking more than they told me to. Accordingly, I had better give up Algebra.[25]

Lowell's stay in Arizona not only produced the desired effects on his mind and body but also introduced him to a subject that would become a lifelong interest. On several of the short camping trips that Evans required his students to take, Lowell visited the ruins of pre-Columbian native societies, as well as the reservations of contemporary American Indians. He was fascinated by what he saw, and his diary contains detailed descriptions of the people and their artifacts. In preparation for the month-long camping excursion—by horse—that traditionally capped off the school year, Ralph read the latest annual report of the Smithsonian Institution's Bureau of American Ethnology. The high points of that journey were stops at cousin Percival's astronomical observatory (Percival was not there, but his associates arranged for Ralph and his companions to view Jupiter through the telescope) and the Grand Canyon ("We sat on a cliff drinking in the changing beauties of this greatest of God's creations and involuntarily our voices sank to little more than a whisper"). But the trip's enduring legacy was a deepening of Ralph's attachment to the Indian culture of the American Southwest. This bond would bring him back to Arizona three years later, supply a framework for his academic work in college, and continue to enrich his life for decades to come.[26]

In early June of 1908, Lowell boarded a train for the three-day trip to Boston. Before leaving, he and another Volkmann graduate sold their horses to "a couple of innocent Easterners." His first day back he bought a whole new wardrobe, because "I didn't have a decent stitch to my name when I got home." Later that month he attended the Harvard-Yale crew races and watched Harvard "lick the pants off Yale" at baseball. Much of the summer was spent in Maine in the company of friends and relatives, and in September Lowell moved into his new quarters in Cambridge.[27]

2

"That manly mass of Noble man"

HARVARD—AND THE WORLD

In 1721, slightly more than eighty years after the first Percival Lowell arrived in New England, Harvard College bestowed an A.B. degree on one of his fourth-generation descendants. Other Boston families had ties reaching farther back into Harvard's past, but none forged as strong and intimate a bond as the Lowells. Over the next 190 years, more than a score of Lowells passed through Harvard's halls as undergraduates; some joined its faculty, and several served on its governing boards. When Ralph Lowell entered Harvard in the fall of 1908, his cousin Lawrence was widely regarded as a likely successor to President Charles W. Eliot, whose appointment in 1869 had been, in large part, the handiwork of John Amory Lowell. Being a Lowell gave Ralph the freedom to make many independent decisions, but selecting a college was not one of them.

CLASS OF 1912

The Harvard that welcomed Ralph was not the one where his father, John, had graduated thirty-one years earlier. The far-reaching reforms fostered by President Eliot had just begun to be felt during John Lowell's stay in Cambridge (1873–1877). John faced a heavy regimen of prescribed studies, oriented toward the classics, philosophy, and mathematics, taught by a small faculty undifferentiated by formal departments. He was also obliged to attend chapel every day. By the time Ralph arrived, a student's presence at religious services was voluntary, and the only required courses were year-long classes in English rhetoric and composition and either French or German. The faculty had been enlarged and upgraded, the curriculum widened. The student body had grown as well: John's freshman class was the first to number more than two hundred; Ralph's class was just over six hundred. The loss in intimacy was accompanied by a rise in diversity. Whereas the bulk of John's classmates were fellow Bay Staters and shared his ethnic background, the class of 1912 included a wider geographical mix and a richer stew of cultural backgrounds.[1]

As Eliot's policies raised the level of education Harvard offered and made it available to a larger and more heterogeneous constituency, the college became divided along social lines. A biographer of Franklin D. Roosevelt (class of 1904) wrote that "[t]he Harvard student body, like a binary stellar system, consisted of two worlds, each revolving around the other in its fixed orbit." Populating the "outer darkness" were the graduates of public high schools in the Boston area and elsewhere who came to Harvard to study and learn. Enjoying the "inner light" were "the fellows from the select private schools," whose primary purpose at Harvard was to cultivate the "aloofness and good taste by which they distinguished themselves."[2]

When he arrived at Harvard, Ralph Lowell fell naturally into the latter group. As a junior he recalled how "scared to death" he had been on his first day as a freshman: "Francis Gray [his longtime friend and roommate] and I wanted to get an invitation to eat at the 'Groton Table,' that being the best table then, and were very much pleased when a crowd of them asked us to lunch with them." And so it was for the next four years, as Lowell mingled almost exclusively with those from his own social class. The Harvard Union, which offered a wide range of facilities and services, had been established in 1901 by Henry Lee Higginson as a "house of fellowship," but Lowell rarely went there.[3]

The housing situation at Harvard accentuated the socioeconomic fault lines. Too busy transforming the intellectual climate to pay much attention to the physical conditions of student life, Eliot left the provision of additional housing to private entrepreneurs. They responded by constructing a half-dozen residential halls on a "scale of outward magnificence recalling the splendor of a Venetian palace." Claverly Hall, opened in 1893, started the building boom on Mount Auburn Street, which soon was known as the Gold Coast. At a time when many of the dormitories in Harvard Yard had no central heating and no plumbing above the basement, Claverly and its neighbors offered suites with private baths and steam heat. The great demand for these accommodations meant that a freshman had to engage in a student-run election before he could get a room. Ralph was in Arizona in March 1908 when he heard the good news that he had been voted into Claverly. He spent three of his four years at Harvard there.[4]

One amenity that Claverly and the other Gold Coast halls did not offer was dining facilities: It was expected that the students would eat at their clubs. Private social clubs dominated virtually every aspect of undergraduate life, and for someone of Lowell's background "the big thing, without which everything else would be dust and ashes, [was] to get into 'the clubs.'" Within days of his arrival on campus, Ralph was informed of his election to the Polo Club, one of only two social clubs for freshmen. It had a rowdy reputation, and when he was told not to make any engagements for the following Monday night Ralph was nervous:

> "Bloody" Monday was going to have a meaning for us after all. We awaited that day with growing apprehension, drinking in the terrible tales about jumping into the river and other diabolical tricks ending up with the fact that we all had to get very drunk. It was to great relief that we learned that we did not necessarily have to drink if we didn't want to. The day came and at last the evening, and supperless and dressed in our worst clothes we climbed into the bath tubs. . . . [Two others] were in the bath with me and we had a pretty good time together. Then the lights were flashed on and we were called forth and made to perform.

Ralph enjoyed the good times afforded by the Polo, but the key dates in a clubman's calendar took place during sophomore year. Ralph passed all the hurdles without difficulty. After being elected to the Institute of 1770, which carried with it subsequent admission to the Hasty Pudding Club, and making it among the first groups of admittees, which placed him in the D.K.E., Ralph was accepted by the A.D. Club. This was the club of his father, his grandfather, and his brother Jack; it ranked with the Porcellian as the most exclusive of Harvard's final clubs. The A.D.'s building on Massachusetts Avenue across from the Yard, with its pool table, smoking room, and dining and bar services, would be the center of Ralph's active social life during his last two years of college.[5]

One of the few areas in which the social lines at Harvard eased to some extent was athletics. Victory over intercollegiate rivals, particularly Yale, thrilled all but the "intransigent aesthetes and the greasiest grinds," and the hunger for victory led to the adoption on the playing fields of a merit system not otherwise conspicuous at Harvard outside the classroom. Ralph first met the man who would become the most famous member of the class of 1912—Joseph P. Kennedy—when both served on the class finance committee in the fall of 1908; but it was the following March, on the baseball diamond, that Kennedy helped shape an important element of Lowell's college years.[6]

The opportunity to play baseball at El Rancho Bonito after his humiliating failures at Volkmann apparently had revived Ralph's faith in his skills, and he tried out for the freshman team. Competing against him for the first baseman's job was Joe Kennedy, who was, as Lowell recalled later, "clearly more proficient at the game than I." The coach was a good friend of Lowell's—Ralph's father had been administrative manager of the baseball club during his college days and had remained a loyal fan of the team through the decades—and the coach "wisely suggested that, since Joe was so far superior to me, I continue to work as manager of the crew rather than warm the bench with the baseball team."[7]

In moving from baseball to crew, Ralph never gave any thought to trying out for the team. He was not strong enough to man an oar, and being coxswain still held too many terrors for him. But in order to become manager, Ralph faced another sort of competition. The position was a prestigious one—the senior manager would receive the coveted "H" awarded to all Harvard team members who competed against Yale in a varsity sport—and there were many like Ralph who wanted to be part of the athletic tradition even if they could not play.* One important test for evaluating managerial applicants was their success at soliciting contributions for the team. Less than two weeks into the fall 1908 semester, Lowell started making the rounds for subscriptions to the team. This is the first recorded instance of an activity for which Lowell would become celebrated: fund-raising. He must have done well, but the appointment would not be made until March and the wait was agonizing. As the day of deci-

---

* Ralph's father had won his letter for managing the baseball team, and his uncle James Arnold Lowell, class of 1891, had won his for managing the football team. Guy Lowell, class of 1892, earned his "H" as a miler on the track team.

sion approached, Lowell wrote in his diary, "If lucky, I won't play [base]ball again for a long time." He didn't have to—the freshman manager's post was his.[8]

By the early 1900s football had emerged as the most popular of college sports, but rowing had the longest history and the greatest prestige. The first intercollegiate sporting event of any kind occurred in 1852 when crews from Harvard and Yale squared off on Lake Winnipesaukee in New Hampshire. Teams from the two schools raced fairly regularly over the next two decades, and in 1876 the Harvard-Yale meetings became an annual fixture on the calendar of commencement activities in June. The Thames River, upstream from New London, Connecticut, served as the site, and crowds of fifty thousand were not unusual by the early 1900s. An observation train traveling along the west bank of the river allowed spectators to keep up with the boats as they traversed the four-mile course, and the last half mile was lined with yachts hailing from New York, Newport, Boston, and the North Shore. Some of the people who would play important roles in Ralph Lowell's early business career, such as James Jackson Storrow (class of 1885) and Robert Herrick (class of 1890), were fervent supporters of the Harvard crew.[9]

College athletics during Lowell's years at Harvard were run largely by students and alumni, with the faculty and administration hovering in the background to maintain academic standards and to keep one eye on finances. In its 1907–1908 report the Committee on Regulation of Athletic Sports took a dim view of the hoopla over the crew:

> Rowing has been called the best sport; but to many persons it seems— for the few men who take part in the race with Yale—the most dangerous. Moreover, the race brings together, outside of all Faculty control, great crowds of students, with nothing to do but wait for the race and console or congratulate themselves afterwards. The race itself [which lasted less than twenty-five minutes] is a short and not always visible spectacle for which those who attend it pay high.

To underline its point the report quoted no less an authority than the president of Yale, who had declared, "I can imagine no other ordinary occupation of human life where you go so far and see so little."[10]

Rowing had another liability: It was "enormously expensive." Training facilities and equipment did not come cheap, and the races brought in no revenues. The proceeds from football and baseball subsidized the crew and other teams, as did solicited subscriptions and generous donations. The 1909–1910 report of the Athletics Committee, while not singling out rowing for special criticism, must certainly have had it in mind when it described the cost of organized sports as "almost scandalous":

> Some expenses bear about the same relation to the health and success of our teams that a silver-mouthed bridle bears to good horsemanship. Captains, managers, and coaches incline to throw aside equipment that is highly serviceable and almost new, and to buy at great expense something wholly new and a shade better; they tend to encourage an exaggerated fastidiousness in hotel accommodations, in food, and in clothing; they too often require for themselves and their men such luxuries of the table and of transportation as none but the rich can afford. . . . It is things like these that give a handle to the enemy of athletic sports, and pamper or even pauperize strong men. . . . When an athlete feels that victory hangs on gratuitous automobile rides, or on the substitution of squabs for chicken at the training table, . . . he is already beaten.

During Ralph Lowell's term as head manager (1911–1912), spending on the crew reversed the upward spiral of previous years, dipping $400 below the record set in 1910–1911 ($16,260), but the gap between receipts and expenditures remained just about the same (approximately $12,000). If Ralph instituted any changes in response to the committee's criticism, they did not attract notice.[11]

In November 1908, just a month after Ralph commenced his studies in Cambridge, President Eliot announced that he would retire the following May, the fortieth anniversary of his election. Years later the poet laureate of Ralph's class recalled the event:

> The Class of Twelve, that manly mass
> Of Noble man, select, refined
> Whom Eliot glimpsed—and then resigned.

In fact, Eliot was in his seventies, and his departure had long been anticipated. It did not take long for the members of the Harvard Corporation to designate a replacement: A. Lawrence Lowell.[12]

Lawrence's selection signaled a retreat from the extraordinarily liberal educational policies of his predecessor. Lowell had been Eliot's most vocal critic on the Harvard faculty, arguing that his free elective system encouraged laziness and indifference to scholarship. "[We] fail to touch the imagination of the students," Lowell complained in 1904. "We awake little spontaneous enthusiasm for knowledge or thought. We arouse little ambition for intellectual power." Philosophy professor George Santayana, also critical of Eliot's system, observed that the typical Harvard undergraduate "does, except when the pressure or fear of the outer world constrains him, only what he finds worth doing for its own sake." Before becoming president, Lowell scored a minor victory when he persuaded the faculty to create the category "With Distinction" in the awarding of the A.B., thereby recognizing outstanding academic performance as "both honorable and desirable" and encouraging students to group their courses in a particular branch of learning. This policy went into effect for the class of 1908. Lowell's more far-reaching reforms, including concentration and distribution requirements, a general examination, and the use of tutors, were phased in gradually during and after Ralph Lowell's years in Cambridge.[13]

Ralph, then, was in one of the last classes to enjoy the freedom and to face the perils of Eliot's elective system. He needed sixteen full courses to graduate, and like so many of his fellow clubmen and sportsmen, he could have put together an assortment of subjects that would enable him to earn his degree without much difficulty. Indeed, he passed up the chance to study with some legendary figures on the faculty, such as George Lyman Kittredge (English), Josiah Royce (philosophy), and Hugo Munsterberg (psychology). He did take George Santayana's History of Modern Philosophy but described it as "the worst course I have ever seen," adding, "It is impossible to understand what Santayana says." He received a C, the same grade awarded for his efforts in Barrett Wendell's History of English Literature from Elizabethan Times to the Present, and A. Lawrence Lowell's Constitutional Government.[14]

Most of the instruction offered at Harvard during this period was "Europocentric, . . . nostalgic, traditionalist, and elitist," and Ralph's courses in history and economics fit the mold. His two history courses carried the story of Western Europe through 1715; his two economics courses were taught by Thomas Nixon Carver, an advocate of individualism, thrift, free enterprise, and social Darwinism. Harvard did not challenge Ralph's inherited conservative beliefs, but it did develop his capacity for analyzing the world around him. Commenting in his diary on Carver's class (entitled Principles of Sociology—Theories of Social Progress), he wrote:

> That course teaches one to think, which to me is the best thing anyone
> can get out of college. School training throws facts at the individual and
> makes him grasp those facts without necessarily understanding the steps
> by which the ends have been reached. When one gets to college, things
> are placed before one in such a way as to enable one to follow out the pro-
> fessor's reasoning in such a way as to arrive at his conclusions almost as
> soon as he does. For example, I got marks at mid-years this year [1911] with
> less work than I have ever done before.[15]

Ralph's grades as a freshman were decent (three B's and three C's). This record was virtually duplicated in his sophomore year (two B's and three C's, one of the latter in Carver's Principles of Economics), except that he also received his first A.

This breakthrough occurred in the full-year introductory course offered by the anthropology department. The "science of man" was a relatively new subject in the Harvard curriculum—the first course open to undergraduates had been offered in 1894–1895. The faculty in Lowell's time were young and as yet undistinguished, but they helped Ralph forge his initial fascination with the Indians of Arizona into the organizing theme of his undergraduate studies and a hobby that would stretch over a lifetime.[16]

Anthropology and the related field of Egyptology dominated Ralph's course work during his last two years in college. In addition, he spent nine weeks during the summer of 1911 in Arizona, traveling on horseback to visit and observe the Indian tribes there and accumulate materials for his senior honors thesis. President Eliot's elective system allowed Ralph to explore anthropology, and President Lowell's emphasis on scholarship gave Ralph's studies a focus they might not otherwise have had.[17]

Ralph's senior year marked not only the culmination but also a broadening of his Harvard experience. One important change was in his living accommodations. During the spring of 1910, when the spirit of Progressivism was very much in the air across the nation, the leaders of the class of 1911 sought to promote class solidarity by asking members to spend their final year in the dormitories in the Yard. A considerable number, including many from the Gold Coast, responded favorably, and the following spring President Lowell altered assignment procedures to encourage the class of 1912 to do the same. So Ralph and several of his friends gave up Claverly for the far less pleasant facilities of Thayer Hall.[18]

Ralph also volunteered for the new senior advisers program that cousin Lawrence had established as part of his campaign to break down the barriers separating students of diverse backgrounds. A senior adviser was to give "newcomers the benefit of his own experience in all things which go to make up the social atmosphere of college." Ralph thought the concept an excellent one that could produce "unity and good-will among the Class of 1915," and he took his responsibilities seriously. Camped on a Navajo reservation in northeastern Arizona in August 1911, he wrote a letter to each of the six incoming freshmen to whom he had been assigned. He stayed in close contact with them over the next year.[19]

The shift to Thayer and his duties as a senior adviser seem to have stirred Ralph's social conscience. In March 1912 a beer night was held for the whole senior class, which Ralph described as a "great success," adding, "There were any amount of fellows I had never met there and I got a new idea of what college life . . . seems to the men that are not overrun with clubs and societies to which they have to give their time. I hope there are more of these nights." Earlier that month, under the auspices of the Phillips Brooks House (founded in 1900 and "dedicated to Piety, Charity, and Hospitality"), he had spoken to a group of young people at the Frances E. Willard Settlement House. It was an odd jarring of worlds for this Brahmin and his audience of "32 Jews and 5 women," but it went well enough: "They were really a very nice crowd, genial and jovial but not fresh or annoying. I don't think my speech was much of a success, because it was on rowing and very few if any of the boys have ever seen a boat race, but after I stopped talking a good many of the fellows crowded around and we talked over the political situation."[20]

Politics in 1912 centered on the three-cornered race for the White House, and Ralph's willingness to venture into unfamiliar territory quickly found its limits. Citing the need to study for an examination, he passed up the chance to hear a speech by the top Democratic hopeful, Woodrow Wilson. Although Lawrence Lowell ended up voting for the former president of Princeton, Ralph could not imagine casting his first presidential ballot for a Democrat. Like many young men, Ralph had been attracted by the magnetism and activism of Theodore Roosevelt, but Roosevelt had veered off on a path Ralph thought too radical. Incumbent William Howard Taft, who carried the Republican label and did not shy away from being identified as conservative, won Ralph's support, along with that of most Harvard students as counted in a straw vote.[21]

The clubmen's outlook carried the day in college elections as well. All of the fall 1911 contests for permanent officers of the class of 1912 were won by graduates of private schools who were either members of top social clubs or recipients of an "H"; in most instances, they were both. A.D. members captured three of the seven prestigious positions. One of these was Ralph's Claverly roommate and triple "H" winner Richard Bowditch Wigglesworth, who prevailed easily in the race for secretary. Ralph himself gained the treasurership comfortably (173–97–75) over two competitors, who were president of the *Crimson* and manager of the musical clubs, respectively.[22]

Ralph enjoyed similar success academically. In his junior year his grades were not good enough for election to Phi Beta Kappa, but by virtue of receiving all A's and B's he still had a shot at it as a senior. He worked hard during the first semester, and in early March his labors were rewarded. "I am about as pleased as a man can possibly be," he noted in his diary. For the rest of his life, his Phi Beta Kappa key would hang conspicuously from his vest pocket.[23]

In order to earn an A.B. with distinction, Ralph faced two final hurdles. He had to complete his thesis and pass a special oral examination. The thesis, a review of his summer with the Indians of Arizona, was read favorably, but the examination in May proved to be an "ordeal." Three of his five inquisitors were anthropology instructors familiar with his work, and the fourth was Carver, who had given him a B in sociology. The remaining member of the panel was George H. Chase, a specialist in Greek art, whom Ralph had not had as a teacher. Ralph thought Chase's questions were unfair, and as he waited in the hall while the committee deliberated, his anger mounted. After ten minutes, the group emerged to inform him he had passed. Ralph shook everyone's hand, but "could hardly keep from slugging Chase when he congratulated me on a very good examination." Lowell graduated magna cum laude, the only man in A.D. or Porcellian to achieve that honor, and the only member of the class of 1912 to combine it with a varsity letter.[24]

His classroom work completed, in early June Ralph spent two weeks with the crew team in New London as it prepared for the race against Yale. On June 18 Ralph was back in Cambridge for Class Day. Robert Benchley, president of the *Lampoon*, delivered the Ivy Oration.* It was, as described in one Boston newspaper, a "delightfully rambling discourse, beginning with a 'peroration' and ending 'lastly and inevitably' with the 'anticlimax.'" Ralph labeled it "as great a success as was expected." But for him the day was difficult. "It was very hard," he wrote in his diary, "to keep a smile on one's face in the Stadium. . . . I have loved college so much, I hate to think it is all over." Commencement on June 20 was a letdown, and as soon as the ceremonies were over Ralph returned to New London for the big race.[25]

Yale's poor record made Harvard the favorite, but this only added to the pressures on the team. Besides wanting to maintain its four-year winning streak, the Crimson wished to avenge the baseball team's double losses to Yale just a few days before. The Harvard-Yale football game the previous November had ended in a scoreless tie, so a victory on the Thames was necessary for the class of 1912 to go out with any glory. On his arrival back in New London, Ralph noted the scarcity of Yale rooters, commenting that the Elis appeared to have deserted their crew now that the race was "a losing proposition." He added, "I am sure Harvard never lost faith in their crews during the long time they got the short end of the deal."[26]

The day went gloriously for the Crimson. Symptomatic of Yale's woes, the team's launch broke down and the Eli coaches spent the afternoon watching the races from the Harvard vessel, never saying a word. It was, Lowell noted, "a novel experience." By the first half mile Harvard had gained a half-length lead, and by midpoint (two miles) those on the launch "knew that there was nothing to the race." Harvard won by five lengths, twenty seconds ahead of Yale.[27]

A few days later, Ralph went to Cambridge to move out of his dormitory. "As I look back at my course [at Harvard]," he wrote in his diary, "I have not a single regret, and I smile at the remembrance of the youth who entered four years ago, fearful that his slightest move would get him disliked among his classmates and frowned on by older men."[28]

---

* Benchley had defeated Frederick Lewis Allen, later the editor of *Harper's* and author of *Only Yesterday* (1931), for this honor.

Ralph had matured while at Harvard, not only intellectually and emotionally but also physically. Weighing slightly over 100 pounds when he entered, Ralph now carried 165 pounds on his five-foot-eleven-inch frame. He moved easily in Boston Brahmin society, but still lacked one useful credential: foreign travel. Many of his friends had been overseas with their parents or on their own during summers while in college, but Ralph had done neither. He rectified this gap in the year after graduation.

The inspiration to travel originated with Ralph's good friend and fellow Brahmin Richard Wigglesworth. "Wigg" hoped that a band of five or so could be put together, but in the end it was only Wigg and Ralph. Lowell had been enthusiastic about Wigglesworth's plans from the start, but the financial requirements of such a trip seemed beyond his family's reach. "So I guess I stay put here in Boston for the rest of my life," he lamented in January 1912.[29]

By spring, however, the funds had been found. It was rare for Ralph's parents to deny their children anything, and given his stellar performance at Harvard they may have seen this trip as his just reward. "Father," Ralph wrote in his diary, "is the most unselfish man I have seen or heard of." He noted that the elder Lowells thought "the experience I will gain on the trip will repay any loss in time that I may suffer in business."[30] The two friends waited to depart until late fall so that Wigglesworth, who had quarterbacked the varsity eleven, could watch the football team play its nine-game schedule. Harvard emerged unbeaten, and on November 28, 1912, five days after the Crimson routed Yale 20 to 0, Lowell and Wigglesworth boarded the Cunard liner *Franconia*, bound for Naples.

Expecting to be away for nine months, each took a trunk, two dress-suit cases, and a hat box. Their stateroom on the second deck of the *Franconia* was typical of their accommodations on the trip: comfortable, but not luxurious. Ralph was conscious of expenses, but the detailed diary he kept offers no indication that any opportunity for adventure or sightseeing was passed up because of the costs involved. The following August, as the trip drew to a close, he estimated his total expenditures at $3500 — this at a time when the average income of American factory workers was $600 a year.

After a two-week voyage across the Atlantic and into the Mediterranean, highlighted by flirtations with two New York debutantes they met the first day out of port, Lowell and Wigglesworth enthusiastically assumed the tourist's role. Before leaving the United States, Lowell had written that he expected to find Italy "a land of pleasure, of music, of art, and of aesthetic beauty." He was not disappointed, but his overall impression of Italians was unfavorable.[31]

Their second night in Naples afforded the young travelers a lesson about European society. After a dinner with some fellow Americans at a fancy hotel, for which Lowell and Wigglesworth had put on dress suits and top hats, they decided to walk back to their place. They quickly became "fair prey for everyone," Lowell noted in his diary:

> Cab drivers followed us, people laughed at us, and urchins jeered us.
> I think the solution of the problem lies in the remark of one cab driver,
> "Gentlemen with tall hats do not walk." We probably offended the natural
> class sense of the people and, by so doing, immediately lost our class and
> became a comedy or comedic imitation of real aristocracy.

These Boston Brahmins would be more careful of their image in the future.[32]

Lowell and Wigglesworth spent most of their time in Naples visiting museums and natural sights. Getting to these places, however, often took them through poor neighborhoods where the houses were "mere hovels," as Lowell described them.

> Here reside the worst people morally in Italy. It is a den of vice and disease.
> The street barely admitted the passage of our carriage while the odors
> that greeted our nostrils were most annoying. It is unbelievable that hu-
> man beings could live in such misery and squalor. . . . We came away with
> the feeling that we indeed had something to be thankful for living in
> America and not in Naples.

While not rejecting Lowell's conclusion out of hand, the Italians and other immigrants packed into the slums of American cities might have wished that Lowell would come to see their living conditions.[33]

After a week in Naples Lowell had formed a negative view of its residents. Neapolitans, he wrote, "may be a happy, smiling people, but . . . I see in them only a dirty, slovenly crowd who are ever trying to steal something or to cheat you in some way or other." His feelings toward Italians in general did not improve after contact with the country's railroad system. The trains always ran late—"it is just a question of the degree of lateness, that is all."[34]

If Neapolitans made Naples "one of the worst places on the face of the earth," Rome and the Romans proved "perfectly delightful." Romans were "much nicer and more polite" than their countrymen to the south, and Rome lived up to its reputation as "the city of history and power, which enthralls the visitor and makes him wonder about life and the inconsistency of things." Not even a run of nasty weather during the ten days he and Wigglesworth spent in the Eternal City could dampen Lowell's enthusiasm for the place.[35]

Not all expectations were fulfilled, however. On Christmas morning the travelers opened the presents their families had sent and then proceeded to Saint Peter's to view the Christmas Day mass. Lowell was "very much disappointed." Instead of a large gathering of the faithful and an impressive service (he had thought "the music and choir would be a thing to remember until one's dying day"), the two Episcopalians found the service conducted in a little chapel with only a small choir and small congregation present. "When I think of the devout crowds that throng our churches at home on this day," Lowell wrote, "I am more and more persuaded that the Roman Catholic Church is rotten at the core and that its day of usefulness has passed forever. When the heart is cold, the body has not long to live." But that afternoon they went to the Church of Santa Maria Maggiore, where the service was beautiful.[36]

Lowell and Wigglesworth returned to the Vatican two more times before leaving Rome. The first visit was for a tour and interview with a high church official. In his account of the meeting Lowell again reflected on the divisions in Christendom:

[Their host said] churches should be more richly decorated than any other buildings because it is to God that we should give the finest fruits of our labors. This is diametrically opposed to the belief we Protestants have in an unassuming place of worship where the individual, shorn of all his pomp and plumage, may quietly and with dignity commune with the Lover of Mankind.

A few days later Lowell and Wigglesworth, along with about a hundred other people from "all walks of life," had an audience with Pope Pius X: "As [the Pope] stood there in the center of the room clad in his white robes trimmed with gold, and said his benediction, a wave of pity swept over me for the simple, holy man who stood there far along in life, knowing that most of the people there had come out of curiosity and not out of true devotion." [37]

Lowell expected his undergraduate studies to serve him well on the next stop: Egypt. His main preparation for Italy had been a visit to "Mrs. Jack Gardner's exquisite palace" on Boston's Fenway, but he had a solid background in Egyptian history, as well as familiarity with desert conditions from his time in Arizona. He looked forward to Egypt as "an intellectual appetizer whose worth I expect to be able to enjoy to the utmost." [38]

"The land of fairy tales and mythical beings" did not disappoint him. The day after the steamer dropped them off in Alexandria, Lowell and Wigglesworth took their first rides on camels as they visited the pyramids. "There is nothing so awe-inspiring, or conducive to serious thought, as the approach to the base of the Pyramid of Cheops," Lowell declared. "The grandeur of the massive pile grips one and holds one enthralled. . . . It exceeds [one's] fondest expectations." The following day they made a call on the Harvard–Boston Museum of Fine Arts excavation camp at Giza—an adventure not open to the average tourist. The camp was directed by Lowell's Egyptology professor, George Andrew Reisner. At Reisner's invitation, they descended by a "rickety rope ladder" into a tomb where a month earlier the expedition had found one of the finest known pieces of well-preserved early Fifth Dynasty wooden sculpture. The tomb's grave furniture and gifts became a prized part of the museum's extensive Egyptian collection. After Lowell assumed the presidency of the museum in 1951, he enjoyed taking guests to the Egyptian room and recounting his 1913 visit; since he had put on a great deal of weight in the intervening decades, he would add good-naturedly, "Some people wouldn't believe a rope would carry me, but it did." [39]

Lowell and Wigglesworth spent three weeks in Egypt, most of it on a boat that took them up the Nile as far as Aswan. Engrossed in ancient history, far removed from the concerns of modern civilization, Lowell felt none of the ambivalence he had experienced in Italy. His immediately positive attitude toward the Egyptians—"happy, smiling, jesting people, not grouchy and disgustingly dirty like the damn Dagos we had to do with in Italy"—remained with him throughout his stay. [40]

At Port Said, Lowell and Wigglesworth boarded a German ship that sailed through the Suez Canal and Red Sea, stopped at Aden, then delivered them across the Arabian Sea to Ceylon, a trip of twelve days. They passed a week on the island, enjoying the lush scenery and bumping into old friends. Some girls they knew from Beacon Hill–Back Bay parties were taking their own tour, properly chaperoned, of course, and the young people shared their tales of exotic lands. One of Lowell's anthropology professors, on his way back from Tibet, also had stories to relate. Adapting to the colonial status of the region, Lowell and Wigglesworth hired a servant, who later accompanied them in India.[41]

During their five weeks in India, Lowell and Wigglesworth trekked all over the subcontinent, from Madurai in the southeast, to Bombay on the west coast, to Darjeeling in the north and Calcutta on the northeast coast. They rode on elephants, hunted tigers, waded in the Ganges, and glimpsed the as yet unconquered Mount Everest. At Agra, the Taj Mahal left Lowell speechless: "Mere words cannot in any way describe its wonderful beauty, and my memory will never need any goad to call it up to view." At Lucknow, where British troops and civilians successfully held out in a four-month siege during the sepoy uprising of 1857, Lowell felt a different kind of emotion: "One comes away with a depressingly grand feeling, and walks a little firmer and more proudly for belonging to a race which was capable of such a sterling fight."[42]

The part of his India trip that Lowell most often described to friends was the visit to Baroda, a city 225 miles due north of Bombay. Lowell and Wigglesworth paid a call on the local maharaja's son, who had been their classmate at Harvard. Jasinthrao had known Lowell only slightly and Wigglesworth not at all, but the Harvard link was all the two Bostonians needed to show up uninvited in this distant land. It was, as Lowell noted in his diary, "quite cheeky." When they stepped off the train, which was not only late but also noisy, dirty, small, and unsteady, Lowell and Wigglesworth discovered that they had arrived just in time for the three-day ceremony marking Jasinthrao's marriage to his twelve-year-old bride. An enormous, fully carpeted tent with two bedrooms, two bathrooms, and a sitting room was set up for the Americans. The wedding procession was led by a band "which played eight bars of 'Fair Harvard' in a fashion that we could scarcely recognize, but which made us feel much more kindly to the little man who was so unpopular in college, but who seemed to be fond of it nevertheless."[43]

As he traveled around India, Lowell recorded the views of the people he met about conditions and prospects there; when he departed in the latter part of March he was ready to express his own feelings. He was not sorry to be leaving because India was, despite the magnificent sights it offered, "a depressing country." In his diary he wrote: "The men of the South are disheartened and sullen, the men of Central India are worse; the native states are insolent, the Bengalis not to be trusted, and it is only in the hills that one meets real men, men who treat one as an equal and do not cringe and smirk to one's face, only to curse one out behind one's back."

Lowell came away impressed by the "immutability of India" and the "almost hopeless task" confronting the English in trying to "lift [the Indians] above their present level." Indeed, the English, with their railroads and education, had only made things worse, "as when one stirs up a quiescent cesspool and the filth that had sunk rises to mix with the purer water above." Everyone was disgruntled, "[f]rom the low caste, stupid Hindu who spends his whole life trying to pay taxes, to the well-educated Brahmin gentleman who finds that his education does not do him any good and that an Englishman will be given a job over him whenever possible."

Part of the problem the English faced was the caliber of the bureaucrats they had sent to govern. "The officials know very little about the men they are over, and they care less. They do not even attempt to get to know the people as they are, to see behind the external curtain and read the man's soul, and until they do this, if they ever do, they will be unable to really sympathize with and rule the people as true justice demands." Underlying everything, however, was the matter of race: "The white race has a natural antipathy towards a man of color, and this cannot be overcome. You can say that they are intellectually your equals and you may be right, but you do not want them in your drawing rooms or in your families." Lowell concluded that England had maintained her power by playing the various peoples of the subcontinent against one another, but while England "will stay, she must never rely on India for help in time of grave trouble." [44]

Burma, where Lowell and Wigglesworth stopped next, offered a welcome contrast. "We liked the happy, genial, little people," Lowell wrote after a three-day visit, "with their pretty religion and quaint ways—they were such a relief after the hard men of India." Indeed, Lowell was quite taken by what he found: "So far Kipling stood me in good stead, but I must say that when he calls Buddha a 'bloom' idol made o' mud,' it rather riles me, for the religion is more beautiful in its forgiveness and peace than is the corrupted version of Christianity that we know today." [45]

After short stays in Malaya and Singapore, Lowell and Wigglesworth moved on to the Dutch East Indies. As usual, Lowell was enchanted by the physical beauty of the land, but here in Java he also found a society that was "at peace and perfectly happy." The trains were clean, they were comfortable, they ran on time; and the Dutch had shown themselves better rulers than the English of a colonial people. "They treat the native not as a slave as the English do, but rather as a younger brother, whose mistakes are to be overlooked rather than punished, and whose simple joys and pleasures are to be encouraged." One of the key elements of the Dutch strategy was "the systematic squashing of all desire for real education," Lowell observed. "Perhaps this is unchristian and wrong, but it certainly is not as hypocritical as the English method of saying, 'Come to my arms brother, we are all members of the Great British Empire,' and then thrusting them away as they take them at their word."

Intermarriage among the Dutch and the "jolly, pleasant, happy race" of natives seemed to be working, Lowell wrote, noting that the acceptance of mixed bloods boded well for the future.* "Java leaves a pleasant taste in the mouth of the traveler, just as the white pit of their famous fruit—the mangosteen—does," Lowell wrote, as he sailed away after two weeks on the island, "and there will ever be the desire to get back there again." [46]

To reach their next destination, the Philippines, Lowell and Wigglesworth had to backtrack through Singapore and travel through Hong Kong. After two weeks they arrived in Manila on May 4. There they found American food, major league baseball scores, and many people they knew from Boston and Harvard. The Philippines was "like getting home again." [47]

They spent almost five weeks in this American dependency, much of it as the guests and companions of the highest official there, Governor General W. Cameron Forbes. On his mother's side, Forbes was the grandson of Ralph Waldo Emerson; on his father's, the grandson of the legendary Boston businessman John Murray Forbes, who shrewdly invested the family fortune (made in the China trade of the late eighteenth and early nineteenth centuries) in America's western railroads. An appointee of President Taft, Cameron Forbes had held his post since 1909; his duties kept him away from the June 1912 commencement at which Harvard awarded

---

* Not that Lowell would ever have considered intermarriage for himself. Two months earlier, he told his mother that he and Wigglesworth had been "shocked" to hear of a friend's engagement to a woman who was part Hawaiian. "These mixed marriages with people of another color and race are rather apt to turn out badly, don't you think? You need not be afraid that I shall fall before a negro lady or a Persian dame." Lowell to Mary Emlen Hale Lowell, January 25, 1913, Ralph Lowell MSS, 1913–1917 Correspondence box, World Tour 1912–1913 folder.

him an honorary degree, lauding him as "a son of Harvard who craved a service for his country, and found it in leading upward a people ruled through him not for our benefit but theirs." Lowell shared his alma mater's esteem for Forbes, calling him "an energetic builder and a man of exceptional ability in finding out the facts of a case and acting on them with firmness and fairness."[48]

The decision to annex the Philippines in 1898 had provoked bitter debate in Boston and elsewhere about the morality of an American colonial empire, and the recently inaugurated Wilson administration was sympathetic to those who wanted to advance the archipelago swiftly toward independence. Lowell opposed such action. He called himself "an Imperialist" and believed that "America and American commerce should expand." The islands did not "cost us a cent, except for the maintenance of the small army and ridiculous navy that we keep out here, and we should have to keep this up whether we had the Philippines or not." Furthermore, he reasoned, "Our whole trade with the East," would be "utterly ruined were we to relinquish the islands," and withdrawal would cause the United States to "lose the respect of every nation in the world."[49]

Lowell was not impressed with the Filipinos. The islands' "tremendous potential for economic development" would "disappear very far into the distance" should independence be granted any time soon. Filipinos, he wrote, did not understand the American sources of their economic progress to date, and were "suffering from a swelled head and [had] suddenly turned into a race of politicians and orators." The fact that "there are no businessmen among them shows conclusively as any one fact can that they are not nearly ready to govern themselves."[50]

In the Philippines Lowell found "all the possibilities that have become certainties in Java." American "brain and brawn" had already accomplished "wonderful things," and he expected the future to be even better. The United States was showing "the world how savage people can be governed without soldiers if only justice be present." In so doing, he added, undoubtedly recalling what he had encountered in Arizona, "we have partially atoned for the disgraceful treatment that our own American Indians have met with." Based on what he had seen in India and the Dutch East Indies, Lowell had one specific recommendation: Vocational education for the Filipinos was, he believed, "vastly more important than merely teaching [them] book learning, which will simply make them mediocre Europeans."[51]

Aside from the Filipinos' misguided interest in independence, the only threat to American control of the Philippines came from Japan. Lowell received a briefing on this military danger from Forbes's chief aide, who was a Harvard graduate (class of 1910) and a member of the crew. The defense plan centered on Corregidor, "an impregnable island in the mouth of Manila harbor, to which the 12,000 American troops could retire and could await the arrival of our fleet." No enemy navy "could get by the rock," he assured Lowell, "and even if the Japs landed an army on the island they could do nothing but wander around and when our fleet came along they would be blown out of the place." Lowell later had a chance to visit "the rock"; as a security precaution, his camera was taken away. Although he was reassured by the preparations under way, he noted one weak point: mountains on the mainland overlooking the fortress that could be sites for enemy artillery.[52]

In late May Forbes embarked on an eleven-day tour of the northern district of the main island of Luzon and took Lowell and Wigglesworth along. Forbes was traveling for political purposes and also hoped to expand his renowned collection of stuffed birds, which he had already presented to Harvard. Traveling on horseback in roadless jungle, the Americans were accompanied by Filipino laborers, who hauled their baggage and set up camp every night. Forbes escorted his guests through the territory of a tribe that less than a decade earlier had practiced head-hunting; as he had done throughout the trip, Lowell took notes on the natives' rites and social patterns. The tribe apparently posed no threat, but shortly before returning to their home base the travelers experienced a different sort of excitement: an earthquake. From this, too, they emerged unscathed.[53]

Back in civilization, Forbes offered Lowell and Wigglesworth posts in the colonial government. Although the jobs were likely to be of short duration—with President Taft's defeat in the November 1912 elections, Forbes's tenure was most uncertain—Wigglesworth was keenly interested. Lowell and Wigglesworth were well matched as traveling companions, but they held widely divergent views of what constituted a good life. Lowell had addressed that question in his diary while preparing to leave Egypt in January:

> [T]wo kinds of life are open to a man, the life of the home, where one
> makes enough money to love and live upon; and the life of power, when

one wastes one's energy for the fame that may accrue to one on history's pages. If there is a Hereafter, we shall not need the praise of the younger generations, nor shall we be any the happier or worthier for having disregarded the home and striven for power. Power is only gained at the expense of others, and power thus gained is scarcely worthwhile.

A few days later, on board the boat taking them to India, Lowell noted that Wigglesworth put his ambitions first, "while I maintain that love and a happy family is the best thing in the world, and easily outshines simply being in the public eye." Wigglesworth had already set his sights on a political career—an ambition he later fulfilled in thirty years of service (1928–1958) in the U.S. House of Representatives—and he thought the time with Forbes would be well spent. With Lowell's encouragement, Wiggleworth tentatively accepted the position, having explained to Forbes that he must first consult with his parents.[54]

As for Lowell, he quickly but politely declined Forbes's offer. Although it was gratifying to hear that the prominent Boston attorney Robert Herrick had recommended him, government service held no attraction for Lowell. He told the governor general that his family needed him.[55]

With Wigglesworth's future still up in the air, the two men left the Philippines on June 9 bound for China. After a few days in Hong Kong, they went on to the Portuguese colony of Macao. Disgusted by the gambling, prostitution, and opium trade on open display, Lowell labeled Macao "the cesspool of the world, the home of crime and disease, a disgrace to Christianity and the flag under which it lives." Everything about the colony sickened Lowell. Touring the home of "the Chinaman who runs the gambling monopoly," Lowell observed that his gardener was Portuguese. "It certainly does rub one the wrong way," he wrote, "to see any man with white blood in his veins working for a yellow man."[56]

Proceeding up the coast, they stopped in Shanghai, Nanjing (Nankin), Tianjin (Tientsin), and then to Beijing (Pekin). In Shanghai they paid a call at the famous Shanghai Club, with its 115-foot bar "lined seven or eight deep with thirsty men, a truly awe-inspiring sight, and a sight that would drive a Prohibitionist into a very early grave." They also visited the Great Wall. In the two weeks they had allotted to China they could barely scratch the surface. On the basis of what they did see, Lowell concluded that the collapse of the Manchu dynasty sixteen months earlier had been a destructive development: "It is a shame . . . the way the old buildings and all the old institutions and customs are being allowed to go to rack and ruin, and one could almost wish that the Republic would be overthrown and that there might be a return to some kind of monarchy which would protect a few temples and allow some of the better customs to go on as of old."

Westerners whom Lowell met in China predicted an upheaval before the end of the year. Lowell took a dim view of the political situation in China, but he enjoyed doing business with the Chinese. "As businessmen and canny merchants [the Chinese] cannot be beaten," he declared. "It is very restful to know that when a Chinaman says, 'Can do,' the thing will be done and will be done absolutely on time." [57]

Lowell and Wigglesworth's last stops in China were two battle sites of the Russo-Japanese War of 1904–1905, Mukden and Port Arthur. Mukden was a swift, decisive victory for the Japanese army, but Port Arthur was under siege for 241 days before the Russian garrison capitulated, thereby effectively bringing the war to a close. In his diary Lowell described the Port Arthur episode in great detail, observing that "no nation except the Japanese could have carried it to a successful end." "I hope," he continued, "we shall never have to fight them, for they would be a hard nut for us to crack." But, he concluded, "Japan is preparing herself for more wars, there is no doubt of that." [58]

After a short stopover in Korea, Lowell and Wigglesworth arrived in Tokyo, where they had arranged to meet some Harvard friends who had just completed their first year of law school. The plan was for all of them to tour together, but Wigglesworth received a message requesting that he return to Manila to become Forbes's assistant private secretary. Lowell was sad to see him go, but he understood his friend's "sense of duty and ambition" and hoped "his experiment" would be a success. [59] (Unfortunately, within a few weeks President Wilson appointed a replacement for Forbes; but Wigglesworth was able to get back to Cambridge in time to enter Harvard Law School that fall.)

With his expanded traveling entourage, Lowell saw Japan's most famous sights as well as some unusual ones. In Yokohama they visited the red light district. "That kind of outing does not really interest me at all," Lowell wrote, "but it is a good thing to see it once and see how the thing is done under government inspection. Now having seen it, I do not care to do any more of such kind of work."

He climbed Mount Fuji and took in countless shrines, but he showed signs of becoming jaded. "Temples are beginning to pall on me, and I haven't the gumption to do them justice in the diary any more." [60] More than simple fatigue, however, lay behind Lowell's rather negative summary remarks as he departed Japan:

The people are clean and their dress is pretty. I like the women who shuffle from the knees down, with their large sashes and their mountains of shiny black hair; I like the children, . . . who run about on their improbable wooden shoes (at least I like them when they are clean); I like the houses with their paper scenes and their immaculate mats; but I do not like the stupid, swell-headed men, despite their veneer of insincere politeness. I do not like the Geishas or the Japanese music—they are slow and uninteresting—and I do not like their interminable plays, or their outlandish food.

Given a choice, Lowell wrote, he would go back to any of the other Asian countries he had visited, "even India," before returning to Japan. [61]

Now traveling alone, Lowell took a boat to Vladivostok and on August 14 boarded the Trans-Siberian Railroad. The train was his home for the next eight days as it slowly but methodically headed westward; he found his second-class accommodations "pleasant and comfortable." Lowell had only limited contact with Russians, but what he saw depressed him:

The people at the stations along the route are really pathetic. They are as poor as can be and all the life and ambition that they ever had has been successfully knocked out of them by the oppression and cruelty with which they are treated. There would seem to be a good deal of truth in the assertion that Russia is only held together by the church, which works on the superstitions of the downtrodden people and does its utmost to keep them down and uncultured. All the excess money they have—and God knows there is little enough—goes to buying candles for their ikons.

Nonetheless, he wrote "Russia has a great future ahead of it and . . . will be a place that feeds the world in the future." On the August 20 the train crossed the Urals, and Lowell's "glorious trip to Asia" came to an end. Two days later the train pulled into the Moscow station, where his parents and his younger brother and sister were waiting on the platform. With one additional entry to record his troubles in retrieving his trunk, Lowell's sixteen hundred pages of travel diaries were finished. ("I saw the manager twice," he complained, "fought with everybody, cursed loudly, was understood by no one. . . . The Russians are the worst businessmen in the world.") More than three decades would elapse before he traveled west of Chicago or again crossed the Atlantic.[62]

3

"Everything in this world of ours is topsy-turvy"

WORK, WAR, AND A WEDDING

I n August 1914, exactly a year after Ralph Lowell completed his grand tour, Europe plunged into the abyss of war. Before it finally ended, more than four years later, the Great War had taken millions of lives, including more than fifty thousand Americans killed on the battlefield, and planted the seeds for an even more destructive conflict. For Lowell personally, however, this calamitous period had a positive side. Although the international crisis put his pursuit of economic success on hold, his matrimonial plans were accelerated, and he was given an opportunity to demonstrate his organizational and leadership skills.

A START IN BUSINESS

As he pondered his future in the months before graduating from Harvard, Ralph considered joining his cousin Lawrence in the world of academia. His professors encouraged him to go on to graduate school, and he thought "teaching anthropology would be a very enjoyable job." But he recognized that scholarship was "a peculiarly unremunerative occupation," and he was not ready to give up the style of life to which he was accustomed. Anthropology would have to remain a hobby rather than a vocation.[1]

Following the long line of John Lowells in the field of law held little attraction. Ralph believed his father was fighting a losing battle to uphold the values of that once-honored profession. "Justice," Ralph observed during his world tour in 1913, "is nearly a thing of the past. . . . [A]ny lawyer can make the worse appear the better reason." In the decades that followed, he barely disguised his impatience with attorneys and their mindset.[2]

In the early and middle nineteenth century the Lowells' business prowess had cemented their position in the upper echelons of Boston society. Ralph decided that a business career offered him the best opportunity for retaining that status. Several of the Boston Brahmins at the turn of the twentieth century, comfortable in their inherited wealth, were critical of the business culture of that era, but A. Lawrence Lowell was not among them. He called business "one of the oldest of the arts and latest of the professions," and once remarked to a Cabot, "I'm getting worried about the Lowell family, George. There's nobody in it making money anymore." Ralph decided to try.[3]

The customary way for young men—even those from the very best families—to start out in business was at the bottom. Lowell's job hunting in the Boston area before his graduation took him to a large shoe manufacturing firm, whose owner agreed to take him on even though he had "no definite position for [Lowell] to work up to." Lowell declined the offer, perhaps because of its vagueness or because he was unenthusiastic about "tackling the shoe business." An invitation to go into insurance prompted another negative response. Financially the package was enticing, "but the agent of an insurance company," he wrote, "is a mere automaton and does not have an opportunity to show whether he has any brains or not. He is the rankest kind of middleman."[4]

Three weeks after receiving his diploma, Lowell found a job to his liking. By interviewing at Curtis & Sanger, dealers in commercial paper and investment securities since 1899, Ralph entered strange yet friendly territory. The Lowells had made their fortunes in manufacturing, not in financial transactions, and Ralph's single accounting course—the only utilitarian course he had taken in college—had been a "nightmare." However, both Curtis and Sanger were Harvard graduates, as was Edward Motley, the partner who interviewed Lowell. A member of the class of 1902, Motley belonged to the A.D. Club and was engaged to the sister of Lowell's closest friend from the Volkmann School. It was agreed that Lowell would start work as a messenger on August 1, take off in late November on his world tour, and return to the job the following fall. Although his wages were only $5 a week, Lowell was "swell-headed and puffed up" by his good fortune.[5]

Lowell remained in this congenial environment for three years, advancing from addressing envelopes to sales. He received a good education in the operations of a brokerage firm, but also became aware of Curtis & Sanger's inconsequential status in the financial world. By 1916 he was eager to associate himself with a bigger and more powerful player.

When Lowell joined the First National Bank of Boston that year, it was in the midst of an expansion that by the mid-1930s would make it the largest financial institution in New England. The investment banking firm of Hornblower and Weeks had laid the foundation for this expansion in 1900, when it gained control of the Massachusetts National Bank (successor to the state-chartered Massachusetts Bank of which Ralph's great-great-great-grandfather had been an original incorporator in 1784) and placed Daniel G. Wing in command. Over the next three-and-a-half decades, "by conquest, alliance and salvage," Wing transformed the bank, which had been on the brink of collapse, and established its "undisputed hegemony" in New England banking.[6]

Wing was an unlikely savior of Boston's oldest bank. Born in Iowa and raised in Nebraska, he had not gone to college; after spending nearly fifteen years at a Nebraska bank, where he went no farther than cashier, Wing became a bank examiner for the federal government and was assigned to Boston. In that capacity, he nearly shut the Massachusetts National Bank in 1899 for insufficient capital. Returning to the private sector the following year at the behest of the bank's new owners, he quickly restored its profitability. "Not knowing the traditions of Boston," it has been said of Wing, "he did not suffer from the limitations of those who did." He took the bank into the familiar fields of safe deposit and trust administration, bought out competitors—including the First National Bank of Boston, whose name he also appropriated—and thrust the bank into entirely new endeavors. Beginning in 1913, Wing made the First National Bank of Boston a potent force in Latin American banking, a role it retains more than eight decades later.[7]

Lowell's ties to Harvard rowing gave him access to Daniel Wing. Robert Herrick, that grand friend of the Harvard crew, was the First National Bank's lawyer, and he recommended to Wing that he take Lowell on. In July 1916 Lowell became secretary to the president.[8]

The midwesterner and the Boston Brahmin did not hit it off. The closest Lowell ever came to explaining why was in 1943. Lowell had recently become chairman of a trust company, and for the first time since the First National Bank's move to its new building in 1924, he attended a meeting in the board of directors' room. Wing had died in 1936, but as Lowell noted, "the room was dominated (as was the bank)" by Wing's portrait. "I felt that he was looking directly at me," Lowell wrote, "and I wasn't quite sure of whether he approved of where I had arrived at or not. I think he felt that I was really not cut out to be a banker, although that might have been because he was against my going in the World War so early." [9]

PREPAREDNESS AND MILITARY SERVICE

During his tenure at the First National Bank, Lowell was more concerned about training to be a military officer, and encouraging others to do the same, than about learning the bankers' craft. While Daniel Wing's eyes were turned southward with a view to expanding his bank's presence in Latin America, Lowell looked east at a Europe consumed by war.

Like most of his social class, Lowell's sympathies in 1914 were with the Allies. The emotional bonds linking the United States with England and France were much stronger than the intellectual ties to Germany, and whatever legitimacy the German cause may have had was lost with its invasion of Belgium. In early 1915 Lowell served as treasurer for the A.D. Club's Ambulance Fund, which raised money to aid an American hospital treating Allied wounded in Paris. But it was a crusade started by a member of the Porcellian that would engage Lowell's energies for the next three years. [10]

Grenville Clark (class of 1903), a lawyer who moved in the most elite circles of his native New York City, was an initiator and mobilizer on a scale that Lowell would never achieve. Outraged by the German sinking of the British liner *Lusitania* in May 1915, Clark convened a series of meetings at the Harvard Club of New York to establish the Military Training Camps Committee (MTCC). In cooperation with General Leonard Wood, the commander of the army's Eastern Department, based in New York, the MTCC began planning a Business Men's Camp, where men in their twenties and thirties would be prepared to serve in a new reserve officers corps. In June, Clark, who had married a Boston Brahmin, traveled to Boston and enlisted Harvard alumni John Wells ("Mike") Farley and Benjamin Joy to take charge of the MTCC's recruitment campaign in New England. Farley (class of 1899) was a law partner of Robert Herrick, and Joy (class of 1905) worked at the National Shawmut Bank. They had to act quickly; the camp at Plattsburg, New York, was to start on August 10.[11]

Boston, with its large reservoir of Harvard graduates, proved to be fertile ground for volunteers. In the view of Harvard philosophy professor Ralph Barton Perry, a participant in the camp and a chronicler of the movement to form similar camps, the "Plattsburg Movement" derived its strength from "the desire of young business and professional men . . . to escape the ignominy of weakness and inaction in the presence of a grave national and human emergency." Another historian of the MTCC observed that "[i]n a time when certainty and conviction were attributes of the educated," the men who responded to the committee's call "looked upon such things as 'right' and 'duty' as tangible imperatives." Among those joining Ralph at the camp were his brother Jim; Richard Wigglesworth; the Harvard football coach; and two sons of Harvard philosopher William James.[12]

Having paid their thirty-dollar fee (five dollars was refundable if the individual did no damage to government property), twelve hundred men gathered in mid-August by the shores of Lake Champlain for four weeks of training by regular army personnel. In addition to bringing their own uniforms, the men were expected to have read a military manual and the army's field service regulations. Upon arrival they were supplied with a rifle and bayonet, a mess kit, a water bottle and cap, a web belt and pack, blankets, a sweater, and a poncho. They slept in tents on collapsible canvas cots. Eager to demonstrate the usefulness of universal military training, General Wood insisted that the camp match the discipline and effort demanded of the regular army.[13]

"They are making us work right up to capacity all the time," Ralph wrote to his mother soon after settling in. Awakened at 5:30 every morning, the men had ten minutes of sit-ups before breakfast at 6:30. At 7:30 they put on their packs, picked up their rifles, and formed into companies for four hours of drill. Ralph had started in the rear line of his squad, but he was quickly advanced to number three man in the front line. This would be the first of many promotions he received in the army. Lunch was at noon. At 1:30 the men worked on special assignments, Jim in the signal corps, Ralph in mapmaking and engineering. "The map-makers have the hardest physical work," Ralph explained, "for they have to hike all afternoon making maps and putting in all the hills, hollows, houses and paths that they come across." At 5:00 P.M. the entire Camp formed under arms again, and with the band playing they drilled in the large parade ground for thirty minutes "under the eyes of General Wood and other high muck-a-mucks." Supper was at 6:00 followed by an outdoor lecture in the twilight on some aspect of military doctrine or national defense policy. The remainder of the evening was spent "smooth[ing] over some of the rough points of our work," and at 9:00 lights were out. Although the men had Sundays off and were free to leave the post, there was "so much to do that you practically have to stay on the job." "It is good hard work, and plenty of it," Lowell concluded, "but I haven't lost any weight and am enjoying myself immensely." [14]

The climax of the training was a nine-day war game in which the businessmen, carrying forty-two-pound packs, fought mock battles all over the Adirondack countryside against the Regulars. What took place at Plattsburg, Perry later wrote, was "a steady process of seasoning and hardening, that tired a man out every day, but made him feel like a giant at the end." Before departing for home, the "Plattsburgers" adopted resolutions urging the creation of a permanent organization to support additional training camps. [15]

The resolutions were Grenville Clark's handiwork, and in early 1916 he implemented them by forming the Military Training Camps Association (MTCA). Mike Farley served on the new group's executive committee, and along with Ben Joy he continued to direct the New England operations of the Plattsburg Movement. With an eye toward running another Business Men's Camp in the summer of 1916, Farley and Joy created an enrollment committee and asked Lowell to be a member. Lowell accepted and also agreed to help find volunteers for the summer training camp for boys aged fifteen to eighteen, which the army planned to conduct on Long Island. He was now an active advocate of universal military training, a cause he continued to champion through decades of peace and war. [16]

Lowell returned to Plattsburg in August 1916 for additional training. Entering the camp as a private, he left as a second lieutenant with a commission in the newly formed Officers' Reserve Corps. That fall he replaced Farley as chairman of the New England division of the MTCA and started promotional activities for the 1917 summer camps. But events overtook the nation and Lowell. On April 2, 1917, President Wilson asked Congress to declare war, which it did four days later, and on receipt of his orders Lowell, promoted to first lieutenant (infantry), entered active service on May 12. [17]

Before donning his uniform, Lowell helped ameliorate one of the local tragedies generated by the European war. Arthur L. K. Volkmann was no friend of Prussian militarism, but his German name and accent made him and his school unpopular in a Boston swept up in the anti-Teutonic hysteria of the period. "Even in his club," a graduate of the Volkmann School recalled bitterly, "old acquaintances turned away or stopped talking when he entered, as though he were an enemy." Volkmann's health suffered and the school's enrollment dropped. In the early spring of 1917 Lowell and other concerned alumni, wanting to "place the few remaining of our beloved teachers with an enduring school," approached Richard Saltonstall, president of the Volkmann School's "hated rival" Noble and Greenough, with a proposal to merge the two institutions under the latter's name. Saltonstall, a neighbor from Chestnut Hill and the father of Lowell's friend Leverett, agreed to let Lowell present the idea before Noble and Greenough's board of trustees. Lowell and a 1914 Volkmann graduate made their case in April, and the plan was ratified in June. As part of the arrangement, the board was expanded to include two Volkmann alumni.[18]*

The troubles at Volkmann's aside, Lowell was so impatient to get into the army that he jumped at the first position offered him, even though it was in Georgia. But army regulations required that he remain within the Eastern Department, and he was assigned to Plattsburg. Over the next three months he received further instruction from regular army officers and shared his own knowledge with new officer recruits. In August, just after his twenty-seventh birthday, he was advanced to major, one of the youngest men in the army to hold that rank.[19]

CHARLOTTE LORING

August 1917 was a momentous month for Lowell in another way—he became engaged. Within days of placing his major's gold oak leaf on his uniform, Lowell returned to Boston, took Charlotte Loring for a walk in the

---

* In the 1960s the Harvard Club of Boston purchased the Volkmann School building on Newbury Street and demolished it to make way for a parking lot. Lowell helped arrange a reunion of the school's graduates at the building before it was torn down; thirty-five people attended. The tablet from over the front entrance inscribed with the school's motto, *Fortiter, Fideliter*, was made into a memorial bench on the Noble and Greenough campus. Diary, June 1, 1965; *Noble and Greenough Graduates' Bulletin*, June 1966.

woods on her family's estate, and proposed marriage. She accepted, and in less than three weeks they were husband and wife. Thirty years later Lowell recalled that "some people wagged their heads and could only hope that such a war wedding would turn out all right." It did.[20]

Charlotte Loring was the enduring love of Lowell's life, but she was not the first. As a middle-aged and older man, Lowell looked distinguished; as a young man, he was handsome. On his sixteenth birthday a friend wrote a poem describing Ralph's effect on the opposite sex:

> A child with curly hair was he
> With dimples round his mouth,
> That captured all the girls who haunt
> The North Shore or the South. . . .
>
> Each summer's closing season sees
> The same pathetic sight,
> At Kin-e-o or York or Mag
> Some heart had felt the blight.

The busy social life of Brahmin Boston fostered contacts between the sexes — always under strict supervision, to be sure — and during his freshman year at Harvard, a girl from Philadelphia stole Lowell's heart. Unfortunately, she was interested in someone else, and Ralph made a "fool" of himself in pursuing her. Undoubtedly there were others during his college years and immediately after, but marriage was unthinkable until he had a secure financial future.[21]

Lowell, who had grown a mustache since graduating from college, saw Charlotte frequently in 1916, her debutante year, but the two probably had common social engagements even before that. With her red hair, Charlotte stood out in most gatherings. Not a striking beauty, she was, to use a favorite term of Ralph's, attractive. While he never spelled out what drew him to Charlotte, it is fair to assume that he was looking for a wife more like his mother than his sister Molly. In 1913, when Lowell heard that Molly had won a scholarship to study painting in Paris, he was happy for her but nonetheless pitied her husband and son: "She will probably spend more on art than ever before. I hope my wife will not try to decorate canvas to the detriment of our meals and household." Charlotte did not disappoint him; beyond her husband and children, Charlotte's only major lifelong interest was her sewing circle, that special Boston institution.[22]

"Outside of Scotland," observed a newspaper in the late 1890s, "there is no more clannish clan on the face of the earth than the Boston Sewing Circle." Sewing circles began in the mid-nineteenth century with the objective of encouraging fashionable young ladies to sew for the poor. Each year's debutantes formed their own circle—Charlotte's was the 1916 Sewing Circle. By the early twentieth century, however, the sewing circles essentially had become lunch clubs that met at members' homes, rather than charitable groups.[23]

References to Charlotte's debutante ball and her sewing circle testify to her family's wealth. Each of her parents alone had access to more money than John and Mary Lowell could touch. A 1902 list of Boston millionaires included Charlotte's two grandfathers; the only Lowell recorded was the deceased Augustus. Marriage would have been impossible for Major Ralph Lowell in 1917 without Charlotte's income to supplement his meager military pay.[24]

The Loring family had deep roots in Massachusetts, but the Cochranes, the family of Charlotte's mother, were more prominent at the start of the twentieth century. Charlotte's grandfather Alexander Cochrane had come to the United States from Scotland as a child in 1847. He made the chemical company founded by his father into one of New England's largest manufacturers of sulfuric acid, dyestuffs, and ammonia. An investment in a company that produced batteries introduced Cochrane to the work of another Scotsman, Alexander Graham Bell, who was the company's technical adviser. Cochrane became an early investor in Bell's telephone company, a move that brought him a great fortune and made him an associate of Boston's two most prominent financiers, Henry Lee Higginson and William Hathaway Forbes. One of Cochrane's daughters married a Forbes, another married a Cushing, and a third married a Loring.[25]

If the Cochranes could be regarded by some as upstarts, the Lorings furnished Charlotte with a New England pedigree comparable to the bridegroom's. Through her paternal grandmother, Charlotte was descended from a signer of the Declaration of Independence (William Ellery of Rhode Island) and related to both William Ellery Channing, a leading nineteenth-century Unitarian clergyman, and Margaret Fuller, a Transcendentalist writer and early advocate of women's rights. Elisha Loring, Charlotte's great-grandfather, amassed his wealth during the middle of the nineteenth century in South American trade and copper mining along the shores of Lake Superior. The career of her grandfather, Thacher Loring, remains a mystery; his 1928 obituary noted only that he had been "for many years closely identified with Boston business interests."[26]

Neither Elisha nor Thacher Loring went to college, and Thacher's son, Lindsley, attended but did not graduate from Harvard. Lindsley fell in love with Charlotte Blake Cochrane while a sophomore and left Cambridge after his junior year to go to work. In working first at his father's shipping firm and then at his father-in-law's chemical company, Lindsley demonstrated little of the business acumen found in the previous generation of Lorings and Cochranes. Nor did he show much interest in civic activities. But by drawing on their ample inheritances, Lindsley and Charlotte bestowed an elegant way of life on their four children.[27]

In 1898–1899, Lindsley and his brother-in-law purchased about 125 acres in the town of Westwood, fifteen miles southwest of Boston. Each family built a large home on the property, and it was here, at Lindsley's "Sunrise Farm" with its spectacular view of the morning sun coming over the Blue Hills to the east, that Charlotte Loring, born in 1897, grew up. And it was here that Ralph Lowell proposed marriage to her on August 14, 1917.[28]

A letter Ralph wrote to his mother in May, soon after assuming his military duties at Plattsburg, suggests that his engagement to Charlotte took the family by surprise. "Despite Aunt Susy's dope," he proclaimed, "I do not write the Fessendens every day (only once as yet), so you needn't get your hopes up in that direction." Ralph's family may also have been surprised by Ralph and Charlotte's decision—probably made on August 21, the day Ralph had to return to Plattsburg—to set their wedding for September 1. "I think she is a perfect wonder to want to marry me right away," he told his mother. "I guess it is the best thing to do, even though everything in this world of ours is topsy-turvy." There would be no time to send out formal invitations, and only the families and a few intimate friends would be present. "Rarely has it happened," a Boston newspaper observed, "that so pretty and well-placed a girl as Charlotte Loring has embarked upon the matrimonial ocean with no prefacing gayeties, but the absence of Major Lowell in Plattsburg was an effective veto on the entertainments friends would have liked to give."[29]

Ralph almost missed the wedding. It was set for noon on Saturday, and he was permitted to leave the army post on Friday afternoon. By leaving on the 4:20 train from Plattsburg, Ralph planned to make a connection in Albany that would bring him into Boston's South Station at 6 A.M., giving him ample time to get home and prepare for the ceremony. According to the railroad schedule, he had two hours' leeway in Albany, but the train left Plattsburg late and fell progressively behind as it headed south. Knowing that if he missed the Albany connection he could not possibly reach Westwood by the appointed hour, Lowell "grew desperate, and finally wired Albany to hold the Boston train, signing the telegram, 'Major, U.S. Infantry.'" Years later Lowell wondered if he could have been court-martialed for his action—but the telegram achieved the desired result. Half an hour after its scheduled departure time, the train to Boston was still in the Albany station. As Lowell "came panting up to it, the conductor, with his watch in his hand, said, 'Thank God, you are here.'" [30]

Ralph arrived early at Sunrise Farm, "much to the dismay of [his] mother-in-law, who belonged to the old school that believes the groom should not see the bride until the ceremony started." Otherwise, the day went smoothly. The wedding took place on the Lorings' magnificent great lawn, Lowell dressed in his uniform and Charlotte in a traditional bridal gown with a full train. Ralph's brother Jim served as best man, and Charlotte's younger brother and sister attended her; there were no ushers. The groom was twenty-seven years old, the bride just four days short of her twentieth birthday. They would celebrate this day together for the next sixty years. [31]

ARMY LIFE

After a two-day honeymoon in New Hampshire, Ralph returned to Plattsburg on Tuesday to resume his supervision of an infantry battalion in training. He rented a room for Charlotte in a house near the post and was able to take lunch and dinner with her. Lowell hoped to be sent to France with his unit when the current ninety-day camp finished up in late November, but the army had other plans for him. Being an instructor came easily to him, and he was assigned to a series of officer training camps to prepare the men who would lead the troops in battle overseas. One of the men who passed through Lowell's command wrote forty years later to tell him what a wonderful job he had done: "You always dealt with the men in a vibrant and refreshing manner. You cast aside the somewhat pedantic method that was employed by too many of those who were merely following the book. You were a natural teacher. You were friendly and helpful. . . . You, sir, were an officer and a gentleman." Although Lowell was disappointed to be left behind, he took it philosophically. "It is all in the game," he wrote his mother, "and a soldier very soon learns to take what is coming to him without grumbling."[32]

With conscription in place and the army undergoing tremendous expansion, Ralph received a transfer that greatly reduced the young couple's feelings of loneliness. In the fall of 1917 a new training facility called Camp Devens was opened in Ayer, about thirty miles northwest of Boston, and Lowell was appointed assistant senior instructor for the training session that commenced in early January 1918. Charlotte stayed with her parents in Westwood. On weekends she would visit her maternal grandparents on Marlborough Street in the Back Bay, and Ralph would come into town on Saturday afternoon and return to Devens the following evening.[33]

With his promotion to major and his move to Camp Devens, Lowell became one of the better known soldiers in the Boston area, and in March he accepted an invitation to address the annual meeting of the Harvard Club. College men in the officers' training program at Devens, he told the alumni, "lead in every requirement excepting discipline and realization of the seriousness of the war, but they are woefully lacking in those essentials." He argued that the blame for this should fall on their fathers for failing to insist on discipline at home and in school.[34]

Lowell served as senior instructor for a another training camp held that spring at Devens, but in July he was shifted to Camp Lee, near Petersburg, Virginia. Charlotte did not accompany him, as she was pregnant. On August 23 while giving a talk to fifteen hundred officer candidates, Ralph was handed a telegram informing him that he had a daughter.[35]

The Central Officers' Training School at Camp Lee was the largest of the infantry encampments established by the War Department in the summer of 1918; at its peak four thousand men were enrolled. As the senior instructor Lowell was the school's second-ranking officer. Its commander was Colonel Henry A. Eaton, a West Virginian who had made a career of the army after volunteering for the Spanish-American War. Not long after taking up his duties, Lowell outlined for his mother the task confronting him:

My job is a very responsible one, and one that I think I will enjoy as soon as I get used to Colonel Eaton. He is an old woman and believes that things can be done only one certain way, and he is there to see that they are done in that manner. All the innovations that we worked out to benefit the men and make them feel that they are being trained to be officers and not enlisted men have been thrown into the discard. But still, . . . it is only a question of getting used to the Colonel and then all will be well.

One of the first changes Lowell made was in the way the men were drilled. They had not worn hats, even though many suffered heatstroke in the brutal midday summer sun. Lowell ordered that heads be covered, and heatstroke ceased to be a problem. This was typical of Lowell's approach to life: Although he revered tradition and generally accepted the customary method of doing things, he was open to change when conditions seemed to demand it.[36]

In mid-September Lowell was promoted to lieutenant colonel, a sure sign that he and Eaton were working well together. Lowell's duties were administrative and instructional. His officers learned battlefield tactics and techniques for motivating the men under their command. Although Lowell regarded Petersburg as "a dirty hole, . . . a shiftless, no account town," he arranged for Charlotte and little Charlotte, as the baby had been named, to move there in late October.[37]

The sudden outbreak of peace in mid-November forced Lowell to make decisions about his future. His rapid advancement in the army made it an attractive career option, and Eaton encouraged him to stay on. But Lowell saw little hope in a severely downsized military. "Officers who have not gone abroad," he observed, "will not be able to compete with those who have." Without a wife and a child he might nevertheless have considered the army, but both of his Charlottes needed to be fed. Resumption of his business career in Boston seemed a wiser course. He wrote to Daniel Wing inquiring about his prospects at the First National Bank.[38]

Wing's response was disappointing though not unexpected. "We can, of course, find a place for you here and should be glad to have you back," Wing wrote on November 15,

> but I am inclined to doubt whether in any position we could give you, you would be contented for any length of time, either with the salary or with the immediate chances for going ahead. You, of course, realize that with a good many officers here, who are your seniors and who have been here a good while, the promotion upward must be necessarily slow.

Noting that economic conditions were likely to stagnate for a year or so, Wing suggested that Lowell remain in the army "until things settle down and you can determine more clearly what is going to happen." Wing added that "the Army is going to need some officers with business training as much as business men are needed anywhere else."[39]

Lowell got the message. Wing's letter was "a gentle hint," Ralph wrote his mother, "that he doesn't want me." Although he vented his frustration in the letter to his mother—"I am afraid that most of the good jobs are being held by slackers that didn't go, and that we must be the goats for a while at least"*—he was polite to Wing. Thanking him for being "frank," Lowell outlined what he was looking for: "a responsible job in Boston which would enable me within the next few years at any rate to enjoy home life and get a thorough rest after the hectic time of the last year and a half. Naturally I want to rise and go ahead as fast as possible in business, but I want to get a good foundation before so doing." He told Wing he would be asking others for advice and checking with other banks.[40]

Lowell was discharged from the army on December 4 and immediately proceeded to Boston. Wing had given him at least one lead, and other possibilities also materialized. At the investment banking house of Lee, Higginson & Co., a meeting with one of the partners (the captain of the Harvard crew of 1900) brought an offer to manage the firm's Stock Department. Lowell accepted, and as of January 1, 1919, his business career was again on track.[41]

---

* At the close of World War II, as head of the Boston Safe Deposit and Trust Company, Lowell instituted a rule that bank employees who served in the armed forces were "entitled to their old positions and [would] not be penalized for time out in the Service." However, he stipulated that there be "a period of a few months of intensive study on our part as well as theirs before they are put ahead to where the older men have arrived." At the outbreak of the Korean War, Lowell declared that all bank employees called into the military would find their jobs "waiting for them," and added, "[P]rovided they return hale and hearty, they will not be penalized in line of promotion." Diary, February 12, 1945; July 31, 1950.

4

"Pumping in orders . . . as fast as we could"

MOVING AHEAD IN THE 1920s

When Ralph Lowell and his Harvard classmates gathered for their fifteenth reunion in 1927, many had already made impressive strides in their chosen fields. Robert Benchley, whose Ivy Oration had been such a hit, was a drama critic for the nationally circulated *Life*, then a humor magazine, and a contributor to the recently launched *New Yorker*. With his chair at the Algonquin Round Table, Benchley sat at the center of what passed for wit and sophistication in the Jazz Age. The frenzy of the era was best symbolized by the bull market on Wall Street, and few played the New York Stock Exchange more successfully than the class of 1912's own Joe Kennedy. His next stop was Hollywood, where he became a movie mogul. Less conspicuously, other classmates were making their way up corporate ladders or winning desirable law partnerships. Ralph Lowell had neither fame nor an imposing job title to flaunt at the reunion. Instead, the 1920s brought him a bigger family and a generally happy home life, as well as a deepening involvement in community activities.

LEE, HIGGINSON & CO.

In moving from Daniel Wing's First National Bank to the investment banking firm of Lee, Higginson & Co., Lowell left a rising institution for the one already at the top of Boston's financial community. Founded in 1848 as a brokerage house "in the purchase and sale of Stocks, Notes, and Exchange," it shifted to private and investment banking by the time of the

Civil War. Its initial financing aided New England railroads and textile mills, but by the late 1860s and 1870s it had expanded geographically. It funded the Chicago, Burlington & Quincy Railroad and the Atchison, Topeka & Santa Fe Railroad; most important, it invested its money, as well as that of its select circle of clients, in the Calumet and Hecla copper mines in Michigan. The profits from these mines vastly enlarged the fortunes of Boston's Brahmins and prolonged them into the twentieth century.[1]

The individual primarily responsible for the Calumet and Hecla investment was Henry Lee Higginson, son of one of the founders and a cousin of the Lowells. Higginson had joined the firm reluctantly, only after finding that he had little talent as a musician and after an honorable military career during the Civil War; the rank of major preceded his name for the rest of his life. Under his leadership Lee, Higginson staked several profitable ventures, including Alexander Graham Bell's telephone company and General Electric. As was demonstrated by his offer of aid to Ralph's grandmother, Major Higginson enjoyed sharing his considerable wealth with others, and his philanthropy was not restricted to family and friends. His gifts to Harvard included Soldiers Field, the Harvard Union, and the funds needed to start the business school. Higginson also founded the Boston Symphony Orchestra (1881) and covered its expenses for nearly forty years. At his death in 1919, he was hailed as Boston's "first citizen."[2]

At the turn of the century, leadership of the banking house passed to James Jackson Storrow, a kinsman of the Lees and Higginsons who carried on the Major's role as a civic benefactor as well. Storrow reshaped the firm in the early twentieth century to counter the increasing domination of the financial markets by New York City (or more precisely, by J. P. Morgan). Rapidly growing businesses with roots in New England, like American Telephone and Telegraph and General Electric, found that their Boston bankers could not satisfy their voracious appetite for funds, and turned to Morgan for sustenance; many moved their headquarters or operations to be closer to their new backers. Under Higginson the firm had relied on a small pool of investors, each with a considerable sum of capital; Storrow created a network of salesmen to sell bonds to a mass of customers with only limited resources. The trend toward concentration of financial power in New York continued, but Storrow's strategy kept Lee, Higginson among the first rank of the nation's investment houses.[3]

With Storrow at the helm, Lee, Higginson & Co. underwent significant expansion during the first two decades of the twentieth century. It admitted additional partners and opened offices in Chicago, New York, and London. It also established a separate Stock Department. Although partners in the firm had been members of the Boston Stock Exchange since 1848 and of the New York Stock Exchange since 1888, trading stocks had become a minor component of Lee, Higginson's business. The firm underwrote stocks and bonds to raise capital for new and growing companies, but disdained as "speculation" the subsequent buying and selling of these securities. Nonetheless, in 1905, as a service to the customers of its expanding retail bond distribution system, Lee, Higginson began offering easier access to the stock market. Significantly, the Stock Department was not directed by a partner, and the actual processing of trades was handled by correspondent brokerage houses in New York.[4]

The layout of Lee, Higginson's new facilities in 1925 confirmed the Stock Department's inferior status. After more than seventy years at the same address on State Street, the firm moved to 70 Federal Street, which had been vacated by the First National Bank. The bond sales department, the partners' offices, the conference rooms, and the expanding foreign department occupied the main floor; the Stock Department, although well equipped and allotted ample space, occupied the floor below.[5]

If Lowell failed to appreciate the partners' condescending view of the Stock Department when he accepted the position as manager, he quickly discerned the situation once on the job and spent the next decade trying to win his bosses' approval of the department's work. Lee, Higginson always had prided itself on its "reputation for faithfully honest advice to its clients," and Lowell tried to associate his department with that tradition. Soon after assuming his job, Lowell wrote in a report to the partners that it was the duty of "reputable brokers" to educate the public about investing in stocks. "Sharks and promoters" were all too ready to take advantage of the "gambling instincts of the people," and unless these charlatans were challenged by expert "financial stock advisers," the public's willingness to save and invest—one of the positive consequences of the war—would "die an abrupt death." Most stockbrokers, Lowell argued, never escaped "the sinister shadow of the stock exchange" with its short-term view of stock price fluctuations. Stocks could be viewed in another way, he declared: "Just as bonds keep steady like the deep water in the ocean, stocks go up and down like the waves, and when they are founded on the deep water of security they do not break." Stocks were a sound investment, he concluded, as long as the recommendations for their purchase and sale came from reputable sources, not

> [the] set of ticker-bound men that grasp at rumors like drowning men at straws. [The financial stock adviser] must be a conservative student of equities and finance. He must be able to forget the rumor-led flurries of the moment and look deeper into the fundamental values of things. If he can do this, if he can "keep his head when all about him are losing theirs," he can be of inestimable benefit to the small investor as well as to the man of larger means.[6]

By not sending out market tipsheets, by keeping a close eye on customers' margin accounts, and by refusing to become involved in the pools and raids that were commonplace on Wall Street in the early 1920s, Lowell hoped to gain stature within Lee, Higginson, both for his department and for himself.[7]

In the first part of the decade, the level of stock market activity was higher than it had been before the war. But for Lowell, with his generally cautious clientele, it was not an especially hectic time, and others in the business thought he might be open to a change. In building up his sales team, Lowell had hired Robert Fisher, a 1912 Harvard classmate and coach of the Crimson football team. Fisher and Joe Kennedy had roomed together in college, and they remained good friends after graduation. Sometime in 1924, at Kennedy's behest, Fisher approached Lowell with the idea of establishing a brokerage house in New York. Gotham held no appeal for Lowell, and he had other reasons as well for not joining the venture. Kennedy was already notorious for his flamboyant stock market operations. Lowell would not have been comfortable with Kennedy's business practices. And even if Kennedy's reputation had been better, there was still the matter of his ancestry. Decades later, Lowell recorded in his diary a lunchtime conversation with friends. The discussion turned to the persistence of Kennedy's Irish accent, despite his years at Harvard and in London as U.S. ambassador to England. Lowell made a note of his own remark: "You can tune a harp and tune a harp, but it's still a harp." This, he observed, caused "amusement." Partnerships across ethnic and religious lines were a rarity in the Boston of the 1920s, and at this stage of his career Lowell was not cut out to be a trailblazer. For a long time he believed that Kennedy bore a grudge against him for spurning his business offer. The word got around Boston charitable circles that if you wanted a contribution from Kennedy, Lowell was not the man to send as emissary.[8]

Kennedy went to New York on his own and scored big.* Despite their best efforts, Lowell and Lee, Higginson could not escape the repercussions of the stock manipulations by which Kennedy and others amassed fortunes. During the winter of 1926, for instance, the market dropped thirty points (or 21 percent) in six weeks, one of the steepest declines in the New York Exchange's history. The drop was precipitated by the collapse of a pool in Devoe & Raynolds, a large paint manufacturer. By using sixteen different margin accounts, a novice trader had acquired all but fifteen thousand shares of the company's stock and then approached a brokerage house to help him squeeze the people selling short. But his allies betrayed him by breaking the pool, and the price dropped so far and so quickly that the brokerage firms holding his margin accounts could not liquidate his assets. A committee eventually was formed to dispose of the stock, and all of the firms lost heavily (one lost $400,000). The problems created by the attempted corner at Devoe & Raynolds led brokers and banks to scrutinize their other loans more carefully, and this prompted the collapse of three other pools and a precipitous decline in overall market prices. As a consequence, Lowell noted, "all those who had stocks on margin, both good and bad, without exception," were put at risk.[9]

These events made for "some very exciting days" in Lowell's department. "It is not at all very pleasant," he wrote, "to have a stream of customers besieging you for advice as to what to do, especially when in addition you have all the worry of the margin accounts on your shoulders and the chance of one or more getting in such shape that an actual loss might result to the firm." But "luckily," Lee, Higginson had comparatively few margin calls to send out and they all "came across in good shape." Some brokerage houses had to work late into the night to clear up their records, but at 70 Federal Street everything went smoothly; by 5:30 P.M. on each day of a big price break, Lowell had a list of the accounts that had fallen below

---

* In a 1962 interview, Lowell commented that Boston "was a small, clear puddle. New York was a big muddy one, and that's what Joe wanted." Reflecting on his own preference for the "smaller puddle," Lowell observed, "Too bad; I might be as rich as Joe today." Ralph Lowell, interview by Richard J. Whalen, October 5, 1962, Richard J. Whalen MSS, John F. Kennedy Library, box 1, Classmates folder.

the required 30 percent margin. "I'll admit," Lowell confided in his diary after the worst had passed, "that I was a very tired young man." [10]

That spring a company closely tied to Lee, Higginson came under attack from stock manipulators. When William C. Durant, the daring founder of General Motors, nearly ran the company into the ground in 1910 with his wildly optimistic plans for expansion, Storrow was called in by a consortium of bankers to straighten out the mess Durant had left behind. Storrow's five-year stewardship at GM reaffirmed Lee, Higginson's reputation for prudent business practices, but Durant launched a counterattack and succeeded in ousting Storrow and his management team in 1916. With automobiles now in his blood, Storrow set up the Nash Motors Company that same year with an initial capitalization of $5 million. At Storrow's death in March 1926, Nash's stock was worth $145 million. [11]

Two months later, bears on the New York Stock Exchange tried to knock the price of Nash Motors to below $52 a share. This provoked, according to press reports, "one of the greatest battles in the recent history" of the Exchange. Nearly 75,000 shares were thrown on the market, but Lee, Higginson held its ground, buying up everything that was offered at $52, and the short-sellers, "unable to complete their coup" had to "beat a hasty and costly retreat." There was "pandemonium" at the Nash trading desk and "business in other stocks was practically suspended as scores of traders milled around the Nash post to watch or participate in the struggle." It was all over in less than an hour. The stock rose to 55½, and Lee, Higginson actually made a nice profit on the day's business. Lowell was in constant touch with New York on the telephone, "pumping in orders . . . as fast as we could." "While the drive was on," he wrote in his diary, "it was about the most exciting half-hour I ever spent." [12]

As speculation swirled around him, it was difficult for Lowell to avoid engaging in some himself. Years later he recalled the day he had wanted to buy a new tuxedo. Before lunch he bought some shares of stock; by the time he got back to his desk, the shares had "advanced so far that I sold them and had money enough to buy my tuxedo." In the winter of 1927, Lowell convinced the partners that Lee, Higginson should begin trading in certain stocks for its own account. [13]

Despite this small victory, he felt badly treated. The bull market of 1926 produced record earnings for the Stock Department, and 1927 promised to be even better, but Lowell's career was standing still. "I ought to move on somewhere," he confided in his diary in April 1927, "where my work is more appreciated, and where I can become a member of the firm and not simply someone's hired man." Too many of the partners were "not in sympathy with the stock business" and failed to understand that not only was Lee, Higginson doing "the largest stock business in Boston, but by far the cleanest and best." A few years earlier, Lowell had turned down a job offer from the fast-growing investment banking firm of Dillon, Read & Co; it hurt that since then, two new partners had been admitted by Lee, Higginson.[14]

In the fall of 1927, Lowell's original employer, Curtis & Sanger, invited him to become a partner. Lowell realized that Curtis & Sanger was "not and never [would] be the house" that Lee, Higginson was, but he believed he would be happy there, "that being one of the firm, I would feel I was getting real results from my own efforts." On the other hand, he "hated to face the idea of cutting loose from the [Stock Department], and giving up all that I have done for the last few years."[15]

On a Sunday afternoon in late 1927, George Cabot Lee, a grandson and son of partners at Lee, Higginson & Co. and the senior partner since Storrow's death, visited Lowell at home. A partnership for Lowell was not yet possible, Lee told him, but he promised that Lowell would have it by January 1, 1929, and urged him to wait. Complicating the matter, however, was the disclosure that the firm would be taking on a new member in the interim. This placed Lowell in a quandary: He had resolved that if anyone else was admitted ahead of him, he would quit at once. A few days later Lowell informed Lee that while he thought the partners were behaving "rather shabbily" toward him, he "would stay, although rather reluctantly." In January of 1928, Lowell was still unsure of his choice: "All my friends are going ahead of me, and I cannot help but wonder whether I made the right decision in staying on the job."[16]

While Lowell waited for his partnership, the stock market zoomed upward and became even more volatile. Lowell wondered whether the unleashing of the bulls on Wall Street was good or bad. He reacted with typical indecision to President Coolidge's January 1928 declaration that the amount of margin buying was not a cause for worry: "I think it was a rather unfortunate statement for him to make just at this time when the public is running away with the market. Still it makes for business, and you might just as well keep things humming while the going is good as worry too much about the day of reckoning until that day appears."

In March, fueled by heavy speculation in Radio Corporation of America stock, the market became "very, very wild" and Lowell expressed concerns:

Tips are rife on practically every stock on the board, and, for the moment, they are all making good. This means that the public is getting a good run for its money and now has taken the bit in its teeth and is running away with things. How long it can continue is anyone's guess, but sooner or later the weakened technical condition of the market plus the passing of stocks from strong to weak hands, will lead to a break the magnitude of which will be in proportion to the excesses which occur before the break starts, but which even from this level would cause tremendous losses to speculators and houses with thinly margined accounts. I am persuading our people to sell right and left and hope to be in good shape when the break comes.

But ten days later, as the market continued "its violent surge forward," Lowell had second thoughts: "It's undoubtedly a dangerous market and the conservative thing to do is to get out and stay out, but it tries one's patience to sell good stocks and then see them go on kiting upwards."

The market maintained its "wild course" throughout the spring; the Stock Department was so hectic that Lowell had to give up keeping his diary. In June the inevitable crash occured. "These were indeed exciting days," Lowell wrote, "as margins melted away almost before one's eyes and frantic customers threw stocks overboard and clamored to know when we thought the bottom would be reached. We didn't lose any money on our accounts here, but there was one that got under water for a brief time one day." Lowell was forced to bail out two of his friends who did get in over their heads; one of them owed Lowell $30,000.[17]

As long as customers made their margin calls, the market's somersaults meant hefty profits for the Stock Department. But the strain on Lowell was great. "Many evenings," he wrote later, after things had settled down, "I got home feeling as though I had been wrung through a wringer." Making it even harder for Lowell was the knowledge that some of the partners were watching over his shoulder. One day a partner "butted in" and asked the clerk in charge of margin accounts to compile "all sorts of figures" for him. This made it impossible for Lowell to get his lists on time; he "blew up" and went to see George Lee.

[I] told him I couldn't work with so much interference and that either I was responsible for the accounts or I wasn't, and I wanted to know what it was. Of course it was a childish thing to do, and I shouldn't have done it, but I did it anyway and won my point, even though I may have appeared in a poor light, blowing off the way I did. Still there is only one way to run things and that is to put one man in charge and back him up to the limit until he proves himself incapable of the responsibility, and that was what I was fighting for and what I won.

But Lowell recognized that his position would never be truly secure until he made partner. Although the stock market suffered another major break in prices in December, Lowell and his department got through the year safely, and on January 1, 1929, his partnership became official.[18]

DOMESTIC TRANQUILLITY—AND TRAGEDY

Lowell looked to his home life for relaxation and comfort, and for much of the 1920s marriage and fatherhood provided both. Having enjoyed their country-based childhoods, Ralph and Charlotte wanted to provide similar surroundings for their children, to the extent their financial means would allow. Writing to his mother shortly before his discharge from the army, Ralph reported that he and Charlotte preferred to "live outside of Boston, where we could have a little ground around our house." The phrase "a little ground" was accurate. In Chestnut Hill and Westwood, Ralph and Charlotte had had scores of acres to call their own; the house they rented in Dedham, about five miles south of Chestnut Hill and three miles northeast of Westwood, sat on a single acre. But for a young couple just starting out it was ample, and they were quite happy in their first home and the community in which it was located.[19]

Settled only a few years after the Puritans established themselves in Boston, Dedham was primarily a farming community for two hundred years. Industrialization began in the nineteenth century, and by the 1920s Dedham and its nearly 11,000 residents presented a mixed picture to the world. Small factories and worker housing dominated the eastern part of the community. In the northwest, where the Charles River loops through the town, large parcels of land had been taken out of cultivation and allowed to return to their natural state; impressive mansions dotted this rural landscape. Closer to the center of town was the historic district, where people still lived in frame houses dating back to the Colonial and Early National periods. Dominating the scene here was the Norfolk County Courthouse, a nineteenth-century stone building with massive Greek Revival columns and a Roman dome. Beginning in the spring of 1921, the state, the nation, and eventually the world came to know this courthouse through the trial of Sacco and Vanzetti.[20]

The Lowells' three-story house at 21 Dexter Street was about a mile northwest of the courthouse. Built in 1911 by a Boston lawyer, it was a Georgian colonial clapboard dwelling with Ionic columns at the front entrance. Much smaller than the Loring home at Sunrise Farm, it was comparable to the house in Chestnut Hill where Ralph had been raised. Almost all of the land was in back; the house sat close to the street, which was one block long and linked with major thoroughfares at either end.[21]

True to Lowell tradition, the house soon swarmed with children. Little Charlotte was joined by a baby brother, John, in September 1919. Ralph Jr. arrived in March 1923, and Mary Emlen made her appearance in December 1925. Two more girls followed: Lucy in October 1928 and Susan in January 1932. Also true to Lowell tradition, running the household was Charlotte's responsibility. She hired and managed the servants: cook, waitress, upstairs maid, governess (as needed), and chauffeur. When the coal furnace required service, she made the arrangements. In 1927, after being laid up at the house for a few days with an injury, Lowell commented in his diary on what he had witnessed: "One thing staying at home does is to show a man that a girl with four children, one of them very small, has very little time to herself. Charlotte is busy all day long, and I don't wonder that she gets tired out. . . . I have a much greater appreciation of all she does for the family than I ever had before."

When the Lowells bought a summer place and moved many of their belongings from one house to another for the season, Ralph's only assignment was to set aside the liquor to be transported. That done, he went to work in the morning and showed up at the other residence in the evening, expecting to find everything in place. Thanks to Charlotte, it was.[22]

Charlotte was a devoted and affectionate mother, and Ralph, within the limits imposed by competing demands and the social conventions of the day, was a devoted and affectionate father. During the week he ate breakfast and dinner with the children, and on evenings when he had no other engagement he played with them before bed. On Saturdays the Stock Exchange was open in the morning and Ralph had to go to his office, but in the afternoon he would set up a movie projector and show films, which the neighborhood children were also invited to view. Sunday was usually a family day. As the children got older, Lowell tried to do something special with each of them, such as going to a baseball game, a tennis match, or the circus. Ralph enjoyed their company and wished he could see them more. "They are growing up fast," he noted in the fall of 1923, "and my problem is to see them and get to know them before they are old enough to become independent and prefer their own friends to playing with their father."[23]

Lowell liked to socialize, and in Dedham he found many opportunities. He had joined the Masons at Camp Devens, but during his early years in Dedham it was the newly formed local American Legion post that best satisfied his need for male camaraderie. Its clubhouse featured bowling alleys, pool tables, a card room, and a reception hall. The post sponsored patriotic activities on Memorial Day and the Fourth of July. When the tumult generated by the Sacco-Vanzetti trial threatened to overwhelm the town police force, the Dedham Legionnaires volunteered to serve as an auxiliary; the offer was declined. Lowell served on a committee that awarded college scholarships to outstanding high school students. He regarded the scholarship program as "one of the more constructive things" the Legion did because it "would help materially in giving young boys the proper start in Americanization."[24]

The Legion was also a lobbying group for veterans. Here Lowell broke ranks. In 1924 the Legion pushed the Bonus Bill through Congress to provide special benefits for World War I veterans. Denouncing the measure as a raid on the national treasury and a piece of class legislation, President Coolidge vetoed it. The House easily overrode the veto, but a close vote was expected in the Senate. Lowell telegraphed Henry Cabot Lodge, the senior senator from Massachusetts, and persuaded others to do the same, urging the Republican lawmaker to stand with the president and his "masterful" veto message. But Lodge, in whom Lowell had been a "firm believer" and for whom he had voted "on every opportunity," joined the two-thirds majority that enacted the Bonus Bill into law. A few weeks later, when the Dedham post adopted a resolution commending Lodge's action, Lowell was in the minority. That fall Lowell marched in a "stupendous torchlight parade" through downtown Boston in support of the president's successful reelection campaign.[25]

Lowell's Legion activities slackened by the mid-1920s. He had become enthusiastic about a purely local Dedham club, the Beefers, founded around the turn of the century. Once a month the club brought together a score of young men to hear each other make presentations on various business topics, historical events, and recent trips they had taken. Enrollment was restricted; a long waiting list testified to the club's popularity. The Beefers entered a team in the Dedham Bowling League (Lowell was on it, and both he and the team fared poorly) and held an annual outing at a beach on Buzzards Bay every summer.[26]

Lowell liked swimming, but unlike many of his social class, he was not a sailor. His favorite sport was tennis, particularly doubles. Although his enthusiasm surpassed his talent, he usually held up his side of the court in an honorable fashion. Despite — or perhaps because of—his hectic schedule, Lowell put on weight during the 1920s and was advised by his physician to exercise more and cut back on second helpings. For Lowell, whose home had many fireplaces to feed, the solution was chopping wood. It was an activity he would keep up into his seventies. In 1940 he described the daily ritual in his diary:

> My wood pile is the joy and delight of my life. I come home every day at 5:30 and work on it for an hour or so, then a hot bath and change for dinner, feeling rested and ready for a quiet evening with a good book. I keep saw, etc. in an open-ended, lighted shed and there I do my work stacking the sawn wood and kindling according to the various sizes. In this way I keep the various fireplaces supplied and have a dandy workout in the cold air as well. You might think this would be monotonous, but such is not the case, for if I tire of cutting small stuff I work on big logs or turn to splitting kindling, and when it is time to stop I carry in as much as I comfortably can. I look forward all day to the wood pile, and begrudge the evenings I have to do other things that keep me from it.[27]

The Lowells attended services regularly at Saint Paul's Episcopal Church in Dedham. As an undergraduate Ralph had adopted a somewhat skeptical attitude toward religion. "The stereotyped forms of religion are for the unthinking masses and for women," he wrote in 1912. "I suppose I am becoming more and more of a Unitarian every day, which shocks my mother a great deal." But now that he was a parent himself, he wanted to provide his children with the security and guidance of the faith in which he had been raised. The Harvard senior who thought that "a thinking man ought to dope out his religion for himself" had become an unabashed admirer of religious leaders. In early 1927 he wrote:

> I have had a real thrill finishing Bishop [William] Lawrence's book, *Memories of a Happy Life*. When a really saintly man sits down and writes from

the heart, the simple, happy things that go to make up an ideal life, the result cannot but be thrilling. In an age when books are written for this or that segment of the community, it is wonderful to find one that is written for everyone in a style which everyone can understand and enjoy. May Bishop Lawrence have many more years of happiness, safe in the knowledge that his happiness is reflected in the happiness he brings to all who come in contact with him.

The following year Lowell agreed to head up the Boston fund-raising campaign for the National (Episcopal) Cathedral in Washington. That "wonderfully beautiful and appealing" edifice, he declared, "will stand as long as the nation endures, as an example of its religious life and beliefs." [28]

If Lowell's club joining and renewed religious faith were typical of the 1920s, so too was his flouting of the Prohibition laws. Ralph had grown up in a stratum of society where social drinking was the norm, and he and his friends had no intention of forgoing a good martini simply because some rednecks and overcharged moralists had amended the Constitution. Liquor was available at most social events the Lowells attended—including the 1922 reunion of his Harvard class in Plymouth, where courtesy of Joe Kennedy the booze "came ashore the way the Pilgrims did." But no drinks were offered when Ralph's uncle James Arnold Lowell came over for dinner. He was a federal judge and presided over many Volstead Act cases; the only liquor he would consume was that manufactured before Prohibition. [29]

In 1927 Ralph and Charlotte purchased the house at 21 Dexter. The following year they completed another real estate transaction. For Ralph as a child, summers had usually meant long vacations at the shore, and he desired the same for his children. Beginning in 1925 Ralph and Charlotte spent summers at the house Mary Emlen Hale Lowell had bought on Nahant, a spit of beach and rock jutting into Massachusetts Bay just a few miles north of Boston. Attached to the mainland by a narrow neck, Nahant was the preferred summer home for Boston's elite for decades beginning in the 1820s. By the 1920s, improved transportation had given Brahmins many other options, but Nahant remained highly desirable; until his death in 1924, Henry Cabot Lodge was the community's best-known resident. In 1928 a house on Swallow Cave Road, a remote part of the peninsula, came up for sale. Within two days of learning that it was available, Lowell bought it, after matching coins with a friend to see who would get to bid on it. Except during World War II, this would be the Lowells' home every year from mid-June until mid-September.[30]

As Lowell and the nation observed Armistice Day in 1928, his acquisitions in Dedham and Nahant and the promise of a partnership in Lee, Higginson within two months showed how far he had come since being mustered out of the army. But if the intervening years had been remarkably good to Ralph and Charlotte, they also generated a great sadness that was never entirely absent from their lives thereafter. They would meet some hard blows and disappointments in the half-century that lay ahead, but none would compare to the loss they suffered on March 5, 1927. "Since then," Ralph wrote four decades later, putting things in perspective, "everything has broken our way."[31]

It was the prime symbol of the 1920s' rush to modernity—the automobile—that brought tragedy to the Lowells. Ralph Lowell's relationship with this catalyst for change is one of the riddles of his life. Although his move to Dedham was made possible by the automobile—the Dexter Street residence was not accessible by foot from the commuter train—Lowell never had a driver's license. Most of his male contemporaries eagerly took to operating a car, just as most people of his generation later took to air travel, but Lowell did neither. His decision not to fly was motivated by fear, but he saw driving simply as a waste of time. By employing a chauffeur he could spend his time in the car reading. He was not averse to using the commuter railroad, or even trolleys and subways, when they were convenient.[32]

One of the attractions of the suburbs for Ralph and Charlotte had been the scarcity of cars. "It is very hard on little children in the city, especially nowadays when there are so many autos that children cannot go anywhere alone," Lowell wrote in 1926. "I like the country much better than the city itself, even though at times it is rather a drag pulling out there after an evening in town, but when the children are considered the scales go way over and stay down in favor of the country." Yet as the number of cars multiplied over and over again, even the generally rustic neighborhoods of Dedham were not immune to the hazards they created. The intersection of Common, Bridge, and High Streets, a half block from the Lowells' house, proved especially dangerous; during the summer of 1924 a fence near the corner was broken five times by cars involved in accidents.[33]

Saturday, March 5, 1927 began on a particularly happy note. It was Ralph Jr.'s fourth birthday, and before Ralph headed off to work he, Charlotte, and the children went through the joyous ritual of opening presents. As Ralph set out to leave, Tonka (their nickname for eight-year-old Charlotte) called after him, "After lunch, Daddy, we will have more presents." Later, she went out to play in the snow that was piled up along the sides of the streets. After sliding down one of these embankments on High Street near Common, Tonka started to cross the road, saw a car approaching, and attempted to retrace her steps. The driver, a novice, swerved to avoid the little girl but instead hit her head-on. Rushed to a nearby hospital, Tonka was pronounced dead on arrival.[34]

Lowell's grief was profound. It was not until a year after her death that his depression began to lift and he was able to make peace with himself. Although he missed her greatly, he felt "certain that little Tonka is happy. There must be some kind of life after death, I am sure of that. I don't know what form it takes, but the soul does exist, somehow, somewhere, and that helps those that are left behind." Ralph and Charlotte's faith in God remained strong, and Ralph believed he had "developed and grown in the last year." Yet even as he saw himself as "a better, less selfish man" than before, Lowell could not understand why in order to make those improvements "it was necessary that an angelic little life should be taken."[35]

Ralph and Charlotte continued to live their lives: They purchased the houses in Dedham and Nahant; they had more children; Ralph received his partnership and took on additional civic responsibilities. They did not, however, forget Tonka. Ralph's diary always marked the day of her death. Ralph and Charlotte set up an award in Tonka's name at her school, and they established a fund in her memory at Saint Paul's. The fund provided flowers for the altar every Easter and flowering plants to be distributed after the Easter children's service.

SERVING THE COMMUNITY

"My life's philosophy is a very simple one," Lowell declared when he was in his seventies. "Most of us are given a great deal, in one way or another, and I believe it is our duty and privilege to return that bounty to our fellow man in whatever way our talents direct us." This was not an idea that Lowell suddenly embraced in the twilight of his years, but one he earnestly put into action for six decades after graduating college. Not having a mountain of money to share, Lowell made his contribution in the form of service on a long list of boards and committees. He offered his time, his energy, his common sense and insights, and his incomparable experience, which grew with every additional membership and year of duty. By the 1960s the sheer number of his directorships made him something of a celebrity. But in the early years Lowell toiled for the most part in obscurity.[36]

In deciding where to help out, Lowell started with organizations devoted to the welfare of the young. He joined the boards of the Massachusetts Society for the Prevention of Cruelty to Children and the North Bennett Street Industrial School, which sought to teach immigrant youths from Boston's North End the manual skills they would need for better-paying jobs. Closer to home, he served as a trustee of the private school in Dedham to which he sent most of his children. He also served on the committee that found a new home for the Noble and Greenough School in 1921 after its trustees decided to make residence an option for students. The site chosen, a hundred-acre Dedham estate, was less than a mile from the Lowells' house on Dexter Street; each of the Lowell boys enrolled there, and Lowell served on the board for nearly forty years.[37]

Also in Dedham, Lowell became treasurer of Saint Paul's. Since the church was one of the biggest landowners in the town and collected rents on a large number of leases, the amount of bookkeeping required approached that of "a very large corporation." This chore, however, actually was handled by Lowell's secretary at Lee, Higginson, whose name was Ruth Perkins. She took on many similar assignments in the nearly fifty years she worked for him. Among the tasks of the church treasurer that Lowell did assume personally was taking home the collection money on Sunday mornings, counting it, and then depositing it in the bank on his way to work on Monday. During cold weather Ralph usually had Charlotte carry the offering in her muff, and on one Easter Sunday the contributions were so large that she could hardly get her hands in with the money. Once in the house she poured it out on the table for counting, as was her custom. But Ralph, Charlotte, and the children had hardly started to count when there came a knock on the door—some friends had decided to stop by on the spur of the moment. Thinking it unseemly to receive guests with money all over the dining room table, Ralph and Charlotte scooped it up and stuffed it under the cushion of the couch. By the time their visitors departed, the Lowells had forgotten about the money, and it was only after Lowell left for the office the next day that the maid found the stash.[38]

Lowell had followed George Cabot Lee in the Saint Paul's post, and at Lee's request Lowell also followed him as treasurer of the Boston Floating Hospital. This peculiar Boston institution was created at the turn of the century by social reformers concerned about the health of children forced to live in crowded, poorly ventilated dwellings. It began as a series of summer boat excursions, intended merely to give the children a temporary escape from their oppressive housing conditions. But almost immediately it was recognized that the boat could also be used to provide medical care and instruction. After operating a makeshift craft for several years, the Boston Floating Hospital Corporation succeeded in raising funds for the world's first vessel designed and built as a hospital ship. Launched in 1906, it had room for one hundred beds and laboratory space for pediatric research. It later became the site of important advances in the fight against infant diarrhea. The hospital charged no fees for medical services and by the mid-1920s was one of the most popular and loyally supported of all the charities in Boston.[39]

The ship operated only in the summer. It was being overhauled in the spring of 1927—soon after Lowell took over as treasurer—when fire broke out, and within a matter of hours only a burned-out hulk remained. From that blaze a legend arose in philanthropic circles about Ralph Lowell. For reasons not clear, the story got around that there had been no insurance at all on the vessel until Lowell became treasurer. Privately at first and publicly only much later, Lowell claimed a more modest form of prescience: since new boilers were being installed, he had thought it prudent to take out $30,000 additional coverage beyond the $165,000 already in place. The dramatic account gained greater currency, and for the rest of his life friends would teasingly refer to Lowell as an arsonist.[40]

The Floating Hospital's executive committee met on the afternoon following the fire and voted to build a new boat, but reversed the decision after the initial shock had worn off. The summer illnesses that the boat was best equipped to treat were no longer a major health problem, and its limited operation period each year made maintaining it prohibitively expensive. Doctors associated with the hospital urged the trustees to construct a land-based facility, and most of the longer-serving trustees supported that idea. The "middle-aged and younger men" on the board, however, thought it unlikely that the necessary funds could be raised for a conventional structure. Lowell belonged to the latter group, and when Children's Hospital and Massachusetts General Hospital, both affiliated with the Harvard Medical School, proposed that the Floating Hospital's insurance money and contributions be used to support beds at these distinguished institutions, Lowell was receptive. By this means, he wrote, "we can carry on the work of our charter and help to the utmost limits of our resources the poor sick babies and children of the city." In March 1928 it seemed as if this plan would be approved, although Lowell recognized that to do so would be "quite a blow to . . . the old guard." [41]

But the ambitions of the Tufts Medical School and a generous benefaction combined to keep the Floating Hospital alive in a new home on land. Thanks to lobbying by Harvard, the original charter granted to Tufts College in 1852 expressly prohibited its granting medical degrees. The ban was lifted in 1867, but not until 1893 were the Tufts trustees prepared to challenge the Harvard Medical School. During the next thirty years the Tufts Medical School surpassed Harvard in enrollments, but in terms of prestige it remained very much in the older institution's shadow. Tufts needed better hospital affiliations, and in the late 1920s its president began talking to the leaders of the Boston Floating Hospital and the Boston Dispensary (founded 1796) about forming the New England Medical Center. Such an association would redound to the advantage of each of the constituent units. When $200,000 became available from the estate of an early investor in Boston's street railways, earmarked for the construction of a new forty-bed facility for the Floating Hospital, Lowell and the trustees signed on. For Lowell the opening of the new building in 1931 was one of the few high points of the Depression decade. [42]

5

"Everything looks very dark tonight"

DOWN BUT NOT OUT
IN THE DEPRESSION DECADE

Twenty-fifth anniversaries are usually a time for reflection, and as the Harvard class of 1912 celebrated this milestone in 1937, the members were asked to describe their outlook on life. Some avoided the question altogether, others responded jokingly. Ralph Lowell was among those who addressed the matter seriously. Noting that he had had "his share of ups and downs" over the past quarter century, Lowell declared that these experiences had "strengthened my belief that what a man gets from life depends on what he puts into it; on his capacity to live in the present, looking forward, not backwards." By any accounting, the 1930s brought many more "downs" than "ups" to Lowell, but he emerged from a steep fall in a far better position than most of his contemporaries. That Ralph came through the decade in relatively good shape undoubtedly was tied to his ability to "look forward," but it also owed much to his being a Lowell.[1]

THE 1929 CRASH AND ITS AFTERMATH

"This recognition of character, ability, and achievement," wrote one of Lowell's distant Philadelphia relatives in a congratulatory letter to the new Lee, Higginson partner in January 1929, "comes at the time of life at which it is most certain to be a stimulus to further effort." Indeed, confident as he was of his own abilities, Lowell was eager to play a leading role in the firm's affairs. But he understood that as the junior man he would need to be patient. While discussions at partners' meetings reaffirmed the weighty and international character of Lee, Higginson's business, in the others' minds Lowell remained identified with the shenanigans taking place on the floor of the New York Stock Exchange. Management of the Stock Department was still Lowell's primary responsibility, and the burden grew as activity and prices on the Exchange rose at a frantic rate during the first half of 1929.[2]

Mindful of his new status, Lowell abandoned a proposal that he had long advocated. He had been urging that the firm handle its own trading on the Stock Exchange instead of contracting it out to two New York brokerage houses. The New York houses received 45 percent of the commissions Lee, Higginson received from its customers, and Lowell estimated that if Lee, Higginson did the buying and selling itself, the Stock Department's profits would increase by a third. But in the spring of 1929, he recommended against this step. The two houses were giving Lee, Higginson excellent service, they were reliable sources of information on what was happening in New York, and any change from current arrangements would be disruptive for six months to a year. In addition, the New York houses were a conduit by which Lee, Higginson financed the margin accounts of its customers. Throwing all this overboard risked the danger that Lee, Higginson "might become known as a stock house, to a much greater degree than we are at present, and this might lead to the demand for a questionnaire from the Exchange." No one thought this desirable and so the existing setup was left alone.[3]

As the stock market rose higher and faster that summer, Lowell prepared a memorandum reassuring his partners about Lee, Higginson's position. He explained that unlike bond sales, which usually were cash transactions, most stock sales were covered by loans, and the only way for a brokerage house to make money was to offer credit. Lee, Higginson, he explained, did not participate in "the more objectionable features of the stock game" (e.g., daily tipping service, pools), nor did it encourage its customers to trade for the commissions this would generate. Consequently, its "accounts [were] well margined. We have in the main first-class securities and we have little turn-over in our individual customers." Lowell's confidence in the Stock Department proved well founded when the market collapsed a few months later.[4]

The events of October 24, 1929—Black Thursday—and the days that followed forced Lowell to shift his base of operations to New York for a few weeks in order to keep up with the fluid conditions there. He was not alone. He canceled a New England Medical Center fund-raising committee meeting scheduled for October 30 because "so many [members] are out of town and so occupied with the unusual action of the stock market." Wall Street was in chaos, but Lee, Higginson, he wrote later, "sailed [through the Crash] without a quiver. Our margin business was well run and contracted with the market without loss to us." Lowell's personal losses are not recorded, but they do not appear to have been substantial. His financial woes began two years later and were less the product of stock speculation gone sour than of misplaced faith in his august partners at Lee, Higginson.[5]

In the interim the collapse of the great bull market actually bolstered Lowell's position at the firm. The Crash confirmed the partners' longstanding fears, but they could not help noticing that Lowell had brought Lee, Higginson through the crisis safely. Furthermore, the slowdown on the Stock Exchange gave Lowell time to explore underwriting projects, which were Lee, Higginson's traditional business. As economic conditions deteriorated in 1930–1931, Lowell worked on projects in the automobile and textile industries that he thought would be profitable once recovery got under way. The automobile scheme would have merged Nash, Packard, Auburn, Studebaker, and Hudson to create a company second in size only to General Motors. "These big things move very slowly," Lowell noted, "and we haven't made a great deal of progress as yet, but the thing is in the fire, and the plan is a good one even if nothing comes of it." Nothing did.[6]

Thirteen months after Black Thursday, another shock hit Lowell's financial world. Relaxing after a filling Thanksgiving dinner, Lowell received a call—he should be at the office the next morning at eight-thirty for an important meeting. Any doubts about the seriousness of the matter were dissipated when he arrived at work to find the leading partners from New York in attendance. "And then the bomb burst," Lowell later recalled in his diary. Kidder, Peabody & Co., "long classed with ourselves in the public mind as the leading bankers in Boston, and safe as the Rock of Gibraltar," could not meet its obligations and would fail the following Tuesday unless it could raise $5 million.[7]

Founded in 1865, Kidder, Peabody had become the exclusive American agent for the English house of Baring Brothers, and as Lowell's comment suggested, was soon Lee, Higginson's strongest competitor among New England's investment banking firms. Kidder, Peabody's problems had been a decade in the making, ever since Robert Winsor, a Harvard classmate of Theodore Roosevelt, became the active senior partner. Sixty years old in

1918, Winsor lacked close ties to the rising generation of bankers in New York and Boston and could not adjust to the changing financial practices of the 1920s; during his tenure, Kidder, Peabody lost its ranking among the ten leading houses of issue. The stock market crash hit the firm hard, and the deaths of Winsor and another partner in 1930 resulted in the withdrawal of their partnership capital, further depleting the firm's cash reserves. Rumors about Kidder, Peabody's troubles led depositors to take out their funds, and in early November the firm appealed for assistance to J. P. Morgan & Co., with which it had a long and close relationship. The New York financial colossus was prepared to help out, but wanted the Boston banking community to join the effort.[8]

All day on that November Friday was spent looking at the problem from "every possible angle." One of the options considered was absorbing Kidder, Peabody, "but it was apparent that there was nothing really left to take over; that the shell of what was once a powerful firm had nothing left to it." Before finally breaking up at six-thirty, the partners agreed to a Morgan-devised plan in which Lee, Higginson and other private Boston banks would put up $5 million as junior security and private banks in New York and commercial banks in Boston would establish a credit line of $10 million. This would allow either for the salvaging of Kidder, Peabody or for its orderly liquidation. Lee, Higginson's contribution was set at $500,000, and Lowell and his partners were impressed by their own magnanimity. "Everyone says we are most generous and we ought to be praised," Lowell wrote. "We are giving a firm that has always been our rivals, and in the past has dealt us some doubtful blows, a half-million dollars to save their reputation and we will never get anything tangible back."[9]

It was obvious within a matter of weeks that the $15 million could not keep Kidder, Peabody afloat. Morgan began the process of liquidating the firm in the winter of 1931, and at the end of March a much smaller entity, based in New York, assumed the Kidder, Peabody name. Lee, Higginson kept its distance from these developments. Lowell commented in his diary:

> [W]e feel that we would get a great deal of unwarranted criticism if we
> undertook to liquidate the firm and shouldered the burden of putting
> their present partners and employees out in the cold. Many people would
> consider us heartless, and that after competing with them for years, we
> had taken advantage of their troubles to strip their partners and cast out
> their loyal employees. It is too bad, we are all sorry for them.

Lee, Higginson, however, could not evade the consequences of the collapse of Kidder, Peabody and other financial institutions. With the American economy continuing to contract and Europe suffering even more, deposits at Lee, Higginson fell during 1931 from $200 million to $16 million. The firm "paid out on the dot, a really remarkable record," Lowell noted later, but it also began to borrow heavily from a consortium of New York, Boston, and Chicago banks.[10]

On October 1, 1931, Curtis & Sanger was declared insolvent. In a financial community by now inured to the failure of firms large and small, the collapse of Curtis & Sanger hardly caused a ripple, but for Lowell it was a poignant development. Upon hearing the news, he went over to their offices, "with tears in my eyes to tell them how badly I felt." Many of the people he consoled had been at the firm when Lowell started as a messenger there. "Several were standing around, stunned by the blow that had fallen. Poor fellows! How many more of us may there be before this depression runs its course?"[11] Curtis & Sanger's demise occurred during another panic period on the stock and bond exchanges, and Lowell favored shutting down both until order could be restored.

> Every day people come in who are going to be sold out by their banks, begging for help and advice. One man [was] in an absolutely blue funk; he said he had reached the end of his rope and that there was nothing left but suicide. I told him that would really not help anyone, that many were worse off than he, and that he ought to get a grip on himself and be a man. Luckily, those that talk of suicide practically never take the actual step.

As 1931 drew to a close, Lowell breathed a sigh of relief. It had been "a most trying [year] for everyone," and the start of a new year held out the prospect of "change and hope." The "general attitude today," he wrote, "is so hopeless and dulled, that any change must be for the better and lead to better things." Less than six months later, Lee, Higginson & Co. was out of business.[12]

IVAR KREUGER AND THE FALL OF LEE, HIGGINSON

Barrett Wendell, Lowell's English professor at Harvard, wrote in his 1918 history of Lee, Higginson (where his son was a partner) that the firm's success over the previous half century could be attributed to "two steadily maintained principles." One, "before committing yourself to any project, you should study it carefully, to make sure that if successful it will actually *supply an economic need.*" And two, "make sure that the men in charge of it are *men who can be trusted.*" Should the project be "wanting in either of these matters," Wendell wrote, to become involved was "hardly better than a vulgar gamble" and thus not worthy of Lee, Higginson's imprimatur. With the development of the firm's extensive network for selling bonds on a retail basis, an additional principle came into play: "to distribute only securities which should stay good, and thus strengthen the country by giving an increasing number of comparatively small investors a genuine interest in our national welfare." During the 1920s Lee, Higginson tied its reputation for integrity to an unfortunate enterprise, managed by an individual unworthy of the firm's confidence. The venture brought heavy losses for Lee, Higginson's customers and destroyed the firm.[13]

Americans fell victim to many financial swindlers in the 1920s, but Sweden's Ivar Kreuger proved to be "the Leonardo of [larcenists]" in that frenzied decade, and Lee, Higginson was his primary banker in the United States. During their nearly ten-year relationship, Lee, Higginson–led syndicates sold more than $250 million of Kreuger's securities to American investors. Worldwide, Kreuger raised $650 million for his scheme to monopolize the global production of matches; at his death—by suicide—in 1932, his assets totaled $200 million. Embezzlement on this scale, John Kenneth Galbraith has noted, "suggested some new and commanding talents." [14]

There was no question that Kreuger possessed an "astonishing gift for making others trust him." His impressive bearing and speech, combined with an ability to direct conversations along paths of his choosing, made him the dominant figure in whatever business meeting he attended. Kreuger's drive for power and fortune was shared by the bankers with whom he did business, but unlike most of them he operated without moral constraints. As one student of his career has observed, Kreuger's "essential philosophy of accounting . . . was that a balance sheet existed mainly to paint pretty pictures for the public. He had an almost poetic approach to annual reports . . . and he believed the function of figures was not to reproduce a situation as it existed, but to create an impression of it as he wished to portray it." A Lee, Higginson partner declared, after the balance sheet fraud was exposed, that Kreuger was "so crooked he could hide behind a corkscrew perfectly." Yet even Kreuger could not have gotten away with as much as he did, for as long as he did, if the people and firms he dealt with had not had their own basic weaknesses.[15]

In 1922–1923, when Kreuger first encountered Lee, Higginson, it was in the midst of a generational and geographical transformation. Storrow had led the firm for more than two decades and was slowing down markedly, and no one in the Boston headquarters was ready to step into his dynamic shoes. Most of the partners continued to operate out of Boston, but a discernible shift of power to the New York office had occurred as Wall Street consolidated its grip on the nation's monetary levers. As the United States was transformed from a borrower nation into a lender nation by the World War, international finance assumed new dimensions and offered new opportunities. The Manhattan partners of Lee, Higginson were eager to get their share.

Following the lead of the New Yorkers, the firm arranged for the chartering of Kreuger's International Match Corporation in the fall of 1923. Before the year was out, International Match had issued its first bonds: $15 million, twenty-year, 6.5 percent gold debentures. Lowell was among the buyers, and his diary reveals an investor quite pleased with his purchase:

> The Swedish Match Company is an absolute monopoly in Sweden and is a large manufacturer of matches in every country in Europe. Because of their organization, control of raw materials, and excellence of skill in manufacture, they can make matches cheaper than any other match company in the world. In fact, their only real competition today is found in North and South America and in Japan. They believe they can capture these markets as well, and have formed the International Match Company—putting in this company certain of their subsidiaries in Europe and guaranteeing its obligations by endorsement of the Swedish Company. . . .
>
> We are selling $15 million debentures . . . of this company under this guaranty, and have made the bonds convertible into common stock at the rate of 33.3 shares of common for every $1,000 bond. This money is to be used in the acquisitions of match companies in the Americas and the Far East, or in building factories of their own in these countries—which ever proves to be the better business judgment.
>
> At present their profit per box in the countries in which they meet competition is ¼ of a cent and each ¼ of a cent addition per box will mean $25 million net profit to the company. The bond looks like a well-secured industrial bond with a very attractive conversion privilege. I bought 10 of these for mother and one for myself.

How many more of the Swede's securities he bought over the next nine years is not known. A. Lawrence Lowell reportedly lost $194,000 in Kreuger investments, but whatever direct financial losses Ralph may have suffered were overshadowed by the mortal blows dealt to Lee, Higginson by the collapse of Kreuger's financial empire.[16]

Lee, Higginson's ties to Kreuger were well established by the time Lowell assumed his seat at the partners' table in January 1929, and Lowell shared his colleague's enthusiasm for the "Match King." Kreuger, Lowell had told the Dedham Beefers in 1928, was "one of the outstanding business geniuses in the world today." It was a conviction he continued to hold almost religiously, even upon hearing of Kreuger's suicide in March 1932. A "marvelous intellect," an "incredibly masterful brain," his international match monopoly a "stupendous dream"—these were Lowell's assessments of Kreuger and his work. Only weeks later—after it became obvious that Kreuger had done "everything crooked it was possible to do" and that Lee, Higginson's failure to protect its customers would cause the firm to fall—did Lowell recognize that Kreuger deserved "to be ranked with the very greatest crooks in history."[17]

An audit of Kreuger's accounts conducted by J. P. Morgan & Co. in the winter of 1932 turned up the first hints of the Swede's deceptions, and on March 12, just back from the United States, he shot himself in his Paris apartment. A Lee, Higginson partner who had accompanied Kreuger on the boat across the Atlantic was one of the select group to learn quickly of his death. While French authorities debated how to make the news public, he sent a coded cablegram to his associates acquainting them with this shocking development. Lee, Higginson kept the information confidential until after the stock market closed at its regular time of noon that Saturday. "I immediately held up any buy orders [for Kreuger company securities]," Lowell recounted in his diary, but "of course [the news] could not be given out to [clients], as our advices are private and we could not take advantage of them by letting people sell on news that was not public property." The firm's behavior on that day drew criticism at subsequent congressional hearings, but even John Kenneth Galbraith, whose history of the stock market crash treats Lee, Higginson with scorn, concedes that the partners acted honorably.[18]

After spending Sunday at the office reviewing the latest cables from Paris ("not so good; . . . not too reassuring"), Lowell and his partners anxiously braced for the opening of the stock and bond markets on Monday morning. The huge amount of sell orders required that trading in Kreuger-controlled companies be delayed for an hour at the start of trading, but there was "no real panic," and "everything considered, things went fairly well." Rumors were "rife," however, that Lee, Higginson was in trouble. The partners paid calls on banks in Boston, New York, and Chicago to assure their creditors that the firm could absorb whatever losses it suffered on its Kreuger holdings; Lowell's assignment was the relatively small Second National Bank of Boston, whose board he had joined in 1931. With the financial system already under tremendous strain, the banking community initially rallied behind Lee, Higginson in the common interest of self-preservation, but by early April all community of interest had broken down.[19]

The facade of unity cracked first in New York. Three weeks after Kreuger's suicide, enough information had surfaced to demonstrate that the "Match King" was a fraud and that Lee, Higginson had abetted, if unwittingly, his massive swindle. Although Lee, Higginson showed enough assets on its books to meet its obligations in "normal times," these were not, as Lowell conceded, normal times, and Charles E. Mitchell, the president of the powerful National City Bank of New York, panicked. Mitchell, whose optimistic public statements and liberal lending policies on brokers' loans had helped fuel the 1929 bull market, thought Lee, Higginson was doomed and wanted to salvage the loans a consortium of banks had given the firm in 1931. At Mitchell's insistence (Lowell referred to him as "that dirty stinker"), the Lee, Higginson partners in Boston came to New York to meet with him and the leaders of J. P. Morgan & Co. and Bankers Trust. Daniel Wing of the First National Bank of Boston, another of Lee, Higginson's creditors, also attended.[20]

On the evening of April 3, Lowell waited upstairs as two of the New York partners and two of the Boston partners conferred with the bankers. It was agreed that Lee, Higginson would have thirty days to pump $5 million of new capital into the firm; in the meantime, the banks would hold off calling in the loans that were then due. As Lowell saw it, there was no chance the money could be found: "[W]e are practically done as a firm." Back in Boston on April 5, he wrote, "Everything looks very dark to me tonight."[21]

Lee, Higginson's agony lasted for another two months. A few days after the New York meetings, a team of Swedish accountants published a report that exposed Kreuger's "gross misrepresentations" of his companies' fiscal position. Although Lee, Higginson was not mentioned and Lowell and his partners felt that they had been deceived along with everybody else, their involvement was viewed with suspicion. Lee, Higginson had based its business on the "integrity and character" of its partners and had built the business up by earning a reputation for offering only "reliable goods." By its failure to uncover Kreuger's misdeeds—indeed, its failure even to make a good faith effort to investigate his finances—Lee, Higginson had betrayed its heritage and was no longer worthy of its customers' trust.[22]

When the thirty-day deadline arrived, the $5 million had not been found. The only question then was whether the firm would file for bankruptcy or be liquidated. For both sentimental and practical reasons, the partners preferred liquidation.* As negotiations began with the big creditors, Lowell and most of his colleagues took the precaution of transferring their personal property to their wives' names. This action raised some eyebrows, but Lowell and the others, as partners in an unincorporated business, faced unlimited liability in the likely event that lawsuits were instituted against the firm. The attorneys for Lee, Higginson took the brunt of the criticism; no one, Cleveland Amory has observed, questioned the "individual integrity of any of the First Family men involved." In a private letter some months later, one of the partners wrote: "There is not one member of my firm who would be capable of a shady act. At the present moment we are voluntarily sacrificing all that we possess in the world in the hope of paying all our creditors in full. I never was prouder of my association with Lee, Higginson & Co. than I am today."

This particular partner did, in fact, lose practically everything, but Lowell appears to have gotten out of the mess almost unscathed. For the next decade Lowell was snared in legal actions resulting from Lee, Higginson's fall, but as the firm's most junior partner and the one with the smallest amount of capital invested, Lowell let others take the lead in handling them. While the lawsuits caused him to worry, they did not result in any significant damage, either to his financial assets or his reputation. Lowell's association with Lee, Higginson caused him embarrassment, but not shame.[23]

Lee, Higginson & Co. announced its liquidation on June 14, and several partners assumed positions with the new Lee Higginson Corporation,

---

* When a friend of Lowell's, who was writing a biographical sketch of him in the 1960s, referred to "the failure" of Lee, Higginson and Kidder, Peabody, Lowell was quick to correct him—both firms, he wrote, "liquidated and did not fail." Lowell to Edward Weeks, December 29, 1965, Edward Weeks MSS, Massachusetts Historical Society, box 1, 1964–1965 Correspondence folder.

headquartered in New York, with branches in Boston and Chicago. For obvious reasons, the leading New York partners were not among them; for other reasons, neither was Lowell. Limiting its mission to the issuance of securities, the corporation did not offer the private banking and brokerage services previously available through the partnership. Since Lowell had not managed to establish himself in investment banking during his three years as a partner, and had no funds to contribute to the corporation's operations, there was little interest in bringing him on board. He and others were left "out in the cold."[24]

Lowell took the midnight train to New York on June 14 and, after checking in with the Lee, Higginson partners there, proceeded to the offices of Clark, Dodge & Co. This firm had handled Lee, Higginson's stock and bond trading since 1890, and Lowell proposed that it take over Lee, Higginson's Stock Department with Lowell in charge. His idea met with a warm reception, and over the next several hours the details of the arrangement were hammered out. Lowell considered it "the greatest bit of salesmanship in my life, . . . selling a whole department, in times like these." He took the midnight train back to Boston and announced to "his gang" in the morning that they were "now working for Clark, Dodge." Advertisements informing the public of the opening of the Boston office of Clark, Dodge appeared in the same day's newspapers as the stories reporting Lee, Higginson's demise. Never again would Lowell play for such high stakes as he had with Lee, Higginson. But he had at least landed on his feet.[25]

POLITICS AND BUSINESS DURING THE GREAT DEPRESSION

In March 1932, while the fallout from Kreuger's suicide grew heavier every day, Lowell went to a meeting of the organizing committee for his twentieth class reunion. The group looked over a list of class members:

> It was most depressing, for nearly every third name was either out of a job or busted. Also we have six classmates in insane asylums. . . . We are getting old, and the depression catches us and ruins us at the age that we should be making our mark in the world and attaining financial independence. Surely we have had a hard break in our generation. First the war to take us away when we should have been getting our start. The war took some of us, and others lost something in the strain and worry of war that made them less fit for the battle of life; and now even those who worked

so conscientiously and hard, and many through no fault of their own, are faced not only with starting all over again but with debts so heavy that they are unlikely ever to overcome them.[26]

Millions of Americans shared Lowell's gloomy outlook in that presidential election year. Voters ousted the incumbent, Herbert Hoover, in favor of Franklin D. Roosevelt. Lowell, a lifelong Republican, had not been part of that majority. Although he was disenchanted with Hoover's "pathetic apathy" toward the widening economic collapse (in 1931 Lowell had concluded that only Calvin Coolidge could provide the "real leadership" the crisis demanded), he had even less confidence in the Democratic Roosevelt. Hoover, despite his failures, was steady and firm in his adherence to the traditional American values—hard work, individual responsibility, small government—in which Lowell believed. Roosevelt, on the other hand, seemed to Lowell to be surrounded by corrupt politicians from his native New York and rabble-rousing southern and western Democrats pushing screwy ideas. Lowell viewed him as slippery and dangerous. While recognizing the psychological boost a fresh president might supply, he could not embrace the risks Roosevelt and his supporters represented.[27]

Four, eight, and ultimately twelve years of Roosevelt's New Deal strengthened Lowell's feeling that his early negative judgment had been correct. Lowell was encouraged at first by the new president's "wonderful" handling of the banking crisis and his support of the Economy Act of 1933, which slashed $500 million in federal spending by cutting pensions and salaries, but his hopefulness soon gave way to despair. For Lowell, the New Deal became nothing but a bunch of "crackpot schemes" that sent the federal deficit skyrocketing and trapped business in a regulatory straitjacket, making recovery from the Depression impossible.[28]

No sector of the American free enterprise system felt the claws of the New Deal's reformist fervor more strongly than the financial community, and Lowell thought this disastrous for the nation. From the law guaranteeing bank deposits, to the legal requirement that issuers of stocks and bonds provide potential purchasers with complete and accurate information (a rule born out of the collapse of the Kreuger empire), to the termination of the New York Stock Exchange's status as a private club, Lowell described the New Deal measures as "drastic," "stringent," and "radical." At a later, more secure stage of his career, Lowell acknowledged the need for, and even the virtues of, these measures, but in the 1930s he could see them only as interference that dampened "the courage of private capital."[29]

Whatever the cause, business for investment bankers and brokerage houses fell markedly during the 1930s, and Lowell had to adjust not only to a much less hectic pace but also to a diminished role in Boston's financial circles. Although Clark, Dodge & Co. billed itself as an investment banking house, most of its underwriting came to it as a junior member of syndicates assembled by other firms; unlike Lee, Higginson, it did not initiate big deals. And whatever arrangements it did enter into were handled by its New York office. The Boston branch was merely a brokerage outlet, totally dependent on customers' buying and selling on the exchanges. Lowell's operation, which occupied the rooms formerly used by Lee, Higginson's Stock Department, was never more than a marginal profit-maker for Clark, Dodge. But the partners liked Lowell and were prepared to keep this, their only branch, going in the hope that the economy eventually would improve. At the beginning of 1937, they admitted Lowell into partnership.[30]

The stock business continued to decline during the next six years, and Lowell had the unpleasant task of paring his staff and cutting the wages of those who remained. Trips to New York became a trial because he knew the partners there would demand further cutbacks. In the fall of 1940, Clark, Dodge made preparations for more slashes should Roosevelt win a third term. "I hope and pray that he is defeated," Lowell wrote. Two weeks after the election, his salesmen's pay was reduced to commissions only, which meant "quite a cut for each of them." America's entrance into World War II depressed business still further. "We are certainly only a shell of our former self here in the office," Lowell wrote in June 1942, "and rattle around like a very dry pea in a very big pod, but this business is down to its last ditch now and we can only hang on and pray that we may be one of the last to survive."[31]*

FAMILY AND COMMUNITY

The Depression dealt a severe setback to Lowell's business career, but thanks to his mother and in-laws it barely affected his family's comfortable way of life. As a matter of fact, the 1930s saw the Lowell family move into even more spacious surroundings. Although Ralph and Charlotte were

---

* After a walk through Harvard Yard in the fall of 1941, Lowell observed, "Even a few minutes in the academic atmosphere seems to calm and quiet one's self—maybe I made a mistake in not staying in anthropology for a life's work." Diary, November 29, 1941.

quite happy in Dedham, they could not refuse an offer from her parents in 1934 to exchange residences. The Lorings, their children either married or away at school, no longer needed such a large house, and they wanted their grandchildren to grow up in a rural setting. With its seventeen acres of landscaped gardens and woods, adjacent to scores of additional acres of family-owned property, the Westwood estate certainly offered a country setting, and the place soon featured dogs, horses, pigs, and hens. It imposed some hardships on the younger Lowell boys and girls, however; in Dedham many of their friends had lived nearby, but their new home was too isolated to encourage casual play. Nonetheless, they developed strong feelings for the area and with the exception of John, the oldest son, they all settled down in Westwood after getting married.

For Ralph it was the Chestnut Hill of his youth all over again—but even better. Sunrise Farm offered the "best views anywhere around Boston," from the sun rising over the Blue Hills in the morning to the flashing beacons of the Boston Harbor lighthouses in the evening. An ample supply of trees nourished Lowell's passion for chopping wood. Ralph, Charlotte, and the children went hunting each spring for lady's slippers, a type of orchid, just as Ralph had done as a boy. "I never dreamed we would own such a beautiful place," he wrote in 1934. When his business and civic career began to blossom in the 1950s, the Westwood home became an important element of his public image.[32]

Three years after moving to Westwood, Ralph and Charlotte had another son, James Hale II, named for Ralph's bachelor younger brother. Born five years after the last daughter and eighteen years after the first son, Jim grew up something of an only child. For his father Jim offered the opportunity to prolong the role of doting parent. John and Ralph Jr. had been away at boarding school, college, and then war, and the girls naturally looked to their mother for guidance. Ralph found Jim a wonderful companion. His outside commitments rose dramatically in the years that Jim was growing up, but he played with Jim as much as his schedule would allow.

The Lowells continued to summer at the home they owned in Nahant. In June 1938 that little community basked in the glow of a visit from the president of the United States. John Roosevelt, the youngest son of Franklin and Eleanor, was marrying Anne Clark, who lived with her widowed mother next door to Ralph and Charlotte on Swallow Cave Road. The ceremony took place at a local church, the reception at the Nahant Club;

Charlotte, Ralph, and his mother and cousin Lawrence were among the guests. Ralph's mother invited Sara Roosevelt, F.D.R.'s mother and a very distant relative, to stay at her home on Nahant, but she had already reserved rooms at a downtown hotel. The president's accommodations were on his yacht anchored offshore. Ralph had a conversation with F.D.R. at the party, but he was too much of a gentleman to raise political issues on an occasion such as this.[33]

The Roosevelt-Clark wedding, magnificent as it was, could not hide the fact that Nahant was, as Lowell put it, "on the skids." The older generation of "Proper Bostonians" who had made the tiny spit of land so fashionable were dying off, and their children were finding summer places elsewhere. Nothing demonstrated Nahant's decline better than the plight of the Nahant Club. As president of the club, Lowell was dismayed by its declining membership. He wrote in March 1940, "[T]he handwriting is on the wall and we cannot keep the club exclusive much longer. Once the bars are let down and the place opened up to the townspeople, our old crowd will move out and the community will suffer as a summer place." The bars did come down, and during Lowell's tenure as president the "old Club" was transformed into a "community club." One of the new members was a woman whose husband was installing a cesspool for Charlotte's parents in Westwood. "The Nahant Club," declared Lowell, "has certainly gone democratic."[34]

The leveling effects of the Depression decade also hit the Lowells closer to home. Ralph's income dropped sharply after Lee, Higginson's collapse, from $60,000 in 1931 to $20,000 in 1941, and while the latter figure still placed the Lowells among the most fortunate of Americans, the family was now forced to think about its spending. To save $150 in annual dues Ralph resigned from the Union Club, which he had joined in 1915 and of which his father and grandfather had been president. Boarding school for the eldest daughter was ruled out as too expensive; Jim's governess was let go, and the boy moved to a room downstairs so that the furnace serving the upper floor could be shut off. A few days after Ralph had bought shoes for six dollars instead of his usual fourteen-dollar pair, Charlotte phoned him at the office to ask if it was all right to buy one of the girls a ski outfit. Much to his chagrin, Ralph had to say no—the one or two wearings she would get out of it were an extravagance the family could no longer afford. "I never thought that at the age of 50 I wouldn't be able to give my children what they wanted," Lowell wrote in his diary. "It is a very discouraging feeling, that of at least partial failure." That same year, in order to preserve the one major asset he expected to pass on to his children, Lowell borrowed money to pay the premiums on his $500,000 life insurance policy.[35]

These economies, such as they were, reflected the high style of life to which Ralph and Charlotte were accustomed. That more severe measures were not necessary probably was due to the generosity of Ralph's mother.[36] The extent of her assistance is undocumented, but it was more than enough to spare her oldest surviving son the indignities the Depression inflicted on so many others.*

Lowell's main focus during the 1930s was his job, but he also performed a range of civic duties. He continued to serve as a trustee of the private schools his children attended, as well as of the Perkins Institution for the Blind and the Massachusetts Society for the Prevention of Cruelty to Children. With the Boston Floating Hospital permanently anchored on land, his duties as its treasurer reverted to routine. Lowell also served on several committees formed to gather money for the needy. His charitable work generated little publicity, except in 1938 when he headed the fundraising drive of the American Red Cross in Boston.

The renewal of war in Europe in 1939 took Lowell's mind away from the depressed state of business and thrust him back to the front lines of the battle for preparedness. The Military Training Camps Association (MTCA) had languished in the two decades following the Armistice, but in May 1940, as German armies swept across the Low Countries and into France, Grenville Clark began mobilizing his old comrades from the Plattsburg Movement. New York remained the campaign's headquarters, but at Clark's request Lowell arranged a meeting at the Harvard Club of Boston, where Clark would present the MTCA program. The forty men who showed up that Saturday afternoon chose Lowell as their chairman. They adopted resolutions for "immediate and concrete measures, short of war, in aid of the allies" and endorsed the "principle of universal compulsory military training in the present emergency and of universal service if we are forced into war."[37]

---

* At her death in 1940, Ralph's mother left an estate valued at more than $600,000, which she put in a trust for her four children. Middlesex County Registry of Probate, Cambridge, Mass., Docket No. 231609.

Working with Mike Farley and Ben Joy, the original Boston stalwarts of MTCA, Lowell found an office for the group and hired a secretary. The group's immediate assignment was to recruit volunteers for the Citizens' Military Training Camp the army had agreed to operate beginning on July 5. Lowell had performed a similar function, without compensation, for three years in the mid-1920s, carrying the impressive title of Massachusetts Civilian Aide to the Secretary of War. It had been a disheartening experience. Quotas went unfilled and the facilities at Camp Devens were a disgrace: Buildings were rotting or burned out, and weeds and trees grew on the old parade grounds. Lowell resigned in 1927. Explaining his decision, he singled out the army's lack of appreciation for his efforts: "They do nothing to help in any way. . . . [T]hey do not show even ordinary decent thanks." [38]

Not much had changed in the spring of 1940. The commander of the local military district was unsympathetic to the training camps idea, believing that "the Army has all the officers it can possibly need." With the War Department "dumping the whole thing in our laps," Lowell and his associates in the Boston MTCA had to scramble to fill the three hundred spots available at Camp Devens. It did not help that there was "practically nothing at Devens" and that recruits over six feet tall were told to "bring their own shoes and trousers." Nor was there "any equipment—certainly nothing modern or mechanized." Uncertain of their success to the very last minute, Lowell's group made the Devens camp one of the four (from a total of nine) that met its goal. "The older men have come through well," Lowell observed, "but not the younger ones; those of 25–30 years of age do not seem to have the same spirit we had twenty-five years ago." [39]

At the time of his second stint for Devens, Lowell fought for universal military training. He helped set up a meeting of about three hundred Harvard alumni, to be held on the campus between the morning and afternoon ceremonies on Commencement Day, June 20, 1940. Governor Leverett Saltonstall presided, and after various luminaries had delivered their speeches, Lowell presented a resolution urging the creation of a registration and classification system for national service. University officials had worried about "heckling and a possible riot," but the gathering attracted only a few opponents and the proposal passed easily. Neither Roosevelt nor the Congress, however, were ready to stand the political heat of university military training, and a narrower, but still bitterly contested, selective service system was enacted. On October 16, the national registration day for the draft, Lowell served as a volunteer at the Westwood town hall, processing the paperwork.[40]

Lowell's two older sons were of draft age and, indeed, were members of the Naval Reserve Officers Training Corps at Harvard. Understandably, Lowell was not eager to see America join the conflict, but as events accelerated in 1941 he saw no alternative. American naval ships carried out presidential orders to shoot German U-boats "on sight," and the crisis in the Far East intensified. In these circumstances Armistice Day 1941 was an occasion for reflection:

> We certainly have made a mess of things since the last war stopped. Conditions at the time made it necessary for us to go into the war and those who gave their lives gave them for the safety of our country. Since then long-haired theorists have tried to argue that we should not have gone into the war and that the whole thing was a mistake, when really the handling of the world, after the armies had saved the world, is what has been futile and botched. Now conditions are again fast getting to the place where we will have to go into another war in order once more to save civilization. And it is just as important now as it was in 1918 that we go in at the right moment and help destroy the menace of dictator-run states. Nor is there any reasonable doubt that we will be able to do so provided we give the effort our whole-hearted support.

Lowell maintained a keen interest in international affairs in the decades of hot and cold war that followed. But for the next third of a century it was Boston that became, even more than before, the center of his life.[41]

TRUSTEE FOR A CITY,
1940-1978

Ralph Lowell marked his fiftieth birthday in July 1940, and while the occasion was duly celebrated, it was not a particularly happy one for him. Some of his gloom derived from the news from Europe— German troops occupied Paris and it seemed the only question was when, not whether, Hitler would send his conquering army across the English Channel. But it was events much closer to home that most disturbed Lowell. The death of his mother in February, at the age of seventy-six, had "left a void" that was difficult to fill. His ties to a comforting past sundered, Lowell saw the future as bleak. "The times have moved so rapidly" that members of Lowell's generation, "even though we do not feel old and believe we are better able to play a part through accumulated wisdom from actual experiences," were considered "too old and too out-of-date for the modern scheme of things." [1]

But the present was the source of most of his despair: Lowell considered himself a failure. Clark, Dodge's Boston office was nothing but "a little jerkwater affair," and Lowell felt that his service to the community had been marginal at best. Economic success and civic leadership having so far eluded him, he saw little prospect of achieving either in the years that remained. His one solace was his family—

"loving" Charlotte and their six "wonderful" children—and it was to their well-being and happiness that he expected to devote the rest of his life.[2]

Lowell fulfilled that commitment, but also a great deal more. In the three decades after 1940, he rose to heights of business achievement and public esteem that had seemed beyond the reach of a frustrated middle-aged man. Lowell's reversal of fortune had a variety of sources. One was his willingness to work hard, especially at tasks others did not care to undertake, and his ability to manage his time efficiently. Lowell knew when to leave details to administrators, while keeping a close eye on the making of policy. This allowed him to take on more jobs than his colleagues would have considered feasible. He subscribed to the idea that "the busier a man is, the more he can do, as the whole thing is really a question of organizing one's work and keeping at it, a little each day, until it practically runs itself."[3] Once Lowell had achieved some recognition and, as a result, additional invitations to join organizations, he found it difficult to say no, both out of vanity and out of a sincere belief that he had something to contribute. He usually did have something to contribute, but as his name became a hot commodity his role was often more symbolic than substantive.[4]

Friendships also played a part in Lowell's ascent. Although his partnership in Clark, Dodge placed him far from the centers of power in Boston's financial network, he knew everybody who counted on State Street (the term commonly applied to Boston's financial district) and in practically every other major sphere of economic and cultural life in Boston. Many of these associations dated from childhood, while others arose from his involvement in the Plattsburg Movement of World War I or the glory days at Lee, Higginson. Through it all the continuous thread was Harvard. His strong ties to his classmates had broadened over the years to include the much larger community of Harvard alumni, both older and younger than he, as Lowell immersed himself in his alma mater's affairs.

And then there was his family heritage. After 1940 Lowell's civic involvement rested on three main pillars: 1) his job as chief executive officer of the Boston Safe Deposit and Trust Company, 2) his various uncompensated services to Harvard, and 3) his trusteeship of the Lowell Institute. The banking and Harvard positions could have been filled by any number of people; the Lowell Institute appointment came his way by the facts of his birth. That he accomplished as much as he did at the institute is testimony to his skill at getting things done, but like so much in his life, the chance to do good came because of his ancestry.

The chronological approach employed so far in this account of Lowell's career is not suitable for the remainder. During the first fifty years, Lowell's story was essentially a linear one, a chain of decisions and developments that led him down a particular vocational path. In the decades after 1940, the focus of his activities shifted from carving out a place in the world for himself to guiding a group of separate, but interrelated, institutions as they faced the challenges of social and economic change. In this period Lowell's career is best charted by a set of overlapping circles in constant motion. The circles represent the most important institutions in Boston in the process of adapting to an unstable environment. Lowell was so intertwined with them, and they with each other, that an examination of Lowell's life after 1940 must employ these institutions as its organizing framework. Boston and its institutions changed more than Lowell did during this era, but the cumulative effect of his many affiliations and heavy responsibilities was to make him more responsive to change than he might otherwise have been.

Although Lowell's growing prominence placed great demands on his time, his ties to his wife and children remained strong. Charlotte, as always, was in charge of running the household, and even though the children were grown and had started families of their own— young Jim slightly later than the rest—managing Sunrise Farm was a full-time job. A poem Charlotte's three daughters composed in honor of the fortieth anniversary of the 1916 Sewing Circle described her routine:

> Some two score years ago we girls were carefree, slim and gay,
> My attire was the latest mode, my nerves not affray—
> Today at 5 A.M. I don my slippers and chemise
> I meet the plumber, oilman too, in nothing else but these.
> The phone is seldom on the hook; Ralph has to wait his turn—
> With six children's news on which to check, I make the wires burn.
> The doorbell rings—it's time for town—the taxi's at the door—
> "Stand back below"—the flying wedge to Boston goes once more!
> And while in town, just close your eyes, imagine what you will—
> I've boxes stacked up to my ears, and pigeons who are ill.
> And what my evening plans will be, heaven only knows—
> But I've a suitcase in my hand for a quick change of clothes.
> Art Museum, Commencement time, receptions by the score—
> With Ralph as busy as he is, there might be many more.
> If I get home—to bed?—OH NO!
> "Your girls have called," they say,
> And if I sit with less than twelve,
> I've had a quiet day.

"I have spent my life waiting for that man," Charlotte told friends in a good-natured way. When asked by a newspaper reporter to describe her chief interests, Charlotte replied: "They are my children and my husband, I do nothing except drop any other project when he calls me to come and see the Matisses as they are being unpacked at the Fine Arts Museum or stand and receive visitors with him. If he has that much enthusiasm and energy, I find that I have, too." When another reporter asked Charlotte to name her "favorite man," her choice was the former president of Tufts University, where

Ralph had been awarded his initial honorary degree, because he was "the first one . . . who realized my husband's capabilities."[5]

Each of Ralph and Charlotte's boys attended Harvard, naturally, and all the girls went to Vassar. College-educated women were not part of the Lowell tradition, but Ralph insisted that his daughters, who were formally presented to society at debutante balls, continue with their schooling. Lucy was an outstanding student, winning a Phi Beta Kappa key to match her father's, but aside from her charitable activities, she made no professional use of her diploma. Emlen and Susan pursued careers in social work and teaching, respectively, after their children started school. The three sons followed Ralph into finance, working in large, well-established organizations. Jim, the most adventuresome of the trio, eventually started his own investment firm.

Except for Lucy, who married a Yale graduate from New York, all the Lowell children found spouses among the Boston-area elite. Emlen's husband was a lawyer in his father's firm, which handled many of Ralph's legal affairs; Susan's and Lucy's husbands worked at Boston financial houses. John and his wife, after spending the early years of their marriage in Westwood, bought a year-round home in Nahant. The other Lowells lived within walking distance of Sunrise Farm. Children and grandchildren were in and out of Ralph and Charlotte's house constantly, and the elder Lowells loved their company.* One New Year's Eve, when Charlotte and Jim had gone to a neighbor's to watch television, Ralph stayed in the house alone with

---

* When a researcher visited Lowell at home in 1962 to collect information for a biography of Joseph P. Kennedy, the interview was interrupted by "a sporadic game of hide-and-seek with two of [Lowell's] spirited granddaughters." Noting that Lowell had twenty grandchildren in all, the researcher commented to an associate, "[W]ho knows, maybe the Lowells will one day outvote the Kennedys again." William Gill to Marjorie Meehan, November 9, 1962, Richard J. Whalen MSS, John F. Kennedy Library, box 1, Classmates folder.

Ralph III, a baby of only a few months. "Could there be a better setup than that?" he wrote. "It may be a premonition of the future—but I am happy to sit here with the radio going, and every now and then listening for that wonderful little boy that bears my name." [6]

Ralph made it a practice to write to his grandchildren on their birthdays, impressing upon them that "as you go along in years, you will find that a great deal of the pleasure you get out of life is due to giving of yourself very freely to those around you and helping in their problems." On his eighty-third birthday in 1973, one of his teenage grandsons reciprocated:

> For many years you have written me a letter on my birthday—now for the first time I'm going to send you a letter on your birthday, serving the same purpose as yours, expressing my thoughts of someone I deeply love and admire.
>
> Not until recently have I realized how much you have meant to me. Not many people are gifted with a grandfather filled with such knowledge as you. When I was in need of some information for a school report the first thing I would do was to come over and talk with you or go and look for a book in your library. If I were in need of a costume for Halloween, all I would have to do is come over and look through your great assortment of costumes.
>
> My interest in baseball has stemmed from you. I find it really fun just coming over to watch a game. In fact you were the one who really got me interested in any kind of sport. Maybe you remember when I used to come over every week and take the *Sports Illustrated* magazine which you had already read. Now I have a subscription to it. [7]

In addition to giving the grandchildren free rein in Westwood, Ralph and Charlotte welcomed them in Nahant. The army had bought their home during the war, and when the government offered to sell it back to them—along with two seventy-foot-high concrete observation towers—Lowell's initial response was negative. Not only was the place in shambles, "looking for all the world like the 'ghost' houses so often shown on *Saturday Evening Post* covers," but Ralph saw no future there: Nahant was "dying as a resort of 'cold roast' Boston." However, after vacationing for a few weeks at a local inn and finding many good friends still around, he and Charlotte changed their minds. Although the army was asking far less for the house than it had originally paid for it, Ralph had to borrow on his life insurance to meet the expenses of renovation. The town was not the Nahant of yore; the tennis club was gone and the Clark house next door was owned by a government official from an Asian nation. But Ralph and Charlotte were happy there.[8]

The practical difficulties of sightseeing with a large family, as well as the expense involved, had kept the Lowells close to home for their vacations when the children were young. But by mid-century both constraints were lifted. Beginning with transcontinental rail trips, followed by annual midwinter cruises, Ralph and Charlotte put a large distance between themselves and the Beacon Hill matron who, when chided for her limited itineraries, replied, "Why should I travel when I'm already here?" In 1961 they took an around-the-world cruise that included many of the places Ralph had visited in 1912–1913; but Cold War politics kept them out of China and the Soviet Union.[9]

Accompanying Ralph and Charlotte on the global tour was his sister Molly. Ralph saw his younger siblings Jim and Olivia frequently because they lived in Chestnut Hill, but get-togethers with Molly were a special occasion. She had spent considerable time in France and Italy before and after the First World War. After her second marriage, in 1924, to the British Earl of Berkeley, a distinguished chemist and one of the richest peers of the realm, she lived at Berkeley Castle, built in the twelfth century above the Severn in the Midlands. Berkeley died in 1942, taking the title to the grave with him in the absence of a close heir. Molly received a generous financial settlement and moved to Italy at the end of the Second World War.

She restored a villa in Assisi, about halfway between Florence and Rome, and renewed her many contacts in the art world, including Bernard Berenson, another Bostonian expatriate. In 1958 Molly took Ralph and Charlotte to lunch at Berenson's famed Villa I Tatti in Settiguano, near Florence. Although the shortage of money that had clouded Molly's early life was no longer a problem (she blamed it for the collapse of her first marriage), Ralph feared her spendthrift ways would yet bring her to grief.[10]

The conclusion of their 1961 cruise exhibited the differences between the free-spirited Molly and her "practical brother." Molly had arranged for a limousine to meet her at the pier, "an expense much looked down on by my brother." Familiar with the long delays that returning travelers faced going through customs in New York, Molly grabbed the limousine company's agent as soon as he arrived and promised him "a good tip" if he got her "off this boat right now before the rush begins." She was the second person cleared to leave, and within an hour of the boat's docking she was in her room at the Cosmopolitan Club. Because a piece of Ralph's baggage had been misplaced, he and Charlotte stayed on the boat for three hours, which caused them to miss the last Boston train. They ended up hiring a car to drive them all the way home to Westwood.[11]

It was Lowell's "peculiar New England conscience," he told himself, that prevented him from using a taxi when he could take the trolley. Although Lowell enjoyed what most of his contemporaries would have considered an extremely comfortable, even extravagant, lifestyle, he saw himself as living "very simply." His financial situation improved markedly in the postwar period, but without large reserves he felt he could not match the spending of his friends and associates. Ralph kept a close eye on household expenses and usually resisted Charlotte's pleas for repairs until they were urgently required. As he grew older and his schedule became more crowded,

Lowell hired a full-time chauffeur to drive him to and from Boston each day, but when time permitted he would take public transportation or, preferably, walk to consecutive engagements within the city. He delighted in strolling through the Common and the Public Garden, counting the squirrels on either side as he went.[12]

There was no way Lowell could avoid the automobile, but he could and did avoid airplanes. As early as 1940 he noted that many of the people he worked with were taking the plane to New York and that while he was "sorely tempted" to try it, he could not bring himself to make the crucial first trip. A decade later, citing the crash of a DC-6, then the most modern commercial aircraft, Lowell declared that, "despite statistics and all claims of safety in flying, one had better stay on the ground except where some real emergency makes time saving almost obligatory." An investment trust to which he was an adviser reaffirmed its position in 1951 that neither airlines nor aircraft manufacturers were "sound enough" to be in its stock portfolio. By the mid-1950s Lowell recognized that a continuing refusal to fly would destroy his chances of operating on the national stage, but by then it was too late to overcome his fears.[13]

Besides a sense of safety, the train gave Lowell the opportunity to indulge his passion for reading. He also liked to read on his cruises with Charlotte. Before their departure Charlotte would mail packages of books to several ports of call so that Ralph would have a steady stream of reading material. His tastes were conventional: He liked mass-circulation periodicals such as *Time, Life, Readers' Digest,* and the *Saturday Evening Post,* and the popular fiction and nonfiction of the day. In his diary Lowell listed the books he had read each month and gave a grade to each. Among the older classics Lowell particularly liked Dickens; during one summer vacation spent at home he indulged in a "regular Dickens orgy," reading seven of his novels. He found Dickens "a grand relaxation from the worries and strains of the present-day world." *The Pickwick Papers,* a special favorite, was "one of the most delightful books ever written." [14]

Even if Lowell liked to retreat on occasion to the nineteenth century, he was no fan of the New England Watch and Ward Society's crusade to maintain a Victorian code in literature and the theater. Having just finished reading Kathleen Winsor's *Forever Amber,* he thought the society's decision in the fall of 1944 to keep it out of Boston bookstores and libraries was ridiculous: "Besides being the very best advertisement for the [book], it is making Boston a laughing stock all over the country. This book is sexy and perhaps a little unnecessarily so, but it is nothing that should be kept from adults."

Fiction was one thing; biography, quite another—at least when the subject was a relative. Godfrey Lowell Cabot, a distant cousin of Ralph's, was the driving force behind the Watch and Ward Society at the peak of its power in the second quarter of the twentieth century. In 1967, after the society had gone into decline, a profile of Cabot was published that contained intimate quotations from his diary and letters to his wife and family. Most critics relished the irony that Cabot's own words might have been "banned in Boston" had the society retained its influence. But Lowell was "appalled." He thought it "a shame that the book was even written, let alone published." [15]

The fine balance Lowell struck between Proper Bostonian parochialism and sympathy for the modern temper was illustrated by his choice of clubs. As a young man making his way in the financial world, he had joined the Union Club, the favorite of lawyers and bankers. He gave up his membership in 1940 to save money but by 1951 could afford club membership again. His options included the Union and two even more exclusive (and equally staid) clubs, the Somerset and the Algonquin. But Lowell decided to follow his brother Jim into the Tavern Club. It was an odd choice. Founded in 1884 by a group of young men of artistic bent, its members had included William Dean Howells, Charles Eliot Norton, Owen Wister, and Barrett Wendell. *Fortune* described it in 1933 as "the city's pleasantest male retreat, where the more Continentally minded members of Boston's great families hobnob with occasional Chicago poets in an atmosphere of canary-colored waistcoats, first names, and a round oak table." Located on a narrow street just off the Common, the Tavern Club was famous for its amateur theatricals and its poor lighting. When a fire in the mid-1950s reduced the place to ruins, it was rebuilt exactly as it had been, dimness and all, but with a modern sprinkler system. Lowell knew about the lighting situation before he joined, and as his vision deteriorated over the years he began bringing a small flashlight to "protest the candlelit gloom under which we eat." Although Lowell went to some of the club's Halloween and Christmas celebrations, he rarely attended the weekly Monday night dinners or theatricals. A decade after becoming a member, he wrote, "I am not really much of a Taverner." Nonetheless, he stayed on, wishing to be associated with an old Boston tradition even if he could not partake of it.[16]

"I have lived my entire life in one area," Lowell reported to his Harvard classmates in 1962. "I have been happily married for 45 years, and I have been in one business field. . . . That is, I suppose, a picture of a 'Proper Bostonian.'" Indeed, by the fiftieth anniversary of his graduation, Lowell, with his distinguished appearance (gray hair, mustache, and Phi Beta Kappa key) and his slew of good works, had become the personification of the type. The Lowell family was long known for its "frostiness," and those who had limited contact with Ralph usually saw a brusque and stern individual. He rarely wasted words and bristled at people whose long-windedness prolonged meetings. He exhibited a high degree of surface irritability, yet he could also be quite warm, understanding, and funny. Lowell, as described by a non-Bostonian who sat with him on a national board, "was the kind of Boston Brahmin who proves to be anything but forbidding as you get to know him. When he looked most formidable, he could make the most disarming remark; his sense of humor was never at fault, and he was awfully good company, but one felt a sense of substance there that was unshakable." No one in his generation could match the dignity of Ralph Lowell's personal presence.[17]

*"Dedicated to the prudent, productive
management of capital"* [1]

BOSTON SAFE DEPOSIT AND
TRUST COMPANY

I n 1943, thirty years after beginning his apprenticeship in the
world of finance by addressing envelopes at Curtis & Sanger,
Ralph Lowell finally obtained a business position that afforded
him recognition and respect. After the collapse of Lee, Higginson and
Kidder, Peabody, Boston had become a minor appendage of New York
City in investment banking. Boston's status in commercial banking was a
little better, thanks to the First National Bank of Boston's aggressive lending policies, but Daniel Wing's successors lacked the resources to compete
effectively against New York and Chicago banks. Some of Lowell's contemporaries on State Street responded by moving adventurously into
the new field of mutual funds and made Boston a leader there. Lowell
lacked this boldness; however, when presented with an offer to lead a well-
established institution, he seized it. Fittingly, his new employer was engaged in the most traditional and honored activity of the Boston financial
community: managing the monetary affairs of people favored with large
inheritances. Trusteeship as an occupation nicely complemented Lowell's
expanding civic involvement.

TRUSTS AND TRUSTEES

The 1875 state charter authorizing the Boston Safe Deposit and Trust
Company "to act as administrator, executor, and in other fiduciary relations" established that company in a line of business that was an "inextri-
cable part of the life" of the city's privileged class. Beginning with the fortunes made in the China trade during the last part of the eighteenth

century, and continuing with the riches amassed in the textile industry in the nineteenth, Boston capitalists were obsessed with preserving their families' wealth and dominant social positions through ensuing generations. Journalist John Gunther, in his classic *Inside U.S.A.* (1947), summed up their outlook:

> Many fathers of the last century and the early days of this distrusted their own children fearing that they would turn out to be either (a) namby-pambies, or (b) radicals which would be worse. Yet they had a strong fixed family sense. Thus they contrived through the medium of the trusteeship to ensure that their sons could not maraud through their family fortune, and at the same time to arrange that the grandchildren would be provided for.

Through trusteeship, fathers could provide heirs with "the appropriate benefits—in the form of income—but prevent them" from touching the principal. Observing that the Commonwealth's courts had long given their blessing to this device, *Fortune* magazine in 1933 commented that "a Massachusetts estate may be tied up beyond the reach of any power but the Communist International." [2]

The key judicial decision regarding trusts was an 1830 opinion written by Samuel Putnam, the father-in-law of John Amory Lowell. Rejecting complaints from Harvard College and the Massachusetts General Hospital about the way an estate they were eventually due to inherit had been managed by its trustee, Putnam laid down what came to be known as the Prudent Man Rule limiting the liability of trustees: "All that can be required of a trustee to invest, is, that he shall conduct himself faithfully and exercise a sound discretion. He is to observe how men of prudence manage their own affairs, not in regard to speculation, but in regard to permanent disposition of their funds, considering the probable income as well as the probable safety of the capital to be invested."

No investment, the judge was saying, is completely secure, and the best guarantor of the property in a trust is the character of the fiduciary. Although Putnam's ruling bestowed considerable discretion and protection to managers of estates, the "Boston trustee" quickly acquired and maintained a reputation for conservatism. Reporting on the stereotype, Gunther wrote, "Most of the great trustees would not, I heard it said, invest in anything that they couldn't see outside the window." The president of one of the city's leading banks in the late 1950s declared: "The Boston trustee needs a very good reason to kick out [of an estate's portfolio] something he once decided was a good thing to buy. After all, what we're trying to do is run a marathon, not a hundred-yard dash." [3]

Trusteeships proliferated in the early part of the nineteenth century. At that time they were one-man operations. Typically, when a person of property turned to his attorney to draw up the legal instruments for transmitting his wealth to future generations, he also designated the lawyer as trustee. In time, what had been a sideline became a specialty for many lawyers who devoted their entire practices to trust management. They soon were joined by members of prominent families "who by character, training, and temperament [had] a peculiar aptitude" for the responsibilities of trusteeship. Trusteeship became a prestigious profession in Boston, with sons following their fathers into the field. Lists of company boards of directors that cited the business affiliations of the members often identified several simply as "Trustee." [4]

The middle of the nineteenth century witnessed the advent of corporate fiduciaries. English common law had long barred a corporation from acting in a fiduciary capacity because "it is a dead body" in which "a confidence cannot be put," but this was dropped in 1744. A Massachusetts court decision in 1816 adopted the revised English rule, and in 1818 the legislature chartered the Massachusetts Hospital Life Insurance Company; while not legally authorized to act as a trustee for estates, the company offered various investment trust plans that allowed its patrons to control the distribution of their wealth through succeeding generations. John Lowell (1769–1840), one of the original incorporators of the company, called it the "savings bank of the wealthy" and "the best institution on earth." [5]

Massachusetts chartered its first corporate fiduciary—the New England Trust Company—in 1869; Boston Safe Deposit and Trust was the second in the field. Although the bulk of Boston estates remained in the hands of individual trustees, dozens of other trust companies were chartered by the state in subsequent decades,* offering their customers "stability and continuity" as well as the convenience of banking services, such as checking accounts and loans. [6]

---

* On the advice of her attorney, the will of Mary Emlen Lowell named her two sons and a bank or trust company of their choosing as trustees for her estate. Their choice of Fiduciary Trust in 1940 undoubtedly resulted from Ralph's friendship with Francis C. Gray (Harvard class of 1912), Fiduciary's president.

During the seventy years between its founding in 1875 and Ralph Lowell's arrival in 1943, Boston Safe distinguished itself in two ways from most other Boston trust companies. First, while many of its competitors emphasized the banking aspects of the business, Boston Safe focused primarily on the administration of trusts.* And second, while many trust companies combined in the twentieth century through mergers and takeovers, Boston Safe went its solitary way.

Whatever the merits of these policies—it is likely they drew in customers looking for a personal touch—they cost Boston Safe its top ranking. In the 1890s the trust department of Boston Safe controlled more assets than all the other leading Boston trust companies combined; by the 1910s it had fallen behind the Old Colony Trust (incorporated in 1890), and Old Colony's narrow lead continued to widen. On the banking side, there was no contest at all: Old Colony's deposits were more than seven times greater than Boston Safe's. The differences between the two institutions in size and dynamism were reflected in the types of directorships held by their presidents. The head of Boston Safe sat on the boards of old-line New England textile firms; the president of Old Colony helped shape the destinies of modern national corporations such as American Telephone & Telegraph and General Electric. Old Colony expanded further in 1929 when it was taken over by the First National Bank of Boston. While maintaining its own identity, Old Colony gained additional business through its connection to the New England region's largest bank.

If Boston Safe was losing the race with its upstart rival, for its shareholders it was still a profitable investment. The company declared its first dividends on June 1, 1877, and never missed a semiannual payment after that—even during the Depression. Its stock value rose from $12/share in 1880 to $30 in 1900 and $67 in 1930. In 1909 Boston Safe moved its operations to the ten-story building it had built at 100 Franklin Street. Constructed in an age when bank offices were designed to inspire awe and confidence, the Franklin Street edifice became a pillar of the financial district.[7]

According to legend, the men of Boston Safe were so conservative they never noticed the Great Depression. Indeed, Boston Safe was the first banking institution in Massachusetts allowed to reopen following the Bank Holiday of March 1933. Deposits increased almost 50 percent be-

---

* Because it made no commercial loans, Boston Safe was not obliged to join either the Federal Reserve System or the Federal Deposit Insurance Corporation. Its awkward situation is neatly summed up in the label often applied to it since the 1950s: "a nonbank bank."

ABOVE, LEFT: John Lowell,
Harvard College, class of 1877.
(Courtesy of the Massachusetts
Historical Society, Boston)

ABOVE: Mary Emlen Hale Lowell,
1882. (Courtesy of John L.
Thorndike)

LEFT: Ralph Lowell and his brother
James Hale (Jim), when they were
students at the Volkmann School.
(Courtesy of John L. Thorndike)

BELOW: Polo Club dinner, spring 1909. Ralph Lowell is in front at right. (Courtesy of the Massachusetts Historical Society, Boston)

ABOVE, RIGHT: Roughing it in Arizona, summer 1911. (Courtesy of Ralph Lowell Jr.)

BELOW, RIGHT: Citizen-soldier Ralph Lowell, Plattsburg, 1917. (Courtesy of the Massachusetts Historical Society, Boston)

Ralph and Charlotte Loring Lowell on their wedding day, September 1, 1917.
Charlotte's younger siblings are in the foreground. (Photo by Bachrach)

The financier on the rise in the 1920s. (Courtesy of Ralph Lowell Jr.)

LEFT: Sunrise Farm, Westwood. (Courtesy of Ralph Lowell Jr.)

BELOW: Charlotte (June 1935) on the steps of the Lowells' Westwood home, "which is to be opened to the public to raise money for the Dedham milk fund." (Photo by Bachrach) (Courtesy of the Boston Public Library, Print Department)

Ralph with his three sons (left to right: John, Jim, Ralph Jr.), Memorial Day 1943. (Courtesy of the Massachusetts Historical Society, Boston)

tween 1929 and 1934, attracted by the banking department's policy of maintaining high liquidity.[8]

In March 1942 James Dean, the chairman of Boston Safe, died. A retired investment banker who became famous in Boston financial circles for getting out of the stock market before the Great Crash, Dean provided the bank with sure-handed direction and a solid public image. His second-in-command, President Lyman Allen, showed no talent for direction or image-making, so Boston Safe's directors launched a search for a new chairman. Dropped into the hopper of possibilities was the name of Ralph Lowell.[9]

Two of the most influential members of the board, Nathaniel F. Ayer and Edward A. Taft, supported Lowell's candidacy. Ayer, a wealthy cotton manufacturer, and Taft, a law partner of Robert Herrick, were old friends of Lowell's and familiar with his unhappy situation at Clark, Dodge. But they were not simply doing a friend a favor. World War II had put a spotlight on Lowell's civic role—he was active in the USO and British War Relief—and they felt this could draw business into the bank. Equally important were Lowell's managerial talents. In the winter of 1942, Ayer and Taft had led the campaign to make Lowell president of the debt-ridden Harvard Club of Boston. Their confidence that Lowell could turn that operation around was rewarded before the end of the year, and now they wanted him for a bigger job.

The board offered the chairmanship to Lowell in early March 1943. For Lowell, who was finding it harder each day to go to the brokerage office and face his "dull and stupid" chores, the Boston Safe proposal was a godsend. "That is a real job," wrote Lowell, "one that carries a great deal of prestige in this city." Lowell set a single condition: "I made it clear that I wouldn't consider it unless I could do the outside things I am now doing." [10]

TAKING COMMAND AND MAKING MORE MONEY

Not since his days in the army had Lowell led an undertaking as large as the Boston Safe Deposit and Trust Company. The bank had about 375 employees, two-thirds of them women in clerical and secretarial jobs. All of the important positions—from assistant trust officer to trust officer to treasurer to vice president and president—were held by men who, with few exceptions, had spent their entire business careers within the organization. Lowell's first full day in his new office established a pattern of reaching out to his workers. Well-wishers inundated him with flowers. ("More than I will ever see again," Lowell commented. "There may be more at my funeral but I will never see them.") At four o'clock he invited all the "girls in the bank" to his office, then shook hands with each one and presented her with a rose. "I think it was a nice little gesture," wrote Lowell, "and served to break the ice."[11]

Lowell spent the first several weeks learning about the bank's operations and getting acquainted with the department heads. He was generally pleased by what he found but soon began offering suggestions to reduce paperwork. Staff meetings were streamlined and other procedures overhauled. For the most part Lowell accomplished these reforms without generating resentment by discussing them thoroughly with the people involved. Indeed, the greatest change Lowell brought to the bank was a sense of openness. Dean had played his cards close to his vest, but Lowell gave subordinates direct access to the top and shared information with them. During the fall of 1943, for example, when Lowell was negotiating with other banks to alter the fee structure on trust accounts, he brought the officers together to let them "know what was going on in the bank" rather than leave them to hear about it from outside." After a "good frank talk," Lowell felt they would be "back of the change almost 100 percent." "I hear that the 'esprit' of the bank is growing," Lowell wrote in October, "which pleases me greatly."[12]

There was, however, one dark shadow hovering over Lowell's administration—President Lyman Allen. Being passed over for the chairmanship did nothing to improve Allen's usually sullen disposition, and Lowell's initial encounter with him presaged later difficulties in their relationship. Lowell's devoted secretary, Ruth Perkins, had moved with him from Lee, Higginson to Clark, Dodge and then to Boston Safe. Lowell wanted her to have the office next to his, but he had a "hard time" persuading Allen to agree. Three years of conflict followed, after which Lowell received the directors' approval to strip Allen of his duties. As of January 1946 Lowell was both chairman of the board and president.[13]

Believing that Boston Safe had coasted for too long on its reputation, Lowell wanted the bank to become a more aggressive competitor for business. Indicative of this new attitude was his launching of a common trust fund. The Massachusetts legislature in 1941 had authorized fiduciary companies to mingle the assets of small estates, thereby facilitating more diversified portfolios and lower administrative costs, but Dean and Allen had not taken advantage of the opportunity. Lowell began looking into it in early 1944, noting that such funds had proved popular in Philadelphia and that Old Colony probably would start one soon. When he met resistance from his vice presidents, Lowell dispatched one of them to the City of Brotherly Love in the hope that he would be "converted by the experiences of the Philadelphia banks." The trip produced the desired result. Lowell observed, "This move should be made after the most careful study, but it does seem at times that this old institution is very hard to move." Four months later he noted that progress on the plan was "painfully slow." It was not until April 1945 that he presented the plan to the board's executive committee, which approved it. Yet even at this slow pace, Boston Safe became one of the early entrants in the common trust fund field.[14]

In addition to pursuing new clients with more vigor, under Lowell's direction Boston Safe moved energetically to expand its banking operations. Lowell made personal solicitations to corporation executives, launched unprecedented advertising campaigns directed at the general public, and employed a man with wide community contacts to drum up fresh business. When the new hire succeeded in attracting deposits from an investment banking firm, Lowell commented, "An account we should have had, but no one ever thought to ask for it, and there must be a great deal of money lying around that we could get in the bank if we only went after it." Healthy profits were to be earned on the banking side during the war and immediately afterwards. Thanks to Lowell, Boston Safe shared in the rewards.[15]

Although Lowell wanted to shed the public image of "staid old Boston Safe," his internal management of the bank was quite traditional. As in his previous business positions, Lowell envisioned the organization as "one big family team in which we are all pulling together with the same aim." Only when an employee displayed gross incompetence and an inability to do better in another job or department did the bank resort to dismissal. To thwart the menace of unionization, Boston Safe instituted a pension plan in 1945. Lowell also made himself a conspicuous figure at the bank's semi-annual dinner-dances and beach parties for the entire staff. Reviewing the summer outing at Scituate in June 1945, Lowell observed:

> I cannot feel I am so old that I cannot mix in at such a party, even if I
> am the "boss." I swam and played ball and had a good time and left early
> enough so that no one need feel embarrassed if they got a bit "edgy." I was

very proud of the crowd, they are a high grade group of people and they love the bank, and it is up to me to see that this feeling is maintained and grows over the years to come.[16]

Lowell's strategy "to keep the bank on its toes and going forward" paid off handsomely for Boston Safe's stockholders. The price they received when they sold their shares was fixed by the board of directors, and when Lowell took over in 1943 the figure was about $75/share. In 1949 the board raised this to $100/share and declared an extra dividend—the first of its kind since 1930.[17]

DOING GOOD AND DOING WELL

One of Cleveland Amory's "latter-day Proper Bostonians" declared, "When I can do a good action and at the same time make money, I find that all my powers are moving in harmonious cooperation." This dual ideal guided Lowell in his management of the bank. Although his first obligation to the company's board of directors and stockholders was to make Boston Safe a more profitable enterprise, he refused to consider the bank "just a cold-blooded money-making machine." As a fiduciary institution, the bank operated under the legal obligation to put the interests of its clients before its own. Furthermore, because it was essentially a supplier of services, Boston Safe developed intimate relationships with the people whose affairs had been entrusted to its care. Lowell emphasized the "human element" in the operations of the bank, which tried to deal both sympathetically and objectively with the "poignant problems" of its customers. Other trust companies followed essentially the same approach, but at Lowell's Boston Safe it was reaffirmed and expanded to demonstrate that good works could also mean good business.[18]

The burden of looking after the needs of a customer, from selecting a suitable private school for a young boy to arranging a winter trip south for an elderly widow, fell on the trust officer in charge of that customer's account. But on occasion Lowell would be called in to assist. In one instance a trust beneficiary told of having friends who wanted to build a house near hers and who expected her to give them a mortgage for the full amount. Sensing the woman's distress, Lowell assured her that "she should always hide behind the bank in things like this so that those asking for her favors would not feel she was a tightwad or ungracious if she turned them down."[19]

Fiduciaries were accustomed to administering strange endowments, such as the $40,000 trust set up at Boston Safe by a lawyer for the care of his cat, but few could match the unusual circumstances of the bequest of Lucy C. Farnsworth. A reclusive spinster heiress living in the small community of Rockland on the Maine coast, Farnsworth died in 1935 at the age of ninety-six; her death was discovered by the milkman, who noticed the accumulation of bottles on her doorstep. Boston Safe did not know it had been named executor of her estate until Farnsworth's will was read. When the bank's officers entered her house for the first time, they found money and securities secreted everywhere—under stairs and carpets, behind pictures, and even in a metal swill pail. The dining-room table was blanketed with brokers' statements, bankbooks, and thousands of dollars in rent receipts. When it was all totaled up, Farnsworth had left behind $1.3 million, which she wanted used for the construction and operation of a library and art museum in Rockland to be named after her father.[20]

The tangled assets of the Farnsworth estate had only just been straightened out when Lowell came to Boston Safe in 1943. He assumed personal supervision of the library and museum project, saying, "It ought to be a lot of fun playing with it." He retained a fellow trustee of the Museum of Fine Arts to advise the bank on the books and art to be purchased, and met with architects and Rockland residents to go over designs for the building. Construction of the $600,000 brick structure began in the spring of 1947; the dedication was held in the summer of 1948. Lowell maintained a keen interest in the affairs of the Farnsworth Museum and went to Rockland every summer for its annual meeting, at which he presided. The collection was built around the art and artists of Maine. By 1963 the museum owned twelve paintings by Andrew Wyeth, more than any other museum in the country. That year it paid $65,000 for Wyeth's "Her Room," the highest price yet paid by a museum for a work by a living American artist. Lowell came to know Wyeth and basked in the artist's growing reputation.[21]

A special endowment of Boston Safe's own making gave Lowell another opportunity to serve the public good. In 1915 the bank combined several trusts that had been left to its care for philanthropic purposes to create the Permanent Charity Fund, and invited potential grantors of benevolent trusts to contribute. The fund's prospectus described the dilemmas facing altruists:

Many people desire to make gifts to charity or to leave money in trust for charitable purposes, but are in doubt as to the proper means of doing so effectively. They believe that it is impossible for them to foresee the charitable needs of the future, and feel that if they leave their money for a definite charitable purpose, the changing conditions of the future may deprive that purpose of its usefulness and leave their gifts without a beneficent object. On the other hand, many persons fear that if they leave their money outright to a charitable institution to be used for its purposes, the management of that institution may not continue conservative and sound, and as a result the very principal of the gift may dwindle or even be entirely dissipated and thus the usefulness of the gift may be impaired or entirely nullified.

The Permanent Charity Fund solved these problems by (1) establishing a continuing seven-member committee (serving without compensation), which was to keep abreast of "changing and progressing charitable needs" in allocating the fund's income; and (2) placing Boston Safe Deposit and Trust Company in charge of the fund's assets, thereby guaranteeing to donors that the principal would be "well cared for and . . . invested wisely and conservatively." The $4 million pledged to the fund (most of it from the bequest of a longtime Boston Safe officer) made Boston's community trust the biggest in the nation. (In 1914 Cleveland had earned the distinction of being the first city to have such a trust.) By 1955 the resources of the Permanent Charity Fund had climbed to more than $15 million, and its annual disbursements exceeded $500,000.[22]

In the mid-1950s, in violation of the spirit if not the letter of its mandate, the fund had settled into a rut. Lowell had supported the 1945 appointment of its director, whom he regarded as the best man available at the time. Under this director the fund assisted traditional health and social service agencies with almost automatically renewed grants. Little changed until 1959, when the fund received a $17 million bequest from a local man whose business affairs were a mystery to everyone in the tightly knit Boston financial community. This doubling of the fund's resources reinvigorated the committee, which eased out the octogenarian incumbent and in 1961 hired Wilbur Bender, a dean at Harvard College, as his replacement. Lowell had worked extensively with Bender at Harvard—where Bender sought to increase the socioeconomic and geographical diversity of the undergraduates—and recommended him for the directorship of the fund.[23]

Bender drew on Lowell's experience as he familiarized himself with his new responsibilities. Both men agreed that beneficiaries should be reviewed and dropped when they became habitually dependent on the fund. Fairly quickly, Bender placed the fund in the mainstream of the 1960s by becoming an active advocate for change. "Anyone with a new idea," he announced, "is welcome to come in and talk, and will be listened to no matter how cockeyed he or his ideas may seem." Lowell thought Bender did an excellent job of bringing up "many worthy causes that don't quite fit the ordinary definition of charity, but for which we have funds." These included neighborhood health centers, day care facilities, and job training programs, as well as a state advisory committee to study racial imbalance in the Commonwealth's public schools.[24]

Sometimes, however, Lowell's more developed sensitivity to the nuances of "giving" put him at odds with the former academic. As part of a national fund-raising campaign in the early 1960s, the Jewish-sponsored Brandeis University, located in suburban Waltham, had applied to the fund for a contribution. Bender recommended against giving Brandeis anything, noting that the university was pitching itself as a national institution in making its appeal for donations—while the fund was devoted to local causes—and that Brandeis had the ability to achieve it goals without assistance from the fund. Lowell pleaded for at least a "token gift," based on the university's "standing in the community and its great progress in the last twelve years." The committee decided to give Brandeis $25,000, which Lowell said "will please them and will be welcomed by the Jewish Community."[25]

In addition to the Permanent Charity Fund,* Boston Safe served as a trustee for the Godfrey M. Hyams Trust. Hyams, a metallurgist and engineer, had made a fortune in copper mining and railroad construction, but he lived in a modest triple-decker in Dorchester, which he shared with his two sisters. The women took a keen interest in the social work agencies of the Progressive Era, and in 1921 Godfrey Hyams established a charitable trust to finance his sisters' benevolence. After his death six years later, the trust received a gift of stocks and bonds worth $7 million, then the largest philanthropic bequest in the Commonwealth's history. By the time Lowell became a trustee in 1943, H. Le Baron Sampson, who had been Hyams's

---

* In 1984 its name was changed to the Boston Foundation.

personal attorney, had established himself as the dominant figure in the administration of the trust. Under the lawyer's management, the trust made grants to a wide variety of social welfare agencies in amounts ranging from a few hundred dollars to $100,000. Although Lowell succeeded in directing Hyams's funds to his favorite charities, particularly in the medical field, the trust remained oblivious to the social ferment sweeping across Boston until Sampson retired in 1970.[26]

During Lowell's tenure the bank also worked with newly established charitable trusts. In 1943 Dr. Elliott P. Joslin, one of the world's foremost authorities on diabetes, arranged with Lowell for Boston Safe to administer the funds of the foundation he was starting to sponsor further research on this disease. For two decades Lowell served as treasurer of the Diabetes Foundation, which built and operated the Joslin Clinic, located near, and eventually affiliated with, the Harvard Medical School. In the capacity of chairman of the bank, Lowell also became deeply involved in the creation and activities of the Retina Foundation, devoted to research on the human eye. When the work of this group was threatened by bickering among its leading doctors in the 1960s, Lowell performed the role of peacemaker. The Blanchard Trust, founded in the 1940s with about $100,000 to distribute annually, had much the same goals as the Permanent Charity Fund and the Hyams Trust. After attending the first meeting of the Blanchard trustees, Lowell wrote, "It's little jobs like this that really make the trust business interesting and great fun." By the mid-1960s, these three community-oriented funds were contributing $3 million a year toward making Boston a better place to live.[27]

The bank's association with these philanthropies yielded not only income—it received fees for managing their assets—but also good public relations. "A bank with a conscience" was how Lowell described Boston Safe in a 1957 article in the *Christian Science Monitor*. In his annual report to the stockholders the previous year, he had focused on the individual's obligation to the community and how the bank encouraged its staff to participate in charitable endeavors. No one, of course, did more of this than Lowell himself, and the personal satisfaction he received from these efforts was enhanced by his belief that the bank also benefited. For instance, Lowell was an enthusiastic supporter of Brotherhood Week activities, designed to bridge religious and ethnic divisions; commenting on his attendance at one of the gatherings he wrote, "One does see a different crowd and that is a good thing not only for oneself but for the bank as well." In 1951 Lowell's service on the board of trustees of Boston University resulted in the shifting of that institution's $4 million custodial account from Old Colony to Boston Safe. "That won't mean much in earnings," Lowell observed, "but it seems only fair if I am to have the burden of the [trustees'] finance committee." [28]

NEW OPPORTUNITIES—AND OLD RIVALRIES

Lowell accomplished much for Boston Safe in terms of greater visibility and higher earnings, and Boston Safe did the same for him. Eighteen months after starting at the bank, Lowell's salary was raised to $35,000, the amount James Dean had been paid in his last years. Additional increases came every few years thereafter; Lowell's salary peaked at $50,000 in 1957, placing him near the middle of the compensation list of Boston's financial leaders. But if he did not strike it rich at the bank, at least his money worries were finally over—from then on, his main complaint was about income taxes.

In addition to providing him with financial security, Boston Safe gave Lowell access to the higher echelons of State Street. His first big break came in January 1947, when he was invited to join the board of the John Hancock Mutual Life Insurance Company. Hancock, with $2 billion in assets, ranked fifth in size among the nation's life insurance firms and was the largest headquartered outside the New York metropolitan area. Noting that the president of the First National Bank of Boston had been elected to the Hancock board at the same time, Lowell observed, "So I am really traveling in high company." Less than a year later, Lowell was asked to join the advisory committee of the Massachusetts Investors Trust. One of the first mutual funds created in the 1920s, it ranked as the nation's largest in the late 1940s. It employed fewer than thirty people but was the biggest owner of common stock in the United States, holding $233 million in more than 130 corporations. The advisory committee lacked the authority of a board of directors, as the trustees were free to reject its recommendations. This led some of the trust's rivals to dismiss the advisory committee as mere "window dressing," to which a spokesman for the trust retorted, "How some of them would love to have this board." In 1949 the committee, whose members were featured prominently in the trust's advertising, included not only an Adams, but also—as *Fortune* noted—"an Amory, a Cabot and a Lowell." [29]

Boston Safe's trusteeship for large stockholdings in the nation's big companies assured Lowell of an honored place at the dinners and luncheons held by the heads of these firms when they came to Boston to meet with State Street's money managers. Similarly, Lowell usually made the rounds of the big financial institutions on Wall Street when he went to New York.

Lowell's increasing prominence in corporate boardrooms opened a new role for him: expert witness. In the spring of 1949 the president of New England Telephone asked Lowell to provide an affidavit for his company in its court appeal of a rate decision by the Massachusetts Department of Public Utilities. Lowell had been snubbed the year before when he suggested that New England Telephone open an account at the bank. He was still irritated and left no doubt of his annoyance. Nonetheless, while noting that he was not an expert on utility securities, he expressed strong sympathy for New England Telephone's regulatory problems. The telephone executive took advantage of this opening to say that Lowell and Lloyd Brace, the president of the First National Bank of Boston, would make the best witnesses for the company's case. Lowell wrote later, "I said that, of course, I would do what I could for them as a public duty."

New England Telephone won its suit and asked Lowell to submit a bill for his testimony. Lowell declined, saying he had done it as a "public service," but the utility's president came to Lowell's office to explain that it was common practice for expert witnesses to be compensated. Lowell asked what the company would consider a fair fee, thinking the answer might be $500. The president's response that $5,000 to $7,000 was the going rate stunned him, but not so much that he didn't think to check with Boston Safe's attorney to make sure that he and not the bank was entitled to the money. Indeed, the fee was Lowell's. [30]

In 1959 Lowell gave expert testimony in a case of national dimensions. The Supreme Court, in agreement with the Justice Department, had ruled that the du Pont Corporation's ownership of 23 percent of the stock of General Motors constituted a violation of the antitrust laws and ordered the chemical giant to dispose of these shares. The Justice Department and du Pont were soon at loggerheads over the means of divestiture. The company's lead counsel, John Lord O'Brian of Washington, whom Lowell knew from his Harvard activities, asked Lowell to make a deposition in support of the corporation's plan. Lowell's views, among others, were cited by the trial judge of the Northern Illinois Federal Court in his decision upholding du Pont. In Boston, Lowell received the news with considerable satisfaction. The judge, he wrote, "favored the testimony of experienced handlers of investments and trusts over the charts and statistics prepared by economists with no practical experience." [31]*

Lowell recognized and accepted the limits of his growing prominence. In February 1952 he was informed that the selection process for filling a vacant seat on the board of the American Telephone and Telegraph Company had come down to him and the First National Bank's Lloyd Brace, and that Brace had been selected. Lowell had no difficulty understanding AT&T's preference for Brace, observing that he was "a younger man filling a more important job." At the age of sixty-two, the yearning for recognition, which the position would have bestowed, was no longer so strong: "I don't want anything more and I certainly do not want to be traveling to New York every other week or so." [32]

Although Lowell was not prepared to bear the inconveniences of national prominence, the competitive fires still burned within him on the local level. He thought the First National Bank's towering position in the New England financial community was unhealthy for all concerned, and it rankled him that Old Colony was able to widen its lead over other trust companies simply by hitching a ride with the First National. The Boston Safe–Old Colony rivalry assumed personal proportions with the appointment of Robert Cutler as Old Colony president in 1946. Lowell and Cutler were friends from childhood, Cutler a few years behind Lowell at both the Volkmann School and Harvard. After his military service overseas in World War I, Cutler joined Robert Herrick's law firm and took a leading role in charitable fund-raising in the 1930s. Cutler went to work at the War Department in 1942 and gained the rank of brigadier general before returning to Boston at the end of the war. Lowell admired Cutler's talents as a public speaker and envied him for his military career. A rivalry had developed between them in their medical affiliations; Lowell was on the board of the Massachusetts General Hospital, and Cutler was on the board (as chairman after 1949) of the Peter Bent Brigham Hospital. Both institu-

---

* The U.S. Supreme Court overturned this ruling, however, and adopted the major elements of the government's plan.

tions were teaching hospitals of the Harvard Medical School, and they often competed for staff and patients. Characterizing Cutler as a "dynamo," Lowell predicted that "Old Colony will go places under his leadership. I will have to work just that much harder because of his being there."[33]

Lowell and Cutler presented different management styles that reflected not only different personalities but also different corporate environments. Boston Safe was a comparatively small organization, which enjoyed the luxury of determining its own course, while Old Colony, benefiting as it did from the merger with First National, had to function within the constraints and expectations of the parent institution. Lowell tried to win the affection of his employees; Cutler was a stern taskmaster. The Old Colony had always been a pressure-cooker operation, and this continued under Cutler. He moved more quickly than Lowell did, both in overhauling the Old Colony's personnel and adding to its board of directors. Yet while Old Colony maintained its considerable edge over Boston Safe in terms of assets, Lowell lifted Boston Safe's earnings to a level nearly equal to that of Old Colony.[34]

Lowell bested Old Colony in the realm of publicity in June 1959, when *Business Week* ran an article entitled, "In Investing, It's the Prudent Bostonian." Although Boston Safe and its president were barely mentioned in the text, Lowell appeared on the cover, along with Paul Cabot, the founder and head of a major investment fund and treasurer of Harvard. "In Boston," the caption read, playing on the old quatrain, "when Paul Cabot speaks to Ralph Lowell, they talk the language of the Prudent Man."[35]

GEARING UP FOR THE FUTURE

During his years at Boston Safe, as throughout his life, Lowell performed a delicate balancing act between paying deference to the past, adjusting to the present, and anticipating the future. The changes he brought to the bank had more to do with tone than substance, but they were significant nonetheless. One of his innovations was to diversify the board of directors. In searching for fresh blood for the board in 1944, Lowell set his sights on James Madden, a rising young corporation executive who possessed superb business skills and the added attraction of being a Roman Catholic. No one of that faith had ever served as a Boston Safe director, but Lowell had identified the region's large Catholic community as a rich, untapped market for the bank's services and he thought the time had come to end the board's exclusively Protestant character. Madden was settling in at a new job and felt he could not accept Boston Safe's offer; Lowell persisted, however, and in 1949 Madden joined the board. A decade later, just after Lowell stepped down as president, Boston Safe appointed its first Jewish director, Sidney Rabb of the Stop & Shop supermarket chain. The board was hopeful, Lowell noted, that "he will bring us a great deal of business." [36]

One more symbolic addition to the board in the 1950s was Gerald Blakeley, managing director of the commercial real estate development firm of Cabot, Cabot & Forbes. Blakeley was instrumental in making Route 128 (the circumferential highway linking Boston's northern, western, and southern suburbs) the most important development zone for new office buildings and light-industrial parks in the post–World War II era, thereby transforming the metropolitan region. It was a sign perhaps of how much the bank needed Blakeley that when Lowell suggested his name in 1956, no one on the executive committee knew of him. [37]

In addition to fashioning a younger and more diverse board,* Lowell also adopted a bolder approach in the way Boston Safe managed the funds in its care. He rejected as "too conservative" the refrain preached at most trust bankers' meetings that the "prime duty of a trustee is to maintain the principal of the account." In pursuing higher returns, Lowell had few qualms about shaking up portfolios to take advantage of quickly changing conditions. During the Suez crisis of 1956, for example, when huge bargains suddenly appeared in the bond market, Lowell urged his trust officers to cut back on stocks netting less than 3 percent and to pick up good bonds yielding over 4 percent. Lowell was a staunch supporter of common stocks and had to overcome strong resistance to them on the part of a cautious staff nurtured by his predecessors on the virtues of bonds and mortgages.†
Lowell's favorable view of common stocks derived from his more than two decades as a broker and his admiration for the success of mutual fund

---

* Another Lowell initiative in the 1950s was to appoint Boston Safe's first women bank officers.
† By the time he stepped down as president, however, Lowell found it necessary to restrain the enthusiasm of the younger officers for common stocks. When his son John, a vice president of Boston Safe, proposed that up to 60 percent of the assets of pension trusts be held in common stocks, Lowell joined with older members of the executive committee in rejecting the idea. "I fear," he wrote, "that the younger men that have not been through a depression are headed for trouble if they go haywire in the present time." A limit of 40 percent was set. Diary, July 29, 1959.

managers. Impressed by the operation he had viewed firsthand at Massachusetts Investors Trust, Lowell gave Boston Safe's Statistical Department a new name, the Investment Analysis Department, and assigned it additional personnel whose focus was to be security research. Boston Safe's more assertive stance toward the stock market during the postwar era— a time when prices were rising—paid off not only in higher incomes for trust beneficiaries but in higher profits for the bank as well. Annual dividends more than doubled (from $16/share to $36/share) during Lowell's fifteen-plus years at the helm.[38]

In the late 1940s Lowell began thinking about finding and training a successor. He would reach retirement age in 1955, and he felt it part of his responsibility to Boston Safe to leave it in capable hands. "The bank has become, what it should not be, a one-man show," he noted. Because of their advanced age and limited vision, the corps of vice presidents Lowell had inherited did not figure in his plans. He had inaugurated a youth movement within the bank at the end of World War II by hiring veterans and college graduates, including his eldest son, John, for entry-level positions, but none in this group would be prepared to take over when Lowell expected to leave. However, Lowell had spotted one individual, a quarter century his junior, who demonstrated great potential.[39]

William Wellington Wolbach went to work at the bank in 1936. His grandfather had served on the board, and his mother's family owned a substantial block of Boston Safe stock. Between his sophomore and junior years at Harvard, Wolbach had a summer job at the bank as an office messenger. Finding the bank exciting, he never returned to school. When Lowell arrived in 1943, Wolbach was about to be made an assistant trust officer. His forte was stock research. Wolbach (to use his own words) "rode the wave of the coming of age of security analysis, just as if I were on a surfboard." He was bright, full of new ideas, conscientious, and a participant in community good works (he served on the board of Children's Hospital and later became its president). In every respect he fit Lowell's definition of "attractive." [40]

Lowell had found his man, but neither Lowell nor the bank's executive committee was quite ready for the shift as Lowell's sixty-fifth birthday neared. It was agreed in late 1954 that Lowell would remain as president and chairman on a year-to-year basis for up to four years. As part of the arrangement, Wolbach joined the board of directors.[41]

This revised timetable would cause Lowell grief. With his retirement now delayed, he took hope that it might be put off again until John, who had been advancing rapidly through the ranks, could take his place. Giving up the leadership of Boston Safe would have been hard in any case, but with the possibility of John's selection, Lowell had even more reason to hang on. It did not happen. Even Lowell acknowledged that Wolbach was "a little more mature" than his son, and the bank's directors thought Wolbach would do just fine.* In January 1959, while retaining the title of chairman, Lowell passed the presidency and the power to Wolbach.[42]

Lowell's final years at Boston Safe proved disappointing in regard to his familial aspirations, but his decade-and-a-half leadership of the bank had given him personal financial security, restored his business reputation, and bolstered his desire to participate actively in community affairs. In Boston's civic firmament, Lowell's star began to glow brightly during his tenure at 100 Franklin Street.

---

* Although Wolbach was only four years older than John, he had been at the bank a decade longer; John's four years in college and four years of military service were responsible for the difference.

7

"Just what John Lowell would have wished"

THE LOWELL INSTITUTE
COOPERATIVE BROADCASTING
COUNCIL

R alph Lowell the young college graduate rejected an academic career as financially unrewarding, but it was in the field of education that Ralph Lowell the civic leader left his deepest imprint. When WGBH-FM and then WGBH-TV went on the air in the early and middle 1950s under Lowell's leadership, they were pioneers in educational radio and television; in 1970, when Lowell stepped aside as active trustee, WGBH was the national leader in educational broadcasting. Although he rarely suggested a program idea, Lowell, more than any other single individual, was responsible for this achievement. He could not have done it, however, without the benefit of family ties, initiatives taken by others, and fortuitous timing.

THE LOWELL INSTITUTE

In the early 1940s the position of Trustee of the Lowell Institute passed to Ralph Lowell. The institute, the family's most important contribution to the intellectual life of Boston, was the legacy of John Lowell (1799–1836), eldest son of Francis Cabot Lowell. John Lowell followed his father into business and then embarked on a political career, but this was cut short by personal tragedy. While still in his early thirties, Lowell lost his wife and two young daughters to scarlet fever in the space of eighteen months. Devastated, he set out on a globe-circling journey—his route would serve as a guide for Ralph's post-graduation trip—and after two years of travel, he died of dysentery in India.

Before leaving Boston, John Lowell had drawn up his will. It set aside half of his estate ($250,000) for a fund to underwrite, in perpetuity, the cost of free public lectures for adult audiences. He left the choice of subjects open, requiring only that one series of lectures each year be devoted to "the historical and internal evidences of Christianity." In a letter composed in the shadow of the Egyptian pyramids and sent to the executor of his will, Lowell elaborated on his design:

> As the prosperity of my native land, New England, which is sterile and un-
> productive, must depend hereafter, as it has heretofore depended, first, on
> the moral qualities, and secondly, on the intelligence and information of
> its inhabitants, I am desirous of trying to contribute towards this second
> object also;—and I wish courses of lectures to be established on physics
> and chemistry, with their application to the arts; also, on botany, zoology,
> geology, and mineralogy, connected with their particular utility to man.

Over the next century, the Lowell Institute brought to Boston audiences scores of experts, both American and European, on a wide variety of topics.[1]

By 1940, when the institute celebrated the centennial of its first lecture, the focus of its activities had begun to shift in other directions. Although the free public lectures—averaging about five series a year plus the special religious series—remained the best known of the institute's good works, an increasing share of its funds were spent elsewhere. The founder's will had suggested establishing practical courses of instruction for advanced students and artisans and, beginning in 1862, the first trustee, John Amory Lowell, furnished the money for a series of free, college-level evening courses at the new Massachusetts Institute of Technology. In 1903, under the direction of the third trustee, A. Lawrence Lowell, this eclectic program was reshaped into a two-year mechanical and electrical engineering course and given the name of the Lowell Institute School for Industrial Foremen. During the same decade, Lowell also set up the University Extension program at Harvard. Here, for a nominal sum, students could attend evening classes in the liberal arts, taught by the Harvard faculty, and upon passing the final examination could count these courses toward a new Harvard degree. Later, this arrangement was expanded to include several other colleges in the Boston area.[2]

John Lowell's will contained several distinctive provisions regarding the institute. It stipulated that none of the institute's funds be spent for buildings. The institute would not have an edifice of its own—it would rent auditoriums. (The public lectures took place in the Back Bay at M.I.T.'s Huntington Hall from the mid-1880s through 1938, when the building was sold. After that the lectures moved down Boylston Street to the Boston Public Library.) The will also mandated that at least 10 percent of each year's income from the endowment be added to its principal. By this directive, the institute would, indeed, endure for the ages. Most unusual, John required that the responsibility for executing his plans belong always to a single trustee. Furthermore, after naming John's cousin John Amory Lowell as the first trustee, the will required that he and all those who followed him choose as their successors some male descendant of John's grandfather, John Lowell (1743–1802), "provided there be one competent to hold the office and of the name Lowell."[3]

Trusteeship of the Lowell Institute came to Ralph Lowell by a zigzag course. John Amory Lowell chose his son Augustus to follow him, and at Augustus's death in 1900 the position passed to his son Lawrence. According to the will, each trustee was to designate his successor within a week of taking over by depositing a sealed envelope containing the individual's name with the trustees of the Boston Athenaeum. Lawrence had no children, and it is not known whom he selected as his replacement immediately upon becoming trustee; his choice in the 1920s was his cousin, architect Guy Lowell. However, Guy, fourteen years younger than Lawrence, suffered a fatal stroke in 1927. Soon thereafter, an envelope with Ralph Lowell's name inside was delivered to the Boston Athenaeum.[4]

Lawrence waited a decade before telling Ralph of his selection and then broke precedent by going public with the news. The Ninety-eighth Annual Report of the Trustee of the Lowell Institute, dated August 1, 1938, and signed by the two Lowells, also disclosed that Lawrence, concerned about his declining health, had granted Ralph "full authority to act in his stead." (The founder's will made no provision for formal resignation.) Lawrence continued in charge, but over the next five years Ralph became acquainted with the institute's work, about which he had previously known little. Ralph was ready to take over when Lawrence died in January 1943.[5]

Twenty years later, Ralph Lowell recalled Lawrence's telling him that "each trustee tried to do something different or new from the other trustees, and how they were at perfect liberty to do almost anything." Asked by an interviewer if he indeed felt free to mold the Lowell Institute as he saw fit, Lowell replied, "Well, of course, when you take over any kind of thing like that, for a time being anyway, you continue in the line in which your predecessors had followed until you find that you're thoroughly conversant with the problem, and then you branch out on your own." * In the fall of 1945 an occasion to branch out presented itself, and Lowell made the most of it.[6]

WASHINGTON-CAMBRIDGE-BOSTON

In June 1945, the Federal Communications Commission (FCC) announced that twenty of the ninety radio channels in the newly relocated frequency modulation (FM) band had been reserved for noncommercial stations, and sent letters to colleges and universities inviting them to apply for FM licenses. Among the recipients was President James Bryant Conant of Harvard.[7]

Several members of the Harvard faculty had long evidenced interest in the educational possibilities of radio, but Conant did not share their enthusiasm. A renowned chemist, Conant had introduced many innovations to Harvard since succeeding A. Lawrence Lowell as president in 1933, but he held the traditionalist's view that the university's activities were best confined to the classroom, laboratory, and library. He saw two crucial pitfalls in a university radio station: It would be expensive to operate, and it might draw Harvard into damaging public disputes. Nonetheless, several weeks after the FCC letter landed on his desk, Conant formed the Ad Hoc Committee Appointed to Consider the Desirability of Applying for an FM Noncommercial Radio Station.[8]

This panel of deans and professors had its report ready for Conant by the middle of October. Determining that the necessary capital ($50,000 to $100,000) and yearly operating costs ($40,000) of a Harvard FM station were beyond the university's means, the committee unanimously recommended that Harvard provide programming for a station "owned and controlled by some noncommercial foundation, located in Greater Boston, [associated with] but independent of the several universities and colleges of that area." Under this arrangement, Harvard could "go forward con-

---

* Lowell was responsible for some "firsts" in regard to the public lectures: making a microphone available to lecturers, having a woman deliver a lecture series, and selecting a Catholic to offer the religious lectures.

structively, but tentatively, in the field of radio broadcasting without imposing an excessive burden either on the University's finances, or on the time and effort of its personnel."[9]

The Ad Hoc Committee cited two local organizations that might hold the station license. One was the World Wide Broadcasting Foundation, which for about a decade had beamed American educational and cultural programs to foreign audiences via shortwave radio. In 1936 the foundation had broadcast forty-five hours of lectures presented during Harvard's tercentenary celebration, and many Harvard faculty were heavily involved in its activities. The foundation was preparing to file for an FM license and had already informally proposed to set aside two hours a day for Harvard-produced programs. Conant, however, opened discussions with the other entity mentioned in the committee's report: the Lowell Institute.[10]

The Lowell Institute's deep roots in Boston, its historic ties to Harvard, and Ralph Lowell's reputation for prudent management influenced Conant's decision. Although the World Wide Broadcasting Foundation gave its listeners excellent programs, it also had sparked several controversies, which was just what Conant wanted to avoid. With the Lowell Institute in charge, Conant could be confident that the highest intellectual standards would be maintained and that Harvard would never be embarrassed—politically or financially. True, the managers of World Wide had considerable broadcasting experience and Lowell had none, but Conant was confident that Lowell, with his many contacts, could put all the pieces together.

In a meeting in Conant's office at the end of October, Conant summarized the report of the Ad Hoc Committee for Lowell. Since the primary function of a noncommercial FM station would be "to serve as an instrument of adult education in the Greater Boston area," Conant inquired if the Lowell Institute would be interested in taking the lead in organizing a cooperative venture with the region's colleges and universities. Lowell also understood Conant to imply that the institute would serve as a major source of funding for the station. Writing up the meeting for his diary a few days later, Lowell noted, "Probably it cannot be worked out as a practical matter, and perhaps the whole idea would have little appeal to the general public, but it is a challenging idea just the same and I am going to study it carefully."[11]

Lowell was intrigued by Conant's proposal because it supplied a remedy for the declining popularity of the Lowell Institute's public lectures. As early as 1911, Lawrence Lowell had remarked about the fall in attendance, noting that the lectures were not as important to the community as they once had been, "when learned men were fewer and the opportunities for study less abundant." Almost four decades later, the plight of the lectures had worsened; Ralph Lowell observed in his annual report for 1947–1948 that "the competition of radio, television, single lectures, and other forms of entertainment" was too great.* Because many of the lectures later appeared as books and thus reached "a much wider audience than appears in the hall itself," Lowell was prepared to continue sponsoring them, but he was on the lookout for new ways to fulfill the institute's mission.[12]

Three months after his session with Conant, Lowell concluded that a Lowell Institute FM station was out of the question. Using figures supplied by the top executive at Filene's, which had considered starting its own station but backed off, Lowell determined that the Harvard committee had grossly underestimated the expenses involved in starting up and keeping a station on the air. Lowell had been prepared to commit $25,000 annually—more than double the amount allotted to the public lectures and a huge chunk of the institute's yearly income, which ranged between $90,000 and $100,000—but according to the data from Filene's this would be far from enough. Further discussions between Conant and Lowell in the winter of 1946 therefore focused on the suggestion that Boston-area colleges and universities produce educational programs for broadcast on commercial AM outlets. This approach offered the twin advantages of far lower costs and access to far larger audiences. With Conant's encouragement, Lowell began contacting AM stations.[13]

His timing could not have been better. The FCC had just issued its so-called blue book, which announced the commission's new policy of scrutinizing a station's local programming before renewing its license. Among the matters to be considered was a station's willingness to deal with subjects unsuitable for commercial sponsorship and to serve the needs of nonprofit groups. In this stiffer regulatory environment, Boston's AM stations were only too pleased to hear of Lowell's plans and to pledge their assistance, including free air time, production services, and publicity.[14]

---

* Lowell began to attend the lectures more regularly after being named Lawrence's successor. A comment in his diary suggests another reason for their declining appeal: Neither Ralph nor Charlotte could follow what the astronomy lecturer was saying. "It is frightening the knowledge people have today which is incomprehensible to the ordinary layman." Diary, January 22, 1940.

Conant and Lowell concurred on the next step: "sell[ing] our scheme" to the other colleges and universities. On May 1 a letter from Conant went out to the presidents of Boston College, Boston University, M.I.T., Northeastern, and Tufts, inviting them to a luncheon at Conant's house. Ralph Lowell, the letter announced, "would like to discuss with this group the possibility of a cooperative venture in adult education, which I [Conant] venture to think will be of interest to you." All those invited attended the May 24 gathering.[15]

Although Conant's letter had indicated that the discussion was to be "highly informal and preliminary," Lowell received firm commitments from all but one of the participants for financial contributions to the joint effort. (The lone holdout was Boston College. As the leader of a Jesuit institution, its president operated with less administrative freedom than the others at the luncheon. The others would need to get ratification from their trustees but obviously felt themselves on stronger ground in acting independently.) The group approved an annual budget of $40,000 ($45,000 if Boston College signed on). Harvard and the Lowell Institute each pledged $10,000; the others pledged $5,000 each. It was further agreed that the project would be guaranteed a two-year trial beginning on September 1, 1946, and that it would be "run entirely" by the Trustee of the Lowell Institute. "Quite a high point in my career," Lowell wrote in his diary. "If it can be worked out it certainly is just what John Lowell would have wished for his Institute."[16]

GETTING STARTED

Lowell's first task was finding a full-time director for the as-yet unnamed venture. He interviewed three local prospects with backgrounds in commercial radio and, on the recommendation of Conant, contacted Lyman Bryson, a former professor of adult education at Columbia University who was then a consultant on education for the Columbia Broadcasting System (CBS). Conant thought Bryson would make an ideal choice, but he could not be lured to Boston. Bryson offered Lowell some suggestions, however; among those he rated highly was a major in the U.S. Army named Parker Wheatley.[17]

Indiana born and educated, Parker Wheatley began his career in educational broadcasting in Chicago during the mid-1930s. He was on the faculty at Northwestern University, in charge of the school's radio activities, when he was called for military service in 1942. As director of educational programs for the Armed Forces Radio Service, Wheatley served under Francis Spaulding, who was on leave as dean of Harvard's Graduate School of Education, and worked with Lyman Bryson. With strong endorsements from Bryson and Spaulding in Wheatley's file, Lowell invited him to Boston for an early August meeting.[18]

It did not hurt Wheatley's prospects that he appeared in uniform, and the session between the Hoosier and the Boston Brahmin went well. Lowell explained that the director would be paid a salary ($10,000) comparable to a full professor's at Harvard and would be responsible for developing programs with the faculties of the member institutions. Finances would be in Lowell's charge, and his approval would be required on programming plans. Near the end of the interview, Wheatley asked, "Are you sure you want a guy like me with a bachelor's degree in philosophy and English from a place [Butler University] most of these great faculty people and scholars have never heard of?" Thirty-five years later, Lowell's response remained fresh in Wheatley's mind: "Major Wheatley, I think it's better that you don't have a Ph.D. These people are a bunch of prima donnas, and you won't have any jealousy with them with your bachelor's degree in philosophy and English. But your experience is the experience that they *don't* have and you *do* have." Lowell's analysis held up—Wheatley developed a close and productive relationship with the professors.[19]

Wheatley assumed the directorship in early September and had to start from scratch. Lacking quarters of his own, Wheatley operated for the first several weeks from a desk placed in the Boston Safe lobby near Lowell's office. By November, space had been rented at the American Academy of Arts and Sciences building on Newbury Street in the Back Bay. In the meantime, Lowell, Conant, and Wheatley had concocted a name for their venture: The Lowell Institute Cooperative Broadcasting Council. On October 24 the presidents of the participating institutions gathered in Lowell's office to be introduced to Wheatley. They agreed to make a public announcement of the council's formation in November and set February 1, 1947, as the target date for the first broadcast.[20]

One loose end remained to be tied up before the council could go public—the status of Boston College. Lowell had heard nothing after the original meeting in May. In early September, when he sent Wheatley's name in for confirmation, he received distressing news: The school had made its own broadcasting arrangements with a new Boston radio station and would not be joining the Lowell Institute group. The inclusion of Boston College was important to Lowell and Conant because, as the foremost Roman Catholic college in the Boston area, it would enhance the council's appeal to the region's large Irish population. Afraid that Boston College's absence would generate "a good deal of comment," Lowell refused to take no for an answer and invited the school to send a representative to the October 24 meeting; although a representative did attend, the question of the school's membership remained unresolved. Not until November 6, the very day the institutions were scheduled to inform their faculties about the council, did Boston College formally notify Lowell that while it would proceed with its separate broadcasting plans (which were dropped after a year's trial), it would also join the council. "This takes quite a load off my mind," wrote Lowell.[21]

Lowell had devised a two-step plan for announcing news of the council. Recognizing that the entire scheme was dependent on the goodwill of the teaching staffs, Lowell wanted to avoid newspaper stories that might lead some professors to feel they were being "put under duress or that their rights had been overlooked in pledging the universities' cooperation." Therefore, only after the presidents had reassured their respective faculties that their participation in the council's programs was completely voluntary* did press releases reach the desks of city editors. Prodded by personal telephone calls from Lowell, the newspapers gave the council excellent coverage in their November 15 editions. "So we are officially launched on an uncharted sea," Lowell noted, "with great hopes that it may be of real value in the field of adult education." [22]

In a foretaste of the future, the inception of the Lowell Institute Cooperative Broadcasting Council rated national attention as well. Although the New York Times gave the story only a paragraph in its weekly roundup of educational news, Time devoted two thirds of a page, complete with a portrait of founder John Lowell. The article displayed some of the magazine's characteristic caustic tone ("The Council is to broadcast learned lectures as a typically Boston bluestocking scheme of adult education"), but it was a favorable treatment overall. "The venerable Lowell Institute," Time declared, "refused to admit its age." [23]

On the evening of February 3, 1947, the Council unveiled its premier

---

* Faculty were not to be paid for taking part in council broadcasts; in the mid-1950s, however, the council began offering honoraria.

programs. At 7 P.M., on station WMEX, *Our Children* featured faculty members from Boston College, Harvard, and Tufts discussing the problems of young people in the home, school, and community. *We Human Beings,* an examination of the psychological nature of humanity conducted by professors at Boston University, appeared at 8:15 P.M. on WCOP. An eminent literary critic, Professor I. A. Richards of Harvard, closed out the evening with a 9:45 broadcast on WHDH entitled *Your Ideas,* which related the philosophy of Plato to the world today. Each program lasted fifteen minutes; the first and last series each ran three times a week, and *We Human Beings* ran twice weekly. Thus the council produced two hours of educational programming a week. In June a faculty group from M.I.T. inaugurated a series entitled *Our Weather,* and a contingent from Harvard began *Crossroads of the Future,* a study of the Middle East. As the council's first anniversary in September neared, Lowell wrote enthusiastically, "[T]he experiment has been a great success."[24]

HOLDING THE COUNCIL TOGETHER

Turning this experiment into something permanent demanded Lowell's frequent intervention over the next few years. A similar cooperative effort in Chicago in the 1930s had fallen apart in discord, and Lowell understood that institutional egos, which were even stronger in Boston, would need to be stroked continually. To ensure the council's success, Lowell was willing not only to make radio announcements plugging its programs, but also to work behind the scenes to keep everyone in harness.[25]

In the beginning, Boston College required the most delicate handling. Sharp sectarianism dominated Boston's religious climate at midcentury, and the Catholic college was a staunch champion of Church dogma. Perhaps unaware of these facts, Wheatley distributed a list of programming possibilities in early 1947 that included the Lowell religious lecture series presented by Harvard psychologist Gordon Allport at King's Chapel—the first Anglican Church in New England and subsequently the first Unitarian Church. Boston College's Jesuit president wrote Lowell to express his discomfort. "A series of lectures originating from King's Chapel," he declared, "might not portray the religious ideals for which Boston College must stand." Lowell replied that the lectures would be removed from the schedule, adding, "I want to be very careful that in this cooperative effort we do not produce any series that will be objectionable to any of the members of the group." A few years later, when a program dealing with population issues touched on the question of birth control—the subject of two bitterly contested state referenda in 1942 and 1948—unhappy listeners contacted administrators at Boston College to voice their outrage. These complaints were passed on to Lowell, who decided to cancel the next program in the series. Explaining the council's policy on religion, Lowell later declared, "It's what you do with an ordinary group of friends: you just don't want to step on their toes." [26]

Boston University (B.U.) posed a different type of problem. Overshadowed in intellectual distinction by the institutions across the Charles River and lacking the cultural base enjoyed by the Catholic college farther out on Commonwealth Avenue, B.U. attempted to make up for these deficiencies by offering a wide array of degree programs and experimenting with innovative approaches to education. It latched onto radio in the postwar period as a place to make a name for itself, and when it joined the council, it took care to preserve its free hand in the field. At the instigation of B.U., the presidents at the council meeting of October 24, 1946, agreed that membership would "not limit the various colleges and universities in their own broadcasting." [27]

B.U. secured a license for its own FM station (WBUR) and a few years later informed Lowell that it would leave the council. The news shocked Lowell, and he considered resigning his seat on the B.U. board of trustees. "It would look bad," Lowell noted, "for a university of which I was a trustee not to belong to the Council." But quitting in a huff was not Lowell's style. Instead, he lobbied B.U.'s president and joined the board's executive committee to improve his negotiating position. Together with Wheatley, he also met with the WBUR staff to forge a better working relationship. These personal efforts were rewarded by B.U.'s decision to stay with the council.[28]

Thanks to Lowell's attention to the special needs of its members and Wheatley's success in generating well-received programming, the council was renewed for another two years and given a larger budget at the end of the trial period in the summer of 1948. Approximately 250,000 listeners tuned in to the three hours of programs the council produced each week. Lowell and Wheatley sought and gained a 25 percent increase in the council's spending ceiling, raising it to $56,250. The ratio of contributions among the members remained the same: Harvard and the Lowell Institute each would pay $12,500; the others would pay $6,250 each. When this two-year extension expired, the council set off on a very different track.[29]

THE COUNCIL'S STATION: WGBH-FM

Pledges of free air time and technical assistance from Boston's AM stations were key to the formation of the Lowell Institute Cooperative Broadcasting Council in 1946, but by the fall of 1949 commercial stations had become far less accommodating. The reason was television. Boston was first exposed to video in mid-1948 when two television outlets began broadcasting, and radio immediately felt the competition for audiences and advertising. Carrying the council's programs became a financial drain on radio stations, not only because the programs were not sponsored but because they drove away audiences for prime-time, commercially sponsored programs. One council series in the 1948–1949 season was canceled because it failed to deliver the audience it inherited from the entertainment program preceding it to the entertainment program that followed. To raise the council's ratings, Wheatley and his staff tried to loosen up their programs, moving away from the formal college lecture style to one "more directly adapted to the medium," but the stations remained doubtful. Not only did stations reduce the total number of hours available, they also moved the council's programs around in their evening schedules almost capriciously, making it difficult for listeners to find them. The average weekly audience for council programs in 1949–1950 was 180,000, a decline of 30 percent from its peak in 1947–1948.[30]

This reversal in the council's fortunes prompted yet another initiative from Harvard. The central player this time was not Conant but his close aide, David W. Bailey. A Harvard graduate (class of 1921) and a former reporter and drama critic for the *Boston Evening Transcript,* Bailey had returned to his alma mater in the 1930s to head its publications office. He also acted as faculty adviser to the student-run radio station, WHRB, which used the university's steam pipes and power system as broadcasting antennae. Appointed secretary of the Harvard Corporation in 1945, he served as Conant's liaison to the council and dealt frequently with Lowell. In the fall of 1950, while Wheatley was busy grappling with the details of weekly programming and at the same time planning the leap to television, Bailey took the lead in convincing Lowell that the council should end its dependence on commercial outlets and operate its own FM station.[31]

A gift to M.I.T. laid the groundwork for what Lowell described as Bailey's "grandiose scheme." Edwin H. Armstrong, the father of FM broadcasting, had donated an FM transmitter to the engineering school, and if M.I.T. officials were unsure how to use it, Bailey could see the possibilities. This equipment, with expert technical assistance from the M.I.T. and Harvard faculties, would allow the council's FM station to get on the air for just $30,000. Bailey proposed that Harvard, M.I.T., and the Lowell Institute each contribute $10,000 toward start-up costs. For yearly budget needs, Bailey looked to expanded membership on the council and larger payments from some of its constituents. The dues of Harvard, M.I.T., and the Lowell Institute would be increased to $15,000 while those of the other schools remained at $6,250. Bailey hoped to get two women's colleges (Simmons and Wellesley) to join, but preliminary discussions were fruitless. The New England Conservatory of Music came in at $6,250, as did the Museum of Fine Arts (of which Lowell was president). But the key to the scheme was the Boston Symphony Orchestra (BSO).[32]

The symphony offered the council two important assets. First, the BSO's membership dues would add $15,000 annually to the council's income. In order to facilitate BSO participation, Lowell arranged for the Permanent Charity Fund (which, it will be recalled, was closely tied to the Boston Safe Deposit and Trust Company) to make a $15,000 contribution to the orchestra. Second, the broadcasting of BSO concerts would add an entirely new dimension to council programming by moving it away from lectures and discussions and into the performance hall.

Affiliation with the council carried benefits for the BSO as well. The orchestra's contract with the National Broadcasting Company called for only occasional appearances, but switching to the council's station would mean regular broadcasts and an opportunity to present concerts in their entirety. The fact that the council would operate on the FM band was a plus—FM provided much better sound quality, especially for music. Furthermore, the BSO's leaders realized that the orchestra's future depended on reaching out to a larger segment of the population. The old families that had supported the symphony for three quarters of a century could no longer do it alone.[33]

Bailey's plan seemingly overcame the financial obstacles, but a legal hurdle remained. Although the council's fiscal accounts were (at Lowell's insistence) audited annually, it was otherwise a remarkably informal group, with no official charter or bylaws. As successful as this flexible arrangement had been in producing programs for broadcast by others, the fact that the council was not a recognizable legal entity made it unacceptable to the FCC as the holder of a broadcasting license. When the Washington law firm that Lowell had retained for the council advised him of this, his immediate inclination was to make the Lowell Institute the licensee. But this would have placed all of the institute's assets at risk from possible libel suits and other legal actions against the station. The attorneys urged that while the Lowell Institute might apply for the license in the interests of speed, the license should be assigned to a new nonprofit corporation established under Massachusetts law.[34]

In April 1951 the WGBH Educational Foundation, Inc., was created. (The initials "GBH" stood for Great Blue Hill—the site of the station's antenna atop a Harvard-operated weather observatory.) The incorporators and original board members were the Trustee of the Lowell Institute, the presidents and treasurers of Harvard and M.I.T., and the president of the BSO. The exclusiveness of the board generated no protest among the other members of the council, which were not only less committed financially to the operation than these four institutions, but probably also quite relieved not to be burdened with legal responsibility for the station. In practice, the chartering of the foundation did not immediately alter the council's broadcasting activities, which continued on a broad cooperative basis under the leadership of Lowell and Wheatley.

The choice of the call letters "GBH" did, however, have an effect in the long run. By opting for the initials of a geographic location (which as few people recognized then as do today—some critics of the station have claimed the letters stand for God Bless Harvard), the incorporators of the foundation undermined public awareness of the link between the broadcasting operation and the Lowell Institute. As long as Ralph Lowell remained active, his prominent role in the community guaranteed that educational broadcasting in Boston would be closely linked to the Lowell name, but as he began to slow down in the late 1960s and control of WGBH gravitated toward the station's professional staff, the connection with the Lowells and their institute became increasingly obscure. Nearly a half century after WGBH's birth, a Lowell still sits on the foundation's board and the institute remains one of its important financial angels, but there is scant appreciation of the station's roots in the Lowell Institute Cooperative Broadcasting Council.

No one could have foreseen the WGBH Educational Foundation's future as a multi-million-dollar operation when WGBH-FM made its initial broadcast on October 6, 1951. Fittingly, the broadcast came from Symphony Hall. Presenting the first Saturday evening performance of the BSO's seventy-first season, it opened with words of welcome from Lowell and Henry Cabot, president of the orchestra. It was the first full-length broadcast of a symphony concert in Boston in twenty-five years. To mark the occasion, Ralph and Charlotte Lowell were given the seats that Major Henry Lee Higginson, founder of the BSO, had always used. Only 15 percent of the households in Greater Boston had FM receivers, but WGBH's premier broadcast was a rousing success. For days afterward, people stopped Lowell on the street to thank him for bringing the symphony into their homes.[35]

During its first year, WGBH-FM broadcast 2,600 hours of programming—ten times the amount that the council had been allotted on commercial stations. On the air every day from 3:30 to 10:30 P.M., except on Friday when it began at 2:10 P.M. to carry the BSO's weekly afternoon concert, WGBH offered listeners a mix of classical music, college lectures, seminar discussions, service programs for preschool children, news, and commentary. Most of the programs were produced by council members, but some came from the British Broadcasting Corporation, French and Dutch radio, and educational stations in other cities. By the end of 1952 a quarter of the families in the Boston region had FM sets—a dramatic increase clearly attributable to WGBH's presence—bringing the size of the station's potential audience to 350,000.[36]

Despite its popularity, WGBH-FM barely survived its inaugural season. Start-up and operating costs outran projections by nearly 50 percent, putting the budget some $50,000 in the red. One component of the council's response was to solicit contributions from WGBH listeners. The campaign, at best a half-hearted effort, netted a grand total of $1,344. On a more appropriate scale, Lowell increased the institute's annual contribution from $15,000 to $25,000 and told other members of the council that he was prepared to pump in even more. But he cautioned them that without additional sources of financial support, the station would be living on borrowed time.[37]

Responding to Lowell's warning, Wheatley turned to the one agency likely to help: the Fund for Adult Education (FAE). An offshoot of the recently reorganized Ford Foundation, FAE had been drawn immediately to the broadcast media as a prime instrument for "the development of mature, wise and responsible citizens who can participate intelligently in a free society." Wheatley's contacts with FAE went back to its beginnings when he and several other educational broadcasters had submitted a proposal for a series of educational radio programs for national distribution.

The FAE directors approved a $300,000 grant for Wheatley's group at their first board meeting in April 1951, but found that the group possessed neither the legal status nor the organizational framework required to administer the grant. Anxious that its initial endeavor in the broadcasting field be managed with the highest standards of financial probity and intellectual distinction, FAE officials decided that Lowell, in his capacity as Trustee of the Lowell Institute, would be the perfect choice to oversee the grant. Lowell agreed to the assignment, although he feared the endeavor would distract Wheatley from the job of getting WGBH-FM on the air. The project was a smashing success—two of the series produced (*The Ways of Mankind* and *The Jeffersonian Heritage*) became classics—and this auspicious beginning deepened FAE's commitment to educational broadcasting.[38]

But when Wheatley approached FAE officials in the late winter and early spring of 1952 to discuss WGBH's fiscal plight, there was no precedent for an FAE subsidy to an individual radio station. WGBH did, however, have several things going for it. FAE staff felt obligated to Lowell for his supervision of the $300,000 grant and thought quite highly of Wheatley's work, both in Boston and with the National Association of Educational Broadcasters. Furthermore, the council and WGBH were already of sufficient national stature—having won several awards, including a prestigious George Foster Peabody citation—that their collapse would have dealt educational broadcasting a severe setback. In May the board of FAE approved a $100,000 donation to the council in recognition of its "significant and unique role in adult education through radio." The funds would be spread out over a period of three years ($50,000 for 1952, $30,000 for 1953, and $20,000 for 1954). These sums, along with the larger dues paid by the Lowell Institute ($25,000 in 1952 and 1953, $40,000 in 1954) enabled the council to balance its books and to set its sights even higher.[39]

"For the benefit of the people as a whole"

WGBH-TV

R alph Lowell did not rush to bring a television set into his home—unlike most Americans who could afford it, including his children and business friends. He enjoyed watching sports on TV, but its other entertainments could not entice this avid reader to forsake his books in the evening or on weekends. Not until December 1952, when Lowell was in the midst of his campaign to bring educational television to Boston, did a TV console arrive in his house—as a Christmas gift from a fellow denizen of State Street. After a few days of watching it regularly, Lowell had even stronger feelings about the goal he had established for himself: "One can see why TV gets such a hold on people and that simply increases the importance of keeping Channel 2 for educational TV if we can possibly do so." [1]

RESERVING SPACE FOR EDUCATIONAL TELEVISION

Because FM radio presented only marginal profit-making possibilities in 1945, the decision by the FCC to reserve FM channels for noncommercial licensees evoked little opposition in business circles. But the allocation of television channels in the late 1940s and early 1950s was a different matter. Entrepreneurs saw television as a potential gold mine, and if educational broadcasters wanted a share of the medium's future, they would have to fight for it.

The FCC gave them a chance when, at the request of the U.S. Commissioner of Education, it held hearings in the fall of 1950 on the question of setting aside stations for noncommercial users. Most of the witnesses in favor came from states west of the Alleghenies, a reflection of educational broadcasting's roots in the nation's large land-grant, public universities. The argument for educational broadcasting in Massachusetts arrived in the form of a letter from the president of the Commonwealth's most prestigious private university and a personal appearance by the state's senior U.S. senator.[2]

Both the letter from James Bryant Conant and the appearance of Leverett Saltonstall were largely Ralph Lowell's doing. Lowell had contacted the two men in response to prodding by Parker Wheatley, who had been one of the leaders of the ad hoc group that organized the educational broadcasters' presentation to the FCC. In his letter Conant issued a strong plea that stations be reserved for educational licensees. But still cautious about broadcasting's financial and other pitfalls, he weakened his advocacy by adding that the recommendation "in itself constitutes no commitment on behalf of Harvard University."[3]

Saltonstall took an unequivocally positive stance, making frequent references to the "sound opinions" of his old friend Ralph Lowell. Quoting from the letter Lowell had written to alert him to the FCC hearings, Saltonstall argued that it would be "very short-sighted to allot all the channels now [to commercial stations] rather than holding some out for future educational use." The senator also cited the analogy Lowell had drawn between the reservation of television channels and another well-fixed aspect of government policy, saying that noncommercial channels were "[i]n a way similar to the Public Park system and the preservation of the natural resources of the country for the benefit of the people as a whole." Admitting that financing for educational stations was a serious problem, Saltonstall told the commissioners he was confident that, should a channel in Boston be set aside for noncommercial purposes, Lowell would go out and raise the funds to get it on the air.[4]

On March 22, 1951, the FCC released a preliminary report outlining a reservation policy for educational stations. Under the commission's formula, one of the four television channels allocated to Boston was to be held for an educational licensee. Lowell received the news with mixed feelings: "That is just what we have been working for, but we haven't the money in sight to build, let alone run such a station at the present time."[5]

If Lowell and Conant were not inclined (as Conant put it) "to rush into the television business," Wheatley (Lowell noted) had "television on the brain." A few days after Saltonstall's testimony to the FCC in December

1950, Wheatley came into Lowell's office excited about the prospect of an educational station in Boston. Lowell wrote later: "He wants me to drop everything and get the colleges and the state and everyone else to get to work on television. What a man! He goes off on a tangent every now and then." His exasperation with Wheatley was all the greater because Lowell was then engaged in pinning down all the commitments needed to get the license for the FM station.[6]

Under pressure from Wheatley to find funding for a television station, Lowell sought Conant's advice, as he had on many occasions during the previous six years. The two decided that the Ford Foundation should be approached about underwriting "an experimental television station which might help solidify [the foundation's] ideas about educational television." They would request a budget of $2.5 to $3 million to build and operate the station for five years.[7]

Lowell took an exploratory trip to New York in the spring of 1951 and found the Ford Foundation moving in a different direction. It was on the verge of announcing plans to support the Television-Radio Workshop, which was to produce high-quality shows for broadcast on the commercial networks with advertising.* This approach seemed to preclude Ford Foundation support for individual educational stations.[8]

Frustrated in his bid for financing in New York, Lowell returned home to prepare for a legal battle in Washington. The FCC had given interested parties a year in which to file statements supporting or opposing specific channel reservations, and the designation of Channel 2 in Boston came under challenge. CBS, heretofore slow in assembling a television network to complement its highly profitable radio web, feared being shut out of three of the nation's biggest markets—Chicago, San Francisco, and Boston—and filed arguments requesting deletion of the educational reservations in each of these cities.

The threat from CBS, Wheatley observed later, "angered Ralph Lowell and stiffened everybody's determination." The Lowell Institute Cooperative Broadcasting Council filed a bulky document with the FCC in May 1951 urging confirmation of the allocation. At Lowell's request, each of the council-member presidents had written a letter naming the council as the vehicle through which his institution would operate in the television field. Lowell also solicited and received letters of support from the state's two

---

* The Television-Radio Workshop produced the award-winning series *Omnibus*.

U.S. senators, several of its congressmen, and the superintendent of schools for the Catholic Archdiocese of Boston. In its brief the council cited its extensive experience in educational broadcasting, its readiness to meet the challenges of television, and its search for the funds to construct and operate the station, asserting that it was "more than reasonably confident that [the funds could] be secured" if Channel 2 were reserved.[9]

On April 11, 1952, the FCC ratified its decision on Channel 2.* It rejected CBS's claim that Channel 2 probably would not be utilized in the "ascertainable future." The commission found reasons for confidence based on the past:

> The educational organizations in Boston have demonstrated their interest in establishing a noncommercial educational television station in the Boston area. They have supported this interest with concrete plans to establish such a station by banding together in an association, the Lowell Institute Cooperative Council [sic]. They have mobilized their resources and, further, have already established a noncommercial educational FM station.

Supporters of educational broadcasting had until June 2, 1953, to take advantage of the reservation. After that date, applications from commercial broadcasters would be entertained.[10]

RACING AGAINST A DEADLINE

Although the Lowell Institute Cooperative Broadcasting Council had played the leading role in winning FCC approval for a Boston educational station, it was by no means certain that the council's corporate affiliate, the WGBH Educational Foundation, would become the licensee. Television was frightfully expensive—it would take an estimated half-million dollars just to get started—and Lowell knew that his colleagues in the council could not provide a penny of it. The money for this experimental venture would have to come from outside sources, and Boston philanthropists were not known for supporting unconventional and unproven projects.[11]

---

* CBS also lost its challenges to educational channels in Chicago and San Francisco.

Financing aside, two other considerations kept WGBH from immediately applying for the license. The first was Lowell's own divided mind about committing himself to such a major effort. When in June 1951 it became evident that Ford Foundation funds would not be available, Lowell noted, "In a way that is a relief and we can now concentrate on our new FM station and really make that the outstanding station of its kind." Later, with WGBH-FM on the air, he told Wheatley, "What do we need a television station for? You're doing a brilliant job with the FM station. Forget the television stuff." In June 1952, after another funding possibility appeared to be fading, Lowell confided in his diary, "I rather fear getting too involved in this TV business as I feel it is too big a thing for me to try to run on top of all that I am doing." The president of the Fund for Adult Education recalled Lowell's telling him during this period: "I've got more trouble than I ever want to have much longer with educational radio. Why in the hell should I bother myself and hurt myself mentally and physically by trying to run an educational television station?"

But Lowell allowed himself to be drawn in deeper and deeper. Finally, in May 1953, WGBH applied for the license, but Lowell's emotions remained confused: "I wonder whether I am taking on more than I can do, and whether it is fair to Johnny [his eldest son] who will succeed me as Trustee [of the Lowell Institute] to present him with such a heavy load. Well the Lowell motto is 'grab your opportunity' and that is what I am trying to do now." [12]

The other question was whether the Commonwealth of Massachusetts would seek the license for Channel 2. The state's commissioner of education had been an ally of the council in the FCC proceedings, and now he wanted the Commonwealth to own and operate Channel 2. But neither Governor Paul Dever nor the legislative leadership was prepared to make that financial and managerial plunge without a full review. To study the issue, in the fall of 1952 they created the Special Commission on Educational Television, on which Lowell was asked to serve. [13]

Lowell's feelings about a Commonwealth-run Channel 2 were marked by ambivalence. He feared that politics and patronage, two elements never absent from Massachusetts state government, would wreck the station. Furthermore, the educational bureaucracy appeared ready to emphasize instructional programming, "from the multiplication table through irregular French verbs on to Home Economics," as a Dever aide later put it.

Lowell acknowledged that educational television could serve as a "21-inch classroom," but his target audience was primarily an adult one, the types of people drawn to the Lowell Institute's public lectures and the council's broadcasts on radio. A state-run station was agreeable to Lowell only as a mechanism for preventing the loss of Channel 2.[14]

The Special Commission's report, issued in early December, recommended that the state build and operate Channel 2. Noting that the search for private financing had been going on for close to a year without yielding any results, the commission declared, "It appears that if the presently available channel in the Boston area is to be utilized, public funds must be used, at least in the initial stages, for the entire cost of construction and maintenance." The commission's preliminary estimates of expenses were $500,000 to $1,500,000 for studio, transmitter, and other equipment, and $150,000 to $750,000 annually for operations. Astronomical as these sums appeared, they were "considerably [lower than the costs of] one high school in a medium-sized community." They were also considerably lower than Channel 2's estimated market value of $5 to $8 million, which meant that if the state did not act by June 2, commercial applicants would be lining up at the FCC. "The tentative allocation of Channel 2," warned the commission, "gives educational television only a fragile hold on this priceless cultural treasure."[15]

The commission's pleas fell on deaf ears atop Beacon Hill. Christian A. Herter, the Commonwealth's freshly elected Republican governor, had, as a congressman from the Beacon Hill–Back Bay–Brookline district, endorsed the Lowell Institute Cooperative Broadcasting Council's 1951 petition to the FCC, but in his new post he was committed to slashing state spending. Hence, Lowell's personal entreaty to include funds for Channel 2 in the governor's budget was rebuffed. Legislative leaders on both sides of the aisle were equally unresponsive. Lowell concluded at the end of February 1953 that only a WGBH application for Channel 2 could save it from commercial interests.[16]

Financial support for a council-owned Channel 2 had been taking shape since the previous spring. In May 1952, a month after the FCC confirmed its reservation policy, Harold D. Hodgkinson, the head of Filene's, approached Lowell with an idea. He thought that the Filene trusts might back an educational television station, as a "fitting and living memorial" for two of twentieth-century Boston's leading citizens, the Filene brothers.

Edward and Lincoln Filene, best known for their retailing innovations and enlightened attitude toward their employees, had been generous philanthropists as well. Hodgkinson was not a native Bostonian (born in Connecticut, he started at Filene's after graduating from Yale in 1912 and worked his way to the top by the mid-1940s), but he had married a Cabot, and he continued the Filene brothers' tradition of active community involvement. The various Filene-endowed philanthropic trusts had been considering a number of possible projects to honor Edward and Lincoln, including a social welfare center building and statues, when Hodgkinson, who had long been fascinated by broadcasting, drew their attention to Channel 2.[17]

In mid-July, Hodgkinson informed Lowell that the Filene trusts were considering making $300,000 to $400,000 available for Channel 2. Lowell discussed Hodgkinson's offer with Conant, and they agreed that the council should not seek the license until it had all the required funds in sight. The generous sum being dangled in front of them fell short of the $600,000 Lowell estimated as necessary to construct the station, not to mention the $600,000 needed annually to operate it. However, in August 1952 the Fund for Adult Education (FAE) decided to launch a national program that would match $1 for every $2 raised locally to build community-based educational television stations. This increased the pressure on Lowell to proceed. The Filene money would entitle Boston to the full $150,000 set by FAE as its maximum contribution to a single station; with approximately a half-million dollars available for construction, the council now had a fighting chance of going all the way.[18]

Lowell kept the Filene offer secret during the fall of 1952 and the following winter as the Special Commission tried to win backing for a state-owned station. When that effort collapsed, he opened negotiations with Herter and other officials about possible state funding for the main share of operating costs for a council-owned station. Talks soon broke down over Beacon Hill's insistence that "over-all control" of Channel 2 be lodged with a new State Board of Educational Television. Lowell and Hodgkinson were unwilling to have politicians looking over the council's shoulders. But they were prepared to heed the state leaders' pleas to apply for the license.[19]

In a meeting at Hodgkinson's office on May 5, attended by Lowell, representatives of the various Filene funds (whose combined commitment now totaled $450,000), and the chairman of the Special Commission on Educational Television, it was agreed that the council would file for Channel 2.* "And so the die is cast and we are in it and after it," observed Lowell, "and no one knows just what it all may mean and whether we can find the financial backing necessary to put it across." Lowell naturally felt "quite excited" about the challenge he had undertaken, but then reminded himself that "I had better be for I certainly have stuck my neck out on this television business." At the end of the month, he dispatched Wheatley to Washington with the necessary paperwork, instructing him to go by train rather than airplane, because he wanted to make sure the material arrived safely. On June 1, 1953, the application was filed and on July 16 the FCC issued the license to the WGBH Educational Foundation. "So we are now in the television business officially, whether we like it or not," Lowell observed. "I confess that I am quite scared at the prospect." [20]

MONEY, MONEY

Two years after receiving its license, WGBH-TV/Channel 2 went on the air. Lowell was involved in nearly every aspect of the preparatory work, from finding a studio (the ladies' squash court at the Harvard Club was considered, but it lost out to an unused skating rink on the M.I.T. campus) to arranging with Boston University's School of Public Relations and Communications for a scholarship program through which students would learn television production while providing WGBH with low-cost labor. But Lowell's principal task was finding the money to get the station in operation and keep it going. [21]

For a time he hoped that others might relieve him of that chore. In the early spring of 1953, a small group of young men organized the Massachusetts Citizens' Committee for Educational Television to raise funds for Channel 2. Although the committee was independent of the council, its leaders consulted with Lowell before going public. However, it was not until December 1953 that the committee established its goal of $450,000, and the kick-off dinner was delayed until March 1954. The campaign did not go well. Lowell had been delighted to see a new generation of civic-spirited people come to the fore. When the young men asked him in May

---

* Hodgkinson had received assurances that Channel 2 would be known as the Filene Educational Station, but in 1955 the new president of Harvard, Nathan Pusey, thought this too commercial and threatened to withdraw from the council. Hodgkinson settled for having the Filene trusts acknowledged as major contributors during station breaks.

1953 whether they needed an advisory committee of more practiced hands, he had said no—it was important for "a young group to take the bit in their teeth and show the rest of the states that Boston was not just a place where a man had to die before he could get anywhere." But the committee soon fell under the domination of an older crowd incapable of generating public enthusiasm. After subtracting the $40,000 advance from the WGBH Educational Foundation, the committee had only $165,000 to show for two years of effort.[22]

Lowell had no choice but to get personally involved. Initially he concentrated his efforts on local charities and corporations, receiving unrestricted gifts from the former (the Permanent Charity Fund kicked in $10,000, the Hyams Trust $25,000) and grants for specific programming from the latter (Gillette paid for programs from the Museum of Science; the John Hancock Mutual Life Insurance Company sponsored a series on health issues). The decision by the Museum of Fine Arts (where Lowell was still president) to equip all its galleries for television furnished Channel 2 with relatively inexpensive programming possibilities. Most dramatically, Lowell increased the Lowell Institute's contributions. Having promised the other members of the council that moving into television would not mean higher dues,* Lowell began to tap the institute's reserve funds, which he had been accumulating to support the council's activities. He gave WGBH $130,000 in fiscal 1956 for its first full year of television broadcasting and another $161,000 the following year. That the WGBH Educational Foundation paid its bills during the early years of television was due mainly to the generosity of the Trustee of the Lowell Institute.[23]

In 1957 WGBH created the job of assistant general manager for finance, a full-time position devoted to fund-raising. The first appointee inaugurated WGBH's annual public fund-raising campaign; after three years he reached an annual goal of $250,000. Beginning in June 1960, the position was occupied by David O. Ives, a journalist with keen public relations skills. Ives's success in reaching out to the Greater Boston community took much of the fund-raising chore off Lowell's shoulders. But Lowell remained WGBH's most prominent figure and the institute an indispensable source of money.[24]

---

* To this day the two-tiered schedule of membership dues adopted in 1951 remains in effect: Harvard, M.I.T., and the BSO pay $15,000 each, while all the rest pay $6,250 each.

At 5:30 P.M. on May 2, 1955, WGBH-TV hit the airwaves with its first two shows. One, directed at small children, presented a guitar player and storyteller from the Tufts Nursery Training School; the other featured the Rembrandt collection of the Museum of Fine Arts. "We are doing what commercial television does not do," Wheatley later explained: "We don't insult people's intelligence and we don't scream at them. We try to govern ourselves by our three R's: respect for the viewer, respect for the performer, and respect for the material itself." [25]

In the winter of 1957 the station's commitment to these principles gained recognition in the *New York Times* and *Time*. Noting that WGBH's annual budget of $400,000 (for both radio and TV) was about the cost of one network spectacular, *Time* declared that the station's "leisurely, professorial pace and erratic showmanship would send Madison Avenue professionals out for triple martinis." Ralph Lowell came in for mention, too, described as "probably the only banker who displays on his wall a citation for achievement in show-business [awarded in 1953] from *Variety*." Having drawn the Lowell connection, *Time* could not resist adding a social comment: "Now that his operation is functioning smoothly, Benefactor Lowell finds it possible to report that through WGBH the Lowells now speak not only to the Cabots, but to some thousands of Bostonians a day as well." [26]

ON THE NATIONAL STAGE

As the *Time* and *New York Times* articles demonstrated, Lowell's role in television not only made him a familiar figure to Bostonians but also admitted him to a bigger playing field. Ralph Lowell never became a household name outside Boston, but within the burgeoning world of educational broadcasting he achieved national prominence. This role, however, would be more symbolic than substantive.

In late 1952 C. Scott Fletcher, president of the Fund for Adult Education, invited Lowell to join the board of the newly formed Educational Television and Radio Center. The National Association of Educational Broadcasters (NAEB) had applied to FAE for $1 million to establish a production unit that would supply noncommercial stations with quality programming. Although Fletcher recognized the need for such an undertaking, he was insistent that it be independent of the NAEB. At a New York meeting in the summer of 1952, where Wheatley was one of the participants, Fletcher outlined his proposal to tie the proposed production unit to the mainstream of authority—educational, economic, and civic—within American culture. That fall FAE arranged for the incorporation of the Educational Television and Radio Center, and Fletcher asked University of Illinois president George Stoddard, Yale University law professor Harold Lasswell (both of whom had been at the New York meeting), Brookings Institution president Robert Calkins, and Ralph Lowell to serve as directors.[27]*

The center acted as Lowell's introduction to the politics of educational broadcasting outside Boston. The board's membership expanded over the years to include prominent businessmen who spearheaded educational television in their communities, as well as national opinion leaders such as James Reston of the *New York Times* and Norman Cousins, editor of the *Saturday Review*. Meetings were held most often in Chicago and New York but sometimes in other large cities east of the Mississippi. They gave Lowell a chance to compare notes with his counterparts elsewhere and to offer suggestions to the WGBH staff on his return home. Stoddard, who had played a key role in galvanizing the educational broadcasting movement prior to the FCC hearings on television reservations, was the board's first chairman, and when he stepped down in 1955, Lowell succeeded him. This transfer of power reflected an important change taking place in educational broadcasting, as leadership shifted from the land-grant universities where the movement had originated to the urban-based businessmen and nonacademic broadcasters who ran the stations in large cities.

Reminiscing in 1964 about his seven years as chairman, Lowell described himself as a "steadying influence" on the board. He generally kept his own counsel as discussion flowed back and forth across the table, intervening only to keep the "thing from getting too serious." A veteran board member saw things somewhat differently:

> He was the most kindly, friendly man I think I've ever associated with on a board like that. He was generally agreeable, but I always got amused by his tactics which the board tolerated. He would listen to discussion for just

---

* Lowell went to Chicago for the directors' first meeting that December. In line with his preference for spending as little time as possible away from home or office—as little as was possible without flying, that is—he took the overnight train from Boston, attended the one-day session, and caught the train back to Boston that evening.

about so long if he was favorable to that. Then he would say, "Are you ready for a vote, those in favor say aye, the ayes have it!" It went just that fast! That's the way he would say it. We would do that over and over as long as he was chairman of the board. Nobody would laugh about it, but afterwards in a little private talk we would talk among ourselves.

Lowell remained chairman until 1962, when the center's bylaws placed him in emeritus status because of his age.[28]

The center had rocky beginnings. To fill the post of president, the original board had followed Stoddard's suggestion and selected Harry K. Newburn, president of the University of Oregon. Unacquainted with the details of educational broadcasting, Newburn failed to develop good rapport with the station managers, who had their own ideas about how the center should function. Newburn's first decision, to locate the center's operations in Ann Arbor, Michigan, did not improve matters. Although Newburn felt at home in the university-town setting, the location intensified educational television's isolation from the rest of the American broadcasting industry.[29]

But Newburn's biggest handicap at the center was the shortage of funds. With FAE grants of $1 million to get started and $3 million more to be stretched over three years, the center operated on a shoestring. On the commercial networks, shows were budgeted at $100,000 or more per program hour; the center spent $3,500 per hour. The quality of the center's productions suffered from the poor recording apparatus then available. Lacking funds to tie the various educational television stations together by wire, the center could not transmit its shows instantaneously but had to send them out to stations by mail. The films and kinescopes used by the center were no match for the crisp pictures on commercial channels.

In the fall of 1956, as the third year of Newburn's five-year contract came to an end, the board heard increasing complaints about the president's failings. The station managers wanted someone with more imagination and a greater willingness to take chances. Lowell, however, was not prepared to dump Newburn. In Lowell's opinion, Newburn had succeeded in getting the center off the ground and had been doing a fairly good, if not spectacular, job of expanding its activities. "[H]e may not be the greatest man in the world," Lowell observed, "but how can we expect to get a real headliner when we cannot offer a longtime contract or any real assurance of any permanence when our whole future depends on relatively short-term grants?" Newburn remained on the job, but after a disastrous meeting with station managers in March 1958 he announced that he would leave the center when his contract expired in the fall.[30]

By the time of Newburn's departure, the center's financial base had been strengthened by a Ford Foundation grant of $6 million to be spread over a period of three years.* But while this new grant meant a doubling of the center's budget, the foundation did not give Lowell what he wanted most—a long-term commitment to support educational television. "The hardest job I had," he recalled later, "was negotiating with the Ford Foundation. They vacillated. Sometimes they think they want to support educational television and sometimes they think they want to wash their hands of it." Indeed, in 1959 the foundation announced a five-year, $5 million "terminal" grant. Throughout his tenure as the center's chairman, Lowell feared that the foundation would pull the rug out from under the center, and with this "terminal" grant he felt it had. The one glaring failure of Lowell's chairmanship was his inability to resolve the center's relationship with the Ford Foundation or to find alternative sources of financing.[31]

Despite this uncertainty, the center made progress in the late 1950s and early 1960s under the leadership of its dynamic new president, John White. General manager of the much-praised WQED-TV in Pittsburgh, White was hired on the recommendation of Leland Hazard, the Pittsburgh businessman who directed the cultural side of the Mellon family's campaign to revive Steel City. If Lowell had any rival as the "grand old man" of the educational broadcasting establishment, it was Hazard, but the two respected one another and when Hazard pushed for White, Lowell readily agreed. Lowell and the new chief executive meshed well. White later described the Bostonian as the "perfect board member—[a man] who knew that boards don't interfere with operations but they're there to defend and stimulate operations."[32]

White's first step was to relocate the center to New York. Soon after his arrival, he became deeply involved in the campaign to rectify one of the major weaknesses in educational broadcasting: the absence of a television outlet in New York City. By the end of 1961, funding had been arranged

---

* In 1956, as part of the Ford Foundation's reorganization, the foundation replaced the Fund for Adult Education as the source of money for educational broadcasting. The FAE was legally dissolved in 1961.

and FCC approval secured. Under White's lead, the center also played an important role in bringing educational stations to Philadelphia and Washington, D.C.

Perhaps White's most significant innovation was "prime time" scheduling. Thanks to the introduction of videotape recording, educational television stations across the country could air the same shows at the same time, making national promotion and publicity feasible. The center seemed well on its way toward becoming the "Fourth Network" as Lowell's tenure as board chairman drew to a close in early 1962.[33]

Two developments kept Lowell from slipping into the background. The first was the Ford Foundation's 1963 decision to hike its grant to the center to $6 million for the coming year. Munificent as the gift was, it created a Catch-22 situation by highlighting the center's dependence on the foundation, making it difficult to enlist other patrons for educational television. As long as the center remained a tail to Ford's kite, the future of the "Fourth Network" would be uncertain. The second development was the reorganization of the National Association of Educational Broadcasters in 1963. Growing differences between stations that targeted general audiences and those that emphasized television's instructional potential led the NAEB to establish separate divisions. The unit designed for the first category hired Scott Fletcher, former president of the defunct Fund for Adult Education, as a consultant.[34]

Fletcher's main responsibility was to promote long-range financing of educational television stations, and he won a grant from the U.S. Office of Education to conduct a preliminary study and a national conference on the topic. The conference, scheduled for early December 1964 in Washington, would be the first gathering of chairmen of the governing boards of the nation's more than one hundred educational stations. Fletcher considered Lowell one of educational broadcasting's prime public relations assets and desperately wanted him at the conference. Knowing the Bostonian's aversion to travel, Fletcher offered him the honor of introducing the conference's featured speaker, the U.S. commissioner of education. Prodded by Ives and WGBH general manager Hartford Gunn, Lowell consented to take the overnight train.[35]

Lowell carried with him a statement, prepared by Gunn and Ives, urging the creation of a presidential commission to study educational television. The originator of the idea was Gunn, who believed that the federal government offered the only alternative to the fickle financial support of the Ford Foundation, and that a presidential commission was the way to start the process of opening the federal pocketbook. A proposal similar to Gunn's was already on the conference's docket, but the force of Gunn's logic, the power of Ives's prose, and the strength of Lowell's presentation stampeded the session. The "Lowell plan" became the basis for the most important of the resolutions adopted by the conferees.[36]

To maintain this momentum Fletcher once more turned to the Boston trustee. "I called Mr. Lowell and said, 'I think that if you agree to become chairman of a committee that would write to the President on a commission, this will work.'" Lowell considered it "quite an honor," although he feared it would mean several trips to Washington. It didn't. The so-called Lowell Committee was all Fletcher's doing; he chose its ten members— distinguished veterans of the educational broadcasting movement—and handled the administrative details. Lowell's only contribution was to chair the group's single meeting, in March 1965, at which the committee composed a letter to President Johnson urging the appointment of a presidential commission. (The meeting took place in Boston. As Gunn later remarked, Fletcher knew "we couldn't get Ralph Lowell on the train again!")[37]

Battles over bureaucratic turf and concerns about a possible conflict of interest resulting from Mrs. Johnson's ownership of radio and television stations in Texas blocked creation of an official government panel, but the president publicly endorsed a privately funded commission. The Carnegie Corporation, which was first alerted to the matter by Gunn and Ives, put up the money, and the Carnegie Commission on Educational Television became a reality. In his December 1964 speech, Lowell had explicitly opposed membership by educational broadcasters on the proposed commission ("We should testify and persuade, not make the decisions"), but WGBH's influence on the commission was clearly evident.[38]

Heading the Carnegie Commission was the chairman of the M.I.T. Corporation, James R. Killian, whose ties to the Lowell Institute Cooperative Broadcasting Council went back to the first meeting of Boston-area college presidents in May 1946. It had been Killian who authorized the transfer of the FM transmitter to the council and encouraged M.I.T. faculty to contribute their technical know-how. Killian consulted with Gunn and Lowell before accepting the post. Joining him on the commission was on individual who had played an even greater role in the council and

WGBH—James Bryant Conant.* The commission's legal counsel was Ernest W. Jennes, the Washington-based lawyer who had handled WGBH's contacts with federal regulators since 1951.[39]

In recognition of his conspicuous role in the Carnegie Commission's formation, Lowell was invited to address its organizational session in New York in December 1965. Lowell's mission was to inspire the commissioners with the majesty of their task, and if the words were strung together by Ives, the sentiments were certainly Lowell's. "I like to think of our station," he declared, "as a bridge between Boston's people and her famed academic and artistic centers. I take great pride in knowing that we have done much to let the people of our region realize the freshness and excitement and beauty and knowledge that is contained behind the walls of our institutions." He reiterated a point from his December 1964 speech: "If we in the United States are to create the Great Society, we must . . . make better use of broadcasting. Television particularly must be used not only to peddle products, but also to put beauty, truth and wisdom into every home in the land." Then, characteristically, he made a familial connection: "No one is more deeply committed to the system of free private enterprise than I am. The Lowells have produced merchants, bankers and manufacturers for generations. But we have also produced poets, artists and educators, and I am very much aware that neither group can long exist without the other." The following April the Carnegie Commission came to Boston to inspect the WGBH operation and to hear Gunn's suggestions for improving educational television.[40]

The commission's report, issued in January 1967, called for a "well-financed and well-directed educational television system, substantially larger and far more pervasive and effective than that which now exists," and recommended that a manufacturers' excise tax be slapped on television sets to pay for it. President Johnson accepted the main outlines of the commission's proposals, including the establishment of a federally chartered, nonprofit, nongovernmental entity, the Corporation for Public Broadcasting (CPB), which could receive and spend governmental and

---

* Conant joined the commission despite his skepticism about "the claims made for television as an educational medium." He was disappointed by the failure of the commission's final report to include adequate safeguards protecting public television from political interference. James G. Hershberg, *James B. Conant* (New York: Knopf, 1993), pp. 741–742.

private funds. But he rejected the recommendation of an excise tax as politically unpalatable. Instead, he urged annual federal appropriations out of general revenues. Johnson's legislative instincts were correct, and in November the Public Broadcasting Act of 1967 passed in the form he favored without much debate.

Lowell played a minor role in these events. In February, at Gunn's behest, he had called a meeting in Boston of the heads of the educational television stations in New York, San Francisco, Pittsburgh, Philadelphia, Washington, and Chicago, to enlist support for the Carnegie Commission's program and to voice opposition to an alternative plan being pushed by the Ford Foundation. In April Lowell accepted an invitation from the Carnegie Corporation to become one of the five incorporators of a national Citizens Committee for Public Television, which would campaign for the president's proposed legislation. Lowell was scheduled to appear at a July hearing before the House committee considering the measure, but he decided to submit a written statement instead; Gunn, however, did testify. Lowell, Gunn, and Ives were invited to the White House ceremony in November at which Johnson signed the act into law. Although Lowell did not go, one of the presidential pens used for the occasion was set aside for him.[41]

Poor health kept Lowell from making another trip to Washington in November 1968 when, for once, he was eager to go. He had been named the National Association of Educational Broadcasters' "Man of the Year," and the award was to be bestowed at the group's annual banquet in the nation's capital. Lying in his hospital bed, Lowell noted, "This is the day I should be in Washington, my last chance of being a 'national figure.'"[42] Two years later, in honor of his eightieth birthday, Lowell's family established the Ralph Lowell Award for Excellence in Public Television, a silver medal bearing his likeness, to be conferred annually by CPB.

CRISES AND TRIUMPH

Lowell basked in the renown that came with his national activities, but his major stake in educational broadcasting was WGBH, and here he faced two great trials. One concerned personnel, the other was a catastrophic accident. Out of these ordeals emerged a television station that would be a pacesetter for the rest of the nation.

Aside from Lowell, no one was more responsible for the success of the Lowell Institute Cooperative Broadcasting Council during its first decade than Parker Wheatley. His genius for recognizing what would work as educational radio programming laid the groundwork for WGBH-FM, and, as Lowell wrote, his "appreciation of the possibilities of educational television and enthusiastic [pursuit] of that" made WGBH-TV a reality. It was Wheatley, Lowell remarked at a 1955 dinner at the Tavern Club celebrating the launching of Channel 2, "who would never give up and kept me pushing along when things looked darkest." Two years later, Lowell fired Wheatley, saying "[T]he "the job has outgrown him and, despite all he did in the early years, the whole movement is too important to be jeopardized by any one man."[43]

Although Wheatley's ouster in the spring of 1957 came suddenly and, for Wheatley, unexpectedly, the roots of the problem reached far back in his eleven-year career at the council. Lowell had assured Wheatley at their initial meeting that his Midwestern background and obscure alma mater would not be a handicap in dealing with Harvard's prima donna professors, but the cultural barriers separating the scion of one of Boston's leading families and the son of an Indiana farmer eventually proved insurmountable. Lowell rarely associated socially with those who worked for him, and his relationship with Wheatley remained more formal and distant than most. Lowell's pragmatic nature, which was evident in his choice of a business career over an academic one, contrasted with Wheatley's artistic bent. (Wheatley, too, had forsaken his youthful ambition—which was to be an actor—but chose an only slightly less theatrical line of work as a broadcaster.) Lowell appreciated the value of what Wheatley was doing but never could overcome the feeling that Wheatley's artistic inclinations made him too emotional and impractical. Lowell's references to Wheatley and his crew at the council—to their faces and to others—as "opera singers" reflected his exasperation at their seeming inability to keep their feet on the ground.[44]

Lowell and Wheatley also differed greatly in their managerial styles. Lowell prided himself on staying on top of issues, acting decisively, delegating responsibility for details to others, and conducting well-focused and short meetings. Wheatley, on the other hand, was capable of "making the most enormous mountains out of the ordinary molehills of executiveship," was "no businessman and [let] little details bog him down," and "waste[d] an awful lot of time in talking and going over and over the same ground."[45]

In a strange twist of fate, it was WGBH's entry into television, which had been Wheatley's objective for so long, that undermined his position in Boston. WGBH-TV required a much larger staff than WGBH-FM, and Wheatley, who "did not want to be 'a boss' in the ordinary sense" but wanted to run the station in a "democratic fashion," seemed "too scatter-brained" to Lowell to administer the operation effectively. Furthermore, the stakes in television were much higher than in radio. WGBH-TV was operating on the frontiers of the newest instrument of mass communication, and innovations emerged almost daily. Leadership of the expanding profession of educational broadcasting was up for grabs, and if Wheatley had his vision of how to proceed, others in the field had theirs.[46]

Although Wheatley had demonstrated real imagination in creating intelligent radio and television programs that appealed to a wide audience, he was unwilling to go beyond certain limits in compromising his academic standards. "I was called classical—and, by some, too classical," Wheatley declared long after leaving the station. "I was functioning as an educator, as a kind of philosopher of this medium, to build something that would be to Boston what the Colosseum was to Rome, the Parthenon to Athens." Wheatley's plan to make WGBH "the best television station in the world" called for staying close to its geographical home base and relying on community support and charitable foundations for its funding. He resisted proposals from staff members that WGBH go heavily into partnership with large corporations to produce shows for national distribution.[47]

Hartford N. Gunn Jr. championed a national focus for WGBH. A graduate of Harvard College (class cf 1948) and the Harvard Business School, Gunn had been hired in 1951 by Wheatley, who was under orders from Lowell to find someone to manage WGBH's financial affairs. Over the next several years, Gunn broadened his administrative duties, recruited many of the television station's new personnel, became Lowell's main source of information about what was going on at WGBH, and developed his own ideas about WGBH's future. Gunn later gave Wheatley "full credit" for establishing the "very high standards" for which WGBH was known, but in the latter part of the 1950s he saw Wheatley's Olympian notions as an obstacle. If Wheatley was perhaps overwhelmed by how far educational broadcasting had come in little more than a decade, Gunn was focused on where it might go in the next decade, and he wanted WGBH to be in the lead. Making the Boston station a center of national program production was essential to Gunn's design and, when Wheatley would not support it wholeheartedly, the WGBH staff divided into hostile camps led by the two men.[48]

Wheatley's dissatisfaction with the programs WGBH was producing under a National Science Foundation grant brought the breach to a breaking point in April 1957, and Gunn informed Lowell, who had just returned from a two-month South Atlantic cruise, that he and several WGBH personnel were prepared to resign if Wheatley remained in charge. Afraid of losing Gunn, whom Lowell saw as both practical and brilliant, and having previously warned Wheatley that he would get rid of him if the station fell into disarray, Lowell fired Wheatley, without giving him a chance to defend himself, and appointed Gunn as his successor.[49]

Wheatley left quietly,* and to the public the turnover at WGBH was presented as both natural and orderly. But more than forty years later he remained bitter about what he considered Gunn's power play to unseat him and Lowell's role as executioner. Questions can be raised about Lowell's decision to fire Wheatley, but one point is indisputable: Hartford Gunn proved a worthy replacement. Gunn was quick to adapt to the latest developments in television technology and mindful of the need to produce entertaining as well as thoughtful programming. Under his management WGBH discovered educational television's first "star," Julia Child. Gunn, in his thirteen years as general manager, established Channel 2 as the nation's preeminent educational station. In 1970 he left the station to become the first head of the Public Broadcasting Service.

Lowell's second great trial at WGBH occurred in the fall of 1961. In the early morning hours of Saturday, October 14, the WGBH studios and offices on the M.I.T. campus burned down. No one was hurt, but the building and equipment, except for the mobile unit, were a complete loss. Gunn and his dedicated staff were able to get WGBH-FM on the air that afternoon for its regularly scheduled broadcasts from the small Symphony Hall studio where the radio station had started a decade earlier. WGBH-TV had to skip its Sunday programming, but the Monday morning shows for

---

* Unable to find a job in Boston, Wheatley was hired as director of public affairs for a new CBS-owned television station in St. Louis. Back in the Midwest, Wheatley worked out an accommodation with commercial television, eventually becoming the host of an offbeat, very early morning interview show, *The People Speak*.

children appeared as usual, just forty-eight hours after the fire was put out. Generous contributions of equipment from local commercial stations and the willingness of the Catholic Television Center to make its studio available were responsible for WGBH-TV's quick recovery. For the few people who missed hearing or reading about the fire—which was covered as a major news event—it was as if nothing had happened. For the next three years the WGBH staff operated out of six locations scattered over Boston and Cambridge. During this time they met all of their deadlines and continued to win awards for their work.

On the weekend of the fire, Lowell was in Bethel, Maine, for a meeting of the trustees of the Gould Academy. Paged at Saturday morning breakfast to take a call from Boston, he received the news with an equanimity that three decades later still amazed the bearer of the ill tidings, David Ives. After being assured that no one had been injured, Lowell remarked: "It's not a total disaster. We will pick up and come back stronger." Lowell returned to his meal and informed his fellow trustees of the Bingham Fund about what had happened. They promptly voted $10,000 for WGBH (Lowell did not participate). And so began the campaign to construct new facilities for Channel 2.[50]

Within days of his return to Boston Lowell wrote, "[W]e may look back on the fire as a blessing in disguise." The Massachusetts Avenue studio was inadequate for the station's expanding activities, but tight finances had made a move to something bigger and better impossible. Not only did the fire necessitate a move, it also created a climate that would allow WGBH to build a state-of-the-art studio. "A fire," observed Edward Weeks, editor of the Boston-based *Atlantic Monthly*, "like a centennial, creates a momentary glare in which people look at you with a fresh concern." Donations flowed into Channel 2's coffers from all over the WGBH viewing area, raised through theater benefits, penny sales, auctions, card parties, concerts, athletic contests, and many other events. This display of civic spirit was unusual in twentieth-century Boston. It revealed the depth of goodwill WGBH had built up over the years.[51]

The popular response and the tens of thousands of small contributions were gratifying and much needed. But to reach its $1.7 million goal, the station also needed large donations in the thousands of dollars. Lowell went all-out, appealing to each of the various corporate and charitable boards on which he served as well as to his friends at other companies. Although the Boston business community responded positively, the two largest local benefactors were the Permanent Charity Fund ($75,000) and the Hyams Fund ($50,000), both of which Lowell served as a trustee. (Lowell made a personal contribution of $10,000, and the Lowell Institute later helped the station meet other extraordinary expenses by increasing its regular assistance to $225,000.) The Twentieth Century Fund, a Filene foundation, put up $125,000. As in the trying days of 1952–1953, a critical impetus came from the Ford Foundation. Jay Stratton, president of M.I.T. and a member of the Ford board, had promised Lowell a few days after the fire that he would seek assistance from the foundation, and he came through with a $500,000 matching grant. On the first anniversary of the fire, Lowell announced that the $1.7 million was in hand.[52]*

Thanks to the intervention of David Bailey, the fire also led to WGBH's return to its Harvard origins. Both Northeastern University and Brandeis University (which had been invited to join the Lowell Institute Cooperative Broadcasting Council as soon as its academic accreditation was formalized in the mid-1950s) made generous proposals to house the new studios. But thanks to Bailey's position as secretary to the Harvard Corporation, Harvard offered WGBH two acres behind the business school on a thirty-year lease at $1 a year. Building from scratch on the Harvard property would be more expensive than the other options, but the site came with the fewest strings and provided the choicest location. The groundbreaking took place the day after Thanksgiving 1962, and at the end of August 1964 WGBH broadcast its first programs from the new facility.[53]

On May 1, 1965 — the tenth anniversary of Channel 2's first broadcast — the WGBH building was formally dedicated and named in honor of Ralph Lowell. James Bryant Conant returned to Boston for the televised dinner, which was attended by more than two hundred of Boston's leading citizens. I. A. Richards, who had inaugurated the council's radio series in 1947, read from Shelley's *Prometheus Unbound;* Julia Child also gave a short talk. Aaron Copeland provided musical entertainment by conducting his *Fanfare for the Common Man.* The citation presented to Lowell noted that he had used "his influence, his prestige, his energies, and his abilities to transform a lofty concept into an effective force for the public good." Applauding Lowell's "foresight, wisdom, integrity and strength of character," the WGBH trustees concluded, "He exemplifies the way in which wise management of money and enlightened philanthropy can benefit a community." Deeply touched, Lowell summarized the occasion as "My Day."[54]

---

* As in the case of the Boston Floating Hospital, insurance ($600,000 on the studio equipment) helped finance the building of new facilities.

"A firm believer in . . . all it stands for"

LOYAL SON OF HARVARD

Harvard," observed Cleveland Amory in 1947, "is a major part of the Proper Bostonian's total existence, of his adult life in some respects even more than his college life." None of the other characteristics Amory ascribed to this subspecies so aptly fitted Ralph Lowell as this one. Lowell spent many an autumn Saturday afternoon in Harvard Stadium watching the Crimson eleven and took the train every other year to New Haven for "The Game" at the Yale Bowl. He also worked Harvard baseball games and track and field meets into his schedule when circumstances allowed, and rode the subway to Cambridge to attend lectures and various Harvard committee meetings. Scarcely a week went by that he was not on campus. His enthusiasm for his alma mater knew virtually no bounds; simply through their association with Harvard, people and ideas were assured of a respectful hearing from Lowell. "I am a firm believer in Harvard and all it stands for," he wrote in the twenty-fifth anniversary report of his college class in 1937. Conceding that "it is hard to explain the force that is Harvard," he offered an explanation juxtaposing venerability with youth: "Old in wisdom but young in ideals, it has continued its steady progress towards greater intellectual leadership, despite carping criticism and narrow individualistic abuse." For sixty years after his graduation Lowell worked diligently to help Harvard maintain its eminence. Few things in his life gave him so much happiness as seeing his sons and grandsons (and granddaughters!) "join its ranks and go forward under [the Harvard] banner." [1*]

---

* In the 1940s John Gunther asked Leverett Saltonstall what he "believed in most." Saltonstall's

CLASSMATES, CLUBS, AND ASSOCIATIONS

Lowell's links to Harvard took several forms, but the oldest and strongest was as a member of the class of 1912. This label identified him as a graduate of Harvard College, unlike people whose Harvard degrees came from the graduate or professional schools—a distinction that Lowell and those of his generation took quite seriously. Although Lowell appreciated the contributions that other parts of the university made to its standing in the academic world, for him the college was heart and soul of the institution.

Lowell never lost the fascination with anthropology that had been nurtured by his professors—and reinforced by nearly three decades of membership on the Overseers' Visiting Committee to the Peabody Museum and the Department of Anthropology. But as he looked back decades later at his four years in Harvard Yard, what he appreciated most was the personal bonds forged there. In 1946, when his eldest daughter was about to graduate from Vassar and appeared impatient to put that period of her life behind her, Lowell recalled how differently he had felt about leaving Harvard. "[W]omen's colleges," he wrote, "seem to miss that something that means so much in male colleges—the feeling of comradeship and friendship that all through life ties one to his college classmates." And indeed, some of Lowell's closest and most enduring relationships were with fellow members of the class of 1912, such as trust company president Francis Gray, attorney Oscar Haussermann, and Chief Justice of the Massachusetts Supreme Judicial Court Raymond Wilkins. Lowell's diaries were sprinkled liberally with references to his classmates—usually so designated—as Lowell met them at social gatherings, heard stories about them, read about them in the newspaper, or saw their obituaries. Lowell took satisfaction in their good fortune, convinced that the explanation lay in their years spent at Harvard.[2]

From his position as class treasurer, which he held from 1912 until his death, Lowell took an active role in class activities. He handled the finances associated with publishing class reports and holding class reunions at commencement time; his duties also included investing the money that members donated for class gifts to the college. In 1962, in recognition of Lowell's

---

response, "Harvard and my family," would have been Lowell's as well. Gunther, *Inside U.S.A.* (New York: Harper Bros., 1947), pp. 477–478.

fifty years on the job, Haussermann composed a quatrain, which he read at the big reunion dinner:

> Here's to dear old Twelve,
> The class which is keen but odd—
> For its monies are managed by Lowell,
> And Lowell keeps books for God!

Although the workload of class treasurer was not taxing, and Ruth Perkins actually handled the bulk of the chores, someone in the class had to accept the responsibility, and Lowell considered it a privilege.[3]

Every June, Lowell cleared his calendar so that he could participate fully in the week-long schedule of events connected with Harvard's commencement. He and any classmates who were in town always got together for a fancy dinner, and Lowell marched with them in the procession of alumni, except when a formal role in the exercises placed him in a position of honor. Class functions sometimes brought out the hidden prankish side of Lowell's personality. In January 1937 Boston newspapers carried a picture of Lowell and four classmates at the Back Bay Station, all dressed in cutaways and top hats and carrying sticks. They were preparing to greet five New Yorkers who were fellow members of the class of 1912's Twenty-fifth Reunion Committee. Their display of sartorial elegance, the papers reported, was designed to refute the common allegation that Boston men were less fashionable than their Gotham counterparts.[4]

The "Proper Bostonians" usually cast off their inhibitions at the annual winter dinner of the A.D. Club, which Lowell attended faithfully. The stories told by Lowell's brother Jim became a staple of these gatherings,* and after John and Ralph Jr. were admitted they often joined their father in regaling the crowd with a song or two. The A.D. Club was dear to the elder Lowell's "heart as the symbol of all the best in [his] college years." When John and Ralph Jr. were quite young, he had written that "[i]f my little boys ever make the Club, I will be a very proud man." The induction of John's son in the 1960s made him the sixteenth Lowell in A.D., the most for any family.[5]

Lowell joined the Harvard Club of Boston in the fall of 1913, just as it opened its elegant new home on Commonwealth Avenue in the Back Bay.

---

* In 1965, while in the midst of his presentation, Jim collapsed and died of a heart attack.

He managed the club's fall 1914 dinner for the Harvard rowing team, which had won the Henley regatta the previous summer, and in January 1915 he was made a member of the club's nominating committee. After his return from military duty, Lowell served a three-year term on the club's board of governors.

Although the Harvard Club functioned primarily as a dining room and lecture hall for the pleasure and enlightenment of its members, it also contributed to Harvard's educational mission. Like many of the other Harvard Clubs scattered across the country (Lowell also joined the Harvard Club of New York and usually took a room there when he stayed overnight on business), the Boston group recruited outstanding local students for the college and helped subsidize those who could not afford the tuition and living expenses. Lowell took a particular interest in the scholarship program and gave generously of his time to interview candidates for assistance. Decades later, one applicant in the 1930s could recall being asked by Lowell what he had done on his own to earn money for college. The student, who was from Beverly on the North Shore, replied that he had reported school events for the local newspaper and dug clams during the summer. Lowell responded: "Dug clams? Tell us about it." Whereupon he was treated to a full description of the way to hold the digger and follow clam holes down through the sand. The boy got the scholarship and always told people he had "dug my way into Harvard with a clam hole." [6]

In the early 1940s the Harvard Club of Boston found itself in a different kind of hole—a financial one—and enlisted Lowell to help dig it out. The depressed economy of the previous decade and the inauguration of the military draft in 1940 caused a significant decline in club membership. This, combined with poor management, had produced a balance sheet that Lowell described as "dripping with crimson ink." By the winter of 1942 the club desperately needed a president prepared to lead and able to commit a great deal of time to its affairs. Two of Lowell's friends who sat on the nominating committee, Nat Ayer and Edward Taft, thought Lowell would fill the bill just fine. As the stock brokerage business demanded little of his attention and his work for the Military Training Camps Association had been rendered all but irrelevant by the Roosevelt administration's mobilization for war, Lowell was eager for an additional outlet for his energies. Not just any outlet, however; in November 1941 he had turned down an invitation to become president of the Massachusetts Society for the Prevention of Cruelty to Children. But when a few months later Ayer and

Taft asked him to rescue the Harvard Club, Lowell accepted. As he told a nephew years afterward, "One doesn't refuse the Presidency of the Harvard Club." [7]

Lowell's five years as president brought a reversal of the club's fortunes. In addition to slashing expenses, Lowell attacked the deficit problem with two bold moves. He supported a 10 percent surcharge on annual memberships and implemented an Adoption Plan, under which the dues of those in the armed forces were paid for by the Club's civilian members. With Lowell's encouragement, the club also set up a War Service Bureau to assist Harvard graduates in securing appropriate war-related positions, and then an Advising Bureau for College Men to help alumni in uniform through the reconversion process. By the time Lowell decided to step down, the club was operating in the black and had wiped out its debts and made substantial improvements to its physical facilities. [8]

So successful was Lowell's tenure that, as he prepared to leave the job in the winter of 1947, he was invited to become president of the Associated Harvard Clubs (AHC). Organized in 1897 by clubs located in the Midwest, AHC had expanded to include scores of Harvard clubs in all parts of the country. AHC annual conventions, held in a different city every spring, typically featured an address by the president of the university and attracted hundreds of alumni. In June 1946 the Harvard Club of Boston had served as host for the gathering and Lowell enjoyed "a few hours in the big leagues" as he chaired a session of fifteen hundred people. The following May he took the train to Milwaukee (the farthest west he had been since his trips to Arizona before and during college) to be installed as the association's president. Lowell had been assured that the job would not be time-consuming, and his year in the office passed uneventfully. [9]

Lowell was also active in the larger and older Harvard Alumni Association (established in 1840). During the 1920s Lowell served on the committee charged with developing an appropriate memorial for the sons of Harvard who had died in the Great War. The panel's decision to construct the Memorial Church across from Widener Library disappointed him. He considered the architect's plans "ugly" and thought it a "a shame to tear down Appleton Chapel which, though itself an eyesore, has been associated with the Yard in the memory of all the living Harvard graduates." Lowell would have liked the memorial to take the form of a large athletic or recreational facility "typifying the youth and spirit of those who fell. For [this]

was a war of young men, the physically strong and perfect of the nation."*
Fifty years later, Lowell's own funeral service was conducted in Memorial Church.[10]

RAISING AND DISTRIBUTING FUNDS

Ralph Lowell's personal finances allowed him to make only a tiny fraction of the monetary gifts to Harvard that his cousin Lawrence did, but he toiled diligently to assist Harvard's fund-raising efforts. In 1925 the Harvard Alumni Association and the Associated Harvard Clubs established the Harvard Fund as a mechanism to encourage annual giving by the college's graduates. Lowell volunteered to be the fund's agent for the class of 1912, which meant that every year for the next fifty years, Lowell sent appeals to his classmates for contributions; the results were not noteworthy, but the effort provided Lowell with another occasion to reflect on how much his college experience had meant to him. During the late 1940s he was involved in a special campaign to raise funds for a new undergraduate library; however, few of the people he contacted responded positively.[11]

If Lowell's reputation as a successful fund-raiser derived from his non-Harvard activities, he did gain some renown as a shrewd investor through his treasurership of the Fund for Assisting Students at Harvard College. Started in 1838 at the instigation of Harvard president Josiah Quincy, the privately organized and managed fund helped "young men of good characters and indigent circumstances" attend Harvard. John Amory Lowell had been among the small group of alumni who founded the fund, and his son John (Ralph's grandfather) served as the fund's treasurer between 1864 and 1880. Ralph's father held that post from 1898 until his death in 1922, when Ralph took over.

The fund began with $11,350 in contributions and it never again sought or received outside support. Its assets of $238,000 when Ralph Lowell took

---

* After World War II Lowell was a member of the committee that planned a memorial for the Harvard dead of that conflict. Students wanted an activities center built, but the administration was unenthusiastic about the idea, and after a long and contentious study, Lowell and the committee decided to place plaques in Memorial Church listing those lost. Ralph Lowell MSS, Harvard University Correspondence box, War Memorial folders.

charge were the product of investments and repaid student loans (usually at 5 percent interest). The bulk of the loans went to upperclassmen, who were not charged interest until the day of their graduation. The loans carried no definite maturity date, and there was "no great effort made in collecting them" beyond sending out reminder letters. Most loan grantees took their obligations seriously. One borrower, a schoolteacher thirty years out of Harvard, remitted the sum owed when he received a reminder notice, reporting that he had mortgaged his house to do so because he "wanted other young men to have the same opportunity" that he had been given. A widow informed the fund that her older son had died in an accident, but that she and her younger son would try to repay the loan because the older boy had "always said he would have been unable to finish college if it had not been for the loan." Lowell and his fellow trustees (which at the time were a Gardiner, a Wigglesworth, a Lyman, and a Codman) told her "to forget about it and that we would consider the loan paid." [12]

During the first century of its operation, the fund (which was commonly referred to as the Harvard or the Lowell Fund of Boston) made more than $450,000 available to more than 6,300 students. In the early 1940s the sum of loans issued averaged less than $20,000 per year. Fund trustees had always worked closely with college officials in distributing the loans. In the late 1940s the college, in line with its policy of making a Harvard education more accessible to students from low-income families, began pressuring the fund to make additional resources available. The level of lending the college envisioned would have entailed dipping into the fund's principal, which in 1950 was close to $1 million. Lowell resisted this step and eventually agreed to an arrangement whereby the fund would use its principal but the college would compensate it for any losses it suffered. Annual lending jumped to more than $100,000 in the late 1950s; by 1959 the total amount lent by the fund reached $1.4 million.

The college had created a financial aid office in 1950 and decided at the close of the decade that the office would operate more effectively if it had complete control of the fund's money. Lowell and the three other trustees (a Gardiner, a Lyman, and Francis Gray, one of Lowell's 1912 classmates), who together had given 123 years of service to the fund, concurred in the decision and arranged for the fund's assets of $2.1 million to be transferred to Harvard. The nearly tenfold increase in the fund's capital since Lowell had assumed its management in 1922 prompted *U.S. News & World Report* to publish an interview with him in July 1959. The magazine described

Lowell as "a leading example of the New England 'prudent man,' who combines Yankee thrift with the ability to put money to work." Key to the fund's success, Lowell explained, was ending its almost complete reliance on bonds and placing about half its book value in stocks. During the next few years *U.S. News* occasionally called upon Lowell to supply investing advice to its readers. It was fitting that Lowell finally achieved some national recognition as a financier through his service to Harvard.[13]

TO THE BOARD OF OVERSEERS

As much as Lowell enjoyed serving Harvard through the fund and the alumni organizations, he also wanted to help govern it. Lowells had played conspicuous roles in running the institution in an almost unbroken line beginning with the election of John Lowell (1743–1802) to the Harvard Corporation in 1784. During his forty years as a Corporation member (1837–1877), John Amory Lowell participated in the selection of six Harvard presidents; and A. Lawrence Lowell occupied the president's chair for twenty-four years (1909–1933).* Ralph's father did not enter the select circle occupied by his ancestors and his cousin; Ralph came closer but ultimately fell short.

Harvard has two governing boards. The far stronger of the pair, the Corporation, is composed of the president, the treasurer (whose primary responsibility, besides general supervision of the university's finances, is guiding the investment of Harvard's endowment), and five fellows. A self-perpetuating body, the Corporation holds legal title to all of the university's property and exercises managerial control over its operations. The Corporation receives advice from the second governing body, the thirty-member Board of Overseers, which is elected by alumni for six-year, overlapping terms. The consent of the overseers is required for major actions proposed by the Corporation, such as faculty and administrative appointments (including the election of new fellows); however, their consent is rarely withheld. Historian Samuel Eliot Morison observed in 1929 that "the duties of the Board are largely confined to ratifying the acts of the Corporation, after discussing them with the President." (The president

---

* See the chart "The 'Lowell Dynasty'" in Samuel Eliot Morison, *Three Centuries of Harvard, 1636–1936* (Cambridge: Harvard University Press, 1946), p. 159, n. 1.

and the treasurer were ex officio members of the board.) The incongruity between the board's limited power and the pomp that surrounded it led one overseer to remark privately in 1944 that "the Overseers do not amount to much, but it is the nicest club in the country."[14]

By the early twentieth century a stint as overseer was often seen as useful preparation for the more onerous responsibilities of fellow. Ralph's father never cleared that first hurdle, although his active involvement with the Alumni Association led to the placing of his name on the ballot for overseer in 1904, 1905, and 1912. John's younger brother and law partner, James Arnold Lowell, fared no better in the 1916 election for the board.

In his first two races for overseer, Ralph made more impressive showings than had his father and uncle, but the end results were the same. He ran eighth in 1929, just two places away from the victors' circle, and sixth in 1937, only forty-one ballots behind the winner of the fifth and final opening. Ralph's brother Jim finished dead last in a field of fourteen in 1933.

Ralph had to wait six years for another nomination. When he saw the list of twelve candidates made public in January 1943, he was pessimistic about his chances of gaining a seat. One seat, Lowell believed, was sure to go to Leverett Saltonstall, the popular governor of Massachusetts; another would go to Joseph Grew, a national hero since his return from Japan, where he had served as U.S. ambassador and been detained after Pearl Harbor. Lowell saw the other aspirants—two New York lawyers, a Cleveland businessman who was president of the National Association of Manufacturers, the mayor of San Francisco, an assistant secretary of state, the Episcopal bishop of Maine, the president of the American Unitarian Association, a medical professor at the University of Pennsylvania, and a Boston-based federal district court judge—as possessing "more general appeal than I can possibly muster." Lowell's gloom was a natural response to his two previous failures and reflected his general despair over his business affairs (the formal offer of the chairmanship of Boston Safe would not be made until March). But in his dim forecast he overlooked one important fact: The bulk of the alumni casting ballots in 1943 had received their Harvard degrees during Lawrence Lowell's presidency. With Lawrence's death that very January, the impulse to perpetuate the Lowell connection may have influenced the voting. It is impossible to explain conclusively the outcome of the contest, which was bereft of issues and conducted without any campaigning. But here we can see once more the interplay of conscientious service and an honored name that so shaped Ralph Lowell's life.[15]

Commencement Day in late May brought the happy news of Lowell's election as an overseer. As he had predicted, Grew (8,566 votes) and Saltonstall (8,549) far outdistanced the other candidates, but Lowell finished a comfortable third (4,490)—seven hundred votes ahead of Mayor Roger Lapham and Judge Charles Wyzanski, who tied for fourth place and filled the last two vacancies. Lowell was chosen to preside at the class of 1912 dinner that evening because of "my new exalted office." [16]

The first half of Lowell's term as an overseer involved more rite than substance. For example, he was invited to the extraordinary commencement of September 1943, at which Harvard awarded an honorary degree to Winston Churchill. But when a matter of some import did surface, Lowell took his responsibilities seriously. One such issue was the question of admitting women to the Harvard Medical School. The idea had been broached as early as 1847, but at that time and on four other occasions over the next thirty-five years, the school's faculty rejected the proposal. Nothing more was heard of it until 1942 when, faced with reduced enrollments because of World War II, some faculty members urged the admission of women students. Responding to this suggestion, President James Bryant Conant appointed a special committee, which returned with a unanimous recommendation that women be accepted solely on the basis of qualifications and without regard to numbers. The Medical School faculty endorsed the report by a vote of 66 to 12 in April 1943. Conant and the dean of the Medical School declined to take a position on the question, and the Corporation postponed making a decision until a new special committee could be formed. The committee modified the previous proposal by opening admissions to a limited number of women of exceptional ability. After the medical faculty adopted this report by another lopsided vote in April 1944, the Corporation accepted it at a June meeting. The Corporation's action was presented to the overseers for their consent at the board's session on June 29, Commencement morning. [17]

That session proved eventful on at least two counts. With the temperature approaching a hundred degrees, the initial motion approved was for the overseers to take off their coats and vests. It was the "first time in Harvard's history," Lowell recorded, "that the Board had met in its shirt-sleeves." Then "the ordinary rubber-stamping process ran into a real snag" when Dr. David Cheever, a retired surgeon and chairman of the Overseers' Committee to Visit the Medical School, spoke against the Corporation's plan for coeducation. He contended that "all the arguments pro and con" about admitting women to the Medical School would "apply equally to the College" and that the board should not act hastily in establishing a precedent.* The overseers agreed to put the matter over until the fall.[18]

Lowell used the delay to solicit the views of Dr. Nathaniel Faxon, general director of the Massachusetts General Hospital. Lowell served as a trustee of the hospital, which was a teaching affiliate of the Medical School. Faxon indicated his strong support for admitting women, saying it should have been done long ago. But after hearing Lowell describe the pitfalls of coeducation, he appeared to Lowell to be much less certain in his position. As for Lowell, he "frankly did not know how" he would go. "My feelings are to vote against it," he wrote in his diary in August, "but I do not see how I can vote against the wishes of the faculty itself."

Conant recalled the September 25 meeting as "the most amusing" he had ever attended. Cheever, whom Conant affectionately characterized as a "gentleman of the old school," presented a wide range of arguments against coeducation, from its harmful effects on the health of women to its linkage with the revolutionary doctrines of the Soviet Union. On the basis of the ensuing discussion, Conant thought he had enough support to gain consent, but not wanting to take any chances he threw himself into the battle, drawing the line on exactly the point that most bothered Lowell. The real issue, Conant insisted, was the relationship of the faculty to the governing boards, and he threatened to go public with a statement that the overseers had blocked approval of a faculty recommendation based on two years of study. In the vote, Cheever's was the only negative voice. Lowell observed, "[A]nother chapter has been written in Harvard University history." [19]

ALMOST TO THE CORPORATION

In November 1946, Harvard Corporation fellow Henry James (class of 1899) informed his colleagues that he wished to resign. The announcement was not unexpected; James, son of psychologist-philosopher William James, had been in poor health for some time and had often talked about

---

* Although it was not widely recognized at the time, coeducation had come to the college under the terms of a spring 1943 agreement between Harvard and Radcliffe, in which Harvard assumed full responsibility for the instruction of Radcliffe students. Classes were soon fully integrated, although women were not admitted to the undergraduate library until 1967. The residential houses went coeducational in the late 1970s.

the strains of traveling to Boston for the twice-monthly meetings of the Corporation. James lived in New York, where he was president of the Teachers' Insurance and Annuity Association. The Corporation maintained the strictest confidentiality concerning its deliberations and usually took no votes until all present were reasonably confident that the results would be unanimous. Nearly a year elapsed before it was ready to submit its choice for a replacement to the Board of Overseers. Without knowing it, Ralph Lowell came within a hair's breadth of being that choice.

Even before James made his intent to resign formal, members of the Corporation had begun a discreet canvass of their friends for candidates "who might be material for Fellows." Lowell's name appeared on many of the lists that were drawn up that fall, along with those of other prominent alumni, mainly Bostonians. Among the people who responded to fellow Grenville Clark's (class of 1903) inquiries was Henry B. Cabot (class of 1917), a Boston attorney and president of the Boston Symphony. Cabot suggested his brother Charles (class of 1922), a judge of the Superior Court of Massachusetts, and Ralph Lowell. "This sounds a little like the Lowells and the Cabots," he conceded, "but, as you know, I am a narrow-minded cuss." [20]

By early December, the tide clearly was flowing toward Lowell. James told Conant he did not believe the search would take long. "Of course," he added, "it is impossible to deny that there may be some paragon whose name hasn't yet been suggested, but I have an idea that Ralph Lowell is an obvious, sound and safe bet, and unless there is some doubt about that and unless some interesting alternative is suggested, why not proceed?" Writing to Clark, James delivered the same message: "One can always spend time, and perhaps a little time had better be spent, in asking whether there is still anybody as yet unmentioned who may be even better. But why spend much time that way; Lowell looks suitable and promising. So I hope that no great amount of time will be spent in trying to peer beyond the now visible horizons." [21]

As Lowell appeared to be the likely choice, Clark arranged for a meeting so that they could "get better acquainted." Although he had known Lowell for thirty years, through the Plattsburg Movement and more recently the campaign for universal military training, Clark felt he did not know him well. Lowell's diary entry on his lunch with Clark at the Somerset Club gives no indication that Lowell realized he was under consideration for the Corporation. They discussed the university's financial problems and ideas for the appointment of a full-time fund-raiser. Clark told

Lowell in confidence that if world conditions became worse, Conant might leave Harvard for a government post similar to the one he had held during World War II. Clark also intimated that there was "a little friction" between the president and the treasurer, William H. Claflin (class of 1915).[22]

A week after his session with Lowell, Clark informed the other fellows that he favored selecting a Boston man, "especially since there does not seem to be any outstanding paragon in New York or elsewhere nearby," * and that he had narrowed his preferences to Henry Cabot and Lowell. Clark, a lawyer, found Cabot's legal training attractive: "I have seen a lot of him and know that he is a first-rate, all-around man. He has excellent judgment and a very clear head." Claiming less familiarity with Lowell, Clark noted that "everything I know or have heard about him is good, [but] as compared with Cabot, my impression is that he has not got as good and clear a head." For that reason Clark leaned toward Cabot; however, he added, "I think either would be excellent and if the consensus is that Lowell is the man, I would not want to argue about it."[23]

That consensus seemed to have taken shape at the Corporation meeting of December 16, which Clark could not attend. The discussion among the six men present revealed that sentiment for choosing a Bostonian was strong but that there was no support for Cabot. Treasurer Claflin offered another possibility, Boston investment counselor John P. Chase (class of 1928), but Claflin's support of his candidacy made Chase unacceptable to Conant. James came away from the session convinced that Lowell was a shoo-in. "Everybody," James wrote Clark, "seems to respect Lowell. Even Claflin didn't belittle him. [Fellow Henry Lee] Shattuck [class of 1901] was very silent but he's previously praised Lowell." Believing that the matter could be resolved at the next meeting, scheduled for January 6, James advised Clark (who again would not be present) that should he write Conant in support of Lowell, those in attendance would proceed to make the ap-

---

* Before 1912 all fellows were residents of the Boston metropolitan area. Robert Bacon (class of 1880) was the first non-Bostonian. He lived in New York, but had been born and raised in Boston and worked for Lee, Higginson before moving to New York in the 1890s to become a partner in J. P. Morgan & Co. He filled the opening left by the death of Judge Francis Cabot Lowell III. The first native New Yorker to be a fellow was attorney James Byrne (class of 1877), elected 1920, whose other distinction was being the first Roman Catholic in the Corporation. Both Bacon and Byrne resigned after comparatively short six-year tenures, citing the burdens that the trip to Boston placed on their busy schedules. Clark, elected in 1931, and James, elected in 1936, were the only other fellows to live outside Boston.

pointment official. "I don't believe," James concluded, "it could be settled better—even by waiting."[24]

Conant confirmed James's appraisal. "As far as I can discover," he wrote Clark on December 20, "everyone has Lowell at the top of the list, or very close to it; and personally he is my own candidate." Noting that James was eager to leave the Corporation as soon as possible and that Claflin was agreeable to an early election, Conant added, "[A] line from you would clear the way" (for Lowell's designation). Conant also assured Clark that in the absence of a "clear signal" from him, he would not press for action on January 6.[25]

In a draft of a letter to Conant, dated December 20—and thus presumably written before receipt of Conant's letter—Clark referred to his earlier memo expressing a preference for Cabot, and then added, "But I understand that there is much more likely to be a consensus on Lowell; and I want to make it clear that I believe he would be an excellent choice, and that he is a first-rate man who would do us all credit." The letter was to serve as Clark's "proxy, so to speak, for Lowell."[26]

This letter was never sent. Clark apparently had stronger doubts about Lowell than he was willing to put down on paper and felt the Corporation was acting too hastily. Putting the draft aside until after Christmas, Clark checked with James to see if he would be willing to stay a little longer so the search could continue. When James consented, Clark wrote a letter to Conant on January 2, 1947, focusing on a topic that all but placed Lowell out of the running: the age distribution of the Corporation's members. Four of the fellows (James, Shattuck, Clark, and Roger Lee [class of 1902]) were in their middle to late sixties, while Conant, Claflin, and Charles A. Coolidge (class of 1917) were in their early to middle fifties. In presenting his resignation, James had made a plea for the infusion of younger blood, and Clark now reminded his colleagues of this goal:

> While Lowell undoubtedly looks good, he is 56 and my impression is that
> if this is decided in January, there would hardly have been enough time to
> canvass adequately the names of younger men. There are obvious advan-
> tages in having at least one member of the Corporation in his forties. . . .
> It is very likely, I suppose, that after such further consideration we would
> come back to Lowell. However, (a) there is always the possibility that by
> waiting a reasonable time, we would make a wiser choice, all things con-
> sidered; and (b) at the least, we would be better satisfied that in filling the
> vacancy with a man past 55, we haven't made a mistake.[27]

Although Clark raised the age issue in the broad context of preventing the Corporation's arteries from hardening, the question of Lowell's age had important implications for the alignments that were taking shape in the Corporation. Conant's efforts over the previous fourteen years to eliminate Harvard's clubby atmosphere and make it a national university of the highest academic distinction had met stiffening resistance from the two youngest fellows, Claflin and Coolidge. With that duo likely to outlast the others, it was critical to Conant that, as the older men left the Corporation, their replacements be sympathetic to his leadership. The president appears to have been confident that Lowell would fit that criterion, and Lowell was, in fact, a great admirer of Conant,* but someone younger could offer Conant support over a longer period. When Clark forced postponement of a decision, Conant seized the opportunity to buttress his position by finding a man who was not only Lowell's junior by a decade, but also from a less traditional Harvard background.

Conant's choice for the new fellow was William L. Marbury. The two men had met in the spring of 1945 when Marbury, as the top legal aide to Assistant Secretary of War Robert Patterson, worked with Conant in drafting legislation to control the development of atomic energy. Conant thought highly of the lawyer and kept in contact with him over the next year or so, but did not think of him in regard to the Corporation until February 1947, when Marbury sent him a report of the Maryland Commission on Higher Education, which Marbury chaired. Arriving at the very time when Conant was looking for a younger man (Marbury was forty-six years old) with solid credentials and views compatible with his own, the report—which Conant described as "outstanding," both for its thoroughness and its advocacy of "very sensible educational doctrine"—thrust Marbury into the struggle to fill the vacancy on the Corporation.[28]

A man with a penchant for shaking things up (he subtitled his autobiography, "The Memoirs of a Social Inventor"), Conant must have found the prospect of Marbury's election intriguing on at least two counts. As a resident of Baltimore, Marbury would break the Boston–New York monopoly on the Corporation, an important symbolic step in making Harvard the truly national university Conant wanted it to be. Harry James, sum-

----

* When Lowell's brother Jim responded to the news of Conant's resignation in 1953 by "blowing his top," saying that for "three-hundred years Harvard had made progress and Conant did his best to wreck it in twenty years," Ralph observed, "Of course, I do not agree." Diary, January 15, 1953; see also September 28, 1943; October 20, 1945.

ming up the case on Marbury's behalf later on, wrote that "a Baltimorian's presumable in-touchness with the South might be a good thing." But more remarkable than where Marbury lived was that he had not graduated from Harvard College; his Harvard degree was from the Law School, which he had attended after receiving his A.B. from the University of Virginia. Only two previous fellows had not been graduates of the college, and both had presented special circumstances. Nathaniel Bowditch (fellow 1826–1838) was a self-educated navigator and mathematician whose brilliance gained him entry into the most elite circles of Boston society; he had been awarded an honorary degree prior to being elected a fellow. Henry Lee Higginson (fellow 1893–1919) withdrew from the college as a freshman after only a few months because of poor eyesight; a generous benefactor of Harvard, he too had received an honorary degree before joining the Corporation. Because Marbury lacked the close identification with Harvard that Bowditch and Higginson had developed, his designation would be a clear signal that Conant's policy of emphasizing Harvard's graduate and professional schools would be continued.[29]

If Conant "discovered" Marbury, Clark made Marbury's selection his personal mission. Clark had known Marbury's father, also a lawyer, and the younger Marbury had served as secretary of the Clark-led lawyers' committee formed to fight President Roosevelt's "court-packing plan." Besides finding Marbury preferable to Lowell because he was "a younger man with much wider experience and unquestionably with first-rate ability," Clark was attracted to him because of his unconventionality, a term that might also be applied to Clark himself. In 1946 Clark had resigned from the Wall Street law firm he had established nearly forty years earlier to devote more time to the cause of world federalism. Clark refused to give up this campaign even as the Cold War grew more frigid;* similarly, now that Conant had found the "best" man for the Corporation, Clark refused to lose him just because his educational background departed from Harvard Corporation orthodoxy.[30]

But if Conant and Clark had settled on Marbury by early March 1947, other members of the Corporation held back. Claflin and Coolidge opposed him because he was Conant's choice, and the others were unenthu-

---

* A federal judge in New York, who knew Clark well, observed to a Boston colleague that Clark was "a man with a one-track mind" and "a Messianic character." Augustus N. Hand to Charles E. Wyzanski, February 18, 1948, Charles E. Wyzanski MSS, Harvard Law School Library, box 2, folder 2–5.

siastic because none of them knew Marbury—a most unusual situation for a prospective new fellow.* With the Corporation divided on Marbury, Lowell's candidacy remained viable, but Clark directed an intensive lobbying campaign at Shattuck, Lee, and James. By the end of May, Clark felt confident enough to call for an informal vote. All but Claflin and Coolidge expressed a preference for Marbury; it is not clear whether the two dissenters supported Lowell or Chase, or merely indicated unhappiness with Marbury. In any case, at the request of Claflin and Coolidge, it was agreed that the official decision would be put off until the autumn "so as to see whether anything would turn up to change anyone's mind." [31]

"Everyone did feel the same in late September," and events moved quickly. With a 5–2 vote in Marbury's favor, Conant was authorized to check with the Baltimore lawyer to see if he was interested; he agreed, Conant reported to Clark, "almost before I could say Jack Robinson." On October 17 Conant telephoned Lowell, in his capacity as chairman of the Overseers' Executive Committee, to review the procedures for selecting a new member of the Corporation. At the regular overseers' meeting set for the 20th, the president would inform the overseers of a vacancy on the Corporation and request their consent to have the fellows proceed to the election of a replacement. With consent granted the president and treasurer would immediately leave the overseers' room and meet with the fellows to vote formally on their choice. The president then would return to the overseers and submit the person's name. The matter would be referred to the Overseers' Executive Committee for a report and action at the next overseers' meeting, a month later.[32]

Lowell naturally speculated about the meaning of Conant's call. He guessed that Henry James was resigning, and thought the opening was likely to be filled by a "young New Yorker." Thomas S. Lamont (class of 1921), the son of Thomas W. Lamont, who was a J. P. Morgan partner and a generous benefactor of Harvard, seemed a good possibility. The younger Lamont was also a J. P. Morgan partner and served on the Overseers' Executive Committee with Lowell. Lamont ultimately would become a fellow, but at this point in late 1947 he and Lowell found themselves challenging the Harvard Corporation.[33]

---

* Decades later, Marbury told an interviewer that at the time of his selection he hadn't the faintest idea what the Corporation was or whom it included. Richard Norton Smith, *The Harvard Century* (New York: Simon & Schuster, 1986), p. 174.

10

"The highest honor there is"

CRIMSON BATTLES AND CRIMSON GLORY

Ralph Lowell probably never knew how close he had come to being chosen a fellow ("a Boston honor not to be compared with anything else," wrote Cleveland Amory), and thus his actions in the weeks that followed the announcement of the Marbury appointment cannot not be attributed to personal bitterness. What was at stake in the battle over Marbury, and in the Harvard controversies that came later, was Lowell's vision of his beloved Harvard.[1]

MARBURY BEFORE THE OVERSEERS

The overseers were "dumbfounded," Lowell noted, when Conant revealed that the choice of a new fellow "was one Marbury, a Baltimore lawyer with an excellent war record under Patterson and a graduate of the University of Virginia and Harvard Law School." Ironically, Lowell had traveled to Charlottesville just ten days earlier with a trainload of Harvard alumni to watch the Crimson football team play the Virginia eleven; the Cavaliers whipped Harvard 47–0. By the time the struggle over Marbury's election ended three months later, Lowell would feel similarly mauled.[2]

Although he began the task of preparing a report on Marbury with the feeling that his selection was a "mistake," Lowell was by character not inclined to mount a challenge to the Corporation. And nothing he heard initially gave him cause to act out of character. He had long conversations—separately—with Shattuck and Coolidge, who both spoke well of Marbury and reasoned that it would be "a good thing to have one member outside of the regular Harvard family." At an A.D. Club dinner, Coolidge revealed the 5–2 vote to Lowell and told him that he and Claflin had favored Lowell. Lowell thought their support was "very flattering" in light of "my age and the fact that the vacancy was a New York one," but he did not feel he had a realistic chance. "It is time for younger men on the Corporation, and that is one thing that I patently can do nothing about." [3]

As the overseers' meeting scheduled for November 24 drew closer, however, Lowell's underlying distaste for the Marbury appointment came to the surface. Lowell believed that a letter written to him by Thomas S. Lamont on November 13 had "really hit the problem on the head." In the letter Lamont declared:

> I think that if the Corporation was going to pick a non–Harvard College man, thereby setting a new and important precedent, it would have been more appropriate for them to have picked a man distinguished either for his deep interest in some aspect of Harvard University, or for his standing as one interested generally in educational problems, or for his outstanding reputation in some professional field—a man whose name and record would mean something to Harvard College men generally.

Reminding Lowell that it was the responsibility of the executive committee "to make a thorough, painstaking and comprehensive check on Mr. Marbury," Lamont added: "Probably in the case of no previous appointment to the Fellows has it been necessary to make such a check. In every previous case, I imagine, the new man has been well-known to many of the Overseers by name and reputation, if not personally."

Lamont assumed that a further examination of Marbury's record would confirm the "general pattern" already known: "an independent, alert-minded fellow but one who has not hitherto been much interested in Harvard." But Lamont, too, was hardly the revolutionary sort: "[E]ven if the Overseers were to feel it an inappropriate nomination, still I see no strong enough reasons for withholding consent." Despite Lamont's weak conclusion, Lowell was sufficiently emboldened by Lamont's criticism of the Corporation to tell him, "confidentially," of the 5–2 vote. [4]

Lowell heard more about the Corporation's divisions in a conversation with the treasurer. Lowell and Claflin, an investment banker, had often crossed paths in the course of their business careers, and during the 1940s, in addition to serving together on the governing boards of Harvard, they were both trustees of the Museum of Fine Arts. And just as Lowell thought highly of President Conant, he thought Claflin was doing "an extraordinary job" as treasurer. "He not only knows his stuff," Lowell noted in 1945, "but has a great understanding of values and the ability to express himself clearly and interestingly." Talking with Lowell on November 18, 1947, Claflin left no doubt about how he stood on the Marbury appointment. He was "very much opposed" and, "off the record, hoped that the Overseers would withhold consent."[5]

Lowell immediately telephoned Lamont to impart this information, which Lowell felt shed a "new light on the whole question." For the first time, Lowell could envision the executive committee's recommending the withholding of consent; should that happen, he observed, "I will have a mean job" on November 24. After speaking to other members of the committee, Lowell contacted Conant to alert him that there "might be a disagreement in the Executive Committee" and that he should be prepared to answer questions about the proposed new fellow at the overseers' meeting. On Friday the 21st, Lowell went to New York on business for the Associated Harvard Clubs; he saw Lamont and they discussed the Marbury situation. Lowell was in New Haven on Saturday for "The Game" but did not have his usual good time. Knowing full well that Marbury was "very definitely [Conant's] selection," Lowell realized that he was, against all his instincts, about to challenge the president of Harvard University.[6]

The Overseers' Executive Committee met on Monday morning, just before the full board was to convene. Lowell and four of the other six members were present: Lamont; Charles C. Cabot, the Massachusetts judge who was Henry Cabot's brother; Edward Weeks (class of 1922), editor of the *Atlantic Monthly;* and Hanford MacNider (class of 1911), an Iowa banker who had held War and State Department appointments in the Coolidge and Hoover administrations. One overseer later told Grenville Clark that MacNider was the key figure behind the committee's "snap judgment," but it is likely that the out-of-towner only steeled the resolve of Lamont and the Bostonians. The group voted unanimously to recommend that consent to Marbury's election be withheld. Lowell immediately informed Conant of the committee's decision; the president, Lowell noted, was "quite upset" by the news.[7]

At the overseers' meeting Lowell presented the committee's judgment that Marbury was not "outstanding enough to warrant being elected when he was not a graduate of the College." Vigorous debate ensued with regard to Marbury's suitability and concerns that the board would establish a bad precedent by turning down the Corporation's choice of a fellow for the first time. Fearing defeat, Conant moved, as he had told Lowell earlier that he would, to have the matter referred back to the executive committee for "further consideration of questions of policy involved"; the committee then would report to the overseers at the next meeting in January. This motion was passed without dissent.[8]

For Conant, "questions of policy" meant, as it had in the debate over admitting women to the Medical School, policy regarding the relationship between the Corporation and the overseers. But Lowell preferred to emphasize a substantive issue. When Overseer Jerome Greene (a former partner of Lowell's at Lee, Higginson, and secretary to Harvard's President Eliot when Lowell was an undergraduate) wrote Lowell urging him to defer to the Corporation's judgment, Lowell raised the question that troubled him most:

> We have a unique situation at Harvard now—it is a great college and a great university. President Conant has pointed out that there is no other situation like this. Columbia has a university which has killed its college. Chicago also has a university that outshines its college. At Johns Hopkins the Medical School has eclipsed the college. It seems to me it is important to maintain both. In fact, I believe the heart and core of Harvard is the college, I believe further that a man who has been a graduate of the college gets a much better understanding and affection for the whole picture than one who has graduated from another college and owes his first allegiance to his own college. At present the 4 members of the Corporation, other than the officers of the University, comprise three from the Law School and one from the Medical School, so no one could question the fact that the graduate schools have true representation on the Corporation. Whether we believe in it or not, there is a wide-spread belief amongst the graduates and undergraduates that the graduate schools are at the moment eclipsing the college. This I think is unfortunate and, if true, would be very serious. I believe this feeling would be heightened by the selection by the Corporation at this time of a man who was not a graduate of the college.[9]

Lowell also heard from a quite irritated Grenville Clark. He thought that as executive committee chairman, Lowell had acted irresponsibly in not contacting him or Conant, the two men "who knew most about Marbury," before the November 24 meeting. When word of Clark's displeasure reached him, Lowell sent him a note expressing regret that he had not had an opportunity to discuss the Marbury appointment with him. But Clark was not so easily assuaged; Lowell's letter, he told an overseer, did not "explain why he didn't get the opportunity, . . . for I was available." Clark's reply to Lowell carried an implicit criticism: "I didn't dream that the matter would take the turn it did without full inquiry of Conant and myself." [10]

In mid-December the two men got together, their first private session since the previous December when Clark was looking Lowell over as a potential fellow. If Lowell had been unaware of the purpose of that earlier meeting, he understood what Clark's intent was now: "to persuade me to vote" for Marbury. Clark told Lowell "all about the discussions in the Corporation, the impasse they reached, and the final selection of Marbury on a 5–2 vote." There is no indication that Clark mentioned his own critical role in blocking Lowell's elevation to the Corporation; if Lowell ever found out, he did not record it in his diary. Writing to the president of the Harvard Alumni Association a few weeks later, Clark blamed Claflin for Lowell's "obstinate attitude." Lowell had been "propagandized to the limit" by the treasurer, Clark said, with the result that Lowell "has dug in his heels on this and, as Shattuck said . . . , acts as if he were 'bewitched' about it." Clark felt the opposition to Marbury was "based solely on parochialism and prejudice," and that while Lowell's "influence" would prompt a "a very few die-hards" to cast negative votes, the overseers would consent to the Corporation's choice. [11]

On December 24, Lamont, Cabot, and Weeks gathered in Lowell's office to hear a presentation from Conant. Also in attendance was the president of the Board of Overseers, Leverett Saltonstall, a man of keen political skills. Then serving in the U.S. Senate, Saltonstall had missed the November 24 meeting of the executive committee. This absence, combined with the fact that Saltonstall was liked and respected by all the important players, placed him in a key position to find a way out of the impasse. [12]

Conant was contrite. He apologized for not having given the executive committee adequate information on the steps and considerations that had led to Marbury's selection. If he had done so originally, he admitted, this unfortunate situation might have been avoided. Conant left no doubt, however, that he remained committed to the man from Baltimore. Lowell was unimpressed by Conant's remarks about Marbury; he reported to Mac-Nider that Conant "did not bring out anything new other than to say that he thought Marbury had a real interest in Harvard College." [13]

Of more importance was what Saltonstall had to say after Conant left. The senator was closer to the university president than anyone else in the room, and he explained that "there was a good deal of feeling between Conant and Claflin as to who was actually running Harvard, and that it had come to a point where this election might very well increase that tension, even to the point of Conant's leaving." For that reason, Saltonstall declared, he would vote for consent.* Lowell thought Saltonstall's portrayal put a "new and mean angle" on the affair. The executive committee agreed to meet again on January 5 to take a vote.[14]

While Conant sought to mollify the executive committee, Clark lobbied the other twenty-four members of the board. He stressed that fewer than half of Harvard's ninety-one thousand living alumni held degrees from the college, and that the Corporation believed it important to have a man under fifty in its ranks. From his canvassing of the overseers, Clark could identify only five sure votes against Marbury, and all of them were on the executive committee: Cabot, Lamont, MacNider, Weeks, and Lowell.[15]

Four executive committee members attended the January 5 meeting. Lowell had letters from the other three: Richard C. Curtis, a Boston attorney, supported Marbury; Lamont and MacNider were opposed. MacNider's letter was characteristically blunt. Conant had telephoned him to relate the outstanding references Marbury had received from four prominent wartime associates—Robert Patterson, George Harrison, John McCloy, and Dean Acheson. Professing to know them all, MacNider stated that "not a one of them has a primary interest in Harvard. . . . My vote remains No."[†] Lowell had gone to the meeting unsure where Cabot and Weeks stood, and when they lined up with him to make it five opposed, Saltonstall repeated the warning he had delivered two weeks earlier.[16]

The relationship between Conant and Claflin, declared Saltonstall, had deteriorated to the point where Conant saw the Marbury appointment as a test of his leadership. The withholding of consent would be interpreted by the president as meaning that Claflin, and not he, was "running the University." Once more Saltonstall held out the prospect of Conant's resigning, which again prompted an anguished entry in Lowell's diary: "That puts a new and revolting light on the whole question. In effect, a pistol is being held at our heads."[17]

---

* In his memoirs, referring to Conant's threat to resign, Saltonstall declared, "Personally, I have never liked that type of argument." Leverett Saltonstall, *Salty* (Chester, Conn: Globe Pequot Press, 1976), p. 88.

† All of these men had earned their law degrees at Harvard, but none had attended Harvard as an undergraduate.

Lowell apparently had discounted Saltonstall's previous alert, but he did not do so now. He arranged a meeting that very afternoon with Shattuck, who had been Saltonstall's source. Along with Cabot and Weeks, Lowell presented the senior member of the Corporation with the following question: "If consent is withheld, will the President take it as a vote against him and possibly resign?" Shattuck was unable to answer it, but agreed to convey the query to Conant.[18]

The following day Lowell, Cabot, and Weeks received, via Shattuck, Conant's response:

> The question at issue is in fact one between the President of the University, together with a majority of the Corporation, on the one hand, and the Treasurer on the other hand. If the election is not confirmed it will be apparent to the Treasurer and the President that a majority of the Overseers think that the Treasurer and not the President ought to run the University.

Conant's carefully worded statement added nothing to what Saltonstall had already said, but coming directly from the president it had greater impact. It was impossible now to ignore the probable repercussion of rejecting Marbury, and Lowell did not appreciate the position in which Conant and the fellows had placed him. "I think," he wrote in his diary, "Conant and the other Corporation members are acting like spoiled children and that what they really need is for someone to lay them over his knee and give them a real spanking."[19]

Accompanying Conant's statement was a request to see each of the three men separately, and on January 8 Lowell went to Cambridge to meet with the president. Assuring his host that the executive committee had never questioned that it was Conant who should be running the university, Lowell declared that for the committee the issue had always been Marbury's qualifications; the committee could not have imagined that Conant would take the withholding of consent as a personal affront. Conant did not fully explain why the matter had come down to a vote of confidence, but he did tell Lowell that "when he died he wanted put on his tombstone, 'I worked ten years with Bill Claflin.'" Lowell was amazed to hear Conant assert that Claflin and Coolidge should not have talked to him about the Corporation's deliberations, but ought to have "lied" instead. Summing up, Lowell wrote: "So there it is, two high-strung, able individuals in each other's hair to a point where only the resignation of one or the other will solve the problem."[20]

But Lowell had not yet given up. The overseers were due to convene on January 12, and the days before the meeting were filled with frantic activity. Another appeal was made to Shattuck to get the Corporation together and devise a face-saving compromise, but he told the executive committee there was no use in reopening discussions. "As a last resort," Lowell brought overseer Charles Wyzanski up-to-date on what was happening, and the two decided that Wyzanski should talk to Conant and propose Saltonstall as an alternative to Marbury. But Wyzanski found Conant "adamant on no compromise. . . . He wanted to have a showdown." The following day, January 10, Lowell saw Saltonstall at a Harvard function. The senator felt there was no possibility of resolving the Conant-Claflin dispute, but he agreed to seek the counsel of Paul Buck, the university provost. This proved a dead end as well: Buck had no knowledge of the Marbury appointment and was unaware of the intensity of the Conant-Claflin enmity. As Lowell traveled to Cambridge on the 12th, he knew he was beaten.[21]

Meeting first, the executive committee focused on how to keep the overseers in the dark about the turmoil of the previous six weeks. Cabot, Lamont, and Weeks each had prepared a draft of the committee's report, and Cabot's was chosen. The report's opening sentences were laced with irony:

> It is the opinion of the Executive Committee that this board should scrutinize appointments by the Corporation to fill vacancies in its own membership far more carefully than it does appointments by the Corporation to other positions. This is due to the fact that no group can be as objective in filling its own ranks as it can be when making outside appointments. There is always danger that a self-perpetuating body will perpetuate its own characteristics to the exclusion of others which would widen its horizon.

Turning immediately to Marbury's "not [being] a graduate of the College," the group left no doubt as to its views:

> This committee believes that at the proper time and with the proper person it would be wise to have one or possibly two members of the Corporation who are not graduates of the College. We do not think that Mr. Marbury's qualifications, distinguished as they are as to ability and integrity, are such to justify a departure at this time from the tradition of members of the Corporation being graduates of the College. Were there no other considerations than those suggested, this committee would recommend that this board withhold its consent to the appointment.

But there was "another very important consideration." The report continued:

> The President of the University has stated to several members of the committee that in this particular instance, and for reasons unknown to us but which he believes to be sound, a failure to give consent would reflect a lack of confidence in him. We regret that our recommendation should have to be based on a question of confidence because that confidence has never been questioned. Obviously the actions of this board should very rarely be exercised merely on a basis of confidence. Yet in this instance we believe it to be for the best interests of the University to overcome our doubts as to the wisdom of the nomination by expressing deep confidence in the President. We therefore recommend that this board give its consent to the appointment.

If the overseers wanted details, they would have to ask questions.[22]

None were asked. When the agenda item on the Corporation vacancy came up at the overseers' meeting, Conant made a few brief remarks and distributed a memorandum and documents describing Marbury's qualifications. After he had finished, he departed—along with Claflin—and the overseers took a five-minute recess to examine the materials. Saltonstall called on Lowell to report on behalf of the executive committee as soon as the session resumed, and Lowell read the statement Cabot had drafted. The question of consent was immediately put to a voice vote and passed without dissent. By Lowell's account, "very few" actually opened their mouths. The president and the treasurer were called back into the room to hear the results, Conant read his annual report, and the meeting adjourned for lunch. "I guess our action," Lowell concluded wearily, "was the best under all the circumstances."[23]

If Lowell ever had any second thoughts about his opposition to Marbury, he never wrote them down. The alumni revolt Lowell had expected did not materialize, but Lowell learned that "Harvard men in Baltimore were quite upset" with Marbury's appointment because he had never joined the Harvard Club there. When Marbury addressed an Alumni Association dinner in the fall of 1948, Lowell dismissed his remarks as "rather wishy-washy." But probably nothing gave Lowell more comfort than a conversation he had with Charles Francis Adams on the subway that December. Adams, a descendant of U.S. presidents, a cabinet member in the Hoover administration, a tireless worker for charitable causes in Boston, and a former treasurer of Harvard, asked about Marbury; Lowell replied that he "knew very little about him, but that [Lowell] personally was still in the wrong with the Corporation." "Don't let that worry you," Adams assured him, "you were in the right and that is all that matters." [24]

As Lowell's remark to Adams suggests, he felt the reverberations of the "Marbury affair" for months and even years afterward. He played the good soldier by keeping the dispute private within the Harvard family; when a *New York Times* correspondent contacted him a few days after the overseers' meeting to confirm a rumor about Conant's encountering trouble at the meeting, Lowell was relieved to be able "honestly [to] tell him there was nothing of the sort." Nonetheless, he thought that Conant was "really down" on him. The president seemed to be seeking his advice less, and Lowell understood that any chance he might once have had of becoming a fellow was gone. Lowell continued to think highly of Conant, but he described weaknesses that he formerly had overlooked:

> Conant's mind and judgment and speed of thought put us all in the shade. That is where he shows his greatness, but like Jim Storrow [Lowell's former boss at Lee, Higginson] he is a little inclined to be short with the slower thinker and, as shown in the Claflin case, he does not like disagreement with his decisions. I suppose a man can't be everything, but it is a shame that Jim cannot mix a little better, unbend a little more, and, in other words, be a little more human. [25]

Lowell's relationship with Conant suffered but was gradually restored as the passions of the moment faded and their common interest in educational broadcasting grew. But Lowell's association with Clark did not recover. It had always been one-sided: Lowell had expressed unbounded admiration for the extremely influential New York attorney, while Clark viewed Lowell as a capable subordinate in the New England regional effort supporting his military causes. Having made Marbury's election another of his crusades, Clark saw Lowell's resistance as an act of betrayal; for months after the overseers' vote, Lowell heard from others that Clark was still angry at him. They had a good talk in May 1949, and Lowell wrote a very flattering letter ("you are one of my real heroes") the following year when Clark resigned from the Corporation, but the two men were traveling on different paths. Clark's devotion to "world peace through world law" held no attraction for Lowell, and Lowell did not support Clark's bitter and futile fight in the 1950s to keep Harvard's Arnold Arboretum intact. Paradoxically, it was Clark, not Lowell, whose long ties to Harvard eventually ended in acrimony.[26]

Although Marbury joined the Corporation in January 1948 (where he remained for more than two decades, succeeding Coolidge as senior fellow when he stepped down in the mid-1960s), the final chapter in the saga of his appointment was yet to come. Conant and Clark had expected Claflin to resign voluntarily; they were still furious about Claflin's blatant attempt to undermine the Corporation's selection of the new fellow—"contrary to the necessary and established custom in the Corporation to accept and stand by decisions once arrived at," according to Clark. By late March Claflin had not acted, so Conant and Clark, with the concurrence of Shattuck and Lee, demanded that he leave. When Claflin complied in mid-April, Lowell blamed himself for the outcome: "I feel very badly that my investigation of the Marbury affair may have been the cause of [the conflict's] coming to a head."[27]

MORE APPOINTMENTS

After Claflin's departure from the treasurership, Lowell figured in the speculation about his replacement. Flattered as he was by the talk, and as much as he would have liked being offered the job, Lowell knew that to accept it would mean too great a financial loss for him. The post went to Paul C. Cabot (class of 1921), brother of Henry and Charles. Cabot had founded the State Street Investment Corporation three years after graduating from college and led it to become one of the most successful Boston-based mutual funds. He made unusual arrangements in assuming the treasurership—he would remain at State Street, and in exchange for investment advice his company would be allowed to cite its Harvard affiliation in advertisements. Nonetheless, Cabot's name sailed through the overseers in October 1948 with no trouble.[28]

Not so in the case of economics professor John Kenneth Galbraith the following June. Galbraith had joined the Harvard faculty in 1934 after receiving his doctorate in agricultural economics from the University of California, Berkeley. Having advanced from tutor to instructor, he was looking forward to further promotion in 1938–1939 when he became an early victim of Conant's tightened rules for tenure. He left Harvard, but in the summer of 1948, after stints at Princeton, the Office of Price Administration (during World War II), and *Fortune* magazine, was invited back to Harvard as a lecturer. That fall he received an attractive offer from the University of Illinois, prompting the Harvard economics faculty, with only one dissenting vote, to put him up for a full professorship. A review committee appointed by Conant endorsed this action unanimously and in January 1949 Galbraith's promotion looked like a sure thing.[29]

But overseer Charles Cabot started making noises. Cabot and Galbraith had crossed swords at the close of World War II as members of the Strategic Bombing Survey, in which Galbraith had been a principal investigator and Cabot one of those responsible for writing the final report. As drafted by Cabot and his colleagues, the report concluded that massive bombing had been a great success. This, however, departed completely from Galbraith's findings that "the aircraft, manpower and bombs used in the campaign had cost the American economy far more in output than they had cost Germany." The chief of the survey was unhappy with Cabot's writing style, which he found unreadable. When Galbraith was given the task of editing the report, he used the opportunity to recast its findings in keeping with his own views. In the ensuing arguments with Cabot's group over wording, Galbraith advocated his position with what he himself later described as "a maximum of arrogance and a minimum of tact." The report in its final form represented a substantial victory for the economist over his legally trained adversaries, but Galbraith's behavior had made him some "lasting and influential enemies."[30]

In March 1949 the Corporation held up approval of Galbraith's promotion in order to consider Charles Cabot's charges of "personality defects" and "intellectual dishonesty." A committee specially appointed by the provost took testimony from Cabot and interviewed people connected with the bombing survey; its report in mid-April concluded that there was no evidence to substantiate the claims of "intellectual dishonesty." The committee acknowledged that Cabot had made a case regarding the "personality defects," but pointed out that these flaws had been known to and considered by the department and the review committee before making their positive recommendations. Accordingly, the Corporation forwarded Galbraith's name to the overseers for their consent.[31]

Lowell first became aware of the controversy in May and hoped that it would not come before the full board until after his term as overseer expired in June. But the chairman of the committee that would review the appointment was Clarence Randall, a Chicago steel company executive and 1912 classmate of Lowell's. Randall wanted to move quickly, and he enlisted Lowell and Lamont to discuss the matter with the economics faculty. Lowell came away from this early June meeting impressed with the department's support for Galbraith and the professors' "sincere belief in his intellectual honesty." If the overseers were to oppose Galbraith's promotion, he told Randall, it would have to be on grounds other than academic ability. And Lowell, it developed, was prepared to do just that.[32]

The overseers traditionally held their last meeting of the academic year on the morning of Commencement Day. Given the tight schedule of the day, substantive business usually was kept off the agenda, but on this June 23 Randall brought up the Galbraith case. He and several other overseers (including Lamont and Sinclair Weeks, who later became secretary of commerce in the Eisenhower administration) were disturbed by what they considered to be an already heavy concentration of pro–New Deal, Keynesian faculty in the Department of Economics, and feared that giving Galbraith tenure would only enhance the liberals' domination.

Although Lowell accepted their defamatory characterization of Galbraith as a "Socialist" (a label that Galbraith would publicly accept decades later), his main objection to the economics professor was not ideological but personal. A. Lawrence Lowell had led the fight against Louis Brandeis's 1916 nomination to the Supreme Court, alleging basic character flaws; similarly, Ralph Lowell joined the fight to deny Galbraith a permanent position at Harvard because his friend Charles Cabot had found him to be "one of the worst men he has ever known." Galbraith, Lowell wrote, was "a very arrogant and rude man to his inferiors and a good deal of a bootlicker to his seniors," traits that had led "many men of judgment" to conclude that he was not "qualified to teach at Harvard."[33]

The overseers started their session at 8 A.M.; at 8:30, when the alumni chorus began practicing immediately outside their meeting-room windows, the overseers "grabbed their top hats" and walked across the Yard to find quieter quarters. They were only moderately successful in shielding themselves from the noise of the growing throng, and inside, Lowell noted, "the debate developed hot and heavy." (Galbraith, who of course was not present, described the scene somewhat more colorfully: "My proposed appointment turned gentlemanly contentment and torpor into ardent and eloquent indignation.") Paul Cabot broke ranks with the Corporation to stand by his brother, and Randall's position was winning supporters. It appeared likely that consent would be withheld, but before a vote could be taken, Charles Wyzanski proposed that the decision be post-poned until fall to allow for further study. This motion carried, probably with Lowell's concurrence, but his diary leaves little doubt as to his feel-ings: "I believe that the Overseers will stand up and vote against this man who may be a scholar but does not seem to be a gentleman." [34] When the matter came before the overseers in the fall, however, Conant lectured them on their proper role and they gave their consent.

Lowell was serving a second term on the Board of Overseers when Co-nant resigned his office in January 1953 to become U.S. high commissioner to the Federal Republic of Germany. ("Many of us who love Harvard," Lowell wrote, "feel there is more to be done as President in the training of generations of youth than in the very important but probably temporary job in Germany. I feel sad at his going.") The Corporation carried out its search for a successor in secrecy, but toward the end of May Charles Coolidge told Lowell privately that Nathan Pusey had been selected. Like most of the Boston-Cambridge community, Lowell knew nothing of the man, but he took heart from Coolidge's description of Pusey's achieve-ments at Lawrence College, a small liberal arts institution in Appleton, Wisconsin. This held bright portents for undergraduate education at Har-vard, leading Lowell to conclude that Pusey "sounds like a good risk." [35]

The overseers formally received Pusey's name on June 1, and the choice ran into strong criticism from at least four members of the board: news-paper columnist Joseph Alsop, literary critic John Mason Brown, nuclear physicist J. Robert Oppenheimer, and Charles Wyzanski. These members argued that Pusey was virtually unknown in his own academic field (Athe-nian political theory) and lacked the scholarly attainment necessary to be an effective leader of Harvard. After listening to the hour-long discussion, Lowell expected a close vote when the overseers met again ten days later. [36]

Happy with Pusey and fearing a devisive debate, Lowell quickly grabbed the floor at the June 10 session and moved that consent be granted. The motion was immediately seconded and the opposition folded. Consent was unanimous after only twelve minutes. Lowell's love for Harvard quickly rolled over to embrace the new president; Pusey may not have been as bril-liant as Conant, and Lowell did not have the same opportunities to work with him, but Lowell was comfortable with his humanistic outlook and grasp of Harvard affairs. In the eighteen years that Pusey stood at the helm, Lowell found himself in sharp disagreement with him only once (in the Memorial Church controversy described in chapter 13). [37]

However, Lowell did oppose the Harvard Corporation on an explosive issue. The university had become a favorite target of U.S. Senator Joseph McCarthy, who accused Harvard of coddling "Fifth Amendment Communists" on its faculty. The Corporation adopted a firm public stance against the Senator's attacks, but Lowell thought the Wisconsin Republican had a point. In 1947, before the Alger Hiss case broke into the headlines and before the Cold War had taken a dangerous turn with the explosion of a Russian atomic bomb and fighting in Korea, Lowell had supported Harvard's decision to recognize a chapter of American Youth for Democracy, a Communist-front organization. Interviewed in the capacity of president of the Associated Harvard Clubs, Lowell had declared: "Harvard has always stood for free speech. I don't believe in what these undergraduates want to do, but I do believe that it is a good thing for Harvard men to come out into the open and air their views." But if it was all right then to let college students vent their immature opinions, Lowell could find no reason in the mid-1950s to tolerate professors who sought the protection afforded by the Fifth Amendment when being questioned by congressional committees. "I think anyone who hides behind the Fifth Amendment is a skunk," Lowell told reporters in January 1954, endorsing the suggestion of Massachusetts governor Christian Herter that Harvard fire faculty who claimed possible self-incrimination. "I wouldn't employ anyone in my bank who used the Amendment. I'd find some way to get rid of them." No such instance came up at Boston Safe, but uncooperative witnesses before congressional panels were not welcome on WGBH-FM programs.[38]

Fifth Amendment issues aside, Lowell was distressed by the witch-hunt mentality of the early and middle 1950s. In January 1951 he signed an appeal supported by nearly 150 prominent Americans, including former first lady Eleanor Roosevelt, theologian Reinhold Niebuhr, and broadcaster H. V. Kaltenborn, warning against the use of "star-chamber tactics" in the fight against communism. Three years later Robert Cutler, then a national security adviser to President Eisenhower, "threw a bombshell" into an overseers' meeting by urging that the overseers oppose the appointment of anyone who was a Communist or ever had been a Communist. According to Lowell, Pusey "very wisely said" that he thought the first part was unnecessary and the second imprudent. Lowell, concerned that Cutler's aggressive stance would antagonize the Corporation, believed "Bobby was all wet" and hoped the resolution would quietly be buried by the executive committee. It was. Later that year, when he learned that Oppenheimer had been denied security clearance, Lowell wrote, "He is an Over-seer and a peculiar fellow, but I believe he is a real American." [39]

A GLORIOUS FORTIETH

Ralph and Charlotte were on a Caribbean cruise in March 1952 when he received word that Harvard would confer a Doctor of Laws degree upon him at the June commencement, making him the first in his class to be so recognized.* His short diary entry revealed his emotions: "The highest honor there is." Among those who would join Lowell as recipients of Har-vard's plaudits were Secretary of Defense Robert A. Lovett, Republican foreign policy adviser John Foster Dulles, retiring fellow Henry Lee Shat-tuck, and Tufts College president Leonard Carmichael, whose institution in 1949 had been the first to recognize Lowell with an honorary degree. The Harvard citation, brief by custom, read, "Worthy bearer of a famous name; a public-spirited Bostonian devoted to the welfare of his commu-nity and his college." [40]

The 1952 Commencement—which, not coincidentally, was the fortieth anniversary of Lowell's graduation—marked the pinnacle of his Harvard career. For not only did he receive his Doctor of Laws in the morning, but in the afternoon it was announced that he had come in first in the ballot-ing for the Board of Overseers, amassing the highest vote total ever recorded in overseer elections as well as the largest plurality. Congratulat-ing Lowell a few days later, Charles Cabot took note of his own position as president of the Alumni Association and declared, "Perhaps our joint battles shoulder to shoulder a few years [ago] weren't as detrimental in the Harvard eyes as we thought they might be." [†] Again, it was probably no ac-cident that Lowell was seated next to Marbury at the Commencement luncheon. This Commencement Day was also Conant's last as president. [41]

---

* Subsequent 1912 recipients were: businessman Clarence Randall (1954); Harvard's Littauer Pro-fessor of Hebrew Literature and Philosophy, Harry Wolfson (1956); and Chief Justice Raymond S. Wilkins of the Massachusetts Supreme Judicial Court (1964).

† Another dissenter in the Marbury and Galbraith battles did well in 1952: Lamont was elected a fellow of the Corporation.

11

"The busiest man in town"

TRUSTEE FOR GOOD CAUSES

Ralph Lowell undertook his first trusteeship in 1913 when, seven months after receiving his Harvard degree, he accepted an invitation to join the Corporation of the Provident Institution for Savings. Established in 1816 by John Lowell (1769–1840) and other benevolent Bostonians to encourage "the practice of frugality . . . among persons in humble life," the Provident had for almost a century looked to a succession of Lowells for guidance.[1] Ralph maintained his association with the bank for more than fifty years, and during that time also served as trustee for about a score of Boston charitable, educational, and medical-related organizations, including Boston University, the Perkins Institution for the Blind, the Massachusetts division of the American Cancer Society, the New England Medical Center, the Community Fund (later the United Way), and the Salvation Army. Bostonians were constantly seeing Lowell's picture in the newspaper at one fund-raising event or another. By the early 1960s, Lowell's title of "Mr. Boston" rested on both his highly public role at WGBH and his ubiquity in the city's good causes.[2]

Lowell's numerous trusteeships, the *Boston Globe* observed in 1965, demonstrated "the validity of the maxim that if you want to get a job done, bring it to the busiest man in town." The question contemporaries often asked was, How does he do so much? Fearful of "exploding the myth," Lowell usually ducked a response, but when pressed he liked to quote a Harvard classmate who explained, "Ralph budgets his time." This explanation was only part of the answer. Much of Lowell's ability to serve on so many boards derived from the fact that few of them placed serious demands on him beyond attendance at occasional meetings.* Extraordinary circumstances might compel Lowell to scrutinize reports and participate in discussions between formal meetings, but by and large he simply went from one meeting to another where individuals who were more deeply involved had set the agenda and dominated the proceedings. On the basis of his experience with numerous groups of a given type, Lowell was adept at identifying the implications of various courses of action and offering suggestions on how to proceed; but only rarely did he initiate new approaches. And he could not have held so many positions had Boston Safe not encouraged it and supplied administrative assistance. At the height of Lowell's civic career in the 1950s, his secretary, Ruth Perkins, spent a healthy part of the work week on his nonbank duties.[3]

If most of Lowell's trusteeships demanded little attention, serving mainly to assault his palate and expand his waistline, two obliged him to become deeply involved. The Museum of Fine Arts and the Massachusetts General Hospital were institutions with national reputations, and Lowell assumed prominent roles as they attempted to adjust to the post–World War II era.

THE MUSEUM OF FINE ARTS

Lowells had figured prominently in the history of Boston's Museum of Fine Arts since its founding in 1870. John Amory Lowell chaired the meeting that took the first steps toward organizing the museum, and in 1875 he donated the monumental Egyptian sculptures from the great temple of Karnak that his cousin John Lowell (the Lowell Institute benefactor), had purchased in the mid-1830s. The Lowell gift formed the nucleus of a growing collection of Egyptian artifacts for which the museum became world famous. After the turn of the century, when the museum outgrew its original accommodations in Copley Square, Guy Lowell designed the new building located between the Fenway and Huntington Avenue. In the early

---

* Such were the numbers that even Lowell could not keep track of all his titles. When he received an appeal for contributions from a nonprofit group, he was careful to check the letterhead to make sure his name was not on it before throwing it into the wastebasket. David O. Ives, Script for All-Staff, April 8, 1988, Records of David O. Ives, WGBH Archives, box cg 334, All-Staff Meeting folder.

1930s A. Lawrence Lowell took the lead in modifying the museum's administrative structure and saw one of his protégés, George Harold Edgell, installed as director.[4]

A. Lawrence Lowell had assisted Edgell's career in art and administration since his undergraduate days at Harvard. Lowell was an early champion of what would later be called "interdisciplinary studies," and Edgell, who received his A.B. in 1909 in history and literature, was one of the first to pursue such a program. After gaining his Ph.D. in fine arts from Harvard in 1913, Edgell joined the faculty and established himself as a popular lecturer in the introductory art history survey course. No one was more surprised than Edgell when President Lowell, in 1921, appointed him dean of the School of Architecture. Edgell initially declined the appointment, noting that he could not have passed any course given in that school except history. But Lowell persisted; he supported his argument with an analogy, saying there was no reason why the director of the Metropolitan Opera Company had to be able to sing, and Edgell eventually agreed. After Lowell retired in 1933, Edgell, perhaps sensing that Harvard would be a different type of place with a chemist in charge, accepted the post of curator of paintings at the Museum of Fine Arts, and in the fall of 1934 he was named director.[5]

In early 1943, after more than forty years as a museum trustee, A. Lawrence Lowell died. Under the museum's charter the Trustee of the Lowell Institute was a member ex officio of the Board of Trustees, so Ralph assumed his cousin's seat. The younger Lowell's association with the museum had been intermittent over the previous two decades. Ralph and Charlotte had become museum subscribers in 1926, and the following year he was asked to join the Visiting Committee to the Egyptian Department; he served until 1940. The yearly donation to the museum was one of the extras the Lowells immediately dispensed with as they tightened their belts after the collapse of Lee, Higginson. Not until 1945 would their names again appear on the list printed in the museum's annual report.

Lowell characterized his first trustees' meeting as "awe-inspiring," a sentiment reflecting the august company. Probably no board in Boston had as many members representing the city's first families; there were a Cabot, a Coolidge, a Curtis, a Forbes, a Gardner, a Holmes, two Paines, and a Shattuck. Most were avid collectors of art and gave generously of their acquisitions to the museum. The board met only three times a year, to review and ratify actions taken by the Committee of the Museum, which was the key decision-making body. Composed of the president, the treasurer, the director, and six trustees serving three-year overlapping terms, the committee held monthly sessions to determine what the museum should buy and which gifts to accept.[6]

Edward Jackson Holmes, the museum's president for nearly sixteen years, died in May 1950. Like his predecessors, Holmes had a passion for art; along with his mother, he was a major contributor to the Japanese collection, helping to make it one of the museum's strongest departments. The vice president, Richard Cary Curtis, also an art lover and the obvious choice to replace Holmes, was too ill to assume the post. After months of consideration, a panel of trustees asked Lowell to take over.[7]

In offering the presidency to Lowell, the trustees were choosing a very different kind of leader. Holmes had devoted his "whole life and thought to the Museum"; Lowell, with his broad range of institutional affiliations — to which the museum was a relatively recent addition — could not be expected to bestow the same intense affection. Holmes had been interested primarily in the "growth and curatorial care" of the museum's collections; Lowell, who admitted having a "limited appreciation of art," was likely to focus on administrative and financial concerns.[8]

As Lowell related the story many years later, he had believed himself unqualified to step into Holmes's shoes. "I don't know anything about art," Lowell had told the trustees. To which they replied, "You know a lot about anthropology, don't you?" When Lowell responded affirmatively, they had their opening: "Well, that's kind of an art." Whatever his doubts, Lowell put up little resistance. "It would be good fun and probably not too hard a job, although these things always take more of one's time than one thinks," he noted in his diary. He could give no definite answer before checking with the executive committee at Boston Safe, but the committee quickly gave its consent. When the appointment became official in January 1951, Lowell wrote, "I certainly felt a little like a fish out of water, but it is a great honor and a wonderful institution.[9]

Welcoming Lowell's election as president, a *Boston Herald* editorial observed that the interesting thing was "not the tradition associated with his name, but the untraditional approach he [took] toward his work." The paper cited the Lowell Institute Cooperative Broadcasting Council and its "energetic [exploration of] the possibilities of educational use of radio," and concluded, "Mr. Lowell appears to be an ideal man to preserve the great museum trust while keeping a decorous eye out for the new and promising."[10]

After taking a year to get acquainted with the museum, Lowell offered two modest proposals in 1952. One called for placing women on the board. Nothing in the 1870 charter or the museum's bylaws barred women from becoming trustees, but no woman had ever been chosen. Women were making their appearance on numerous other nonprofit boards, and they had long been significant contributors to the museum's endowment and collections. Lowell thought the time had come to acknowledge their role. Rather than ask any serving trustee to step aside or wait for a vacancy to occur, Lowell urged amending the 1870 charter to expand the board. The state legislature took the necessary action in 1953, and in February 1954, Mrs. Henry Mather Bliss and Mrs. Roger Haydock Hallowell were elected. Coming from the same Brahmin circle as the rest of the board, they settled easily into its activities.[11]

Lowell's other idea was to attract "a lot of working men and women to our Museum" by keeping it open one evening a week. His original plan was based on the expectation that people would stop off at the museum right after leaving work; hence closing time was to be pushed back from five to seven in the evening. Introduced in the fall of 1952, the extended hours failed to lure many visitors; apparently most people preferred to go directly home for dinner after the day's work. Accordingly, the museum experimented with staying open until ten once a week beginning in January 1954; this proved to be a more popular format and was retained.[12]

The museum had followed well-worn precedents in adding women to the board and setting up evening hours, but it took the lead in preparing for the age of television. Shortly after Lowell became president, the museum joined the Lowell Institute Cooperative Broadcasting Council and WGBH-FM went on the air, but Director Edgell was noticeably unenthusiastic about these developments. Council membership entailed "an additional expense and possibly it is justified," he had written in his 1950 report to the trustees, but Edgell did not believe that radio was a useful medium for the museum's educational work. "[W]hen it comes to the arts," he declared, "the eye is vastly more important than the ear." A year later, as prospects improved for a television station run by the Broadcasting Council, Edgell changed his tune and welcomed the museum's place on the council. With Lowell and Edgell pushing the plan, the board agreed in 1954 to rewire the entire museum to permit televised broadcasts direct from its galleries.[13]

Television aside, however, Lowell grew increasingly concerned about Edgell's "letting things rather coast in the Museum." In 1951, Lowell's first year as president, attendance had reached an all-time high of more than 642,000, thanks in large part to the special exhibition "Treasures from Vienna." The following year the number of visitors dropped to 530,000, a total Edgell labeled a "satisfactory" increase over the 1949 and 1950 figures (476,000 and 502,000, respectively).* Lowell was not prepared to interpret the data so favorably. But even more disturbing to him was the decline in annual subscriptions. The usual income from subscriptions (less than $40,000) was small in proportion to the museum's operating budget of $800,000, and the drop-off was by no means sharp (less than $2,000). But the trend reinforced Lowell's fear that Edgell no longer possessed the energy required to keep the museum moving forward. The director's report for 1952 addressed the problem, stating that the dip in annual subscriptions pointed up the need to "start an intensive drive for membership in the Museum." In the past, Edgell explained, "the Director has sent out a good many letters sporadically appealing to individuals . . . [to join]. These letters produced considerable results, but in comparatively small volume. It might very well be time now to start a drive and send out appeals not in driblets, but a hundred thousand." But over the next year Edgell did nothing to implement his proposal.[14]

The director turned sixty-six in March 1953, and Lowell broached the subject of retirement with him that fall. Lowell handled the matter delicately, but over the next nine months Edgell gave no indication of stepping down. With the approval of his fellow trustees, Lowell told Edgell in May 1954 that the board would wait no longer. "I know it is a shock to him," Lowell wrote, "just as the prospect of my being kicked upstairs in the bank next year is a shock to me.† I am glad that is over. I now can enjoy my meals again." Seven weeks later, Edgell died unexpectedly after a brief illness.[15]

The trustees lost little time in finding a replacement. Edgell and all but one of his predecessors had established close ties to the museum before becoming director, and given Lowell's usual preference for looking inside an organization for new leadership, one might have expected the choice to be a familiar face around the museum. But most of Edgell's top staff were too old to be considered, and there was little enthusiasm on the board

---

* Edgell's successor as director claimed that the annual attendance during this period ranged somewhere between 275,000 and 375,000, "although it was otherwise recorded." Museum of Fine Arts, *The Museum Year 1971–1972*, p. 8.

† As it turned out, Lowell was able to arrange a four-year delay of his own retirement.

for the younger man Edgell favored. Since the trustees had been pondering Edgell's retirement for almost a year, they knew who was available and whom they wanted. A month after Edgell's death, the position was tendered to and accepted by the director of the City Art Museum of St. Louis, Perry T. Rathbone.[16]

A graduate of Harvard College (class of 1933) and of a special Harvard program on museum administration, Rathbone was no stranger to Boston and the Museum of Fine Arts, although he had been away for two decades. He had directed the museum in St. Louis since 1940 and had made a name for himself as a "consummate showman." Chroniclers of his career invariably made the point that Rathbone shared more than his first two initials with the nineteenth-century impresario P. T. Barnum. The St. Louis museum was one of the few in the country financed directly from municipal revenues, and Rathbone used "bizarre, unmuseumlike methods" to lure citizens to see what their tax levy was supporting. A show celebrating the 150th anniversary of the Louisiana Purchase, "Westward the Way," was enlivened by a band of Comanches performing tribal dances. A knight in shining armor astride a horse traveled the downtown streets to publicize the "Treasures from Vienna" exhibit, which attracted higher attendance in St. Louis than anywhere else on its American tour.* Edgell once had told a Boston trustee that the "best museum was the one seen by the fewest people." Rathbone assumed that it was a major part of the director's job to use his ingenuity to bring aesthetic enjoyment to people who might otherwise pass it up. Lowell, who had employed publicity agents to increase attendance at Lowell Institute lectures, agreed. He and the rest of the board were ready to shed the museum's image as an aloof and elitist institution restricted to serving the true connoisseur of fine art. In truth, the elitist image was not entirely fair: The museum had been the first in the country to provide interpretive guides, a service it began in 1907, and it offered extensive educational programs to the public. But the trustees were now prepared to attack the image problem head-on.[17]

There was more to Rathbone than his circus techniques. Although he lacked Edgell's Ph.D. in fine arts, he had good taste and had done an excellent job of building up every part of the St. Louis museum's collection. To supplement the public money the institution received, Rathbone or-

---

* Although the two cities were roughly the same size, the exhibit drew 83,000 in Boston and 290,000 in St. Louis.

ganized a volunteer fund-raising group; their efforts made the museum the first in the country to purchase a Rembrandt after World War II. American museum directors of earlier generations had been primarily scholars or amateur collectors; Rathbone saw himself as belonging to a new profession of museum administrators. Under his leadership the City Art Museum began making its way up the list of notable American museums, and the trustees of the Museum of Fine Arts brought him to Boston to maintain their institution's position near the top of that list.[18]*

Rathbone took over as director on May 1, 1955, and he lost little time in making changes. Museum publications, previously black and white on grainy paper, came out in glossy color. With the approval of the trustees, Rathbone and Mrs. Hallowell put together a Women's Committee (later called the Ladies' Committee) to solicit new museum memberships. The first concerted membership drive in the museum's history was launched on January 1, 1956; by the end of the year enrollment had jumped from 2,200 to 4,900, and contributions had more than doubled, from $40,000 to almost $95,000. In November 1955, to publicize an exhibition entitled "Sport in Art," Rathbone demonstrated his flair for the unconventional by featuring a fashion show and a performance by the soon-to-be Olympic champion figure skater Tenley Albright." [19]

Lowell became an instant fan of Rathbone's. In addition to moving quickly on the specific problems Edgell had failed to address, Rathbone brought a new spirit. "Many people congratulated me on what we are doing to put life into the old Museum," Lowell observed after the opening of the "Sport in Art" show. "There were also some elderly people who shook their heads over 'such goings on,' [but] I think the net of it all is good." A few years later, a friend of Lowell's started "blowing off about the modern . . . museum heads, none of whom, including Perry Rathbone, knew anything about art, and are opening the museums to hordes of people who know no art and have no interest in it." Lowell told him he "disagreed with everything he said." [20]

For about a decade after Rathbone's arrival, Lowell and the board allowed him great freedom at the helm. (In the "Boston tradition" trustees would "place the running of an institution in the hands of a responsible ad-

---

* No one questioned the preeminence of New York's Metropolitan Museum of Art. After a visit there in 1954, Lowell observed, "We may have good museums in Boston, be we only have 'examples' compared to their marvelous collections." Diary, February 3, 1954.

ministrator, and let him attend to his business without interference.") And Rathbone delivered: Among his achievements were higher attendance, increased contributions, more educational programs, and improvements to the appearance of the galleries. At one point Lowell used the influence of his position to win approval for a 1958 show on primitive art, which was actually handled by the staff at Harvard's Peabody Museum. But Lowell was generally content to restrict himself to fulfilling the social obligations of the president. Over the years he and Charlotte stood at the heads of countless receiving lines at openings of special exhibitions and other ceremonial events. Between 1951 and 1968 the museum placed greater demands on Lowell's evening hours than did any of his other institutional affiliations.[21]

The one area in which Lowell sometimes challenged Rathbone's judgment was modern art. The museum's bylaws clearly intended the trustees to have a major voice in decisions concerning new additions to its collections, and Lowell and his colleagues were not shy about expressing disdain for some of what passed for art in the contemporary world. Lowell would apply terms like "monstrosity" and "wild" to the items under consideration. He backed buying the museum's first Picasso in 1958 but was less than enthusiastic about it—only Rathbone's going into "practical hysterics" carried Lowell and the committee along with him. The full board discussed modern art at a meeting in the fall of 1963, and Lowell was relieved by what he heard: "There seems to be a feeling that there is a swing back to more conservative art, which would be all to the good."[22]

Traveling exhibitions featuring modern art were a particular bane for Lowell. He felt the 1959 show containing pieces from New York's recently opened Guggenheim Museum was "the worst collection of junk I have ever seen." At a meeting of the board a few weeks after the show opened, Lowell told his fellow trustees to go see the exhibition and "then go home and have a drink." Reviewing the DeStael show in 1965, he wrote, "I tried hard to make some sense out of his pictures, but must admit they are all beyond me." The following year Lowell thought the paintings and sculptures loaned to the museum for special exhibition by Susan Morse Hilles (who joined the board in 1968) were "unbelievably horrible. I even had to go to the Egyptian collection to counteract its effect."[23]

If Lowell was unhappy with the direction of modern art, he also recognized that the museum building needed modernization to display its holdings to best effect. His beloved Egyptian collection was a case in point.

Most of the objects were still exhibited as originally installed when the Huntington Avenue building opened in 1909. Lighting improvements and minor alterations in placement had been made over the decades, but a number of magnificent pieces were lost in the clutter. In the early 1960s, with the trustees' approval, Rathbone launched a major renovation of the Egyptian galleries, a task that involved moving 130 tons of granite and limestone. As the first stage neared completion in 1963, the trustees issued their first-ever "Year-End Appeal" to museum members, asking for help to meet the extraordinary costs of the project. By 1966 (when Lowell sought refuge from the Hilles show by fleeing to the Old Kingdom), the job had been completed.[24]

The 1960s were a time of dramatic change at the museum, both physically and financially, and Lowell was at the center of it. Not only did many galleries undergo facelifts, but the first new additions to the building since 1927 were constructed. And the museum broke new ground in the way it raised the funds to carry on its work.

During the early 1960s the museum had been bringing in more than 730,000 people a year. Faced with continuing deficits in the operating budget, the trustees decided in February 1966 to tap this flood by instituting a general admission charge of fifty cents. The Museum had charged admission when it opened in 1876, with the exception of four days each month when entry was free. (The free days were stipulated in the agreement with the City of Boston by which the museum acquired title to its first home in Copley Square.) However, the sums collected never amounted to more than a tiny fraction of the museum's expenses, and in the spirit of unity fostered by World War I the fee was abolished in January 1918. In the 1950s and early 1960s, the museum charged only for special exhibitions.[25]

The new charge went into effect on July 5, 1966, and Lowell was present when the museum doors opened. "I thought it would help the morale of the Museum if I were there, just as a symbol in case anything happened," he wrote. The president's presence turned out to be a public relations triumph. He had his picture taken with the first paying visitors—two teenage girls—and was interviewed by a reporter for a local television station. The next morning's *Globe* carried the picture, and a column published a few days later put the spotlight not on the new fee but on Lowell. His attendance, the writer declared, was

> characteristic of the man and his clan. If there were going to be any beefs
> about the admission charge, he as chairman of the trustees, who made the

decision, was going to be there to listen to them and to explain them. In a lot of enterprises this unpleasant chore would have been turned over to the salaried director of the Museum or to a public relations man. The Lowells don't operate that way, and between talking to the Cabots and, indirectly, with God, seem also to find the time to talk to John Q.

Patronage did decline by 100,000 visits during the next year, but this was less than the 25 percent drop-off that had been feared.[26]

As bold a step as imposing an admission fee was, it generated only hundreds of thousands in income when the museum needed millions. During the 1870s the museum's original board of trustees had made a successful appeal to the general public for funds to construct the Copley Square building, but none of the subsequent boards had conducted a broad-based campaign for money. Believing that such efforts would be demeaning and might undermine their control, the trustees preferred to rely upon the generosity of a small number of individuals—usually themselves—to finance the museum. This policy reinforced the widespread perception of the museum as, in Rathbone's words, "a private institution catering to the privileged few, a kind of culture club for Boston Brahmins, which they almost alone supported."[27]

With his show-business approach, Rathbone had removed some of the barriers separating the museum from the public; yet the very crowds that he attracted added to the museum's operating expenses. When he presented the board in 1961 with his ambitious plans for expanding the museum, Rathbone forced the trustees to recognize that their traditional fund-raising methods were inadequate to the demands of the museum's future.[28]

The museum's hundredth anniversary was to be celebrated in 1970, and in 1964 the board established the Centennial Development Fund to seek $13.4 million from the public. Lowell chaired the committee responsible for getting the campaign under way; in addition to helping choose a professional fund-raising firm for consultation, he had to find a permanent chairman for the fund and solicit contributions from his fellow trustees. Despite his long experience with responsibilities of this sort, Lowell found it to be an ordeal.

The Centennial Development Fund opened its office in one of the museum's temporary exhibition galleries in August 1965, but it was not until the following February that it had a chairman. Lowell looked on and off the board for a leader, but as one trustee put it, "a 'drive' was so completely foreign to the practices and temperament of the Museum . . . that it was not easy to find among its existing trustees and long-time supporters any-one who was eager, or even willing and able, to assume" the post. The board eventually turned to George C. Seybolt, a New Yorker who had come to Boston after World War II and quickly worked his way to the presidency of the Underwood canned-food company. Seybolt had joined the Visiting Committee of the Department of Decorative Arts and Sculp-ture in 1964. Given his background and short association with the mu-seum, his selection to chair the drive was most unusual. Elected a trustee just about the time he accepted the job, Seybolt proved to be a dynamo, fully capable of energizing a force of eight hundred volunteers. Even so, he succeeded in raising only $10 million of the $13.4 million goal (the for-mer being the figure Lowell had initially thought possible).[29]

Lowell reached the $1.5 million goal that had been set for contributions from trustees—giving $50,000 himself—but only after a great deal of anx-iety and disappointment. He believed that the board had let him down badly, and out of this experience he lent his support to a revamping of its membership. Future trustees would be selected not merely for their ap-preciation of art but for their willingness to donate money themselves or to raise funds from elsewhere.[30]

As he neared his seventy-seventh birthday in the spring of 1967, Lowell decided to step down from the presidency when his term expired the fol-lowing February. The museum had become the center of his activities over the previous two years, and he was exhausted. As president he had played a prominent role in the big kick-off dinner for the Centennial De-velopment Fund held in January 1967, and now that the drive was well un-der way he felt the time had come for "a younger man to take over." The person Lowell wanted to succeed him turned him down on grounds of poor health, and as a stopgap, Seybolt agreed to take the job.[31]

Lowell's seventeen years as president formally ended on February 15, 1968, and the newspapers evaluated his tenure by a recital of statistics. Membership had climbed sevenfold, attendance had risen by more than 40 percent, and the number of education programs had more than doubled. In his annual report, Rathbone also relied heavily on impressive numbers (although he used 1955 as his base) and went on to observe that Lowell's tenure had seen "immense changes in the Museum's outlook and charac-ter." The changes, he continued, "could not have been accomplished with-out Mr. Lowell's leadership, his liberalism, his benign and generous spirit." Privately, Rathbone was even more effusive in his praise. He expressed gratitude in a letter to Lowell:

Your belief in me, my policies and innovations have given me the determination and the courage to pursue our programs of recreating the Museum for a new generation. Had I ever questioned your backing, I could
not have accomplished what I have. In exploring new avenues of development, new areas of support, your judgment of what was possible and
what was right, has always provided me with the sense of security essential to the task.[32]

If Rathbone and Lowell took satisfaction in the significant changes they
had wrought at the museum—in 1970 Rathbone received an honorary degree from Boston College for remaking "the Old Lady of Huntington Avenue into a liberated Woman"—the years immediately leading up to and
following the museum's centennial demonstrated how difficult it was for
an old-line institution to keep pace with a dramatically changing Boston.
Holding the freshly minted title of President Emeritus, Lowell was more
of an observer than a participant in the events of the early 1970s. But to a
large extent it was his leadership that was being judged during that period—and judged harshly.[33]

In mid-March 1970 Lowell, Rathbone, and the trustees waited in the
museum's boardroom for a group of black artists to appear. Showing up
half an hour late for the meeting they had requested, the artists pressed demands for a separate curator of black art, three galleries, and a $100,000
annual budget under their control. Overall, Lowell calculated, they wanted
the museum to spend $7 million as reparations for a "century of nonrep-
resentation" in its collections and administration. Lowell, who noted that
the group's leader kept his beret on ("a symbol of disrespect for us all"),
was not impressed: "We have paintings by blacks, and I have never heard
the question of the color of the artist when we like a picture."[34]

This was not the museum's first brush with the growing activism in
Boston's black community. Two years earlier, in response to complaints
that it was ignoring local black artists, the museum had hired a part-time curatorial aide to help organize exhibitions for Elma Lewis's Afro-American
Center for the Arts in Roxbury. A few weeks after the confrontation with
the black artists, the museum held a show, previously scheduled, entitled
"Afro-American Artists: New York and Boston." It attracted only a modest turnout, especially in comparison with the crowds that thronged the
show by Andrew Wyeth (Lowell's favorite contemporary artist) a few
weeks later. Precisely what and how much the museum could do to forge
links to Boston's growing black population was by no means clear.[35]

In a display of the guilt that plagued liberal and elite consciences during this period, an ad hoc committee of the museum board prepared, and the trustees accepted, a report in the fall of 1970 that belittled what Rathbone had worked toward and accomplished over the previous fifteen years. The museum, the report declared, continued to be seen as a "rich, austere, acquisitive, dignified and not particularly welcoming institution, deeply representative of the Boston 'establishment,' culturally, financially and socially." Without supplying specific examples of how it was to be accomplished, the report called upon the museum to "penetrate more deeply into the lives of the people of Boston and take a larger part in the life of the city." [36]

The trustees' committee assigned no blame in describing the museum's failures, but a February 1972 article in the *Boston Globe* pulled no punches. Rathbone came in for most of the criticism; his beguiling charm, the author charged, hid his lack of administrative skills. The director's policy of aggressive acquisition and popular exhibitions had overtaxed the museum's capabilities, both financial and managerial; the museum "loom[ed] up as a great rigid lumbering institution, a huge turtle carrying its shell wherever it [went]." As harshly as the article treated Rathbone, more remarkable was its censure of the museum's former president for allowing the director to plow on unchecked. Lowell, according to the author, belonged to the "somnolent school, the backseat Brahmin boards that chaired Boston's institutions in the days of the city's economic eclipse." Never before had Lowell been attacked in the press, and how ironic that it involved a place where he had stood for change. Having spent a lifetime making adjustments to the present, it hurt Lowell to be tagged (in his words) a "Brahmin reactionary." [37]

MASSACHUSETTS GENERAL HOSPITAL

As president of the Museum of Fine Arts Lowell functioned with a maximum of publicity: His name and picture appeared frequently in the newspapers as the museum held gala openings for its new exhibitions. At the Massachusetts General Hospital (M.G.H.), on the other hand, Lowell toiled in relative obscurity, helping one of the world's great medical facilities continue its pioneering work in teaching, research, and patient care. It was just as well for his reputation that his M.G.H. duties attracted little attention, for while he helped move the hospital forward, his duties also caused him great frustration.

The Lowell family had a long association with the hospital. While some of Boston's first families, such as the Warrens, Shattucks, Bigelows, and Homanses, established virtual dynasties on the hospital's medical staff, the Lowells sat in the boardroom. John Lowell (1769–1840) was an original incorporator in 1811, and Ralph's great-grandfather, grandfather, and father all served as trustees. Election to the M.G.H. board was unquestionably the most prestigious honor that Ralph's father received, and Ralph's own election in 1940 represented his breakthrough into the higher echelons of Boston trusteeship. His candidacy had been advanced by one of his parents' Chestnut Hill neighbors, who shared his father's passion for raising special breeds of hens.[38]*

Composed of twelve members, the M.G.H. Board of Trustees was a small group by the standard of most nonprofit organizations.† Successful lawyers and businessmen typically filled the ranks of the elected trustees, along with a sprinkling of physicians. This was no sinecure; unlike many other institutions, where the "doctors run the hospital and the trustees run the errands," policy making, as well as many administrative details, was very much in the hands of the trustees.[39]

The board met on alternate Fridays from September through June and once a month during the summer. Sessions began punctually at 9 A.M., and during the next hour the trustees would work their way through an agenda of committee reports. Until government agencies began insisting on thorough recordkeeping, the board seldom bothered with the formality of voting. Almost all decisions were arrived at by consensus, sometimes with delays until unanimity could be achieved.[40]

In nearly thirty years on the board, Lowell dealt with a variety of assignments. He managed merger talks with other hospitals, negotiated labor contracts with unions, kept long-winded doctors from dominating

---

* Lowell's Harvard classmate and roommate Francis C. Gray was also a trustee, as was Phillips Ketchum, a partner in Robert Herrick's law firm.

† Eight of the members were elected by the self-perpetuating M.G.H. Corporation and held office until resignation or death; four were appointed by the governor for annual terms. While the latter group was of uneven quality—it often included the chief executive's personal physician—it also included, through the end of Lowell's tenure, the only female, Jewish, and black trustees.

and prolonging the meetings of the Committee on Research (composed of trustees and doctors), oversaw the construction of several new buildings at M.G.H.'s main campus in Boston's West End, and supervised the preparation of the hospital's post–World War II planning report. To find the money to pay for M.G.H.'s ambitious expansion schemes, Lowell enlisted the talents of David C. Crockett. Initially hired in 1946 on a temporary basis to organize the hundredth anniversary celebration of Ether Day (marking the first use of anesthesia—an M.G.H. discovery), Crockett proved an indefatigable fund-raiser. He retired officially in 1974 but more than two decades later was still visiting the hospital regularly and keeping an eye out for potential donors.[41]

In banking Lowell had a well-deserved reputation as a conservative, but when it came to M.G.H.'s finances he was anything but. To the amazement of his fellow trustees, Lowell advocated borrowing to improve the hospital's facilities. The other trustees thought the idea unworkable because no bank would lend money to a nonprofit institution whose assets did not satisfy legal definitions of adequate collateral. But Lowell argued that the hospital's steady stream of contributions and bequests was always adequate to ensure that the "well . . . would fill up again." The naysayers prevailed until the late 1960s—just as Lowell was preparing to step down from the board—when new laws made hospitals more attractive to lenders and investors.[42]

Lowell pushed two other visionary ideas that came to fruition much later. The first was improving M.G.H.'s ambulatory care services. Lowell was one of a group of trustees and doctors who believed that upgrading the hospital's outpatient clinics would not only improve M.G.H.'s financial condition but also bind its physicians closer to the hospital for the benefit of the community. In the early 1950s the hospital studied prepaid insurance plans and organized group practices, among other options, but most doctors were averse to such radical arrangements. It was not until the 1970s and 1980s that M.G.H. constructed a modern ambulatory care facility and adopted managed health care.[43]

Lowell's other bold notion was not realized until the 1990s. Boston had several fine hospitals, but only the Peter Bent Brigham Hospital shared M.G.H.'s world-class status. Both teaching affiliates of the Harvard Medical School, the two institutions competed for research funds and developed overlapping specialties in patient care. In early 1950, citing the goals of "avoiding duplication and increased efficiency," Lowell proposed to Harvard president James Bryant Conant that the Brigham be "consolidated" with M.G.H. in the West End. Already thinking about leaving Harvard, Conant was not about to tackle this radical suggestion, especially when it met a cool response from both M.G.H. president Francis Gray and Brigham president Robert Cutler. Lowell pressed no further but anticipated that the "seed I planted may possibly bear fruit later on." His kernels were forgotten, but in 1993, when the American health care system was in the midst of revolutionary change, M.G.H. and the Brigham's successor, Brigham and Women's Hospital, announced their intention to combine many of their operations. Although the two institutions would retain their separate identities and elaborate campuses, they expected significant cost savings from the elimination of redundancies.[44]

From 1946 until he became an honorary trustee in 1968, Lowell chaired the M.G.H. board's McLean Hospital Committee. Located on several hundred green acres in suburban Belmont, McLean was M.G.H.'s primary unit for treatment of the mentally ill. While the lush surroundings supplied a salutary setting for treatment, McLean's geographic isolation and the failure of psychiatry to match the advances made by physical medicine in that era made McLean something of an administrative stepchild. Lowell thought M.G.H. shortchanged McLean both in funding and in the quality of the staff it sent there; the trustees usually devoted no more than five minutes of their biweekly meetings to McLean's affairs.[45]

Even before assuming the chairmanship, Lowell feared that McLean was resting on past laurels rather than operating on the frontiers of medical science. On the advice of friends at the Harvard Medical School, Lowell persuaded the M.G.H. trustees in 1944 to promote brain research as a means of restoring McLean's lost luster, and he shepherded through the Hyams Trust an application for $50,000 to build a new laboratory. The laboratory opened in the spring of 1946.[46]

The research facility proved a mixed blessing for Lowell. On the one hand it fulfilled his hope of making McLean once again an institution that mental illness experts would cite when discussing advances in their field. On the other hand, it became a constant source of headaches for Lowell because administrators responsible for patient care resented the funds and attention lavished on the research scientists. The chemical experiments performed in the laboratory were not tied to the daily clinical work carried out by the psychiatrists; indeed, a solid case could be made that there was no reason to locate the laboratory at McLean except to benefit the institution's image. Lowell was, naturally, protective of the laboratory, and he accepted the chore of smoothing out disagreements.[47] *

What McLean lacked for much of Lowell's tenure as chairman was dynamic professional leadership, such as Rathbone brought to the Museum of Fine Arts. Lowell was unimpressed with the medical director he inherited, and when the director was obliged to resign in 1948 because of a sex scandal, eight years passed before the selection of his permanent replacement, Dr. Alfred H. Stanton. Prior to accepting the directorship, Stanton had prepared a devastating report detailing the hospital's woes: too few psychiatrists; no social workers, vocational counselors, or rehabilitation experts; no group therapy; and a research program "seriously skewed" in favor of chemical and physiological studies to the detriment of the psychological and social sciences. Over the next six years Stanton made significant strides in overcoming these deficiencies, but he was a poor administrator and McLean's financial accounts went badly into the red. In 1963 the trustees forced Stanton out and appointed as their new director Dr. Francis de Marneffe, a McLean staff psychiatrist.[48]

With de Marneffe, a skilled manager and an adept player of bureaucratic politics, McLean finally found leadership and stability; he would remain in the post for a quarter century. In order to increase the hospital's income and improve its training of doctors during their psychiatric residency, de Marneffe proposed to raise patient charges substantially, admit only patients with a reasonable chance of being cured, and encourage those already in long-term care to seek custodial assistance elsewhere. Although Lowell could see the advantages of de Marneffe's strategy, it pained him to contemplate McLean's losing its historic role as the refuge for Boston's best families. The implementation of the director's proposals moved slowly during Lowell's last years on the M.G.H. board. To win wholehearted support for his new approach, de Marneffe would have to wait for the installation of Lowell's successor as McLean Hospital Committee chairman, his younger cousin George Putnam.[49]

---

* Lowell served as a sort of mother hen for the laboratory's brilliant Catalan director, Jordi Folch-Pi. Because Folch-Pi's English was often incomprehensible, Lowell not only ran interference for him in administrative matters but also looked after details of his personal life. In 1976 the lower two floors of McLean's expanded research center were named in Lowell's honor.

12

"They ought to be planning to take over the Herald*"*

BUSINESS DIRECTORSHIPS

S urveys conducted by Standard & Poor's in 1965 and again in 1966 and 1967 named Ralph Lowell as the "nation's busiest corporate executive." Well beyond his seventieth birthday, past the age when many men have been retired for a decade, Lowell was serving on the boards of more than forty organizations.[1] But if the title Standard & Poor's bestowed upon Lowell was imposing, it was also misleading. Most of the directorships Lowell held were of charitable groups; of his associations with business enterprises, scarcely a handful absorbed more than a token amount of his time. As was demonstrated by his being passed over for the board of AT&T, Lowell did not play in the major leagues of American capitalism.

Lowell's only directorship of a national corporation was at the John Hancock Mutual Life Insurance Company. Yet even with policyholders all over the country, the insurance giant was very much a Boston institution. Its board was dominated by Bostonians, and Lowell and his brethren took a hometown outlook in guiding its operations. John Hancock was much more likely to commit money to risky local projects such as the refinancing of South Station, construction of the Boston Common garage, and a housing development in the West End than to similar projects in other cities. The local projects were seen as necessary investments in Boston's future.[2]

The close ties between John Hancock and Boston's elite caused the company great embarrassment in the early 1950s. In 1945 a Dallas promoter persuaded scores of wealthy Bostonians ("The list of people . . . reads like the vestry of the Arlington Street Church," observed one business magazine) to invest more than $8 million in several oil-producing ventures. A new firm, the Texmass Petroleum Company, was incorporated to manage the properties located in the Lone Star State, and in 1947 Texmass borrowed $3.5 million from John Hancock and $4 million from another Massachusetts-based insurance company. Texmass could not get the oil flowing, however, even after the infusion of another $1 million from the Boston investors. By the close of 1948 it was clear that Texmass was going to be a costly loss for all concerned. Lowell, whose absence from the investment group may have been the fortuitous consequence of his not having any spare funds to put in, could afford to be smug. "It is another case of a lot of amateurs thinking they know something about the oil business," Lowell noted privately, "which they evidently did not."[3]

A congressional investigation threw an unwanted spotlight on the bad debt on John Hancock's ledgers. The managers of Texmass had sought a $10 million loan from the federal Reconstruction Finance Corporation, and in 1949 the R.F.C., ignoring the statements Texmass had filed with the Securities and Exchange Commission indicating that the company was unlikely to make any money, had approved the request. In the spring of 1950, a Senate subcommittee investigating allegations of widespread corruption and favoritism at the R.F.C. spent a day collecting public testimony about the Texmass loan. The mess was now out in the open and the pressure was on John Hancock to admit its errors and offer some sacrificial lambs.[4]

Lowell and his fellow directors would not bend. Because he had not been on the investments committee when the Texmass loan was voted, Lowell was not a direct target of the finger-pointing, but he refused to be part of any vigilante action. There were, in fact, some avenues of escape for John Hancock from its financial commitment to Texmass; however, the board refused to take any of them, even after being requested by the Senate subcommittee's chairman to do so. While John Hancock's backing out of the Texmass deal would have served the Senator's purpose of "getting the R.F.C. off the hook," it would also, as Lowell observed, have left John Hancock "tagged as withdrawing from a moral obligation and letting down over 300 Boston investors who stand to lose a great deal of money." The directors "voted to stand by our guns."[5]

John Hancock's brush with national politics passed quickly (the corruption at the R.F.C. was part of a larger phenomenon known as the "Truman Scandals"), but the loan to Texmass also ignited a policyholders' suit against the directors for violation of their fiduciary duties. The directors, it was alleged, had made the loans to "close friends, relatives, and business associates solely for the purpose of bailing [them] out." Again, the board held its ground; it issued a statement in January 1951 absolving the committee members of any wrongdoing. Lowell wrote, "I am satisfied proper precautions were taken and that it was a proper loan to make, but was a little worried about the hard work we had at getting all the facts." At John Hancock's annual meeting in February, the policyholders endorsed the board's statement; in November, Federal District Court Judge Charles E. Wyzanski, Lowell's once-and-future colleague on the Harvard Board of Overseers, dismissed the suit on procedural grounds.[6]

If Lowell stood by his peers in the public controversy over Texmass, he clashed in private with some of them over John Hancock's general investment strategy. Known for its prudent management of policyholder premiums, John Hancock traditionally had placed almost all of its funds in government bonds; in public utility, industrial, and railroad bonds; and in real estate mortgages. But these fixed-return investments were not keeping pace with inflation in the late 1940s, and John Hancock began putting more of its money into corporate stocks. State regulations permitted—but certainly did not encourage—acquiring such assets, and John Hancock proceeded with great caution on this new tack.[7]

Lowell was an enthusiastic supporter of the equities-buying program. "I believe one can be a real conservative and still invest in common stocks," he declared in 1948, but several John Hancock directors disagreed. Whenever the market took "a little drop," they got "cold feet" and wanted the company to pull back on its purchasing plan; whenever the market went up, they wanted to cash in the profits. Lowell preferred a steady, long-term policy in regard to stocks. The total investment was small—amounting to 2 to 5 percent of the company's funds—but his stance tagged him as one of the bolder members of the board.[8]

At the Amoskeag Company, where Lowell held another directorship, he provided a restraining influence, but to little effect. Originally established in the mid-nineteenth century as a textile manufacturer, by the 1940s Amoskeag had shed its factory operations and become an investment trust, which took over corporations that captured the fancy of its longtime chief executive, Frederick C. Dumaine. At first glance Dumaine was an unlikely person for Lowell to link up with. Dumaine's buccaneerish techniques made him a reviled figure among employees and most stockholders of the companies with which he was involved; furthermore, given his French-Canadian heritage, he was, as *Fortune* noted, an "improper Bostonian." But a "Proper" Bostonian had given Dumaine his start when he was in his teens, and Dumaine liked to stock his board with Brahmins, who were quite happy to oblige him. When Lowell joined the Amoskeag board in 1947, he found "a nice crowd of old-line Bostonians" that included the venerable Charles Francis Adams; two of Lowell's former partners at Lee, Higginson; and George Peabody Gardner, once A. Lawrence Lowell's private secretary and now a director of AT&T and General Electric.[9]

The eighty-year-old Dumaine, Lowell observed after attending his first Amoskeag directors' meeting in 1947, "is the whole works and the trustees almost all rubber stamps." It was not unusual for these sessions, of which there were only four a year, to be wrapped up in fifteen minutes. It was typical of Dumaine's "autocratic" ways that when he engineered what was arguably the biggest coup of his career—seizing control of the New Haven Railroad in 1948—Lowell found out about it in the newspapers.[10]

Dumaine held his power to the end (he was chief executive from 1905 to 1951). Although he looked more and more like an "Egyptian mummy," he continued to run Amoskeag "the way he wants to and takes no suggestions." But Lowell had to concede in January 1951, "[S]o far he has managed it extremely well." Dumaine died in his sleep that May after spending a busy day on the telephone transacting business. Learning of Dumaine's passing, Lowell described him as "perhaps the last of the old 'barons.'" "His rise was rapid, and though considered ruthless by many and heartily disliked by his labor, he did have a managerial genius and saved many large New England situations—then selling out to others who afterward were not so successful. . . . I was fond of the old man—he was a fighter and never gave up."[11]

Dumaine's anointed successor was his son, Frederic C. (Buck) Dumaine Jr. Like his father, Buck got ahead without benefit of a college diploma; after flunking Harvard's entrance examination, he received his business education as "Dad's errand boy." But if the elder Dumaine had been "full of vitriol" and "hate[d] publicity as heartily as he hate[d] operating deficits," Buck, who was forty-eight when his father died, adopted the persona of a modern corporation executive. "I am young enough and can smile enough to do things a little smoother," he told *Time* in the spring of 1951.[12]

Whatever his public style, Dumaine tried to dominate the Amoskeag board in the manner of his father. After one 1953 meeting Lowell wrote that "Buck told us nothing as per usual." After another he observed that

"Amoskeag is probably the most rubber stamp committee on which I serve." However, after Amoskeag lost control of the New Haven in 1954 following a tough proxy fight, Dumaine faced a palace revolt: Two of the trustees resigned to protest his failure to consult with the board's executive committee. Lowell, who had come to the session prepared to quit, decided to remain after Dumaine promised to "mend his ways." [13]

Resignation was frequently in Lowell's mind from 1956 onward as he watched Dumaine try to make Avis Rent-a-Car a profitable competitor to the dominant Hertz system. Lowell doubted Dumaine could pull it off, and he was enraged by Dumaine's neglecting to keep the board fully informed. Once, when Lowell expressed his frustration at a trustees meeting, Dumaine came to his office the next day to apologize. Dumaine's display of remorse and his pledge to treat the trustees better soothed Lowell's feelings, but Lowell was a realist: "I am afraid this will only last for a few months," he wrote. As it turned out, Dumaine kept his word, but the news he reported was dismal. Lowell contemplated leaving on several occasions, but always decided against it because he did not want to be seen as "desert[ing] under fire." Finally, in 1962 Amoskeag sold its controlling stake in Avis, absorbing a $2.25 million loss.[14]*

Lowell did not resign from the Amoskeag board until nine years later, in the fall of 1971. During those nine years he opposed several of Dumaine's proposed deals, particularly those involving New England railroads. He thought about leaving but always decided against it because he liked Dumaine personally and wanted to perform the useful function of critic of Dumaine's plans. By the late 1960s his reason for staying was that he had "resigned from so many things that I do not have enough to do." The strain of trying to curb Dumaine finally proved too much, however, and Lowell decided to get out "before something unfortunate happens." He retained only one business directorship.[15]

THE *BOSTON GLOBE*

Lowell's last business directorship was also his most important. He had held it since March 1949, when the two surviving trustees of the Eben D.

---

* Under new management, Avis went on to become one of the great success stories of the 1960s. Its "We Try Harder" advertising campaign remains a classic, and in 1965 ITT purchased Avis for $36 million, about six times the amount Amoskeag had received three years earlier.

Jordan estate invited him to fill the opening in their ranks. Set up during the 1890s, the Jordan trust held several parcels of Boston commercial real estate and a half-interest in the *Boston Globe*. The trust sold the land and buildings within a decade of Lowell's becoming a trustee, but still held the investment in the *Globe*—vastly increased in value—when Lowell resigned after more than a quarter century on the board. Unlike Lowell's other estate trusteeships, this one required Lowell to become directly involved in the running of a business because of the Jordan estate's large stake in the newspaper. This assumption of responsibility could not have come at a more dramatic moment: Boston's newspapers, like those in other cities, were entering an era of momentous demographic and technological change. In the early 1960s the *Globe* emerged as front-runner in the bitterly contested Boston market, and by the 1970s the paper had become the most important medium of news and opinion in the region.

The *Globe*, which first hit the streets in 1872, was the handiwork of two men: Eben D. Jordan and Charles H. Taylor. One of the great pioneering retail merchants of the second half of the nineteenth century—his Jordan Marsh department store was New England's largest—Jordan was an original investor in the *Globe*. When it teetered on the brink of bankruptcy a year after its founding, he bought up all the stock and put in additional capital to keep it going. Taylor's political and journalistic experience proved to be a perfect complement to Jordan's financial resources. "My aim," Taylor declared later, "has been to make the *Globe* a cheerful, attractive and useful newspaper that would enter the home as a kindly, helpful friend of the family." In striving to reach a family- and home-centered audience, rather than the customary male- and office-based readership of nineteenth-century daily newspapers, Taylor was an innovator. Features attractive to women and children became staples of the *Globe*, as did extensive coverage of neighborhood clubs and social events. Taylor realized that people liked to see their names in the paper, and the *Globe* did its best to satisfy them. While other newspapers gave big play to foreign datelines, the *Globe* preferred to print stories about the people next door. When Lowell joined the *Globe*'s board, Taylor's disciples were still publishing a paper that read more like a small-town weekly than a large metropolitan daily. "In a city as self-centered as any parish," declared a media critic in 1944, "the *Globe* was as parochial as it knew how to be." [16]

Taylor made the *Globe* a profitable enterprise, and before the merchant's death in 1895 Jordan rewarded him by allowing him to purchase a half-interest in the newspaper. In his will, Jordan named Taylor one of the three trustees of his estate and "suggest[ed]" to the trustees that the estate's 50 percent share in the *Globe* "be retained . . . as a permanent investment." By the time Lowell became a trustee in 1949, the relationship between the *Globe* and the Jordan estate had been firmly established. Management of the paper rested with Charles Taylor and later with his son, William O. Taylor. Upon the elder Taylor's death in 1921, W.O. (as he was known) also succeeded him as a Jordan trustee and in that position helped select other trustees as vacancies occurred. Trustees of the estate served on the *Globe's* board of directors, for which they received no compensation, and where they rarely questioned the Taylors' decisions. The Jordan estate received half the company's dividends, but for all intents and purposes the *Globe* was the Taylors' to run.[17]

What the Taylors put out, the *New York Times* noted somewhat condescendingly in 1921, was a "popular newspaper." The *Globe* was aimed at the broadest segment of the market: the middle class, the upper part of the lower class, and the lower part of the upper class. Charles Taylor's success in reaching these groups had made his paper, the same *New York Times* editorial observed, "a very valuable property." By midcentury, however, the *Globe* faced an uncertain future. Some of the difficulties it confronted were common to newspapers nationally, such as the development of television, the spread of suburbia, and rising labor costs, but others were peculiar to Boston.[18]

The biggest threat to the *Globe's* well-being was the intensity of the competition it faced (see Table 1); only in New York City, with a circulation area four times as large, were there so many papers. The winnowing had already begun. The century-old *Evening Transcript,* the paper delivered to homes on Beacon Hill and in the Back Bay, staggered through the Depression decade and gave up in 1941. At the other side of the spectrum, the sensationalistic *Post,* which in 1918 claimed the highest circulation (540,000) of any morning paper in the country, saw its sales decline sharply as its lower-class Irish readership climbed the economic ladder. The family trust that owned the *Post* made no secret that it was seeking a buyer for the money-losing paper. The popular, syndicated feature–laden *Record, American,* and *Sunday Advertiser* were only marginal earners; as the New England outposts of the Hearst empire, their primary purpose was to promote the newspaper mogul's political views.[19]

For the *Globe,* the huge newsstand sales of the Hearst sheets were less of a worry than the challenge for dominance of the middle-class market presented by the *Herald* and the *Traveler,* which were published by the

Herald-Traveler Corporation. Although the evening *Traveler* brought in the higher profits of the two, it was the morning and Sunday *Herald* that was known for editorial excellence. Founded in 1846, the *Herald* reached a more refined audience than the other Boston papers. It won two Pulitzer prizes during the 1920s and gained two more in the post–World War II era for its editorials on foreign policy and national defense. The *Herald* was, not surprisingly, the Boston newspaper Ralph Lowell read every morning.[20]

TABLE 1
CIRCULATION OF BOSTON'S NEWSPAPERS, 1949

	Morning	Evening	Sunday
Advertiser	—	—	682,000
American	—	190,000	—
Globe	117,500	163,500	392,000
Herald	127,500	—	249,000
Post	338,500	—	276,000
Record	380,000	—	—
Traveler	—	222,500	—

Source: *Editor and Publisher Market Guide, 1950*

Unlike the other papers, which were controlled by people with journalism in their blood, the *Herald* was owned by businessmen who saw it as an investment. Sidney Winslow, chairman of the board of the United Shoe Machinery Corporation, one of Boston's largest companies, owned 23 percent of the Herald-Traveler stock. The First National Bank of Boston voted sizable blocks of stock, and other individuals with close ties to Winslow and First National also held substantial chunks. The stockholders expected the *Herald* to pay healthy dividends and to expound the views of "sound business interests," which put a priority on lower taxes at every level of government. To carry out these policies, in 1940 Winslow and his associates handed management of the *Herald* to Robert B. (Beanie) Choate.[21]

Most sketches of Choate's career at the *Herald* point out that he worked his way up from reporter to Washington correspondent, to managing editor, and finally to publisher. What is often overlooked is that, able and aggressive as he was, Choate did not climb to the top solely by his own talents. His father, Charles F. Choate, founder of the prestigious Boston law firm of Choate, Hall & Stewart, had successfully defended United Shoe Machinery in a major antitrust suit filed by the federal government. Robert, after graduating from St. Mark's School, starting at Harvard, and serving in the army in France during World War I, began his career at the *Herald* in 1920 at the age of twenty-one; the paper was his consuming passion until his death forty-three years later.[22]

Choate's *Herald* operated very differently from the Taylors' *Globe*. The Taylors steered clear of controversies, particularly local ones, on their editorial page. The *Herald* was outspoken on a wide range of issues; it kept up a barrage of criticism of Mayor James Michael Curley and attacked the book and stage censorship that made Boston a laughingstock across the country. The *Globe* was known as a somewhat paternalistic organization, where employees, once hired, almost never were fired; at the *Herald* Choate constantly pushed and prodded his staff, contributing to a high turnover rate. And while the Taylors were under little pressure from the Jordan beneficiaries and trustees to increase profits, Choate's stockholders demanded good returns. Consequently, Choate's personal ambition to play the kingmaker's role in Massachusetts Republican politics depended on his ability to maintain a steady flow of black ink. In the late 1940s Choate concluded that Boston was oversupplied with newspapers and that the best way to ensure the *Herald*'s future was to forge a cooperative relationship with the *Globe*.[23]

Choate's tentative and vague proposals to merge the *Herald* and the *Globe* in some fashion met a cool response from W. O. Taylor. Although he usually cited concerns that any such combination would expose the *Globe* to damage suits from other newspapers under the antitrust laws, Taylor's objections were more personal. He did not trust Choate or his business associates, and he cherished the *Globe*'s independence. It was because of his financial acumen that W.O. was his father's chosen successor, but W.O. was also a traditionalist. In 1929, when it seemed that the *Herald* would fall into the hands of a powerful, New York–based corporation, W.O. had issued a statement declaring that the *Globe* was not for sale: "The *Globe* is a New England institution. My father left it in trust for me and I shall keep that trust for my heirs." Twenty years later, when Choate came calling, Taylor's position had not changed. Around the same time Taylor also turned down Joseph Kennedy, who hoped to merge the *Globe* and the *Post*.[24]

For W.O. and his son, Davis (who was a *Globe* director and increasingly shared his father's managerial duties), the critical problem facing the *Globe* was the need for a new plant to house its editorial offices and printing presses. At midcentury the *Globe* occupied the same building on Newspaper Row (along Washington Street) where it had opened for business nearly eight decades earlier. The purchase of adjacent structures over the years had provided additional workspace, but the setup (a "rabbit warren," as Lowell described it) was inefficient and costly. The *Herald* had moved into new quarters in 1931, and with more modern mechanical equipment was able to produce a paper that was both larger than the *Globe* and typographically more pleasing. These advantages helped the *Herald* augment its circulation while the *Globe*'s stagnated. The downtown location also hampered distribution of the *Globe* to a readership increasingly fanned out over the metropolitan region.[25]

W. O. Taylor appreciated the need for a new building, but—like Lowell—he was not one to act hastily. Although he had been putting funds aside for years to pay for it, he knew that the astronomical sums required would force the *Globe* to seek outside financing for the first time since his father and Eben Jordan had recapitalized the company in the mid-1870s. W.O. did not relish the prospect, and he postponed it until he thought the time was right. When at a May 1950 directors meeting a proposal was made that plans be drawn up for a new building, Taylor was "dead set against it," arguing that the newspaper business in Boston was too uncertain for the *Globe* to put itself into debt. All of the papers had lost circulation in the postwar period, and although the *Globe*'s advertising showed gains, higher operating costs were putting a strain on profits. Taylor knew the *Post* was losing money hand over fist and wanted to see what happened to that competitor before committing the *Globe* to huge loans.[26]

Lowell agreed with Taylor. He realized that the *Globe*'s obsolete facilities were a serious drag on earnings, but felt that W.O. was doing a remarkable job of coping with the problem. "The *Globe*," Lowell observed, "is an exceptionally well-run paper." Rather than plunge the *Globe* into expensive and risky construction, he preferred to pursue another line of action.[27]

What Lowell wanted was "getting together with the *Herald*." The *Herald*'s profits had fallen off markedly in the postwar years, although they remained higher than the *Globe*'s, and Lowell envisioned a deal that would put the Taylors pretty much in "the driver's seat." Lowell vigorously championed the idea through the first half of the 1950s, but W. O. Taylor's opposition proved an intractable obstacle. "The old man [he was seventy-nine]," wrote Lowell in January 1951, "has been through so many battles with the other papers during his long life that he cannot see any good in any of them."²⁸

Lowell continued to meet with Choate on an irregular basis about the prospects for an agreement, as he had done since becoming a director. However, resigned to the fact that a *Herald* merger was out of the question as long as W.O. remained active, Lowell went along with the slow-moving plans for a new *Globe* facility. In 1953 the paper began assembling parcels of land in Dorchester along the Southeast Expressway, then under construction, and purchased another building adjacent to the Washington Street complex to make the *Globe*'s holdings more attractive to a future buyer. With his father's blessing, Davis Taylor visited recently constructed plants in other cities to gather ideas for the design of the *Globe*'s new building.²⁹

But Lowell remained allied with W.O. in opposing Davis Taylor's effort to win a definitive commitment to a new plant. If anything, the newspaper picture was more confused and dangerous in 1953–1954 than it had been at the start of the decade. The *Post* was about to fold. It had fallen into the hands of an aggressive, unpredictable, and underfinanced publisher, who seemed determined to take as many Boston papers down with him as he possibly could. In the face of this challenge, W.O. refused to magnify the *Globe*'s vulnerability by going into debt. For Lowell, the *Post* threat confirmed his belief that the *Globe* should not proceed on a multimillion dollar spending plan until it had explored "every possibility of combining with the *Herald*."³⁰

The *Globe* directors were at an impasse over the paper's future. For the first time in the newspaper's history, serious divisions surfaced between the Taylor and Jordan representatives on the board. Lowell became the pivotal figure in this conflict, but he was not its source. As a trustee and director he usually was willing to defer to a strong and capable chief executive, although without relinquishing his independence and right to criticize. He was disappointed by the Taylors' refusal to consider a merger with the *Herald* but was not about to contest W.O.'s leadership. He respected the "old man" too much to contemplate such behavior. Moreover, he hoped that after W.O. faded from the scene Davis Taylor would prove more responsive to his advice. So Lowell was prepared to bide his time, believing that the *Globe* was essentially the Taylors' to run. In this he differed from Sidney Davidson.

The first Jordan trustee with neither Boston roots nor family ties to the trust, Davidson—a New York lawyer specializing in trusts and estates, who had been chosen at the insistence of Eben Jordan's granddaughter—was not typical of the Taylors' business associates. Complicating their response to Davidson was his penchant for power. Davidson had difficulty playing second fiddle to anyone. The longstanding Jordan-Taylor relationship meant little to him; he continually pressed W.O. for more information on the *Globe*'s operations and looked for an opening that would allow him to push the Taylors aside.[31]

Lowell shared Davidson's desire for more data, but by the summer of 1953 he began to realize that Davidson wanted far more than that. Interrupting his Maine vacation to meet with Lowell in Boston, Davidson argued that W.O. was "breaking up" (referring to both his age and declining health) and that the Jordan trustees "should move into the *Globe* in a big way, and should be well paid for so doing." The *Globe* was something of an anomaly in that it paid its outside directors no fees (although Lowell and Davidson were compensated from the estate's income for their duties as Jordan trustees). In the fall of 1953 the board voted to begin paying such fees. The sum involved was nominal, but a clear precedent had been set.[32]

Although Lowell readily accepted the fees, he could see where Davidson was heading and it disturbed him greatly. Davidson knew "nothing about running a newspaper," and if he tried it "would be fatal for the *Globe*." The paper "should earn more money," Lowell wrote, "but the way to do it was to get back of the Taylor boys and help them." Believing that Davis and his cousin John Taylor (a *Globe* director since the beginning of 1954) could not function "with Sidney snapping at them all the while," Lowell came reluctantly to the conclusion that sale of the Jordan estate's *Globe* stock was the only solution. Davidson, lacking Lowell's support for a coup against the Taylors, became a strong advocate of selling. In May 1954 Davidson informed W.O., Davis, and John Taylor that the Jordan trustees and the Taylors could not continue to run the *Globe* together, and that "one should sell out to the other."[33]

Unhappy with having his hand forced by Davidson's behavior, Lowell sought additional grounds on which to justify divestiture to himself—without much success. A review of the financial projections for the new building revealed that the investment it would require from the Jordan estate would not bring an "attractive" return. "It doesn't look to me," Lowell wrote, "as if a newspaper was really a sound investment for a Trustee. However, the Jordan will is pretty strong in advising us to keep the half interest in the paper and that of course has great weight." Since the sale of the *Globe* stock would require a radical overhaul of the estate's assets, Lowell discussed the paper's prospects with at least two of the Jordan beneficiaries. He expressed his opinion that the estate's investment in the *Globe* (about 30 percent of its assets at market prices) was "too large" and that there was no longer any "sentimental reason" for retaining a half-interest. Yet Lowell's own feelings appear to have been governed by sentiment: "I also told [them] that if the beneficiaries wanted to remain as they are, I certainly would be against selling." The trustee received mixed signals from the Jordan heirs. One seemed to agree that too much of the estate's value was tied up in the *Globe,* while the other voiced confidence in the Taylors' operation of the paper and the wisdom of maintaining the estate's stake in it.[34]

On August 23, 1954, at a morning conference between Lowell and Davidson prior to a meeting of the *Globe* board of directors, the two men tentatively decided to offer the Jordan stock to the Taylors for $2.5 million in cash. At the directors' meeting itself, discussion focused initially on plans to have engineers make test borings at the Dorchester site for the proposed new plant and on yet another plea from Lowell for merger negotiations with the *Herald.* After endorsing the test borings and finding little sympathy for his plea for further merger negotiations, Lowell left to keep another scheduled appointment. Davidson then announced both his desire to be manager of the *Globe* and his and Lowell's intention to dispose of the Jordan half-interest should that desire remain unfulfilled. Davidson's boldness upset Davis and John Taylor, who, after getting W.O.'s consent, sent a letter to Lowell and Davidson asking them to put in writing their offer to sell the Jordan estate's stock to the Taylors for $2.5 million.[35]

Lowell read the Taylors' letter with dismay. "It is unfortunate," Lowell observed, "but it would be very difficult to efficiently run the newspaper with Sidney butting in all the time and that he seems determined to do." Even as the *Globe* took still another step toward the new plant—selling the company's properties on Newspaper Row and leasing them back for significant tax savings—Lowell and Davidson, as requested, made a formal proposal to sell the Jordan holdings in the *Globe.*[36]

The Taylors were not eager to buy. For more than a half century, they had enjoyed total control of the *Globe* while owning only 50 percent of the paper—it was not easy to accept the end of so idyllic an arrangement.

More important, the Taylors lacked ready access to the large sum required to purchase the Jordan stock. Finding the money would have been difficult under any circumstances in the mid-1950s, given the shaky state of Boston newspapers, but to do so when the *Globe* was about to enter the credit market in search of huge construction loans seemed almost impossible. The future of the *Globe* had not been so uncertain since its earliest years.

The Jordan-Taylor partnership survived the crisis. W. O. Taylor, who had dedicated his whole life to the *Globe*, made one last contribution to the paper as he neared death. His health had been declining for some time, and soon after the Lowell-Davidson proposal came to the table in the fall of 1954, he fell seriously ill. Lowell and Davidson, not wanting to complicate matters at this difficult time for the Taylor family, decided to put the sale on hold until W.O.'s health improved. In January 1955, W.O. showed no signs of recovery. Lowell and Davidson agreed that Davis Taylor should replace his father as a Jordan trustee and that the estate should retain its *Globe* stock pending construction of the new building. Two months later the other *Globe* directors voted to increase Lowell's and Davidson's compensation for service on the board to $5,000 a year.[37]

In July 1955, W. O. Taylor died. Of the many tributes that the *Globe* printed, Lowell's was first. "W.O.," he declared, was "one of America's finest publishers and one of Boston's foremost citizens." Characteristically, as Lowell paid respect to the past he also looked to the future: "[W.O.] was fortunate in having a son, W. Davis Taylor, equipped with ability and the same ideals, who will continue to publish the *Globe* according to the same high and creative standards which have guided the *Globe* since 1872."[38]

Lowell's public endorsement of Davis Taylor reflected private confidence in the new publisher's ability to run the newspaper. But Lowell persisted in his own agenda. In April 1955 Lowell gave Davis and his cousin John a stern talking-to about the *Globe*'s finances, pointing out that the paper "made so little money that it really was not a proper investment for outside money." (In the early and middle 1950s, the *Globe* paid annual dividends to the Jordan estate of $100,000. If the Jordan holdings indeed had a market value of $2.5 million, this represented a return of 4 percent.) According to Lowell, the younger Taylors were "bank[ing] on the new building to cure all their ills," when instead "they ought to be planning to take over the *Herald*." Two weeks after W.O. died, Lowell thought he had won a commitment from Davis Taylor to meet with Choate. But in September, when Taylor finally agreed to invite Choate to lunch, he told Lowell that his purpose was to inform Choate that "any possible combination with the *Herald* would be a great mistake." [39]

Like W.O., Davis and John Taylor valued their heritage. The *Globe* was independent, not only politically but also financially. Linkage with the *Herald* would entail borrowing money, and if they had to go into debt to safeguard their paper's future, the Taylors much preferred to do it for a new plant. Their family had built the *Globe* and they did not want it to lose its identity, as was bound to happen in a merger with the *Herald*. Lowell's resistance to these sentiments is surprising because at the same time, he was trumpeting the independent stance of Boston Safe. It was a source of pride for him that the bank's growth had always been achieved internally and that the bank had no wish to combine with another institution. Perhaps he felt the *Globe*'s prospects were so bleak that the Taylors could not afford the luxury of remaining independent. But by the close of 1955 he was prepared to give the Taylors the chance to prove what they could do. [40]

The *Globe*'s year-end figures for 1955 were excellent, the best since Lowell had joined the board. On December 9 Davis Taylor called on Lowell at his Boston Safe office to seek his support for an immediate green light on the new plant. Five days later, the *Globe*'s directors approved the construction contracts and instructed Taylor to tell Choate that "we could not go further with negotiations with the *Herald*." "So now that is clear," wrote Lowell, "we are on our way for the new building for the *Globe*." [41]

Having voted for the project, the directors then had to find the money to pay for it. Lowell wavered between cautious optimism and deep pessimism as he went over the figures in early 1956. On the basis of the paper's 1955 performance Lowell thought the company could handle the debt without much difficulty, but if the economy suffered a recession during the next five years he feared "the whole thing might well blow up." The Taylor family and the Jordan estate each had agreed to put in a million dollars; but because of the risk involved, they made their commitments in the form of loans rather than equity capital. When at the last minute Davis Taylor needed an additional loan of $250,000 from the Jordan estate, Lowell assured him he could count on it. [42]

But the bulk of the $12 million had to come from the outside, and here the *Globe* encountered resistance. Insurance companies were the most likely source for a mortgage, but the first one Davis Taylor approached offered little encouragement. The off-the-cuff response by New England Life's top loan officer was that instead of building a new plant, the *Globe* should merge with the *Herald*.[43] *

Taylor, however, found a more favorable reception at John Hancock. Ironically, at just about the time that Taylor was looking for a loan, the *Post*, in a front-page column written by its publisher, had criticized Boston financial institutions for failing to invest in local firms. John Hancock, proud of its commitment to the Boston region, was sensitive to the *Post*'s attack and may have considered the *Globe* request in this context. At any rate, the insurance firm's staff recommended issuance of a $4.5 million mortgage.

The approach to Hancock placed Lowell in an awkward position. As a director of both the *Globe* and the life insurance company, Lowell was confronted with an obvious conflict of interest. When the loan proposal was presented to the Hancock board, he left the room as the other directors discussed and voted on it. The proposal carried unanimously. With additional funding secured from two large Boston commercial banks, the *Globe* made its building plans public in mid-May 1956.[44]

The *Globe* announcement stirred Robert Choate into action. Choate's way in life may have been advanced by his family ties, but he was also a fighter. As one profiler of his career observed, Choate had "all the proper Boston credentials—St. Mark's, Harvard, Somerset Club, etc. But he is no character out of *The Late George Apley*. Quite the contrary, he is Boston's most iron-handed, politically active publisher, and his critics and enmities are many and bipartisan." Summing up Choate's approach to both business and golf, his lawyer commented, "Whatever he did, he played to win." The *Herald* publisher had dedicated himself to a merger with the *Globe* and he refused to accept as final the *Globe*'s break-off of talks in December 1955. At a lunch at the Somerset Club in January 1956, where he played host to Davis and John Taylor and a director of the Herald-Traveler Corporation, Choate made yet another plea for combining the newspapers, pointing out the advantages for everyone concerned. When the Tay-

---

* This opinion was not uncommon. At about the same time, Joseph Kennedy was telling associates: "Economically, Boston is a monopoly newspaper city, like almost every city in the country. The Hearst papers are going to fold within a couple of years, and that will leave the *Globe* and *Herald-Traveler* to fight it out. After they have ruined each other, I'll come in and pick up the winner." Richard J. Whalen, *The Founding Father* (New York: New American Library, 1964), p. 411.

lors remained unmoved, Choate warned that the *Globe* was in "a fight to the death" and that the *Herald* would "hit the [*Globe*] with everything it could get its hands on to drive [it] out of business."[45]

Choate began delivering on his threat in May, when he dropped in on Paul Clark, president of John Hancock, to grouse about the *Globe* loan. He based his complaint on Lowell's dual role as a *Globe* and Hancock director. According to Choate, the Hancock had rejected a *Herald* request for financing a few years earlier because of Sidney Winslow's membership on the Hancock board; Choate thought Lowell's position should have similarly disqualified the *Globe*. Perhaps Clark disagreed with Choate on the parallels between the two cases, or perhaps he did not recall the past as Choate did, or perhaps Clark was upset by Choate's hostile tone and menacing manner (the *Herald* could make a public stink about the apparent conflict of interest). Whatever it was, Clark gave no ground to Choate, showed him the door, and slammed it after him. Told of the meeting, Lowell wrote that Choate "is making a fool of himself and also showing up as a poor sport."[46]

Choate's tirade at John Hancock came on the heels of other bad news for the *Herald* publisher: In January, an FCC examiner had recommended that the *Herald*'s application for Channel 5, the last available television station license in the Boston area, be rejected.* With the newspaper's profits down in the postwar decade, Choate and his stockholders saw television as the company's financial salvation. But the *Herald* had two competitors for the license from outside the publishing business, and the examiner urged that it be given to one of these applicants. Desperate, Choate sought to influence the FCC's final decision through lobbying in Congress and private meetings with the FCC chairman—meetings that the commission would later admit did "violence to the integrity of the [agency's] processes." In April 1957 the FCC overruled the examiner's finding and awarded Channel 5 to the *Herald*. Recognizing that Choate's control of the television station would give him the means to carry out the threats he had made at the Somerset luncheon, the *Globe* joined with the two losing applicants to challenge the FCC action in the courts.[47]

Lowell endorsed the *Globe*'s legal battle plan with trepidation. He remained hopeful that some accommodation with the *Herald* could be

---

* The *Herald* had opposed the reservation of Channel 2 for an educational licensee in 1952–1953, hoping that this would improve its chances of getting a station.

worked out—if not a merger, then an agreement to divide the morning and evening markets and to have both papers printed in the *Globe's* new plant—and he did not want to antagonize Choate. He also knew that Choate would "not play fair"; indeed, Lowell noted in 1958, the struggle between the *Globe* and the *Herald* had become "a war with no known or respected rules on the part of the *Herald*." After the FCC reaffirmed the *Herald's* control of Channel 5 in September 1959, Lowell urged dropping the lawsuit. "We have been licked," he told his fellow directors, "and should take it like men and quit." To persist would harm the Taylors' reputation: They would be known as "bad losers." Although the Taylors' initial impulse was to continue, Lowell prevailed. The decision to withdraw, however, was made with the knowledge that the other parties would carry on the fight.[48]*

As the *Herald* took apparently permanent possession of Channel 5 in the fall of 1959, Sidney Davidson once again began pushing for the Jordan estate to sell its *Globe* stock. He claimed to have found a buyer and argued that the $7–10 million in proceeds could more profitably and more safely be invested elsewhere. Lowell reluctantly agreed. Although he felt "sad" about breaking up the "80-year partnership between the Jordans and the Taylors," it would have been irresponsible to pass up this opportunity.[49]

But as in 1954, the Jordan-Taylor partnership endured. Davidson's find was Samuel I. Newhouse, an aggressive acquirer of newspapers who had built a reputation for slashing employee rolls and running his papers simply as business enterprises—practices alien to the Taylors. Newhouse expressed interest in buying or entering into a partnership with the Taylors. But the Taylors were no more willing to have Newhouse as their equal partner than they were to sell out to him totally. With Newhouse judged unacceptable, the well of potential purchasers ran dry because most other newspaper chain owners insisted on undisputed managerial control. This would be impossible at the *Globe* given the Taylors' resolve to keep their half-interest. Tempers in the *Globe* boardroom flared as Davidson saw his plans blocked, and Lowell's most important contribution toward resolving the matter was to go off on his annual two-month winter vacation, with everyone's understanding that nothing was to be done in his absence. By the time he returned in mid-April 1960, Davidson had decided that in-

---

* In 1972, as a consequence of this litigation, the FCC took Channel 5 away from the *Herald* and gave it to a new applicant who promised a much wider range of community-based programming.

stead of dumping the *Globe,* he would prod the Taylors and their editors to put out a better newspaper.[50]

The failure to unload the *Globe* stock in 1960 became a big stroke of economic good fortune for the Jordan estate. The *Post* had finally passed away in the fall of 1956, and the *Globe* picked up the bulk of its circulation (see Table 2). In the spring of 1958 the *Globe's* new plant opened; no longer would a *Globe* employee, as had been the custom every day for the previous eighty-six years, climb a ladder propped against the building on Washington Street and tack the headlines on a wooden signboard. Many other fond traditions also disappeared with the move to the modern facility, but the *Globe* was now much better able to reach its readers and service its advertisers. A robust dynamism emerged in the *Globe* organization, starting from the top down. Davis and John Taylor had been badly shaken by the Channel 5 episode and their obvious lack of political clout; they responded by giving the newspaper a sharper editorial identity. Lowell had assessed the Taylors correctly: They certainly did know how to run the paper.[51]

TABLE 2
CIRCULATION OF BOSTON'S NEWSPAPERS, 1963

	Morning	Evening	Sunday
Advertiser	—	—	470,000
Globe	198,000	151,500	504,000
Herald	186,000	—	306,000
Record American	447,000*		
Traveler	—	167,500	—

* Published throughout the day.
Source: *Editor and Publisher Market Guide, 1964*

The *Herald* could not keep pace, despite its move to a new plant (two thirds the size of the *Globe* facility) in late 1959. Several downtown Boston stores closed in the late 1950s, taking with them the advertising that usually had gone to the *Herald.* The flow of population to the suburbs made classifieds a hot item, and the *Globe* had long ago sewed up this market. On the news side as well, the *Herald* fell behind the *Globe.* Ironically, the main cause of the *Herald's* distress was the very television station that was its benefactor. The profits from Channel 5 were being used to subsidize the money-losing paper, but Choate and his managers, distracted by the mechanics of operating the station and the continuing battle over its license, could not keep the *Herald* competitive in the face of the *Globe's* revitalization. When Choate died suddenly in December 1963, the *Herald* was in a downward slide that continued until 1972, when Herald-Traveler lost Channel 5 and sold the paper to the Hearst Corporation. The paper was reincarnated as the *Herald American*.*

In the meantime, the *Globe* made major strides toward becoming a first-rate newspaper. A new editor with fresh ideas was appointed in 1965. Under his leadership the *Globe* adopted and, in some respects, pioneered the latest trends in journalism. The paper moved into investigative reporting, winning its first Pulitzer prize, for "meritorious public service," in 1966 for its disclosures about the background of a friend of the Kennedy family who had been nominated to the federal bench by President Johnson. The following year the *Globe* reversed a longstanding policy of Charles Taylor by endorsing a candidate for political office. It took an increasingly activist editorial line; in 1969 it was the second major newspaper in the country to call for unilateral American withdrawal from Vietnam, and in 1973 it was the first to call for Richard Nixon's resignation as president following the Saturday Night Massacre. In 1975 the *Globe* won its second Pulitzer for meritorious public service for its coverage of the Boston school desegregation conflict.

Lowell's contribution to the *Globe's* improvement was passive but, nonetheless, vital. The Taylors supported their editors' and reporters' efforts to make the paper over, and Lowell backed the Taylors. Although Lowell was uncomfortable with many of the *Globe's* bold, liberal editorial positions and even became the target of its criticisms of the Museum of Fine Arts, he never attempted to interfere with editorial content.[52] By the time he resigned as trustee in 1976, the newspaper was a pillar of American journalism and immensely profitable. It was also a powerful voice for a cosmopolitan and vibrant Boston.[†]

---

* In 1980 the Hearst Corporation purchased the highly profitable Channel 5 from its local owners and sold the *Herald* to the Australian publisher Rupert Murdoch.

† In 1993 the *Globe* was sold to the New York Times Company for $1.1 billion. The agreement stipulated that the *Globe* retain its autonomy.

13

". . . and to the Cohens and Kellys too"

TOWARD A MORE TOLERANT BOSTON

B oston, wrote Walter Lippmann in 1916, is "the most homogeneous, self-centered, and self-complacent community in the United States." No one better symbolized the unyielding resistance to cultural pluralism among Proper Bostonians in the first part of the twentieth century than A. Lawrence Lowell, with his vice presidency of the Immigration Restriction League, his opposition to the appointment of Louis Brandeis to the Supreme Court (the spark for Lippmann's statement), his attempt to exclude blacks from Harvard's residence halls, his policy of setting a quota on Jewish admissions to Harvard College, and his defense of the Massachusetts judicial system in its treatment of Sacco and Vanzetti. Lowell was, as Brandeis put it, representative of a class of "men who have been blinded by privilege, who have no evil purpose, and many of whom have distinct public spirit, but whose environment—or innate narrowness—has obscured all vision and sympathy with the masses." [1]

Almost fifty years after Lippmann penned his condemnation of Boston, an interviewer from Columbia University commented to Ralph Lowell on his cousin's "sense of superiority over Jews and Italians." "He was a good deal of a snob, you know," responded Ralph, "and I'm not a snob." Although he subsequently tried to take the bite out of his words ("I don't mean to say that President Lowell was really a snob, but I think my generation is a more liberal generation than they were back in that time"), there was no question that by the mid-1960s Ralph Lowell had established a reputation very different from that of his controversial relative. "I had a great compliment the other day," he told the interviewer, "when one of my Jewish friends said, 'You're the only fellow I know who has never had any feelings against the Jews, the colored people, or anybody else.'" Ralph

Lowell was widely praised for helping to lower some of the barriers that kept Boston's residents divided and mutually hostile. To accomplish this, however, he had to overcome the prejudices that pervaded the environment in which he grew up.[2]

THE IRISH AND THE JEWS

For most of Lowell's lifetime, no division in Boston was deeper or more treacherous than the gulf separating the Brahmins and the Irish. "Boston is probably the only city in America," observed John Gunther in 1947, "where, in order to have a frank political talk with anybody, you have to begin with the question, 'Are you a Catholic?'" Although the "NO IRISH NEED APPLY" signs of the nineteenth century were largely gone by the 1920s, the lines of ethnic and religious demarcation remained firm; and the young Ralph Lowell was not one to challenge them. Intent on following his grandfather, father, and older brother into the A.D. Club at Harvard, Lowell did not challenge the social conventions that kept those with less exalted pedigrees from serious consideration. A decade out of college, Lowell understood that a business partnership with Joseph Kennedy was not socially acceptable, and he stayed at Lee, Higginson.[3]

By the 1940s, however, Boston's Irish had carved out several profitable areas of enterprise. Confronted by the growing economic clout of the children of Erin, the old bastions of Brahmin power began opening doors. At the socially prestigious, if financially inconsequential, Provident Institute for Savings, where a seat on the board had been bestowed on Lowell early in his career, the first Irish Catholic finally was elected a trustee in 1944. Lowell approved: "Boston is no longer a Yankee city and it is high time that this is recognized and a proper representation of the other elements in the community given a say in its affairs commensurate with their proportionate position in the community." At Boston Safe, Lowell accommodated this new reality by hiring an Irish American to seek business in that community and by adding a Catholic to the board.[4]

In addition to laying down a welcome mat on State Street, Lowell went to meet the Irish on their own turf. The more successful ("lace curtain") Irish had established the Clover Club as the pinnacle of their social order, and the anthropologist in Lowell long hungered to attend one of the club's lavish Saint Patrick's Day dinners, where the required attire was "Black tie or Roman collar." In 1946, Michael T. Kelleher, the Provident's first Irish trustee—whom the *Globe* later called "Boston's outstanding ambassador of good will"—invited Lowell to be his guest. Lowell did not record his impressions, but after attending the annual dinner of the Eire Society a few years later, he commented, "I think I was the only Protestant there, at least I was the only one that didn't kiss the Archbishop's ring or cross myself at the invocation." Lowell saw himself as building bridges by his very presence and sympathized with the Irish quest for social acceptance.[5]

There was no question that Lowell felt more at ease with the lace curtain Irish than with their lower-class brethren. Soon after becoming trustee of the Lowell Institute, he chose an expert on Irish literature to give a series of lectures with the aim of "attracting the better Irish elements here in Boston." In 1945, however, Lowell had to hire a guard for the professor lecturing on Russian religious history. Someone had sent a telegram threatening violence if the series was not halted, leading Lowell to muse: "There seems to be a great deal of feeling against Russia and anything to do with her. Can it stem back to the mass of ignorant Catholics we have here in Boston?" It may have been this class outlook that made Lowell such an admirer of William Cardinal O'Connell, the Catholic Church's leader in Boston since 1907. Lowell usually spoke well of people who had just died, but his comments about O'Connell—whom he knew only at a distance— following his death in the spring of 1944 were especially favorable: "[A] really fine man, broad minded and liberal. As a prince of his church in this Catholic city of Boston, he made himself a leader in all good civic enterprises and frowned on the low grafting Irish politicians who formerly controlled the city." Most students of O'Connell's career would have problems with Lowell's choice of the words "broad minded" and "liberal." It was probably the cardinal's dignified bearing—some critics felt it verged on pomposity—and his insistence that the Irish earn the respect they sought that made O'Connell attractive to Lowell.[6] The two men carried themselves the same way and often viewed political and social issues through similar conservative lenses.

If Lowell felt comfortable with the cardinal, he did not know at first what to make of Richard Cushing, O'Connell's successor as the leader of Boston's Catholics. Breezy and approachable where O'Connell had been urbane and aristocratic, Archbishop (later Cardinal) Cushing never tried to hide his working-class origins, and his speech always betrayed his South Boston roots. But in time Lowell got to know Cushing far better than he had ever known O'Connell. Together the Brahmin and the blacksmith's son would help Boston make progress in easing more than a century of religious and social conflict.[7]

In the beginning, however, Cushing's elevation seemed to provoke more conflict in the city, not less. One point of contention was a place where the Lowells and their caste traditionally had held sway: the Perkins Institution and Massachusetts School for the Blind, which occupied a thirty-four-acre campus beside the Charles River in Watertown.* Incorporated in 1829, the Perkins Institution had long been a pacesetter in the field and was best known for its education of the deaf-blind. As its full name suggested, the school was a joint private-public endeavor, its private endowment supplemented by state subsidies. Gubernatorial appointees sat on the board of trustees, but the majority of trustees were chosen by the members of the corporation, most of whom represented the Commonwealth's oldest and finest families. Lowells had been among the original incorporators, and Ralph's father had been a member of the corporation in the years before his death. In the early 1940s, A. Lawrence Lowell and Ralph's aunt Lucy and brother Jim were on the corporation. When Ralph's uncle James Arnold Lowell left the board of trustees in 1925, Ralph was elected to replace him; he remained there until 1956, serving for a decade as vice president.[8]

As a state-supported institution, the school was ostensibly nonsectarian. It had a chapel on the grounds, however, and six mornings a week the students were required to attend services consisting of Christian prayers and hymns. On Sundays, community groups arranged for the transportation of the children to nearby Protestant and Catholic churches. The Catholic Guild for the Blind, which was administered by an order of nuns, provided religious education to Catholic children at the Perkins one afternoon a week. In late 1945 or early 1946, the guild asked the Perkins board for permission to construct a Catholic chapel on the property.[9]

The executive committee of the board considered the guild's request at a meeting near the end of January. After an extended discussion, Lowell proposed a resolution to make the Perkins chapel available to "any and all sects . . . on Sundays and holy days." This was designed to address the nuns' concern about assuring the availability of Catholic masses, while also maintaining the unifying character of the daily morning exercises. The

---

* Founded by Dr. Samuel Gridley Howe, it was named for Thomas Handasyd Perkins, a famous Boston-based China trader, who furnished much of its original funding.

Ralph Lowell and Paul Cabot in the heart of Boston's financial district.
(Reprinted from the June 6 issue of *Business Week* by special permission.
© 1959 by McGraw-Hill Companies)

ABOVE, LEFT: Ralph Lowell is flanked by Claude M. Fuess (left) and Lawrence G. Brooks, leaders of the Massachusetts Citizens Committee for Educational Television, in April 1955, shortly before WGBH-TV went on the air. At the far right is WGBH General Manager Parker Wheatley. (Courtesy of the Boston Public Library, Print Department)

BELOW, LEFT: Lowell seeking bids for a croquet set, blender, and Instamatic camera during the 1968 WGBH televised auction. (*Boston Globe* photo)

ABOVE: One board Lowell did not join—the Harvard Corporation. After all the dust had settled following the struggle to name a replacement for Henry James, the members were (left to right around the table): Charles A. Coolidge; Roger I. Lee; Treasurer Paul Cabot; President James B. Conant; Henry Lee Shattuck; Grenville Clark; and William L. Marbury. The man with the mustache sitting in front of the left window is David W. Bailey, Secretary to the Governing Boards and a key figure in the development of the Lowell Institute Cooperative Broadcasting Council. (Courtesy of the Harvard University Archives)

BELOW: Ralph and Charlotte admiring a statue at the Museum of Fine Arts exhibition of Turkish art treasures in November 1967. (Courtesy of the Boston Public Library, Print Department)

ABOVE, RIGHT: Lowell and fellow trustees of the Massachusetts General Hospital at the December 1949 groundbreaking for the research building. Trustee Chairman (and Lowell's Harvard '12 classmate) Francis C. Gray is the tall man directly behind Lowell. (Courtesy of the Boston Public Library, Print Department)

BELOW, RIGHT: Ralph and Charlotte in the *Boston Globe* composing room as the presses in the newspaper's new building are put into operation in May 1958. (*Boston Globe* photo)

LEFT: The Lowells with Cardinal Cushing at the August 1967 charity football game at Harvard Stadium. (*Boston Globe* photo)

BELOW: Longtime baseball fan Ralph Lowell gets the autograph of Los Angeles pitcher Sandy Koufax, a fellow honoree at the 30th Annual Dinner of the Massachusetts Committee of Catholics, Protestants, and Jews, May 1967. (*Boston Globe* photo)

"Mr. Boston" in the 1950s. (Photo by Bachrach)

adoption of Lowell's motion left Robert Hallowell, the institution's president, and Gabriel Farrell, its director and an ordained Episcopalian minister, "heartbroken." They feared that the chapel issue was just "an opening
wedge on the part of Catholics" and that "we [the trustees] will rue the day
we passed it." For Lowell it was a matter of accepting reality: "I agree that
the Catholic Church is the church militant and that they are out to gain all
the ground they possibly can, but that is their privilege and more power
to them."[10]

The matter came up before the full board in mid-March, and this time
Lowell lost. With some people absent and others switching their votes,
only Lowell and a Roman Catholic priest, who held a gubernatorial appointment, were recorded in favor of allowing the chapel to be used for
Sunday denominational services. In a visit to Lowell's office the previous
week, Hallowell and Farrell had convinced him that the old system of sending Catholic children on Sundays to the local church was working well; thus
his concern was not so much that the legitimate religious needs of the children were not being fulfilled as that the result had been achieved by the
"use of maneuvers" and seemed to reveal the presence of "bigotry." The
board opted to maintain the status quo, and the nuns decided not to press
the issue.[11]

During the late 1940s Lowell twice encountered the power of the
"church militant" at the Massachusetts General Hospital. In one instance,
the hospital coveted a nearby Boston public school building that the city
was closing. M.G.H.'s president, Francis Gray, did his best to arrange for
the purchase, but the municipal authorities transferred the building to the
Catholic Archdiocese for its parochial school system. The episode "just
shows," lamented Lowell, "that in this city there is no use trying to do anything against the desires of the Catholic Church." In 1947–1948, Lowell
and the hospital dueled with the Church over birth control and lost once
more. Although Protestant divines had spearheaded the movement for
passage of the 1879 Massachusetts law "Concerning Offenses against Chas-
tity, Morality and Decency," by the 1940s the Catholic Church was the
foremost advocate of keeping the act unamended on the statute books. In
1940 a petition drive was launched to make it legal for a doctor to treat a
married woman to prevent pregnancy for the protection of her life or
health. The M.G.H.'s director, Nathaniel Faxon, was prominent among
the signers. The voters of Massachusetts defeated the referendum when it
appeared on the ballot in 1942, but birth control advocates tried again in

1948. Lowell, a longtime supporter of birth control, feared that the membership of a Catholic priest on the M.G.H. board (by gubernatorial appointment) would be a bar to Faxon's signing the new petition; but a way was found to avoid offending the cleric and the director's name was as conspicuous as it had been before. At his wife's insistence Lowell himself avoided a highly visible role in the birth control campaign and declined an invitation to become vice-chairman of the Planned Parenthood Committee. The Church mobilized its forces against the referendum in 1948, sending it down to a decisive defeat.[12]

The battle over birth control reopened old wounds in the Protestant-Catholic relationship. (An Episcopal bishop, making an appearance in favor of the petition at a legislative hearing, was subjected to such intense harassment that he refused to continue with his testimony.) But the impressive dimensions of the Catholic Church's triumph encouraged it to be magnanimous in victory. An important sign of the Archdiocese's growing self-confidence was a speech given by Auxiliary Bishop John Wright in March 1950. Cushing's closest adviser on political issues, Wright was the guest of honor at a dinner at the Copley Plaza hotel given by one thousand Catholic men.* Although the front-page newspaper accounts of the gathering gave little hint of the thrust of Wright's remarks, Lowell referred to it in his diary as "a great speech for toleration—the Catholic majority must be tolerant of the minority in the interests of all." Two days later the *Herald* ran a long editorial recounting the life of the Reverend Jean Lefebvre de Cheverus, the first Catholic Bishop of Boston (appointed in 1808), who had been the subject of Wright's address. Noting how Cheverus had enjoyed friendships with many Protestants and had done "as much as any man to extend the toleration of Roman Catholicism in America," the *Herald* suggested that it would be a nice gesture if "the non-Catholics of this community erected some fitting tribute" to Cheverus.[13]

Harold Hodgkinson of Filene's took up the *Herald*'s challenge and raised money from his fellow Protestant businessmen to place a tablet in honor of Bishop Cheverus on the *Pilot* building on Franklin Street. (The *Pilot* was the newspaper of the Archdiocese.) Fifteen hundred people attended the June festivities at which the tablet was unveiled; Lowell introduced Hodg-

---

* The occasion was Wright's appointment to the newly created position of bishop of Worcester. Wright later was appointed cardinal and went on to be the highest-ranking American in the Roman Curia during the 1970s.

kinson, who made the presentation to Cushing. "It was really quite a historic occasion," Lowell later wrote. "There was a feeling of good fellowship attending the whole ceremony. A really nice gesture on the part of us Protestants to the memory of a truly great priest."* The *Pilot* printed a photograph of Lowell and the other luminaries on its front page.[14]

The reaching-out on both sides continued in a variety of ways through the 1950s. One example was Lowell's growing attachment to Boston College. At the middle of the decade, this Jesuit institution was the only school in the Lowell Institute Cooperative Broadcasting Council that had not given special recognition to Lowell, either in the form of an honorary degree or a position in its governance structure. Appropriately, it was the School of Business Administration that took the first step by inviting Lowell to join an advisory council of prominent local businessmen that the school was reactivating. Lowell's association with that group, as well as his interest in the work of the Citizen Seminars sponsored by Boston College, led the college's president in 1960 to ask Lowell to serve on the newly created Board of Regents; the mission of the board was to assist the president in planning for the future and raising funds to increase the school's meager endowment. In 1962 Boston College bestowed an honorary Doctor of Laws on Lowell, calling him "the beloved first citizen of Boston." It also described him as "an eminently 'serviceable man,'" applying a phrase first used by the nineteenth-century Episcopalian bishop of Massachusetts, Phillips Brooks.[15]†

A few years later Lowell assisted Cardinal Cushing's campaign to raise $50 million for Catholic charities. The owner of the Boston Patriots of the American Football League offered to donate the gate receipts of a preseason exhibition game. But the location that offered the best prospect of holding a large crowd—Harvard Stadium—had previously been declared off-limits by the president and fellows of Harvard. They were uncomfortable about opening this citadel of amateur sports to professional teams, and when Lowell wrote to President Nathan Pusey requesting that an exception be made, Pusey showed little enthusiasm for the idea. He agreed to review the matter, however, and a month later informed Cushing that

---

* Lowell further contributed to this ecumenical spirit by inviting the first Catholic to deliver the annual religious lecture of the Lowell Institute.

† When the Jesuits relinquished legal control of Boston College in 1972, Ralph's son John joined the new board of trustees.

the stadium would be available: "We give our permission in the present instance out of respect for your position in the community and for your leadership of social and religious causes. We recognize the larger issue here of attempting in some measure to serve the community and to help the charities in which you and Mr. Lowell are interested." Lowell and Charlotte sat next to Cushing at the game; this was the first time the cardinal had been in the stadium.[16]

Lowell may also have scored a first with the legendary James Michael Curley. Whereas A. Lawrence Lowell appeared in the former mayor's 1957 autobiography as ungracious and bigoted, Ralph Lowell was portrayed as a symbol of changing times. "I met Ralph Lowell at the Harvard Club one night," Curley recalled, "and he said, 'How do you do, Governor.' It is a far cry from the days when the Back Bay Hatfields fought the Roxbury McCoys."[17]

Ralph Lowell was a student at Harvard when John Collins Bossidy, a graduate of Holy Cross College, wrote the quatrain that captured the popular view of Brahmin Boston:

> And this is good old Boston
> The home of the bean and the cod,
> Where the Lowells talk to the Cabots,
> And the Cabots talk only to God.

The verse was often reprinted and recited with an extra "only" inserted in the third line, making the Lowells appear even snootier than the author intended. Ralph worked conscientiously to overcome this image. Sitting between two labor union officials at a Cancer Society luncheon, Lowell found it difficult "to develop any conversation, but we finally did get underway and I had a very interesting time." On another occasion Lowell took as a "real compliment" the remark of a union president relayed to him by a friend. "How come he's a banker?" the union man was overheard to say. "That S.O.B. is a regular fellow."

Indicative of the public identification of Lowell with Boston's improved ethnic and religious climate was a popular story about the leader of the local longshoremen's union. His mother was surprised one afternoon to find him shaving and asked what he was doing home from work so early. "I'm going to give a speech at Boston College," he replied, "with Ralph Lowell, the banker, and some big-shot professor from M.I.T." "Oh, my God, John," his mother exclaimed, "You've been drinking again."[18]

In breaking away from old Brahmin prejudices, Lowell learned to respect the Irish more quickly than the Jews. The high intensity of the Yankee-Irish conflict in Boston was produced by the peculiar circumstances of the city's history, and the passage of time and the progress of the Irish toward better economic conditions helped relieve tensions. Anti-Jewish bias, however, had much deeper and wider roots.* The mature Lowell considered some Jews as friends, but he had a difficult time discarding traditional Jewish stereotypes.

Growing up in the higher reaches of Boston society at the dawn of the twentieth century, Lowell was exposed to some of the most virulent anti-semitism to be found anywhere in America. This prejudice never assumed the rhetorical, pictorial, and violent excesses to be found in less genteel environments, but it was strong and rampant nonetheless.† Jobs in Brahmin firms and membership in Brahmin clubs were closed to Jews. Jewish students were a conspicuous presence at Harvard, but the social divisions held there as well. Because these Jews were his classmates, Lowell felt some bond with them, but a sense of distance prevailed.[19]

Lowell's early references to Jews almost always cast them in an unfavorable light. Referring in 1907 to a Volkmann School friend who was not Jewish but had a prominent nose, Lowell wrote, "[He] looks and acts [forward and pushy] like a Jew." He dismissed as "hopeless" a German Jew he met on his Arizona trip in the summer of 1911: "That bird talks very poor English, and has the worst table manners imaginable." Dining with his Phi Beta Kappa brothers the following spring, Lowell reported having "a ter-

---

* The antisemitism of the "Protestant Establishment" was probably even stronger than its anti-Catholicism. Writing to A. Lawrence Lowell in 1920, the Wall Street banker J. P. Morgan noted the "strong feeling among the Overseers that the nominee [for the vacancy on the Harvard Corporation] should by no means be a Jew or Roman Catholic, although naturally, the feeling in regard to the latter is less than in regard to the former. . . . [T]he Jew is always a Jew first and an American second, and the Roman Catholic, I fear, too often a Papist first and an American second." Lowell assured Morgan that there was "no suggestion [of a Jew] at the present time" and went on to defend his preference for a Catholic lawyer from New York who had been his classmate in college. The overseers ratified the appointment; the first Jewish member of the corporation would not be chosen for another half century. Morgan to Lowell, March 2, 1920; Lowell to Morgan, March 3, 1920, quoted in Nitza Rosovsky, *The Jewish Experience at Harvard and Radcliffe* (Cambridge: Harvard University Press, 1986), p. 32.

† Antisemitism took violent forms in Boston among lower-class Irish youths. See John Gunther, *Inside U.S.A.* (New York: Harper Bros., 1947), pp. 515–516; Nat Hentoff, *Boston Boy* (New York: Knopf, 1986), pp. 16–21, 28–31, 65–72, 97–98.

rible Jew opposite me who made such a noise over his eating that I could hardly down any food myself." Over the next four decades Lowell sprinkled his diaries with similar stereotypical and negative characterizations of Jews.[20]

Such characterizations were fairly standard in mid-twentieth-century America. What stamped Lowell as being somewhat different was his attempt to move beyond them. If he felt like "a fish out of water" at the seventieth anniversary dinner of the Combined Jewish Philanthropies with its "crowd of Jewish bankers and brokers," the remarkable thing is not that he left early, but that he went at all. Although Lowell may have socialized on a personal level almost exclusively with fellow Brahmins, he felt an obligation to associate with Jews and others in the interests of community harmony. To be sure, many of these "brotherhood" activities were connected to his work—he was always seeking to broaden Boston Safe's customer base—but it would be inaccurate to view his behavior only in crass commercial terms. For Lowell, toleration and understanding were not simply good business, they were a prerequisite for civic involvement. He was sensitive to the barriers Jews faced. When, in the mid-1950s, Governor Herter held a luncheon for the visiting Israeli ambassador at the Somerset Club, Lowell remarked, "A rather peculiar place to stage it—in normal times try to get a Jew into the Somerset Club!" At about the same time, when Lowell and his fellow trustees of the New England Medical Center held a meeting in Maine, the center's medical director, a Jew, was denied a room at the inn where the sessions were to be held. Asked by another trustee what their response should be, Lowell said the manager should be informed that they would all leave unless they were all accommodated. The inn complied with the demand. Some years later, he was surprised by the main course at a luncheon at a Boston hotel hosted by a national magazine: "I had never seen ham served before at such a gathering. I wonder how some of my Jewish friends liked that?"[21]

Lowell took great pleasure in events that highlighted the ability of Bostonians from disparate backgrounds to rise above their differences. In 1949 he was asked to serve as an honorary pallbearer at the funeral of a Jewish state court judge. Mayor Curley and another Jewish judge acted in a similar capacity, and when the three of them emerged from the service together they formed what Lowell called "quite a red, white and blue trio." In the spring of 1953, Lowell was surprised and hurt when Harvard's Board of Overseers passed him over and chose Charles Wyzanski as board president. Wyzanski "is a grand fellow," he wrote, "but it is quite a departure to make a Jew president, and here is where they picked one over a Lowell." But Lowell's pain had subsided by the fall when Wyzanski officiated at his first major ceremonial event—Pusey's inauguration. "So Harvard," observed Lowell, "founded by Congregationalists, has its first Episcopalian President, installed by a brilliant Jew. That is Harvard at its very best." (Lowell was chosen board president for 1957–1958, his last year as an overseer.)[22]

Nowhere was Lowell's commitment to a pluralistic society put to a sterner test than in his ties to Harvard. In 1958, for instance, President Pusey created a "tempest" by announcing that Memorial Church was a Christian church and therefore off-limits to private, non-Christian ceremonies such as marriages and funerals. Lowell unhesitatingly adopted a liberal stance. Not one to criticize Harvard in public, he did not join the many protests against the ban, but his diary left no doubt of his views: "Technically the [action of Pusey and the Corporation] was correct, but many of us feel that the Memorial Church is more than a 'Christian' church, a symbol of Harvard and all that it stands for, disregarding creed and color." He was pleased to see the ban quickly rescinded.[23]

If Lowell was sure of his position within the intellectual and moral confines of Harvard Yard, he faced a dilemma on the social turf of the Harvard Club in the Back Bay. Harvard's Jewish alumni, barred from membership in the most elite Boston clubs, such as the Somerset and the Algonquin, looked to the Harvard Club as an attractive alternative. Their numbers so increased over the years that in 1945 one of Lowell's classmates told him he had overheard one Jew tell another that Lowell was president of "the largest Jewish club in Boston." Lowell did not appreciate the irony. The conspicuous Jewish presence, combined with the widespread feeling that the Jews, in contravention of club rules, were using the club for business purposes, created a backlash among the still predominantly Yankee membership. The prospect of a decline in the number of Yankee members posed a threat to Lowell's efforts to restore the club to financial health. During his years at the club's helm (1942–1947), Lowell steered a careful course between the groups' competing interests. But when the issue apparently came to a head in 1958, he sided with those who favored a revival of the ballot box for voting on applicants. By this device, he noted, "a member of the [elections] committee can blackball a candidate without exposing himself to the whole committee."[24]

Although it was not until 1959 that Boston Safe elected its first Jewish director, Lowell had long been identified with two institutions established in the 1930s to foster better relations between Christians and Jews. One was the annual Goodwill Dinner held at Temple Ohabei Shalom in Brookline. An effort at outreach by the Jewish community, the midwinter event became a fixture on Lowell's social calendar by the 1940s. "I am not sure whether they mean to ask me each year," Lowell wrote in 1949, "or whether they sort of have a bear by the tail and feel they cannot very well drop me. Anyway, I thoroughly enjoy these affairs and love to get in their beautiful temple for even a few minutes." The following year the Brahmin banker heard himself introduced as "a Lowell who talks to Cabots, and to Cohens and Kellys too." [25]

In 1943 Lowell joined the executive board of the Massachusetts Committee of Catholics, Protestants and Jews. Founded in the mid-1930s by Ben Shapiro, a member of the Temple Ohabei Shalom congregation, this organization was not affiliated with the National Conference of Christians and Jews, nor was it endowed with sufficient resources to maintain an office or paid staff of its own. Nonetheless, under Shapiro's vigorous leadership, it was for more than three decades the most important group in the Commonwealth dedicated to better relations across religious lines. In the mid-1940s, for example, as the national press drew attention to violent antisemitic acts committed by Boston Irish youths, the committee helped prepare a collection of articles on democracy and citizenship for distribution in the public schools; in conjunction with this project, the Lowell Institute sponsored a special course of lectures entitled "Inter-group Understanding, Respect, and Goodwill." On a more personal level, the committee brought teenagers from various Boston neighborhoods together at Fenway Park, where they dined with some of the city's business leaders; Lowell was a regular participant. The committee was best known for its annual dinner in the spring, which was televised locally during the 1950s and 1960s. Every year a distinguished member of each faith received an award, presented by someone who represented a different faith. In 1950 Lowell made the presentation for Notre Dame football coach Frank Leahy (formerly the coach at Boston College). Lowell found these occasions "thrilling." In 1967 he was honored, along with baseball pitcher Sandy Koufax and U.S. Senator Edward Kennedy, at the committee's thirtieth annual dinner. [26]

A decade earlier Lowell had been named the first recipient of the "Man of the Year" award established by the *Jewish Advocate*, a Boston newspaper.

"An illustrious scion of a most distinguished clan," the citation declared, "Ralph Lowell embodies the attributes of breeding, learning and morality that form the essence of the exemplary man. He typifies aristocracy in love with democracy." In his diary Lowell described himself as "touched and honored," going on to observe: "Some of my friends will undoubtedly be amused at the source of this great honor, but as I said to one of them, 'It's the Jews that first appreciate real accomplishments.'"[27]

ALONG THE COLOR LINE

Thanks, in part, to the example set by Lowell and many others, by the 1960s the Irish-Brahmin antagonism had been muted and antisemitism was in clear retreat. Discrimination still survived in the most exclusive boardrooms and social clubs, but the affluence of the post–World War II decades and the homogenizing effects of the consumer culture helped reduce the ethnic and religious hatreds that had made Boston a divided city. Yet even as the old cleavages shrank, a new fissure emerged, and Lowell found himself in the front lines in the battle to patch it up.

Before the Civil War Boston was a cradle of abolitionism. But at the turn of the century, Bostonians generally shared the national sentiment that African Americans were inferior and incapable of being integrated into American life. If Boston's blacks were better off than either their southern rural or northern urban counterparts, it was largely because their numbers were few and the fears of the city's Yankee leadership were concentrated on the huge waves of immigration from Ireland and southern and eastern Europe. Lowell's Harvard class included two blacks, but he had little contact with them in school and did not seek them out after graduation. In his college diaries he used the words then widely employed in white society, "coon" and "nigger." Describing a black employee at Harvard who Lowell thought treated his cousin Lawrence—then president— in a "rather fresh and pretty lofty" manner, Ralph wrote, "That seems to be the way with niggers; as soon as they get to know anything and are petted a bit, they get fresh and unbearable." Blacks were virtually invisible in the diaries Lowell kept irregularly for the next quarter century; the last time he used "coon" or "nigger" in a diary was in 1940.[28]

Until the mid-1940s Lowell, like most northerners, thought the "colored problem" (the terminology he then used) was confined to the south. But the war years stripped him of that innocence. Segregation in Massachusetts may not have been mandated by law—indeed, it was specifically prohibited by state law in several important forms—but discrimination in employment and housing and separation of the races in most social settings were the norm. Through his service as a director of the Greater Boston Soldiers and Sailors Committee (better known as the USO), Lowell became aware of some local issues related to race.

The committee operated several facilities in the metropolitan region where men in uniform stationed in or passing through New England could go for assistance on various personal matters or just to have fun. In October 1941 a center was opened on Ruggles Street in Boston's Roxbury neighborhood, which because of its location was staffed solely by blacks and attracted an exclusively black clientele. The following May the committee put the finishing touches on the Buddies Club on Boston Common, a considerably larger and more elaborate hangout for servicemen, which became very popular. Here the personnel and patrons were all white.[29]

In late 1942 the USO committee came under pressure to add black hostesses (that is, dancing partners) to the staff of the Buddies Club. Leading the campaign were two black lawyers and committee directors, Ray W. Guild and Matthew Bullock. Guild was president of the Coordinating Council of Colored Organizations for National Defense and a former president of the Boston chapter of the NAACP; Bullock, a onetime football star at Dartmouth, was active in Republican politics and a member of the state parole board. Lowell found Guild "a very dangerous and disagreeable man" ("He is very light colored and must be a large percentage white, which probably gives him a heavy inferiority complex"), but his impressions of Bullock were much more favorable. "Bullock is colored and fights for the rights of his race, as he should," Lowell wrote in January 1943. Later he observed that Bullock "acted with utmost fairness and never lost his temper even when the debate was against him to the point which would have tried anyone's temper. He is a great credit to his race and a fine character."[30]

Guild, Bullock, and other directors threatened to resign if their demands were not met. After discussing the matter for several weeks, the committee agreed in May 1943 to assign black hostesses to the Buddies Club. The USO's executive secretary had argued that the Ruggles Street facility satisfied the needs of black servicemen, but Guild refused to accept the idea that "Boston wants to go backwards from its traditions just because at present we have many coming from southern parts of our country, and who are not accustomed to see Colored people in public places." Although Lowell feared "trouble" would result from the vote, he went along "in the interests of peace all around." "The colored question is a very pressing and vital one," he noted, "and loaded with dynamite."[31]

How loaded became evident in a matter of days. The committee's decision was not reported in the daily press, but when it reached the staff at the Buddies Club many of the senior people, all of them volunteers, indicated they would quit. Lowell and two other committee members met with this group and found themselves

> assailed from all sides. [They] are sincere in their belief that mixing the races to this extent will not work. We recognize all the problems, but believe that Negroes will not take advantage of their rights and cause trouble, and that they will dance with the colored hostesses and not with the white ones. I am hopeful that after the ladies have had time to think the thing through, they will appreciate the many advantages to be gained by trying the plan, and I think we won a few of them over this evening, but it was a tough evening.

At a committee meeting a month later, Lowell proposed delaying implementation of the black hostesses plan. It was not clear, he claimed, whether "colored people themselves wish[ed] to push it" at that point. In July Bullock indicated that he did want to "push it," leading Lowell to predict that "there may be a good deal of trouble and hurt feelings before the thing is finally settled." He added, "It probably means giving up dancing at the Buddies Club and having that part of the program somewhere else."[32]

Rioting in New York's Harlem in early August confirmed both Lowell's fears about a racial tinderbox and his feelings about how the black hostesses issue should be handled:

> It no doubt means giving up formal dancing, but that is probably a good thing anyway, for these Buddies Club dances attract a large crowd to the Common where the "teenage" problem is at its worst in Boston. There are plenty of dances being given for servicemen and cutting them out in the Common ought not to be a hardship and at the same time should go far towards solving the very perplexing Colored situation.

If dancing at the Buddies Club with black hostesses present was, indeed, to be permitted, it would take place under strict rules. Meeting with the committee in mid-August, the police commissioner initially declared his opposition to putting black hostesses at the Buddies Club, but withdrew his objection when it was explained to him that there would be "no mixed dancing, but that colored boys could dance with colored girls." Shortly thereafter, a white hostess showed up at the Ruggles Street center. The committee issued firm instructions that this was not to happen again, and the "colored leaders [were] all up in arms."

By December the black hostesses had been introduced to the Buddies Club, but they soon left. The white hostesses "high-hatted them to such an extent" that they were instructed by black leaders not to go back again. The blacks now demanded that "a separate club" be established where, in Lowell's words, "everything goes and there is no discrimination in any way between whites and colored." This Lowell and the committee could not accept. The deadlock continued for the duration of the war, with the result that the USO facilities continued to be segregated.[33]

While the battle raged over the Buddies Club, Lowell also had to contend with a racial issue at the Harvard Club. Nothing in the club's rules explicitly barred blacks from membership, but the Elections Committee had wide discretion in its consideration of applicants. No man publicly identified as black had been a member of the club since its founding in 1908. (It is possible that no blacks applied—whether they did cannot be determined, as there are no surviving records.) But in the summer of 1943, the Harvard Club was asked to consider the candidacy of an eminent black Bostonian: William Henry Lewis.

Born shortly after the Civil War in Virginia, Lewis had come to New England to seek higher education and stayed for the rest of his life. He graduated from Amherst in 1892 and from Harvard Law School in 1895. The class orator and captain of the football team as an undergraduate, Lewis continued to play football while in law school and was the first black named to Walter Camp's All-America team. He served as assistant coach for the Harvard team for fifteen years. As a young man he was militant on racial issues (denied a haircut in a Cambridge barbershop, he successfully fought for a state law barring racial discrimination by businesses), but by the turn of the century he had aligned himself with the accommodationist approach of Booker T. Washington. After working in the Justice Department during the Taft administration, Lewis became a renowned criminal defense lawyer. When he died in 1949, a *Herald* obituary described his brilliance as a lawyer: "His eloquent delivery and rapier-like mind could hold an entire courtroom spellbound by the hour with alternate pathos and wit." Lewis's honorary pallbearers included Governor-Elect Paul Dever, Mayor Curley, Charles Francis Adams, two federal judges, and two judges of the Massachusetts Supreme Judicial Court.[34]

In August 1943 Lewis approached Lowell, as Harvard Club president, about becoming a member. At the age of seventy-four, all but retired and recently widowed, Lewis wanted a place where he could find companionship. Because he understood the difficulties posed by his interest, Lewis did not make a formal application; rather, he asked Lowell to explore how his candidacy would be received. While agreeing to do so, Lowell told the attorney that he thought it "very doubtful" that he would be admitted. Lowell pointed out that "it was not against him personally, but that it might start a precedent that would cause hard feeling in the Club and lead to a lot of resignations."[35]

Lewis's possible candidacy received strong endorsements from at least three prominent attorneys who were willing to put their views on paper, but the Board of Governors advised him not to proceed. "Although individually most of the Governors are in favor of electing him," Lowell observed, "we reluctantly felt it would cause a good deal of adverse feeling in the Club."[36]

Two years later, backed by Charles Francis Adams, Lewis submitted a formal request for membership. This took the question out of the hands of the Board of Governors and put it with the Elections Committee. Lowell's initial reaction was that the committee would "throw him down," but in May 1946 Lowell learned that the panel had tentatively agreed to accept him. Although the committee was interested in having the governors' opinions, Lowell insisted that Lewis was now the committee's "problem" and that the governors would back the committee however it decided. Lewis's name was to be posted "just like anyone else's," and "if several men objected he should not be elected; conversely, if no one objected or only one or two, then it was for [the committee] to decide whether or not to elect him."[37]

In the fall of 1946 Lewis's membership was approved, and the "old colored football player and coach at Harvard" telephoned Lowell to tell him how pleased he was. It meant more to him, he said, than the two honorary degrees he had received. When Lowell told him that he had "very little to do with the election," Lewis replied, "I know, but you could have blocked it, and I am very grateful." Perhaps Lowell could have, but if he did not exactly cover himself with glory in this episode, it is worth noting that the Harvard Club of New York had no black member until 1958. Lewis's admission generated no protests, and the club sent an official delegation to his funeral.[38]

Even though Lowell's role had been largely passive, the fact that Lewis had been admitted during his presidency marked him—in the context of mid-twentieth-century America—as someone with advanced views on racial issues. In 1948 Lowell was asked to serve on the advisory panel to the recently established Massachusetts Fair Employment Practices Committee. When he inquired why the heads of the bigger banks had not received similar requests, Lowell was told that he and Alan Forbes of the State Street Trust Company were seen as "the most liberal-minded bankers in the town." Lowell was intrigued by the request, but doubted he could get authorization from Boston Safe's directors because the appointment might "very easily lead to embarrassing situations." Whatever the reason, Lowell did not join the state advisory panel, which eventually was formed of prominent clergymen and other nonbusiness civic leaders.[39]

Sixteen years later, his active business career over and his philanthropic credentials firmly established, Lowell agreed to serve on another state advisory committee. The purpose of this committee was to study racial imbalance in Boston's public schools. Lowell had not taken a public stance on racial issues, either locally or nationally, during the decade leading up to his selection.* However, his work for the local chapter of the United Negro College Fund, the financial support given by the Hyams Fund to the Roxbury-based Freedom House, and his involvement with the Massachusetts Committee of Catholics, Protestants and Jews made him a logical choice. Among the other members of the advisory committee were Cardinal Cushing, the suffragan bishop of the Episcopal Diocese, the president of the Massachusetts Board of Rabbis, and the presidents of four area colleges. Together, the twenty-one men and women on the committee represented a cross-section of Boston's elite.†

---

* Although sympathetic to the objectives of the civil rights movement in the south in the early 1960s, Lowell was troubled by the use of civil disobedience and believed that northern whites had no business involving themselves in the protests. Diary, August 22, 1963; April 1, 29, July 5, 11, 1964; David O. Ives to author, March 17, 1994.

† An article in a national magazine, emphasizing the blue-ribbon nature of the group, mentioned only two members by name (Cushing and Lowell) and included a picture only of Lowell. "Rebalancing Boston," *Newsweek*, April 26, 1965, pp. 60–61.

The committee's report, hammered out by the group in February and March 1965 and released in April, demanded the end of racial imbalance in the schools "because it was right—educationally." Without dissent, the group proposed changes in the Boston School Committee's open enrollment policy and methods for siting new schools, and offered specific plans for "the exchange of students" between existing schools. While Lowell expressed some private misgivings about the report—"the professionals have sort of run away with it and tried to do more than the original plans called for"—he felt that the study had been "worthwhile." [40]

Conflict over Boston's racial future flared up in the aftermath of the advisory committee's recommendations, fueled mainly by the resistance of school committee members and their white neighborhood supporters to the busing proposals. Although black-white issues dominated the headlines, there was an undercurrent of class animosity: Louise Day Hicks, leader of the antibusing forces, denounced the advisory group's recommendations as the "pompous proclamations" of hypocrites whose own children attended private or suburban, all-white schools. Dismissing these sentiments as the ravings of "a stubborn, bigoted woman," Lowell was ready to back any of her rivals in the 1967 mayoral election. She lost, inspiring in Lowell "some hope for Boston." [41]

His ray of optimism proved unfounded; darker days along the color line lay ahead for Boston. Court-ordered school busing inflamed passions, incited violence across the racial divide, and rekindled the glowing ashes of the old cultural and economic antagonisms. The *Globe,* with its strong endorsement of busing, became a prime villain in the eyes of those hostile to the ruling. For Lowell, who had spent decades trying to accommodate differences and soothe the agony of change, the last years of his life proved painful as he watched Boston go to war with itself. [42]

14

"The perfect man for the job"

RESHAPING BOSTON POLITICS

owells originally made their name in Boston as politicians. John Lowell (1743–1802) and his son John (1769–1840) were vigorous partisans in the ideological battles of the Revolutionary and Early National eras. Francis Cabot Lowell's son John (1799–1836) carried this political tradition into the next generation by serving on the Boston City Council and the state legislature. But with the increasing democratization of politics, most of the later Lowells found the pursuit of elective office unappealing. Ralph's uncle James Arnold Lowell, his father's younger brother, won seats on the Newton Board of Alderman and in the state House of Representatives; however, politics in genteel Chestnut Hill was far different from the raucous brand practiced in the city of Boston.*

Immediately after graduating from college, Ralph took an active interest in the Republican Back Bay–Beacon Hill ward committee. But when he moved to Dedham after World War I he became active in a hallowed New England political institution not based on party affiliations. The major decisions in Dedham were made not by elected officials but by the open town meeting, in which all residents were entitled to speak and vote.

Among the more contentious questions in Dedham in the early 1920s was how to commemorate the twenty-four men from the town who had died in the World War. The Dedham town hall had been constructed as a memorial to the Civil War dead, and many in the community believed that something of a similarly utilitarian nature should be built in observance of the more recent conflict. However, a committee charged with

---

* James Arnold Lowell was appointed a federal judge in 1922 by President Harding.

studying the matter opted for a simple stone monument. This proposal failed to generate much enthusiasm, and a new committee was selected. Lowell served as its secretary.[1]

After six months of deliberations, the committee recommended constructing a park on twenty-three acres of town-owned marshland close to the business district. The site would be filled in and recreational facilities built to form a beautiful, permanent, and fitting memorial to Dedham's fallen heroes.* However, at an estimated cost of $100,000, the project would require a property tax increase. Many in the town questioned the wisdom of sinking public funds into a "bottomless swamp," and in the spring of 1925 a spirited debate took place in the town meeting. Lowell strongly defended the proposal and urged those present to reject the opponents' effort to put the issue before the voters in a referendum. After defeating the motion for a referendum by a vote of 195 to 326, the town meeting adopted Lowell's resolution authorizing the committee to proceed with its plans. Lowell then asked permission to address the gathering and appealed to everyone to unite behind the memorial, which was to be named War Memorial Park.[2]

His plea went unheeded. Although the state legislature and the governor approved the legislation necessary for Lowell's committee to borrow money for the project, the opposition kept up its unrelenting fire. Wary about pushing ahead under these conditions, the park's supporters agreed to let the matter be settled by a referendum. In May 1926 the voters of Dedham rejected the War Memorial Park, 584 to 1981. Not until May 1931 was a memorial to Dedham's World War dead completed; it took the form of a monument.[3]

The struggle over the war memorial revealed deep political fissures in Dedham, and in November 1926 the town changed the form of government it had used since its founding nearly three centuries earlier. The New England town meeting has often been celebrated as a birthplace of American democracy, but by the 1920s Dedham and other communities were questioning its viability. The obvious problem was numbers: Dedham had 4,900 voters on its rolls, but the town hall auditorium could accommodate only 600 people. From Lowell's perspective, however, the

---

* This approach was similar to the one Lowell favored for Harvard's war memorial (see chapter 9).

difficulty was not so much quantity as quality. In decades past, communities like Dedham had been fairly homogeneous and property ownership widely distributed, with the result that town meetings usually could be counted on to forge a sustainable consensus. But the growing "preponderance of uneducated and foreign citizens," Lowell wrote, had turned the proceedings into "a real farce." Groups with strong views on one or two issues "packed" the meeting hall to "the exclusion of other townspeople." The widely adopted remedy was the representative town meeting, in which the town was divided into districts and the voters elected town meeting members; the number chosen was far greater than that found on city councils but much smaller than the total adult population. Dedham conducted its first elections for town meeting members in March 1927, and Lowell finished fifth among the winners in his district in a field of almost ninety candidates. But coming as it did just days after his daughter's death, this victory brought no satisfaction to Lowell and he was not active in town politics during his remaining years in Dedham.[4]

The shift to Sunrise Farm in Westwood in the 1930s meant a return to the open town meeting format, but Lowell did not become as involved there as he had in Dedham. His personal economic misfortunes during the Depression decade and his preoccupation with national and global issues in the 1940s and 1950s overshadowed community concerns. Not until the mid-1950s did Lowell find himself drawn into local politics again. And that was in a place where he had no vote: Boston.

A CITY IN DECLINE

"The Hub of the Solar System," as Oliver Wendell Holmes called Boston at the middle of the nineteenth century, was a city in trouble at the middle of the twentieth century. By the most common standard of municipal progress—population growth—Boston stood at an all-time high (the 1950 census counted more than 800,000 residents), but by every other gauge the city was going downhill and had been for decades. By 1960 Boston's population had dropped below 700,000, a loss of 13 percent, the steepest fall for any major American city in the 1950s. Boston's difficulties and their causes were hardly unique; urban physical obsolescence and suburbanization, for example, were national phenomena. But these problems were intensified in Boston because of its distinctive economic, social, and political characteristics.

If Boston's claim to be the Hub of the Solar System was met with great amusement elsewhere, there was no questioning Boston's central place in the New England regional economy. But New England failed to keep pace with national economic growth for most of the first half of the twentieth century, and Boston keenly felt the slippage. Changes in long-distance railroad rates, which had heretofore favored New England, inflicted harm on the Port of Boston unmatched since the Jeffersonian Embargo of the early 1800s. Mainstays of the region's business, such as shipbuilding, furniture manufacture, and silverware crafting, fell victim to competition from other parts of the country or to changes in consumer tastes. But it was the virtual disappearance of the textile industry—an enterprise intimately associated with both New England and the Lowells—that epitomized the region's plight. Enticed to the south by more profitable conditions (cheaper power, a work force accustomed to low wages, and state government hostility toward labor unions), New England businessmen abandoned the communities to which they had been attached for generations with scarcely a look back.

Paralleling and, to some degree, contributing to the deterioration of Boston's economic core was the fraying of the city's social fabric. After decades of enduring the arrogance and—to use a term applied by psychiatrist Robert Coles—"cruel spitefulness" of the dominant Yankee culture, the Boston Irish became more assertive about their own traditions. When Yankee Boston celebrated March 17 as Evacuation Day (the anniversary of the British Army's departure from Boston in 1776), Irish Boston conspicuously marked the date as St. Patrick's Day. As the Yankees retreated into suburban enclaves and the Irish established their own separate institutions, most notably a large parochial school system, the lines of communication between the most powerful economic group and the largest demographic group were stretched to the breaking point.[5]

It was in politics that the Irish could demonstrate most effectively the force of their numbers, and it was in the person of James Michael Curley that they took revenge on the haughty Yankees. Curley's "basic source of power," John Gunther observed in 1947, "was his identification with all the resentments closely cherished by the Irish underpossessed." By waging war on the "codfish aristocracy" (a label he called "a reflection on the fish"), Curley built a political career that spanned the first five decades of the century and placed him in the mayor's office for four terms.[6]

Curley savaged the Yankees in every way he could. His most potent weapon was the power to tax. Although their homes and personal property in suburbia lay beyond his grasp, the Yankees' offices and businesses were in Boston, and Curley skewed the city's real estate assessments to place a disproportionate share of the tax burden on downtown commercial buildings. Homeowners and apartment dwellers got off easy and rewarded Curley on election day, but the city paid a price for accepting the political leadership of this "last of the buccaneers." Viewing Curley's tax policies as confiscatory, the Yankee-controlled financial institutions refused mortgages for new structures in the central business district; when the John Hancock Insurance Company took the bold step of building new headquarters there in the late 1940s, its huge tax bill discouraged downtown construction for more than a decade. Between 1930 and 1958 Boston's tax base shrank 25 percent, and properties typically sold at prices considerably below their assessed valuation.[7]

Lowell personally owned no real estate in Boston, but as a banker and trustee he knew the hazards of doing so. The buildings owned by Boston Safe Deposit and Trust were marginal earners at best, and after Lowell became a trustee of the Jordan estate in 1949, he took the lead in selling off the Boston properties in its portfolio, reinvesting the proceeds in stocks and bonds. The Lowell Institute had long owned the buildings at 2, 4, and 6 Commonwealth Avenue, but Lowell sold them within five years after taking over as Trustee. Although the institute carried them on its books at a value of $226,500, Lowell thought he had done quite well by accepting an offer of $135,000. In 1959 Lowell sold a parcel the institute owned on Franklin Street, again at a figure below the book value. "We do not want Boston real estate," Lowell wrote in his diary, "the way the city is going."[8]

As Curley and the Yankee businessmen traded potshots through the 1920s, 1930s, and 1940s, Boston continued to deteriorate physically. The once-bustling waterfront was now little more than a collection of derelict piers; Scollay Square, where Lowell had often gone to the theater as a youth, became a tawdry entertainment district where Lowell could not feel comfortable taking his family; the fashionable shops on Tremont Street facing the Common were replaced by miscellaneous cut-rate businesses; and many formerly ritzy townhouses in the Back Bay now functioned as rooming houses. If one site epitomized Boston's decline at midcentury, it was the corner of Federal and Franklin streets in the core of the business district, where the squat, pillared edifice of Lee, Higginson once had stood. Only a parking lot remained. Tourists still came to visit the historic sites, but the city's past was blackening its present and threatening its future. The Yankees, nostalgic for the days when they dominated all aspects of Boston life, would not supply the needed economic stimulus; the Irish, nursing old grievances, persisted in electing politicians who gave the Yankees little reason to alter their attitude.[9]

HALTING EFFORTS AT CHANGE

In 1948 Lowell was invited to become a director of the Boston Chamber of Commerce. His acceptance owed more to a desire to increase Boston Safe's visibility among businessmen than to any expectation that this group could steer the city's economic turnaround. In its early years, the chamber (founded in 1909) had been led by giants such as James Jackson Storrow and Edward A. Filene; by the 1940s it was dominated by men with little vision and even less power. In 1949–1950 the president of the chamber was the head of a family-owned company that supplied food and equipment for bakeries, restaurants, and soda fountains. After listening to him speak at a chamber luncheon meeting, Lowell observed: "He seems to be one of those wonderfully optimistic go-getters that we produce here in America. He sketched in glowing terms all that the Chamber is doing and how wonderful and faithful all the various committee members are. It was a good deal like shaking hands with one's self." The lack of inspiration at the top was matched by lack of harmony below. "The Chamber should be a great help to the city," Lowell noted in 1948, "but there are so many cross-currents and political feet to be stepped on, that very little can be accomplished."[10]

Some of those divisions were rooted in the way the Common and Public Garden split the downtown commercial district, but as in practically everything else about Boston, social and cultural fault lines were also involved. When Lowell became one of the chamber's four vice-presidents in the early 1950s, he dismissed his selection as "just a little window dressing they are doing to keep one of the 'Puritan' crowd in amongst the preponderantly Catholic Chamber."[11]

Although the business sector at midcentury lacked any spark, the political scene was beginning to stir. In the 1949 mayoral contest, Boston voters rejected the seventy-four-year-old Curley's bid for a fifth term. (Nevertheless, he received the highest ballot count of his eight mayoral contests.) The victor among the five candidates was a veteran municipal employee making his first race for elective office: John B. Hynes. Hynes had come to the public's attention in 1947 when, under the provisions of a special state law, he served as acting mayor for five months while Curley was in jail after his conviction on mail fraud charges. Lacking Curley's flamboyance, Hynes fulfilled his responsibilities competently and burnished his reputation for honesty. Republicans as well as anti-Curley Democrats saw Hynes as an attractive candidate against Curley, and his campaign for mayor received generous financial support from the downtown business community. Among the Republican contributors were Brahmins such as Henry Lee Shattuck, Henry Parkman, and Robert Cutler. Lowell probably contributed as well, but he recorded no comments about the bitterly fought contest until it was over. "Here in Boston," he wrote, obviously referring to his colleagues on State Street, "everyone feels well over Hynes' unexpected victory over Curley, which will probably mean the end of the 'old grey mayor.'"[12]

Lowell accurately assessed Curley's future—the 1949 election was his last hurrah. He challenged Hynes in a rematch in 1951 and was defeated by a record margin; his candidacy in 1955 was widely taken as a joke, even by Curley himself. When he died in 1958 he had ceased to be a factor in the city's politics. But his legacy persisted, and Hynes, try as he might, could not overcome the mistrust and pessimism that Curley's long career had sowed among Boston's business leaders. They liked Hynes personally, but the mayor could not supply the resolute leadership the city needed.[13]

The drawn-out struggle to build on the abandoned freight yards of the Boston and Albany Railroad demonstrated Hynes's weaknesses. The twenty-eight-acre site in the Back Bay had been on the market for two years when, in early 1953, real estate developer Roger L. Stevens announced plans to buy it and construct a $75 million complex of office buildings, stores, apartments, and a hotel. Despite the project's breathtaking size, Stevens's record inspired confidence; he was the leader of the syndicate that had purchased the Empire State Building for the highest price yet paid for a single building. The mayor was ecstatic. This plan, he announced, "certainly explodes any myth that Boston is all done for and isn't a good financial risk."[14]

Hynes could not have been more wrong. In the summer of 1953, Lowell made note of a conversation about the planned project with a New York developer. The developer "really went to town, saying that if you wanted to know the wrong way to do anything, no matter what, the place to come to is Boston." The events of the next two years vindicated that appraisal. The fact that neither Stevens nor his bankers were Bostonians highlighted how little faith Boston businessmen had in their own community. Stevens's insistence on substantial tax concessions from the city placed the mayor in a political bind. (No investor, Stevens claimed, would put funds into Boston with its "present high tax rate and unsound real estate base.") Hynes attempted to strike a deal with Stevens, but merchants, hotel operators, and owners of other commercial properties bitterly opposed any special treatment for the Back Bay project. The Chamber of Commerce was badly divided over the issue, and after Hynes negotiated a novel tax arrangement with Stevens, the state Supreme Judicial Court, in a 1955 advisory opinion, declared it unconstitutional. Stevens backed out and another two years would pass before anyone else expressed interest in his plans.[15]

Lowell had supported Hynes's efforts to keep the Stevens project on track, and in 1955 he made a $200 contribution (through Cutler) to the mayor's reelection campaign. The incumbent's leading challenger was John Powers, a South Boston politician who was the Democratic minority leader in the Massachusetts Senate. Powers struck themes reminiscent of Curley, attacking Hynes as "consistently subservient [to] State Street and the banking interests," and Lowell and his associates viewed the contest as one between "good government and a return to the old days of Curley and company." Hynes defeated Powers with a good but not impressive showing (his margin of victory was about the same as in the contest with Curley six years earlier). Lowell was encouraged: "We are off for what should be an excellent four years for Boston."[16]

LOOKING FOR LEADERSHIP

Lowell's optimism in the immediate aftermath of Hynes's triumph was understandable, but the reality of Boston's problems soon dampened his spirits. At the inauguration in January 1956 the mayor reiterated his pledge to the business community to curb municipal spending, but the following year he was at the door of the State House pleading for a $45 million loan from the Commonwealth. Hynes may have restored integrity to the very top of Boston government, but he brought neither economy nor productivity to the bureaucracy; the city operated in the red every year of his administration. The state came up with the necessary legislation after Hynes agreed to the oversight provisions demanded by politicians (especially Powers) and businessmen alike, but the mayor had lost his luster. A 1960 survey of business executives in six cities found Boston's business leaders the unhappiest by far with their community's political climate.[17]

Various mechanisms were set in motion in the mid-1950s to help businessmen transform this climate, but none proved effective. The most ambitious and enduring was the Boston College Citizen Seminar. The Jesuit institution's School of Business Administration, its roots strong in the city's Irish neighborhoods but weak in the corporate offices, seized upon the metropolitan area's economic problems as a means of attracting attention to itself. A one-day conference in May 1954 was well attended, and plans were laid for a series of seminars to which labor union officials and politicians, as well as business leaders, would be invited. In October 1954, Lowell and some 250 others attended the first seminar. Hynes delivered what Lowell termed a "masterful speech." Lowell was pleased by the "great turnout," which he said "encourages one to think that something constructive can be done for Boston under the leadership of our excellent mayor."[18]

Lowell became a faithful attendee of the seminars, which met about three times a year, and chaired the session held in November 1956. But the practical achievements of the forum were slim, apart from providing a social setting where prominent individuals from different sectors could get together. One critic dismissed the seminars as "essentially prayer meetings which produce little except an ego-warming splash of publicity in the next day's papers." Lowell's observations were not as caustic, but they pointed in the same direction. The seminars were useful, he noted, in creating the feeling that "something should be done about Boston" and that the participants "had at least some responsibility toward seeing it done." But, Lowell concluded, "there must be leadership to carry them forward to see that their results are attained."[19]

Leadership was the crucial element and no one was prepared to provide it. Pittsburgh's Leland Hazard* addressed this issue at an early Citizen Seminar, in May 1955. Hazard had headed the businessmen's group that, in cooperation with Pittsburgh's Democratic mayor, had forged a postwar urban renaissance in Steel City. The message Hazard delivered was simple:

---

* For information about Hazard and Lowell's common interest in educational television, see chapter 8.

To emulate Pittsburgh's success, Boston needed active leadership by a small group of "men of influence and power." Such a group could not wait for some kind of official appointment from the governor or mayor. No one appointed us, Hazard said, "we appointed ourselves." It was a message the Boston business community either did not understand at the time or could not accept. At the January 1957 session of the seminar a leading real estate developer endorsed Hazard's call for leadership from "those persons who represent the highest level of economic power in the community." But instead of advocating independent action, the speaker recommended gaining mayoral recognition first. Lowell thought this would work: "If the real five leaders could be persuaded to take the job on, something really constructive could be done for the City of Boston. If Mayor Hynes really comes through he will have done a great thing." [20]

Hynes, however, decided to ask not five but one hundred individuals to join his new Committee on Civic Progress in February 1957. Its mandate was broad: to mobilize support for "any program or proposal which will be beneficial to the city and to the community." Lowell was among those appointed, and he served on the fifteen-member executive committee; his major contribution was to help engineer a change in the chairmanship to bring in someone more dynamic than the mayor's original choice. But the committee's unwieldy size and ill-defined agenda proved insurmountable handicaps. Even after breaking free of its formal ties to the mayor, the committee "remained only a hundred eminent names on a letterhead." [21]

A basic weakness of the Committee on Civic Progress was the absence of a shared faith among Boston's business leaders that the city had a future. Not even the announcement in January 1957 that the New Jersey–based Prudential Life Insurance Company was prepared to resurrect the Stevens plan to build on the Back Bay railroad yards could shake off the widespread sense of gloom. Lowell despaired of finding a way to reverse the city's deteriorating financial and physical condition, but he was too much of a civic booster to let his concerns appear in print, especially in a national publication. Thus he told a *Fortune* reporter in the spring of 1957, "I feel like a doctor who knows the worst is over, the turn for the better has come. Things are beginning to boil in Boston." But Lloyd Brace, president of the powerful First National Bank of Boston, was also interviewed for the same article and undercut Lowell's comment. Brace, whose business interests ranged far beyond the metropolitan area and even the New England region, declared that it was impossible to build in the Hub and make

a profit. The Prudential, he claimed, was willing to do it only for the prestige. Referring to plans by New York developer William Zeckendorf to
build a complex of offices and shops near South Station, Brace remarked,
"I don't know where he'll get the money." The president of the New
Haven Railroad, which owned the property in question and stood to gain
if Zeckendorf went ahead, agreed with Brace: "A wonderful place and a
wonderful project, but the taxes are too high." [22]

In the weeks following the appearance of the *Fortune* article that June,
events in Boston seemed to vindicate Brace's pessimism. In the middle of
the month the New York owners of R. H. White's department store, a
downtown fixture for more than a century, announced they were closing
the block-long, five-story building. They had previously informed City
Hall that they would not undertake a needed $1 million modernization
project without a 50 percent reduction in the store's tax assessment. When
Mayor Hynes offered them only 33⅓ percent, the store was shuttered. Two
months later the state legislature, following the lead of Powers and other
prominent Democratic politicians, defeated a sales tax bill supported by
the Democratic governor and the Boston Chamber of Commerce. Lowell
and most businessmen saw the sales tax as the best way to relieve the pressure of the ever-rising property taxes, but Powers denounced it as class
legislation. Boston, wrote Lowell, had suffered a "bad blow." [23]

Few took the defeat of the sales tax harder than Harold Hodgkinson,
the chief of Filene's. Fearing that Boston was "headed for the rocks," he
approached Lowell in the summer of 1957 with the idea of forming a small
emergency committee of politicians and businessmen to work out a compromise on new revenue sources for the city. Hodgkinson wanted Lowell
to lead it. "I consider you," he told Lowell, "the Number One citizen of
Boston and believe they all would come at your invitation, and that you
would get results." Lowell demurred, insisting that he was "no politician
and could be tied in knots by them." A few weeks later the pair met with
two other concerned business leaders to discuss the need for "immediate
action"; they agreed to work through a reinvigorated Committee on Civic
Progress. [24]

This was not the first time Lowell had rejected a conspicuous role in
turning Boston's fortunes around. Two years earlier, attorney Donald J.
Hurley, a partner in a prominent downtown law firm, had asked Lowell
to succeed him as president of the Chamber of Commerce. Citing the tremendous demands the job would put on his time (and the need to fly),

Lowell declined, adding in his diary, "I am not a politician." He felt that Hurley was much better suited for the post, by both his professional training and his Irish ancestry. Indeed, Lowell thought Hurley had done an excellent job in his unprecedented two-year stint as chamber president. When Lloyd Brace came to Lowell in the fall of 1957 and asked him to take over the Committee on Civic Progress and breathe some life into it, Lowell suggested Hurley instead. Since Hurley had been Brace's second choice, the two bankers agreed that they would serve as co–vice chairmen under Hurley.[25]

The words "civic progress" seemed a parody of reality during the final twenty-four months of John Hynes's decade-long tenure in City Hall. Progress was not entirely absent: The city used federal subsidies available under the Housing Acts of 1949 and 1954 to clear tracts of land for redevelopment in the South and West Ends; the Mechanics Building, where Ralph and Charlotte Lowell had attended the flower show every spring, was demolished to make way for construction of the Prudential Center and a municipal auditorium in the Back Bay; and the federal government had announced plans to construct a new office building in Boston. But each project still faced obstacles. No financing had been found for the high-rise luxury apartment houses that were supposed to replace the West End tenements. Prudential had reached a tax agreement with the city for its fifty-two-story tower and other structures in the complex; but the agreement was of questionable legality, and unhappy property owners threatened court action. And while the federal authorities had no financial or tax problems standing in their way, they were undecided whether to locate their building in the Back Bay or in a projected Government Center complex Hynes wanted to construct at Scollay Square. None of these projects was entirely firm when Hynes left office.[26]

UPSET VICTORY

The main concern of Lowell and other business leaders in the 1959 election year was not the uncertain future of urban redevelopment but the deteriorating condition of municipal finances. In a recent contract settlement the Hynes administration had granted police and firemen what the leaders of the Committee on Civic Progress considered to be overly generous pay hikes. "[W]e are very much worried and frustrated," Lowell wrote, "[by the unwillingness of] the Mayor or Council to . . . cut down expenses and shave our terrible taxes." It was clear that the tax levy, which had stood at just under $60 per $1000 of assessed valuation when Hynes became mayor in 1950, would exceed $100 in 1959. In crossing that symbolic barrier, Lowell observed in February, "Boston [was] fast headed for real trouble." Indeed, before the year's end one of the bond-rating services lowered its evaluation of Boston's debt from A to Baa. Back in 1946 the city's bonds had been considered "excellent as its beans and cod"; now they were rated the lowest in the country for cities with populations greater than 500,000.[27]

The upcoming mayoral election offered the business community little hope that the city's finances would be improved any time soon. The mayor's chair had been all but conceded to Massachusetts Senate president John Powers, the man Hynes defeated in 1955 and the key opponent of the sales tax two years later. In anticipation of running again in 1959, Powers had built up a huge campaign treasury and put together a large personal organization of volunteers. There seemed to be no stopping him. Most Democrats lined up behind Powers, including the Commonwealth's junior U.S. senator, White House aspirant John F. Kennedy, who praised his "vigorous leadership." Even the Boston *Herald*, which in 1955 had likened Powers to Curley, got aboard the bandwagon, as did several Republican politicians.[28]

In April Powers was a guest at a Somerset Club lunch attended by twenty-five "leading Bostonians." Obviously not intimidated by the setting or his fellow diners, the Senate president reiterated his unalterable opposition to the sales tax. He claimed he would bring down the tax rate by doing away with the abatements on property assessments that commercial property owners—including some of the "leading Bostonians" in his audience—had exacted from the municipal government. "So you can imagine," Lowell wrote, "he was out of step with his audience. Things look bad for the old city."[29]

Nothing seemed to being going right for Boston in 1959. Lowell usually came away from the Boston College Citizen Seminar feeling upbeat, but a May session on transportation left him "really blue about the future of Boston." The four experts who addressed the meeting were split four ways, "a most discouraging" experience. As the September preliminary election for mayor approached, Lowell struck an uncharacteristically gloomy note in late July:

All the groups trying to help Boston are really not getting anywhere due to lack of leadership that could effectively tell the politicians that are ruining the city where they got off. My hope that we could save the city is fast diminishing and I don't know the answer, unless four or five men under the leadership of Lloyd Brace would really take things in hand as they did in Pittsburgh. With Johnnie Powers likely to be our next mayor, it is difficult to feel optimistic over the future of Boston.[30]

If Lowell found any reason to for optimism after the first round of balloting, he made no note of it, and at first glance the results were not promising. As expected, Powers easily outdistanced his four challengers, gaining 34 percent of the vote. This was not the 50 to 60 percent his campaign managers had expected, but it still put him 12 percentage points ahead of the surprise runner-up, John F. Collins, who finished 2,500 votes ahead of the third-place candidate. The rules in effect since 1951 now called for a face-off between Powers and Collins. This had happened in two prior contests and in both the winner of the preliminary round had emerged victorious. So the betting money was still on Powers.

A few of the people in Lowell's circle, notably Henry Lee Shattuck and Robert Cutler, had been in Collins's corner since the start of his candidacy, but most of the men on State Street knew little about him. He was, after all, a Democrat, though something of a maverick; as a backbencher in the state legislature Collins had opposed a measure supported by organized labor and the Democratic governor. After an unsuccessful race for attorney general in 1954, Collins won a seat on the Boston City Council the following year, despite being struck down in the midst of the campaign by polio; thenceforth he would be confined to a wheelchair. Although Collins left the council in 1957 to accept the sinecure of registrar of probate for Suffolk County, the fires of ambition burned deep within him and he took on the challenge of beating Powers.

The Powers-Collins contest has become the stuff of Boston legend: how the poorly financed, straight-talking Collins, exuding the "carefree, sunny charm of a curly-haired parochial choir boy grown older," bested the power-hungry, wheeling-dealing Senate president. Several factors contributed to the remarkable upset: Collins's adept use of the underdog role, his more effective performance on television, and his success in linking Powers to shady political arrangements and unsavory characters. It is often claimed that the election turned on the arrests of several bookies in an East Boston barroom, which displayed a prominent "Powers for Mayor" sign, on the Friday before the balloting; this association of Powers with the Mob fueled a last-minute advertising blitz by the Collins campaign. Whatever the reason, the upstart won with nearly 56 percent of the vote.[31]

One of the more intriguing aspects of the 1959 election was the part played by "leading Bostonians." As the April lunch at the Somerset Club reaffirmed, Powers and the State Street group had very different ideas on how to attack Boston's financial problems. Nonetheless, many of these "leading Bostonians" contributed to his campaign chest, explaining afterward with "exquisite Puritan honesty," as one magazine writer put it, that they simply had thought Powers was going to win. If Lowell gave to anyone, he did not record it. And if, as some have contended, the State Street group hedged its bets by making contributions to Collins in the final weeks before the election, Lowell's diary contains no mention of the shift.[32]

To the extent that State Street had a leader in the 1959 drama, it was Lloyd Brace of the First National Bank, the single most powerful figure in the financial community. If Lowell had not left the First National in 1917 to join the army, it is conceivable that he would have held the position — and influence — eventually achieved by Brace, his junior by thirteen years. As the bank's president from 1948, Brace operated in a national arena* that was closed to Lowell; and Lowell, by the mid-1950s, believed that nothing could be accomplished on the local scene unless Brace gave Boston his attention. Brace was less than supportive of the effort by Hurley and Lowell in 1954 to beef up the Chamber of Commerce, and his gloomy remarks to *Fortune* in 1957, prophetic as they turned out to be, demonstrated scant regard for the need to bolster Boston's image.[33]

However, the admission by Mayor Hynes early in 1957 that municipal finances were badly in the red seems to have galvanized Brace into action. In February of that year, Brace helped broker a peace treaty between Hynes and Powers (it soon fell apart) and proposed forming a twelve-to-fifteen-member group, composed of representatives from the business community and the state and city governments, that would meet once a week to "troubleshoot" Boston's problems. When the politicians spurned the idea, Brace helped create a new group in the winter of 1958–1959 known

---

* Among Brace's directorships were AT&T, General Motors, the National Industrial Conference Board, and the Rockefeller Foundation.

as the Coordinating Committee, which linked six major business and civic organizations (the Greater Boston Chamber of Commerce, the Greater Boston Economic Study Committee, the Committee on Civic Progress, the Boston Real Estate Board, the Boston Retail Trade Board, and the Boston Municipal Research Bureau). The creation of the Coordinating Committee was kept out of the press; unlike its constituents, this panel, of which Lowell was a member, preferred to operate totally in private.[34]

The Coordinating Committee remained on the sidelines through the preliminary skirmishes of the 1959 mayoral contest, but after Powers and Collins emerged as the finalists the committee extended secret invitations to each man to meet in separate one-hour sessions. Both meetings were held on October 13 at the Sheraton Plaza Hotel (a holding of the corporation directed by one of the committee members). Brace served as moderator.

In his presentation to the group, Collins laid out the three major themes of his campaign: first, a policy of "no hire, no fire" to begin cutting municipal spending; second, a limited statewide 3 percent sales tax to relieve the tremendous tax burden placed on the city's property owners; and third, an ambitious urban renewal program. Spending cuts and property tax relief had long headed the business community's agenda, and Lowell naturally was pleased by what Collins had to say. But Lowell badly misjudged both the man and his prospects. "Collins," he wrote, "is in a wheelchair, a polio victim, but he doesn't strike me as having much personality or force, but he would work with business to save the city. Unfortunately I do not think that he can beat Powers." Others at the meeting may have recognized the underdog's potential, but whether they acted on this discovery remains in dispute.[35]

The committee's session with Powers went as expected. An air of mutual hostility hovered over the encounter as the Senate president once more rejected a sales tax and argued on behalf of "reform" of the property tax abatement system. Lowell summed it up afterward: "Powers put on quite a show, answering all our hopeful questions in the negative." One participant recalled Lowell's saying, "Gentlemen, we all know double-talk and even triple-talk, but I don't know what that was." In his diary, Lowell observed: "We were pretty discouraged when we got through. The old city will be older and poorer under Mr. Powers as Mayor."[36]

Lowell remained pessimistic during the final weeks of the campaign. A meeting of the executive committee of the Committee on Civic Progress produced "a good deal of talk and argument, but really got nowhere." Businessmen, he predicted, would wait out the election and then "they will really get down to work on the major problems of the city, cooperating with the new mayor if possible—if not, trying to sell the public on the desperate situation the city is in and go over the mayor's head." [37]

Lowell stayed up late at his Westwood home on November 3 and watched the election returns on WGBH. Confessing that he was "dumbfounded" by Collins's unexpected triumph, Lowell declared, "There is hope for Boston." [38]

THE VAULT

The next morning the executive committee of the Chamber of Commerce held its regularly scheduled meeting. Erskine White, president of the New England Telephone and Telegraph Company, revived the idea of creating a steering committee of ten to twelve men, each the top officer of his company, to coordinate the work of the half-dozen or so groups seeking to reverse Boston's economic decline. "With Collins as Mayor," Lowell noted, "there is hope that he will play with business and really do something about our zooming tax rate and general sickness of the city." All would depend, however, on the makeup of the group, and here Lowell was dubious: "Several of our top men are not really interested in the city and this must be a real working committee." [39]

Three weeks later the executive board of the Committee on Civic Progress was granted an interview with Collins. The meeting took place under a cloud: The city's bond rating had just dropped, and rumors were spreading of a scheme by bankers to force the municipality into bankruptcy. Collins left no doubt that he would treat any such attempt as a criminal conspiracy and that he would carry out the three-point program on which his campaign had been based. Despite the perils facing Boston, Lowell came away from the session much encouraged: "Collins in effect asked for our cooperation and backing and declared he would give his all to help cure the troubles of the City of Boston. . . . It is up to us to carry on and that very quickly." [40]

Others took the lead in putting together the businessmen's group, but when they were ready to announce their plans to the public, the person they wanted as chairman and spokesman was Lowell. On December 17 Brace, White, Gerald W. Blakeley (the head of the commercial real estate development firm of Cabot, Cabot & Forbes, and a Boston Safe director), and attorney Edward B. Hanify (a partner in the prestigious Ropes & Gray), came to Lowell's office and requested that he head a reconstituted "Coordinating Committee" of sixteen men, which was "to make one last try at saving the City of Boston by backing, helping, and steering Mayor Collins." Lowell was "the perfect man for the job," they told him, because he "liked the men who make up the city and are not 'old Bostonians'" and because Lowell had "no enemies."[41]

Lowell hesitated, citing the need to discuss the matter with his wife. Although he had a lighter business schedule since stepping down as president of Boston Safe in January, he had recently promised Charlotte that he would avoid additional responsibilities. His next birthday would be his seventieth, and they both agreed he should cut back. But when he presented the proposal to Charlotte, they decided that he should accept. The job would entail none of the evening functions that Lowell found increasingly tiring, and the committee's mission was so important that Lowell felt to beg off would be shirking his duty.[42]

The coordinating "group" ("we want to get away from the word 'committee'," Lowell noted) gathered for the first time at the Boston Safe building on December 21. In addition to the four men who had called upon Lowell a few days earlier, the attendees included most of the city's economic leaders. Much has been written since then to the effect that this group represented, as one political scientist declared in 1960, the "return of political responsibility to the Yankee businessmen." Yet most of these men were Yankees only in the geographic sense. Many were not Massachusetts natives, and at least three of those from Massachusetts were Irish Catholics. Lowell was the only certifiable Brahmin (although others joined later), and the only member closely identified with the venerable (and expanding) Bostonian profession of managing other people's money. Brace and some of the others made the committee a force that politicians had to reckon with; Lowell gave it the historical legitimacy Bostonians craved.[43]

The members authorized Lowell to meet one-on-one with the mayor-elect and to issue a press release announcing the group's formation. Lowell had trouble getting hold of Collins, but on December 24 they had a "pleasant" half-hour meeting. The press release went out in conjunction with their meeting, and the next morning it was front-page news in both the *Globe* and the *Herald,* complete with a photo of Lowell. Because it was Christmas Day, most readers probably missed the story, which suited

Lowell and his associates just fine; having gone public with a statement of their aims ("to review long range objectives as well as immediate issues facing Boston") and of their plans to meet regularly with Collins, they could now slip back into the shadows and operate behind closed doors.[44]

Indeed, the nickname by which the coordinating group soon was known—The Vault—underlines the exclusive and secretive nature of its role. Lowell was unintentionally responsible for the label. As head of the group he made the arrangements for its biweekly meetings with the mayor, and the Boston Safe building was the natural choice, both for convenience and for privacy. The group usually met in the board of directors' room on the sixth floor, but sometimes it moved to a conference room in the basement, adjacent to the bank's giant vault. A newspaperman came up with the tag "The Vault," and decades after Lowell left the committee and Boston Safe vacated the Franklin Street building, the term is still being used.[45]

Over the next eight years Collins and the Coordinating Committee forged the partnership that built "the New Boston." The businessmen helped recruit expert local personnel for the municipal government. They used their economic clout to win confirmation of the mayor's controversial candidate for director of urban renewal: Philadelphia-born, Yale-educated Edward Logue. Collins, Logue, and the Vault together paved the way for the huge Government Center complex at Scollay Square and overcame the last obstacles to construction of the Prudential Center in the Back Bay. John Hancock, whose chairman was a Vault member, supplied the financing that finally started redevelopment in the West End. The mayor's cost cutting allowed him to lower the tax rate, and in 1966, after an expensive lobbying campaign financed by the Vault, the state legislature enacted a sales tax to relieve the pressure on local property owners. Collins's two terms changed the direction of Boston politics, brought a new focus to campaign issues, and started an economic upswing that continued, with only a few interruptions, for the next thirty years.[46]

For Lowell, whose seven-year chairmanship of the Coordinating Committee was mainly titular, pride in Boston's progress was tinged by regret at what had been lost. International-style skyscrapers, many of them built by banks, including Lowell's own Boston Safe, were changing the appearance and character of the downtown district. No admirer of these glass behemoths on aesthetic grounds, Lowell was also distressed by their effect on the old dining clubs, which lost business to the skyscrapers' executive dining rooms. The clubs—including the Tavern—were "now almost deserted." In 1968 Lowell, while attending a board meeting, was observed looking out the window on the twenty-fifth floor of the John Hancock building. The big tax levied on the building when it was new in the late 1940s had frightened off further construction in the city, but in 1967 John Hancock had announced plans to build an even taller home across the street. Noting Lowell's interest in the scene below, a friend jokingly asked, "Don't you know Boston by now?" "Maybe," Lowell replied, "but I want to look at it once again before it disappears."[47]

15

"Keeping the faith"

GRAND BOSTONIAN

The Boston where Ralph Lowell grew up, the setting for his business and civic activities, had largely disappeared by the time he celebrated his eightieth birthday in 1970. Much of the change was physical. The municipal government was no longer housed in the century-old City Hall of French Second Empire design, but in a stark, spanking new concrete structure that sat alone on a forbidding brick-paved, wind-swept plaza. The Back Bay, while reviving from its decline into seediness, stood in the shadow of the fifty-two-story Prudential Tower. The rich character of Boston's downtown, which had meshed the financial citadels of State Street, the tenements of the North End, and the bustle of the harbor, had been defaced by an elevated highway. And the Hub of the Solar System was ringed by a beltway (Route 128) that diverted travelers and commerce from the central city. Only in numerical population did Boston resemble the city Lowell had known as a young man. In 1970 it had 640,000 residents—about the same as in 1910, when Lowell was a Harvard undergraduate. (The city had lost 160,000 since its peak in 1950.) A decade later, two years after Lowell's death, the figure stood at 560,000—just where it had been when the century began and Lowell was ten years old.

Even more pronounced was the social transformation of Lowell's Boston. The near monopoly that "Proper Bostonians" had held over the city's charitable and cultural institutions was broken; the ever expanding need of such agencies for money and the emergence of new fortunes brought a fresh cast to elite boards. As the composition of the Vault revealed, economic power was now largely in the hands of those who worked their way to the top of corporate hierarchies rather than those who inherited their

274

positions. Bastions of the old wealth remained, but talent and ambition mattered more than a family name. The same phenomenon appeared across the river at Harvard. When rebellious students, much to Ralph Lowell's disgust, drove President Nathan Pusey into early retirement, the Harvard Corporation publicly solicited names of possible replacements and in January 1971 chose a man who did not have a Harvard College degree.

The following month John Lowell left Boston Safe to join Welch & Forbes, a venerable firm of trustees with strong ties to Charlotte's family. His move, which rated little notice in the press, illustrated how much Boston had changed in just the dozen years since Ralph had stepped down from the presidency of the bank. Ralph's successor, William Wellington Wolbach, was of "Proper Bostonian" descent, but the same enthusiasm that led him to forgo a Harvard diploma in the 1930s to learn the banking business firsthand characterized his response to the frenetic business climate of the 1960s. For Boston Safe to survive, Wolbach believed, it would need to offer a broader array of services, and to pull that off it must break with its customary practices. Among Wolbach's innovations were pursuing growth through acquisitions, hiring outsiders to fill top managerial positions, leaving the Franklin Street building for a glass-walled skyscraper, and subordinating the revered name Boston Safe Deposit and Trust to that of a new corporate entity, The Boston Company. Ralph and John were uncomfortable with all of these changes. Wolbach had largely ignored Ralph even before he vacated the chairmanship in 1966, and recognizing John's unhappiness with the drift of things, Wolbach dropped him lower and lower in the bank's lengthening organizational chart. Deeply embittered by Wolbach's treatment of his son, Ralph felt John had no choice but to go elsewhere. Ralph lived to see Wolbach stripped of his power in the mid-1970s, and three years after Ralph died the Boston Company was sold to a unit of American Express. Boston Safe Deposit and Trust had passed into the hands of strangers.[1]*

Change, although less wrenching, also occurred at the Lowell Institute. In 1959 Ralph designated John his "unofficial co-trustee," and the two worked closely together to revamp the lecture format. Instead of personally making arrangements (with the assistance of a salaried curator) to hire a lecturer for a series of talks at the Boston Public Library, the trustee

---

* In 1992 American Express, which had paid $47.2 million for the Boston Company eleven years before, sold it to the Pittsburgh-based Mellon Bank for $1.45 billion.

would underwrite lectures organized by and held at institutions such as the Museum of Fine Arts, the Museum of Science, and Massachusetts General Hospital. For the annual religious lectures mandated by the will, the Lowells delegated responsibility to the Boston University School of Theology. As a result this series was moved from King's Chapel, in the heart of downtown, to Marsh Chapel, on the B.U. campus out beyond Kenmore Square. Somewhat defensively, Ralph assured the Athenaeum overseers that "the Founder would feel that the spirit of his intent . . . had been met" by these changes.[2]

In 1970 the Lowell Institute remained WGBH's biggest financial supporter, providing about $200,000 a year (roughly 50 percent of the institute's annual income), but this contribution represented an increasingly smaller share of the station's income as budgets rose to the $10 million range. When general manager Hartford Gunn left WGBH to take over the Public Broadcasting Service, and Lowell assumed the newly created position of chairman of the board so that Gunn's successor could have the title of president, the broadcasting operation showed few signs of its roots in academia. Just as Parker Wheatley had feared and Gunn thought unavoidable, corporate grants (like the one negotiated in 1970 with the Mobil Oil Company for *Masterpiece Theatre*) were becoming the mainstay of educational television. And as WGBH focused on producing programs for national distribution, it relied less on the participation of college professors through the Lowell Institute Cooperative Broadcasting Council. The university presidents still sat on the WGBH board, but broadcasting professionals, not academics, conceived and executed the programming ideas.[3]

Although Lowell's reverence for tradition kept him from welcoming enthusiastically most of the change that went on around him, he recognized the impossibility of holding rigidly to the past. In 1962, in the fiftieth anniversary report of his Harvard class, Lowell proclaimed that his "political convictions [bore] the same name" they had twenty-five years earlier (that is, he was still a Republican), but that he was now "perhaps more liberal, perhaps more middle of the road." As he told a reporter for the *New York Times* in 1965, referring to the acquisition of Picasso and Brancusi pieces by the Museum of Fine Arts, "I don't believe in all this modern stuff myself, but I'm not always right." He was open to new ideas. To be sure, Gunn and David Ives had to overcome his initial resistance to the "crazy" proposal that WGBH raise funds by conducting televised auctions. But Lowell was willing to give it a try and even served as an auctioneer. With her usual supportiveness, Charlotte became an ardent bidder in the annual auctions—at all hours of the day. One year at three o'clock on a Sunday morning, she was still phoning in her bids on the very last item to be sold—a batch of huge hats.[4]

Lowell was committed to the idea that—in his words—"You are put here to do something for your fellow man and to take an active part in your community and its problems." This commitment exposed him to the inevitability of change and taught him the wisdom of trying to direct it rather than oppose it. He understood that individuals whose backgrounds differed from his own would guide the city in the future. And he knew that it was crucial, for a smooth transition, that he "mix with the crowd that's coming up." Thanks to his willingness to do that, Boston was unexpectedly successful in coming to grips with its history.[5]

Even as he acknowledged on an intellectual level the need to accept change, it was painful for Lowell to recognize that his sons could not duplicate his role. But it was no longer possible for anyone to be a "Proper Bostonian" in the traditional sense, as described in *Fortune* magazine in 1933: "The Bostonian is an energetic and forceful man with a strong sense of property, a conviction of the moral justification of the accumulation of wealth and, above all, with the power to achieve his earthly as well as his heavenly ends."[6] From Henry Lee Higginson to James Jackson Storrow to Charles Francis Adams to Ralph Lowell, Boston had a succession of "Number One Citizens" whose devotion to the community was undisputed and whose contacts and influence allowed them to make a contribution. In the mid-1950s Hartford Gunn was advising some New Yorkers who wanted to set up an educational television station, and he asked Ralph to recommend someone who could be "a 'Lowell' for New York." Ralph replied that "a Ralph Lowell could not exist in New York City because the pace is too fast."[7] By the 1960s Boston was still not "as fast" as New York, but the world of *The Proper Bostonians* and *The Late George Apley* had largely disappeared, and the title of "Mr. Boston" could not be passed on. The opportunities Ralph had were not available to the next generation, although his children continued the family tradition of active community service. Ralph Lowell and his Boston were a good fit. No one, Brahmin or otherwise, has come close to matching it since or is likely to do so ever again.[8]

Lowell's career peaked in the 1950s and early 1960s; by 1970, retirement rules had removed him from almost all of his charitable and business trusteeships. In February 1973, while leaving his office at Boston Safe's new building, Lowell slipped and took a fall that knocked him unconscious and fractured his hip. He spent the next several months at Massachusetts General Hospital, slowly regaining his strength and undergoing a regimen of physical therapy. Pain, limited mobility, and increasing deafness marked his final years. In 1976 Lowell gave up his last business directorship, the *Globe;* he submitted his resignation as chairman to the WGBH board, but it was not accepted. He remained Trustee of the Lowell Institute and let John handle the details. In the spring of 1978 the chauffeur-driven car in which Ralph, Charlotte, and his nurse were riding was involved in an accident. Thrown from his seat, Ralph suffered a broken leg. On May 15, after ten days in the hospital, too weak to resist pneumonia, Ralph Lowell died at age of eighty-seven. His funeral service, at a crowded Memorial Church in Harvard Yard, featured three hymns: "The Battle Hymn of the Republic," "Onward Christian Soldiers," and "Ten Thousand Times Ten Thousand." The last had been sung at both his parents' funerals—and as Ralph wished, continuity was maintained.[9]

Ralph Lowell received many honors in his life, but none was more fitting than the last: In 1973 he was awarded the title "Grand Bostonian," along with six other distinguished citizens. The award was newly established to commemorate the 150th anniversary of Boston's city charter. Recipients had to have reached the Biblical three-score and ten years and led lives that "mirrored the spirit and the dignity that has made [Boston] and its people so extraordinary." The others named were Arthur Fiedler, longtime conductor of the Boston Pops; Archibald MacLeish, former librarian of Congress, retired Harvard English professor, and twice winner of the Pulitzer Prize for poetry; David McCord, veteran administrator of Harvard's annual fund-raising campaigns and prolific composer of essays and verse about Boston; John W. McCormack, whose half-century in politics had started on the streets of South Boston and culminated in the speakership of the U.S. House of Representatives; Samuel Eliot Morison, former Harvard history professor and historian of the university, whose boyhood on Beacon Hill paralleled Lowell's in the Back Bay; and Paul Dudley White of Massachusetts General Hospital, the world-famous cardiologist best remembered for treating President Eisenhower after his 1955 heart attack. Of the seven, only Ralph Lowell had pursued a career in business, and only he had consciously directed his talents and energy to improving his beloved Boston.[10]

Ralph's decades of civic involvement flowed directly from his abiding sense of custodianship of the Lowell heritage, of "keeping the faith." "It's a tradition in America," he told an interviewer in 1964, "that families such as mine can do [good works]." While he took pleasure in seeing his children continue the tradition, Ralph realized that he was, in fact, the last of a line. A minor provision in his will reflected that reality. Portraits of seven generations of Lowells, stretching from Ralph back to the Reverend John Lowell of colonial Newbury, had long graced the walls of his Westwood home. Aware that subsequent generations might be unable to provide appropriate residential settings for this collection, he charged the executors of his estate with finding a suitable site. They chose Lowell House at Harvard so that every year a new class of undergraduates could draw inspiration from the family's example.[11]

NOTES

PROLOGUE TO PART ONE

1. "The Lowells of Massachusetts," *Life*, March 18, 1957, p. 127.
2. Will Jarvis to Ralph Lowell, September 27, 1956, Charlotte Loring Lowell MSS, Massachusetts Historical Society, box 8, folder 8.2.
3. Ferris Greenslet, *The Lowells and Their Seven Worlds* (Boston: Houghton Mifflin, 1946).
4. Ralph Lowell, *Reminiscences* (New York: Columbia University Oral History Collection, 1964), p. 93; Ralph Lowell, diary, November 20–23, December 10, 1956, Ralph Lowell MSS, Massachusetts Historical Society (hereafter cited as Diary).
5. Diary, January 28, 1957.
6. Lowell, *Reminiscences*, p. 94.

CHAPTER 1

1. Ferris Greenslet, *The Lowells and Their Seven Worlds* (Boston: Houghton Mifflin, 1946), pp. 241–260, 303–310, 329–331, 334–409.
2. A. Lawrence Lowell, "John Lowell, 1824–1897," in *Later Years of the Saturday Club, 1870–1920*, ed. M. A. DeWolfe Howe (Boston: Houghton Mifflin, 1927), pp. 143–145; Thornton K. Lothrop, "Tribute to John Lowell," *Proceedings of the Massachusetts Historical Society*, 2d ser., 14 (May 1900), pp. 177–188; *Proceedings of the Bar and Bench of the Circuit Court of the United States, District of Massachusetts, Upon the Decease of Hon. John Lowell* (Boston, 1897), pp. 14, 48; *Dictionary of American Biography*, s.v. "Lowell, John."
3. Edward Weeks, *The Lowells and Their Institute* (Boston: Little, Brown, 1966), p. 77; *Dictionary of American Biography*, s.v. "Emerson, George B."
4. Fortieth Anniversary Report of the Harvard Class of 1877 (1917), p. 155; Robert A. Silverman, *Law and Urban Growth: Civil Litigation in the Boston Trial Courts, 1880–1900* (Princeton: Princeton University Press, 1981), pp. 109–110.

5. William D. Sohier, "John Lowell," *American Bar Association Journal* 9 (March 1923), pp. 185–186; Silverman, *Law and Urban Growth*, pp. 110–112, 116.

6. Robert Asher, "Workmen's Compensation in the United States, 1880–1935," (Ph.D. dissertation, University of Minnesota, 1971), pp. 505–540.

7. John Lowell, "Some American Causes Célèbres: II. *Attorney General of Massachusetts v. Tufts*," *American Bar Association Journal* 8 (December 1922), pp. 745–746, 771; Jerold S. Auerbach, *Unequal Justice* (New York: Oxford University Press, 1976), pp. 40–73.

8. Henry Simpson, *The Lives of Eminent Philadelphians* (Philadelphia: Wm. Brotherhead, 1859), pp. 350, 746–754; Frank Willing Leach, *Emlen Family* (Philadelphia: Historical Publication Society, 1932); James A. Willcox, *A History of the Philadelphia Saving Fund Society, 1816–1916* (Philadelphia: J. B. Lippincott, 1916), pp. 103–104; E. Digby Baltzell, *Puritan Boston and Quaker Philadelphia* (New York: Free Press, 1979), pp. 165, 170.

9. John Lowell to George Emerson Lowell, December 7, 1882, in possession of John L. Thorndike; Baltzell, *Puritan Boston and Quaker Philadelphia*, pp. 365–368.

10. Mary Lee, *A History of the Chestnut Hill Chapel* (n.p.: The History Committee of the First Church in Chestnut Hill [Mass.], 1937), pp. 12–19; M. F. Sweetser, *King's Handbook of Newton, Massachusetts* (Boston: Moses King Corporation, 1889), pp. 310, 318–320; *Atlas of the City of Newton* (Philadelphia: G. M. Hopkins, 1874), plate T.

11. Molly Berkeley, *Winking at the Brim* (Boston: Houghton Mifflin, 1967), pp. 10–11; Bainbridge Bunting, *Houses of Boston's Back Bay: An Architectural History, 1840–1917* (Cambridge: Belknap Press of Harvard University Press, 1967), pp. 105–106.

12. Sohier, "John Lowell," p. 186.

13. Delmar R. Lowell, comp., *The Historic Genealogy of the Lowells of America from 1639 to 1899* (Rutland, Vt.: author, 1899).

14. Ralph Lowell, untitled MS [1974], Walter Muir Whitehill MSS, Massachusetts Historical Society, box 39 (Individuals), Ralph Lowell folder, p. 1.

15. Diary, July 27, 1976.

16. Lucy Lowell (Ralph Lowell's aunt), diary, February 7–9, 1902, Lucy Lowell MSS, Massachusetts Historical Society; Diary, January 13, 1927; March 7, 1962; July 23, 1970; Ralph Lowell to Ralph Lowell Wales, May 25, 1971, Charlotte Loring Lowell MSS, Mass. Historical Society, 1972 box, folder W; Ralph Lowell, untitled MS, Walter Muir Whitehill MSS, box 39 (Individuals), Ralph Lowell folder, pp. 1, 4.

17. John Lowell to Ralph Lowell, June 13, 1910, Ralph Lowell MSS, 1909–1912 Correspondence box, 1910 folder; Ralph Lowell, undated composition, Ralph Lowell MSS, 1907–1908, Diary Transcript box, El Rancho Bonito folder.

18. Berkeley, *Winking at the Brim*, pp. 3–4, 6–9, 11–12, 17–18, 22, 24, 48; Ralph Lowell to Mary Emlen Hale Lowell, April 23, 1913, Ralph Lowell MSS, 1913–1917 Correspondence box, World Tour 1912–1913 folder.

19. Diary, June 26, 1912; Lucy Lowell, diary, June 26, July 2, 1912; Fifteenth Anniversary Report of the Harvard College Class of 1908 (1923), pp. 349–350; William G. Lennox and Stanley Cobb, "Epilepsy," *Medicine*, 7 (1928), p. 109; Ellen Dwyer, "Stories of Epilepsy," in *Framing Disease: Studies in Cultural History*, ed. Charles E. Rosenberg and Janet Gordon (New Brunswick, N.J.: Rutgers University Press, 1992), pp. 249–250, 256–257.

20. John Lowell, Will and Inventory, file #45040, Middlesex County Registry of Probate, Cambridge, Mass.; George B. Emerson, Will and Inventory, file #65481, Suffolk County Registry

of Probate, Massachusetts State Archives, Boston, Mass.; John L. Thorndike, interview by author, January 10, 1994; Henry Lee Higginson to John Lowell, May 6, 1902, in possession of John L. Thorndike; Diary, May 7, 1911; Berkeley, *Winking at the Brim*, pp. 12, 19–21, 25, 30–31.

21. Samuel Eliot Morison, *One Boy's Boston, 1887–1901* (Boston: Houghton Mifflin, 1962), p. 44; Richard T. Flood, *The Story of the Noble and Greenough School, 1866–1966* (Dedham, Mass.: Noble and Greenough School, 1966), pp. 23, 37, 41, 53; Raymond R. Baldwin, "The Volkmann School," *Noble and Greenough Graduates' Bulletin*, March 1940; Diary, March 3, 11, 1905; January 31, March 26, April 2, May 12, 30, June 1, 1906; March 21, April 22, 1907.

22. Ralph Lowell, Class of 1912, Transcript of Courses and Grades, Harvard University Archives (hereafter cited as HUA).

23. Sybil Ellinwood, "East Meets West in the Field of Education," *Journal of Arizona History* 15 (autumn 1974), pp. 269–271, 276–277; Leverett Saltonstall, *Salty* (Chester, Conn: Globe Pequot Press, 1976), pp. 4–5; Donald Myrick, "Recollections of an Arizona Ranch School in 1911," *Journal of Arizona History* 12 (spring 1971), pp. 51–63; Diary, October 30, 1907.

24. Ralph Lowell to Mary Emlen Hale Lowell, September 14, 1907, Ralph Lowell MSS, 1849–1908 Correspondence box, 1907 folder; Diary, October 5, 7, 8, 9, 13, 1907; March 25, 1908.

25. Ralph Lowell, undated composition, Ralph Lowell MSS, 1907–1908 Diary Transcript box, El Rancho Bonito folder.

26. Diary, December 2–7, 1907; February 8, March 9, 19, April 25–May 26, 1908.

27. Ibid., June 6–10, 24, 25, 28, 1908.

CHAPTER 2

1. Samuel Eliot Morison, *Three Centuries of Harvard, 1636–1936* (Cambridge: Harvard University Press, 1946), pp. 323–438.

2. Frank Freidel, *Franklin D. Roosevelt: The Apprenticeship* (Boston: Little, Brown, 1952), p. 52; Bernard Bailyn et al., *Glimpses of the Harvard Past* (Cambridge: Harvard University Press, 1986), p. 61.

3. Diary, April 28, 1911; Morison, *Three Centuries of Harvard*, p. 418.

4. Morison, *Three Centuries of Harvard*, pp. 418–419; Doris Kearns Goodwin, *The Fitzgeralds and the Kennedys* (New York: Simon & Schuster, 1987), p. 209; Bainbridge Bunting, *Harvard: An Architectural History* (Cambridge: Belknap Press of Harvard University Press, 1985), p. 184; Diary, March 12, 1908.

5. Bailyn et al., *Glimpses of the Harvard Past*, pp. 84–85; *Harvard Graduates' Magazine* 19 (June 1911), pp. 759–763; Robert Cutler, *No Time for Rest* (Boston: Little, Brown, 1966), p. 56; Cleveland Amory, *The Proper Bostonians* (New York: Dodd, Mead, 1947), pp. 297–310; Diary, October 5, 21, 28, 1908; April 28, 1911.

6. Bailyn et al., *Glimpses of the Harvard Past*, p. 86.

7. Lowell to Edward M. Kennedy, January 20, 1965, Charlotte Loring Lowell MSS, July 1964–February 1965 box, folder K; Diary, February 25, March 1, 1909.

8. Diary, October 12, 21, 1908; March 2, 3, 4, 15, 1909; *Harvard Graduates' Magazine* 17 (June 1909), pp. 114–115; 20 (March 1912), p. 474.

9. Bailyn et al., *Glimpses of the Harvard Past*, p. 61; Morison, *Three Centuries of Harvard*, p. 414; Ronald A. Smith, *Sports and Freedom: The Rise of Big-Time College Athletics* (New York: Oxford

University Press, 1988), pp. 26–29; *The H Book of Harvard Athletics, 1852–1922* (Cambridge: Harvard University Press, 1923), pp. 68–72, 80, 88, 105; Diary, May 3, 1941; October 14, 1942.

10. Reports of the President and Treasurer of Harvard College, 1907–1908 (1909), p. 120.

11. Reports of the President and Treasurer of Harvard College, 1909–1910 (1911), p. 87; *Harvard Graduates' Magazine* 19 (March 1911), p. 430; 20 (March 1912), p. 454; 21 (June 1913), p. 807.

12. Ralph Lowell, undated compositions, Ralph Lowell MSS, 1907–1908 Diary Transcript box, El Rancho Bonito folder; Henry Aaron Yeomans, *Abbott Lawrence Lowell, 1856–1943* (Cambridge: Harvard University Press, 1948), pp. 83–91.

13. Morison, *Three Centuries of Harvard*, p. 429; Freidel, *Roosevelt*, p. 53; Samuel Eliot Morison, ed., *The Development of Harvard University* (Cambridge: Harvard University Press, 1930), pp. xlv-xlvi; Yeomans, *Lowell*, pp. 65–80, 121–158.

14. Diary, April 8, 1909.

15. Bailyn et al., *Glimpses of the Harvard Past*, p. 91; Lawrence T. Nichols, "The Establishment of Sociology at Harvard," in *Science at Harvard: Historical Perspectives*, ed. Clark A. Elliott and Margaret W. Rossiter (Bethlehem, Pa.: Lehigh University Press, 1992), pp. 197–199; Diary, April 28, 30, 1911.

16. Curtis M. Hinsley, "The Museum Origins of Harvard Anthropology, 1866–1915," in *Science at Harvard*, ed. Elliot and Rossiter, pp. 121–145; Diary, February 29, April 9, 1912; March 5, 1941; December 2, 1944; February 21, 1948; January 11, February 6, 1949; Ralph Lowell, *Reminiscences* (New York: Columbia University Oral History Collection, 1964), p. 25.

17. Morison, ed., *Development of Harvard University*, pp. 241–243; Diary, July 1–September 1, 1911.

18. Bunting, *Harvard: An Architectural History*, p. 309 n. 25; Goodwin, *Fitzgeralds and Kennedys*, p. 214; *New York Times*, November 5, 1911.

19. Diary, May 22, August 9, 1911; Charles R. Lanman to Lowell, September 6, 1911; W. R. Castle Jr. to Ralph Lowell, December 20, 1911, Ralph Lowell MSS, 1909–1912 Correspondence box, 1911 folder; *Harvard Graduates' Magazine* 19 (December 1910), pp. 270–271.

20. Diary, March 14, 3, 1912.

21. Ibid., January 27, February 27, March 18, 25, 26, April 25, 1912; *Harvard Crimson*, March 18, 27, 1912.

22. *Harvard Crimson*, December 14, 19, 1911.

23. Diary, January 26, 27, 29, March 7, 1912.

24. Ibid., February 1, 15, May 31, 1912; Roland B. Dixon to Lowell, June 5, 1912, Ralph Lowell MSS, 1909–1912 Correspondence box, 1912 folder.

25. Diary, June 3, 18, 1912; *Boston Globe*, June 18, 1912; *Harvard Graduates' Magazine* 21 (September 1912), p. 124.

26. Diary, June 20, 1912.

27. Ibid., June 21, 1912; Thomas C. Mendenhall, *The Harvard-Yale Boat Race, 1852–1924, and the Coming of Sport to the American College* (Mystic, Conn.: Mystic Seaport Museum, 1993), pp. 273–274.

28. Diary, June 25, 1912.

29. Ibid., January 21, 1912.

30. Ibid., July 23, April 14, 28, 1912.

31. Ibid., Preface.

32. Ibid., December 14, 1912.

33. Ibid., December 16, 1912.

34. Ibid., December 18, 20, 21, 1912; Ralph Lowell to Olivia Lowell, December 21, 1912, in possession of John L. Thorndike.

35. Diary, January 2, 3, 1913; Ralph Lowell to John Lowell, January 1, 1912 (actually 1913), Ralph Lowell MSS, 1909–1912 Correspondence box, 1912 folder.

36. Diary, December 25, 1912.

37. Ibid., December 26, 28, 1912.

38. Ibid., Preface.

39. Ibid., January 6–8, 1913; Harvard University–Museum of Fine Arts, Egyptian Diary, January 8, 1913, Vol. II–Giza, Part 2, typescript, copy in Egyptian Department, Museum of Fine Arts; Dows Dunham, *The Egyptian Department and Its Excavations* (Boston: Museum of Fine Arts, 1958), pp. 45, 47; minutes of the Board of Trustees, Museum of Fine Arts, September 19, 1978, Ralph Lowell MSS, 1970–1979 Correspondence box, Letters of Condolence folder.

40. Diary, January 6, 1913.

41. Ibid., February 8–15, 1913.

42. Ibid., March 11, 15, 1913.

43. Ibid., February 28–March 1, 1913.

44. Ibid., March 23, 16, 1913.

45. Ibid., March 25, 28, 1913.

46. Ibid., April 6, 1913.

47. Ibid., May 4, 1913.

48. Ibid., June 8, 1913; *Boston Evening Globe*, June 20, 1912, Peter W. Stanley, *A Nation in the Making: The Philippines and the United States, 1899–1921* (Cambridge: Harvard University Press, 1974), pp. 99–101.

49. Diary, May 8, 9, 1913.

50. Ibid., May 11, June 8, 1913.

51. Ibid., June 8, May 14, 1913.

52. Ibid., May 8, 17, 1913.

53. Ibid., May 19–June 1, 1913; William Cameron Forbes, journals, May 20–June 1, 1913, William Cameron Forbes MSS, Massachusetts Historical Society.

54. Diary, June 1, 2, January 27, February 2, 1913; Forbes, journals, June 1, 1913, William Cameron Forbes MSS.

55. Diary, June 2, 1913.

56. Ibid., June 14, 1913.

57. Ibid., June 20, July 4, 1913.

58. Ibid., July 1–3, 1913.

59. Ibid., July 17, 29, 30, 1913.

60. Ibid., July 18, 21, 1913.

61. Ibid., August 12, 1913.

62. Ibid., August 17, 20, 22, 23, 1913.

CHAPTER 3

1. Diary, February 29, April 9, July 18, 1912.

2. Ibid., March 13, 1913.

3. Frederic Cople Jaher, "The Boston Brahmins in the Age of Industrial Capitalism," in *The Age*

of *Industrial Capitalism*, ed. Frederic Cople Jaher (New York: Free Press, 1968), pp. 198–202, 214–215; Henry Aaron Yeomans, *Abbott Lawrence Lowell, 1856–1943* (Cambridge: Harvard University Press, 1948), p. 14; Cleveland Amory, *The Proper Bostonians* (New York: Dodd, Mead, 1947), p. 44.

4. R. B. Hobart to Lowell, January 30, 1912, Ralph Lowell MSS, 1909–1912 Correspondence box, 1912 folder; Diary, January 25, July 18, 1912.

5. Diary, January 26, 27, 29, July 15, 1912; July 5, 1949.

6. N. S. B. Gras, *The Massachusetts First National Bank of Boston, 1784–1934* (Cambridge: Harvard University Press, 1937), pp. 21, 151–154; "Boston," *Fortune*, February 1933, p. 102.

7. Gras, *Massachusetts First National Bank*, pp. 159–203.

8. Diary, May 3, 1941; October 14, 1942.

9. Ibid., December 17, 1943.

10. Ralph Lowell MSS, 1913–1917 Correspondence box, 1914 and 1915 folders.

11. Gerald T. Dunne, *Grenville Clark: Public Citizen* (New York: Farrar, Straus, Giroux, 1986), pp. 3–41; J. Garry Clifford, *The Citizen Soldiers: The Plattsburg Training Camp Movement* (Lexington: University Press of Kentucky, 1972), pp. 54–69.

12. Ralph Barton Perry, *The Plattsburg Movement* (New York: E. P. Dutton, 1921), p. 25; Clifford, *Citizen Soldiers*, p. 58.

13. Francis Russell, *The Great Interlude* (New York: McGraw-Hill, 1964), p. 13; Ralph Lowell MSS, Military Training Camps 1917 box, Plattsburg folder; Michael Pearlman, *To Make Democracy Safe for America* (Urbana: University of Illinois Press, 1984), p. 58.

14. Ralph Lowell to Mary Emlen Hale Lowell, August 15, 1915, Ralph Lowell MSS, 1913–1917 Correspondence box, 1915 folder.

15. Pearlman, *To Make Democracy Safe for America*, p. 58; Perry, *Plattsburg Movement*, p. 42; Clifford, *Citizen Soldiers*, pp. 88–91.

16. Clifford, *Citizen Soldiers*, pp. 98–102, 109–114, 186–190; Lowell to Edward Weeks, December 29, 1965, Edward Weeks MSS, Massachusetts Historical Society, 1964–1965 Correspondence folder.

17. Clifford, *Citizen Soldiers*, pp. 166–171; John W. Farley to Lowell, October 31, 1916, Ralph Lowell MSS, 1913–1917 Correspondence box, 1916 folder.

18. Diary, February 7, 1946; January 13, 1974; Raymond R. Baldwin, "The Volkmann School," *Noble and Greenough Graduates' Bulletin*, March 1940; Richard T. Flood, *The Story of the Noble and Greenough School, 1866–1966* (Dedham, Mass.: Noble and Greenough School, 1966), pp. 53–55.

19. Ralph Lowell MSS, Military Training Camps 1917 box, Plattsburg folder; Clifford, *Citizen Soldiers*, pp. 234–236.

20. Diary, September 1, 1948.

21. Poem dated July 23, 1906, Charlotte Loring Lowell MSS, June 1978–September 1979 box, Data on Fiftieth Wedding Anniversary folder; Diary, November 22, December 26–31, 1908; January 1–3, 5, 1909; Ralph Lowell to Mary Emlen Hale Lowell, January 25, 1913; June 11, 1913, Ralph Lowell MSS, 1913–1917 Correspondence box, World Tour 1912–1913 folder.

22. Ralph Lowell to Mary Emlen Hale Lowell, [July or August 1913], Ralph Lowell MSS, 1913–1917 Correspondence box, World Tour 1912–1913 folder.

23. S. Foster Damon, *Amy Lowell* (Boston: Houghton Mifflin, 1935), p. 105; Amory, *Proper Bostonians*, p. 355.

24. Sidney Ratner, ed., *New Light on the History of Great American Fortunes* (New York: Augustus M. Kelley, 1953).

25. *National Cyclopedia of American Biography*, s.v. "Alexander Cochrane."

26. *Boston Evening Transcript*, October 9, 1889; *Boston Herald*, January 9, 1932; April 26, 1928.

27. Twenty-fifth Anniversary Report of the Harvard Class of 1894 (1919), pp. 295–296; Fiftieth Anniversary Report of the Harvard Class of 1894 (1944), pp. 344–345.

28. Diary, August 14, 1959; August 14, 1965; August 14, 1967.

29. Ralph Lowell to Mary Emlen Hale Lowell, May 26, 1917; August 28, 1917; Charlotte Loring to Ralph Lowell, telegram, August 25, 1917, Ralph Lowell MSS, 1913–1917 Correspondence box, 1917 folder; newspaper clipping, [September 2, 1917], Ralph Lowell MSS, Scrapbook (1917–1918).

30. Diary, August 31, 1942; September 1, 1966; August 31, 1976.

31. Ibid., September 1, 1966; Lucy Lowell, diary, September 1, 1917, Lucy Lowell MSS, Massachusetts Historical Society; newspaper clipping, [September 2, 1917], Ralph Lowell MSS, Scrapbook (1917–1918).

32. Daniel N. Casey to Ralph Lowell, March 16, 1957, Charlotte Loring Lowell MSS, box 10, folder 10.7; Ralph Lowell to Mary Emlen Hale Lowell, October 23, 1917, Ralph Lowell MSS, 1913–1917 Correspondence box, 1917 folder.

33. Diary, January 5, 1940.

34. Newspaper clippings, n.d., Ralph Lowell MSS, Scrapbook (1917–1918); William J. Robinson, *Forging the Sword: The Story of Camp Devens* (Concord, N.H.: Rumford Press, 1920), pp. 91, 151.

35. Diary, August 23, 1923.

36. Ralph Lowell to Mary Emlen Hale Lowell, July 21, 1918, Ralph Lowell MSS, 1918–1929 Correspondence box, 1918–1919 folder.

37. Ibid.; Ralph Lowell MSS, Military Training Camps 1917–1940 box, Lecture Notes folders.

38. Diary, November 11, 1968; Lowell to Daniel G. Wing, November 18, 1918; Lowell to Charles E. Cotting, November 18, 1918, Ralph Lowell MSS, 1918–1939 Correspondence box, 1918–1919 folder.

39. Wing to Lowell, November 15, 1918, Ralph Lowell MSS, Military Training Camps 1917 box, 1917 folder (Camp Lee, Va.); Ralph Lowell to Mary Emlen Hale Lowell, November 17, 1918, Ralph Lowell MSS, 1918–1939 Correspondence box, 1918–1919 folder.

40. Ralph Lowell to Mary Emlen Hale Lowell, November 20, 1918; Ralph Lowell to Wing, November 18, 1918, Ralph Lowell MSS, 1918–1939 Correspondence box, 1918–1919 folder.

41. Wing to Lowell, November 21, 1918; J. A. L. Blake to Lowell, November 22, 1918; John R. Macomber to Lowell, November 27, 1918, Ralph Lowell MSS, 1918–1939 Correspondence box, 1918–1919 folder; Diary, December 30, 1930.

CHAPTER 4

1. Barrett Wendell, *Lee, Higginson & Company* (Boston: Merrymount Press, 1921), pp. 7–17, 20–21, 25; Bliss Perry, *Life and Letters of Henry Lee Higginson* (Boston: Atlantic Monthly Press, 1921), pp. 272–273.

2. Fritz Redlich, *The Molding of American Banking*, vol. 2 (New York: Johnson Reprint Corp., 1968), p. 387; Perry, *Higginson*, pp. 239, 267–268, 291–384; Wendell, *Lee, Higginson*, pp. 19, 21–23.

3. Wendell, *Lee, Higginson,* pp. 28–29, 32–36; Redlich, *Molding of American Banking,* vol. 2, pp. 387–388.

4. Barrett Wendell, "History of Lee, Higginson & Co., 1848–1918" (typescript, 1918), Lee, Higginson & Co. MSS, Baker Library, Harvard Business School, p. 8; Marshall W. Stevens, "History of Lee, Higginson & Co." (typescript, 1927), Baker Library, Harvard Business School, p. 33.

5. *Boston Evening Transcript,* December 28, 1925.

6. Wendell, *Lee, Higginson,* p. 46; Ralph Lowell, untitled MS [1919?], Ralph Lowell MSS, 1849–1908 Correspondence box, N.D. folder.

7. Diary, March 27, 1922; August 14, 1923; Stevens, "History of Lee, Higginson & Co.," p. 33.

8. Lowell to Edward M. Kennedy, January 20, 1965, Charlotte Loring Lowell MSS, July 1964–February 1965 box, folder K; Richard J. Whalen, *The Founding Father: The Story of Joseph P. Kennedy* (New York: New American Library, 1964), pp. 25–26, 38, 66, 74, 383; Doris Kearns Goodwin, *The Fitzgeralds and the Kennedys* (New York: Simon & Schuster, 1987), pp. 211–212, 269, 275, 322–325; Diary, September 15, 1945; December 14, 1960; David C. Crockett, interview by author, April 8, 1993.

9. *New York Times,* February 16, 17, 20, March 2, 5, 1926; Diary, April 7, 1926.

10. Diary, April 27, 1926.

11. Henry Greenleaf Pearson, *Son of New England: James Jackson Storrow, 1864–1926* (Boston, 1932), pp. 143–144; *Dictionary of American Biography,* supplement 4, s.v. "Nash, Charles W."; *New York Times,* March 14, 1926.

12. *Boston Evening Globe,* May 13, 1926, *New York Times,* May 14, 1926; Diary, May 26, 1926.

13. Ralph Lowell, untitled MS, n.d., Ralph Lowell MSS, Diary Transcript 1946–1949 box, Miscellaneous Transcripts 1946–1947 folder; Diary, February 26, March 1, 1927.

14. Diary, December 13, 15, 23, 1926; January 4, 19, April 26, 1927; January 2, 1928.

15. Ibid., January 2, 1928.

16. Ibid.

17. Ibid., January 7, February 2, March 12, 22, 25, 28, April 10, June 30, 1928; John Kenneth Galbraith, *The Great Crash 1929* (Boston: Houghton Mifflin, 1954, 1988), pp. 11–15.

18. Diary, June 30, 1928; Galbraith, *Great Crash,* pp. 15–18.

19. Lowell to Mary Emlen Hale Lowell, November 20, 1918, Ralph Lowell MSS, 1918–1919 folder, 1918–1939 Correspondence box.

20. Francis Russell, *Tragedy in Dedham: The Story of the Sacco-Vanzetti Case* (New York: McGraw-Hill, 1962), p. 3.

21. Electa Kane Tritsch, ed., *Building Dedham* (Dedham: Dedham Historical Society, 1986).

22. Diary, February 3, 1927; November 18, 1944; Stanley C. Paterson and Carl G. Seaburg, *Nahant on the Rocks* (Nahant, Mass.: Nahant Historical Society, 1991), pp. 353–354; John Lowell, interview by author, March 16, 1995; Mary Emlen Lowell Wheeler, interview by author, April 11, 1995.

23. John Lowell, interview by author; Wheeler, interview by author; Diary, April 30, 1924; August 11, October 29, 1923; November 23, 1950; Susan Lowell Wales to Ralph Lowell ("Old Gent"), August 3, 1955, Charlotte Loring Lowell MSS, box 6, folder 6.1.

24. Diary, June 9, 1927; May 11, 1924; *Massachusetts Bay Tercentenary—Dedham* (Dedham, Mass.: Dedham Transcript, 1930), pp. 53–56.

25. Diary, May 21, June 11, October 31, 1924.

26. Ibid., January 15, May 19, 1927; June 4, October 16, 1924.

27. John Lowell, interview by author; Diary, January 13, 1927; July 15, 1928; July 25, 1963; January 4, 1940.

28. Diary, January 21, 1912; January 16, 1927; April 18, 1928.

29. Ibid., January 29, 1928; January 24, 1931; Whalen, *Founding Father*, p. 58.

30. Cleveland Amory, *The Proper Bostonians* (New York: Dodd, Mead, 1947), pp. 198–199; Paterson and Seaburg, *Nahant on the Rocks*, pp. 59–327; Diary, July 7, 1928.

31. Diary, March 5, 1966.

32. Lowell, interview; Crockett, interview.

33. Diary, December 30, 1926; June 17, October 2, 1924.

34. Ibid., April 25, 1927; February 29, 1928; *Dedham Transcript*, March 11, 1927.

35. Diary, April 25, July 12, September 20, 1927; February 1, 29, 1928.

36. Fiftieth Anniversary Report of the Harvard Class of 1912 (1962), p. 351.

37. Diary, May 5, 1926; January 14, 1927; January 28, 1976; Richard T. Flood, *The Story of the Noble and Greenough School, 1866–1966* (Dedham, Mass.: Noble and Greenough School, 1966), pp. 67–70.

38. Diary, January 19, 1927; *Dedham Transcript*, January 22, 1980.

39. Diary, December 23, 1926; Herbert Black, *Doctor and Teacher, Hospital Chief: Dr. Samuel Proger and the New England Medical Center* (Chester, Conn: Globe Pequot Press, 1982), pp. 24–31.

40. Black, *Doctor and Teacher*, pp. 31–33; minutes of the trustees of the Boston Floating Hospital, June 16, December 8, 1926; January 12, May 11, June 1, 1927, New England Medical Center Archives Minute Book (May 10, 1922–February 24, 1932); *Boston Evening Globe*, June 2, 1927; *Boston Globe*, June 3, 1927; Diary, June 2, 1927; Lowell, remarks at New England Medical Center Hospitals dinner, February 25, 1965, Ralph Lowell MSS, 1951–1969 Correspondence box.

41. Diary, June 2, 1927; January 12, February 7, March 20, 1928; minutes of the trustees of the Boston Floating Hospital, June 2, 3, November 29, 1927; January 4, February 8, March 19, 21, June 13, 1928; "A History of the Boston Floating Hospital," *Pediatrics* 19 (April 1957), p. 638.

42. Black, *Doctor and Teacher*, pp. 33–41; minutes of the trustees of the Boston Floating Hospital, October 21, December 5, 1928; January 19, February 13, April 30, May 10, June 7, 12, October 1, December 31, 1929; January 8, 1930; *Boston Globe*, September 19, 1931.

CHAPTER 5

1. Twenty-fifth Anniversary Report of the Harvard Class of 1912 (1937), pp. 466–467.

2. George Wharton Pepper to Lowell, January 7, 1929, Ralph Lowell MSS, 1918–1939 Correspondence box, Lee Higginson Letters 1929 folder; Diary, March 8, 1928.

3. Diary, September 17, 1923; Albert A. Cree to Lowell, March 26, 1929; Ralph Lowell, untitled MS [1929?], Ralph Lowell MSS, 1918–1939 Correspondence box, Lee, Higginson & Co. 1929–1942 folder.

4. Ralph Lowell, untitled MS, July 5, 1929, Ralph Lowell MSS, 1918–1939 Correspondence box, Lee, Higginson & Co. 1929- folder.

5. Lowell "Reflections on the 1929 Stock Market Crash," [1929?], Ralph Lowell MSS, 1918–1939 Correspondence box, Lee, Higginson & Co. 1929– folder; Diary, April 5, 1932; minutes of

the trustees of the Boston Floating Hospital, New England Medical Center Archives, Minute Book (May 10, 1922–February 24, 1932), p. 160.

6. Diary, May 2, July 9, 1931.

7. Ibid., December 1, 1930.

8. Vincent P. Carosso, *More than a Century of Investment Banking: The Kidder, Peabody & Co. Story* (New York: McGraw-Hill, 1979), pp. 13–42, 50–57, 66–69.

9. Ibid., pp. 71–79; Diary, December 1, 1930.

10. Vincent P. Carosso, *Investment Banking in America* (Cambridge: Harvard University Press, 1970), pp. 312–317; Diary, January 22, 29, February 9, 1931; April 5, 1932.

11. Diary, October 1, 1931; *Boston Globe*, October 1, December 15, 1931.

12. Diary, October 1, 2, December 31, 1931.

13. Barrett Wendell, *Lee, Higginson & Company* (Boston: Merrymount Press, 1921), pp. 18 (italics in original), 46.

14. John Kenneth Galbraith, introduction to Robert Shaplen, *Kreuger: Genius and Swindler* (New York: Knopf, 1960), pp. x, viii.

15. Shaplen, *Kreuger*, pp. 10, 17, 52; Jerome D. Greene to Henry James, May 12, 1932, James Family MSS, by permission of the Houghton Library, Harvard University, Jerome D. Greene folder, bMS AM 1095.2(5a).

16. Shaplen, *Kreuger*, pp. 74–75; Diary, October 14, 1923; Cleveland Amory, *The Proper Bostonians* (New York: Dodd, Mead, 1947), p. 34.

17. Diary, January 23, 1928; March 13, April 14, 1932.

18. Shaplen, *Kreuger*, pp. 210–227; John Kenneth Galbraith, *The Great Crash 1929* (Boston: Houghton Mifflin, 1954, 1988), p. 132 n. 2; Diary, March 4, 12, 1932.

19. Diary, March 13, 14, 1932; *New York Times*, March 15, 1932.

20. Diary, March 15, 17, 20, 25, April 5, 1932; Galbraith, *Great Crash*, pp. 37–40.

21. Diary, April 5, 1932.

22. *New York Times*, April 6, 1932; *Boston Herald*, December 28, 1925; Bliss Perry, *Life and Letters of Henry Lee Higginson* (Boston: Atlantic Monthly Press, 1921), p. 449; Wendell, *Lee, Higginson*, p. 46; Max Winkler, *Foreign Bonds: An Autopsy* (Philadelphia: Roland Swain Co., 1933), pp. 95–101; U.S. Senate Committee on Banking and Currency, *Stock Exchange Practices*, 73d Cong., 2d sess., 1934, S. Rept. 1455, pp. 121–124.

23. Diary, April 14, July 12, 1932; January 19, 1933; January 30, April 17, 1942; Ralph Lowell to Mary Emlen Hale Lowell, April 17, 1933, Ralph Lowell MSS, 1918–1939 Correspondence box, 1929–1936 folder; Amory, *Proper Bostonians*, p. 59; Jerome D. Greene to Joseph P. Chamberlain, July 2, 1932, Jerome D. Greene MSS, HUA, Lee, Higginson & Co. folder, HUG 4436.18; Jerome D. Greene, "Chance and Change: Recollections of a Varied Life," Jerome D. Greene MSS, HUA, HUG 4436.33, pp. F-180–184. James Bryant Conant, *My Several Lives* (New York: Harper & Row, 1970), pp. 147–148.

24. *New York Times*, June 15, 1932; Diary, July 12, 1932; Edward Weeks, *Men, Money, and Responsibility: A History of Lee Higginson Corporation* (Boston, 1962), pp. 26–27.

25. Diary, July 12, 1932.

26. Ibid., October 2, 1931; March 25, 1932.

27. Ibid., March 6, 1933.

28. Ibid., March 9, 20, 1933; April 5, June 24, 27, 28, September 14, 21, October 10, November 5, 6, 1940; February 13, April 28, November 17, 1944.

29. Ralph Lowell, "Whither," [late winter 1934], Ralph Lowell MSS, Diary Transcript 1946–1949 box, Miscellaneous Addresses, Speeches? folder.

30. Carosso, *Investment Banking in America*, pp. 393–398; *Clark, Dodge & Co., 1845–1945* (1945); Diary, October 10, 1932; January 19, March 20, 1933; December 21, 1939.

31. Diary, January 10, 27, February 7, 14, March 1, April 18, May 2, 11, 16, 23, June 23, July 6, September 11, October 20, November 20, 27, 29, December 5, 19, 1939; January 2, 25, February 28, March 5, 6, 7, 19, 21, April 30, July 18, September 2, 9, 20, 26 30, October 2, 10, 22, 28, November 8, 19, 20, December 11, 16, 19, 1940; January 31, February 11, 13, 19, 25, April 17, 21, 25, May 5, 22, June 12, 24, July 3, 9, 10, 14, September 2, 15, October 23, 28, November 14, 15, December 1, 28, 1941; January 5, 26, 30, February 19, March 23, May 18, 24, June 4, 15, 16, 23, 24, 29, July 10, August 21, September 28, November 20, December 24, 1942.

32. Ibid., November 14, 1934.

33. *Boston Globe*, June 17, 18, 19, 1938; Stanley C. Paterson and Carl G. Seaburg, *Nahant on the Rocks* (Nahant, Mass.: Nahant Historical Society, 1991), pp. 384–390; Sara Delano Roosevelt to Mary Emlen Hale Lowell [1938], in possession of John L. Thorndike; John Lowell, interview by author, March 16, 1995.

34. Diary, March 6, 1940; March 29, April 30, June 14, 29, July 3, July 9, September 13, 1941.

35. Ibid., September 16, December 19, 1940; April 11, 1942; January 14, March 20, 27, October 17, December 27, 1941.

36. Ibid., November 19, 1934; Ralph Lowell to Mary Emlen Hale Lowell, April 17, 1933, Ralph Lowell MSS, 1918–1939 Correspondence box, 1929–1936 folder.

37. Gerald T. Dunne, *Grenville Clark: Public Citizen* (New York: Farrar, Straus, Giroux, 1986), pp. 120–124; Diary, May 25, 29, 1940.

38. Robert C. Davis to Lowell, January 25, 1924, Ralph Lowell MSS, Scrapbook (June 1923–June 1932); Diary, May 2, 7, 8, September 19, 1924; January 19, 1927; May 27, June 5, 10, 1940.

39. Diary, June 12–15, 19, 21, 22, 25–29, July 2, 3, 5, 1940; J. Garry Clifford and Samuel R. Spence, *The First Peacetime Draft* (Lawrence: University Press of Kansas, 1986), p. 115.

40. *Boston Herald*, June 21, July 24, 1940; Diary, June 20, July 11, 19, 24, 31, August 1, 2, September 6, 12, 16, October 16, 1940.

41. Diary, November 11, December 8, 1941.

PROLOGUE TO PART TWO

1. Diary, December 31, 1940; undated entry following December 31, 1941.

2. Ibid., October 15, 1941; undated entry following December 31, 1941.

3. Ibid., April 18, 1928.

4. Ibid., January 24, 1963.

5. Poem, June 7, 1956, Charlotte Loring Lowell MSS, box 8, folder 8.15; *Boston Globe*, May 13, 1966; December 22, 1968.

6. Diary, December 31, 1950.

7. Ralph Lowell to Tascha Lowell, November 23, 1956, Charlotte Loring Lowell MSS, box 8, folder 8.4; Ralph Lowell to Theodore H. N. Wales Jr., November 13, 1956; Ralph Lowell to Mary Emlen Wheeler, December 17, 1956, Charlotte Loring Lowell MSS, box 8, folder 8.2; Ralph Lowell Wales to Ralph Lowell, [1973], Charlotte Loring Lowell MSS, 1973–1974 M–Z box, folder W.

8. Stanley C. Paterson and Carl G. Seaburg, *Nahant on the Rocks* (Nahant, Mass.: Nahant Historical Society, 1991), pp. 398–407, 412; Diary, July 11, August 2–4, 8, 1946; January 8, March 30, June 21, July 20, 1947; June 16, July 2, 1948; March 9, 23, June 15, 1949.

9. Cleveland Amory, *The Proper Bostonians* (New York: Dodd, Mead, 1947), p. 23; for detailed descriptions of these trips, see Lowell's diaries for 1949–1961.

10. Molly Berkeley, *Winking at the Brim* (Boston: Houghton Mifflin, 1967), p. 164; *Dictionary of National Biography, 1941–1950,* s.v. "Berkeley, Randal Mowbray Thomas"; Diary, July 14, 1958; Molly Lowell Berkeley to Ralph Lowell, January 29, 1957, Charlotte Loring Lowell MSS, box 9, folder 9.4.

11. Berkeley, *Winking at the Brim,* pp. 164–165; Diary, April 14, 1961.

12. Diary, July 4, August 14, 1944; January 31, 1945; September 12, October 6, 1949.

13. Ibid., October 14, 1940; March 7, 1949; August 2, 24, 1951; September 27, 1951.

14. Ibid., January 19, 1941; February 12, 1944; August 25, 1946; December 16, 1951.

15. Ibid., October 18, 1944; November 7, 1967; Leon Harris, *Only to God: The Extraordinary Life of Godfrey Lowell Cabot* (New York: Atheneum, 1967); Amory, *Proper Bostonians,* pp. 327–331.

16. "Boston," *Fortune,* February 1933, p. 34; Alexander W. Williams, *A Social History of the Greater Boston Clubs* (n.p.: Barre Publishing Company, 1970), pp. 19, 39–41; Robert Cutler, *No Time for Rest* (Boston: Little, Brown, 1966), p. 70–72; Diary, July 19, 1940; April 16, 1945; March 25, 1947; October 28, 1949; September 29, 1958; December 15, 1961.

17. Fiftieth Anniversary Report of the Harvard Class of 1912 (1962), p. 350; Amory, *Proper Bostonians,* p. 30; Everett Case, Oral History, "Public Television's Roots" Oral History Project MSS, State Historical Society of Wisconsin, box 1, folder 9, pp. 29–30; transcript of Ten O'Clock News, WGBH-TV, May 15, 1978, Ralph Lowell MSS, 1970–1979 Correspondence box, Letters of Condolence folder.

CHAPTER 6

1. William W. Wolbach, *Boston Safe Deposit and Trust Company* (New York: Newcomen Society, 1962), p. 7.

2. Ibid., pp. 9–14; John Gunther, *Inside U.S.A.* (New York: Harper Bros., 1947), p. 519; Robert F. Dalzell Jr., *Enterprising Elite* (Cambridge: Harvard University Press, 1987), pp. 101–103; Donald Holbrook, *The Boston Trustee* (Boston: Marshall Jones Company, 1937), pp. 7–8; "Boston," *Fortune,* February 1933, p. 35.

3. *Harvard College v. Amory,* 9 Pickering 461 (Massachusetts Supreme Judicial Court, 1830); Peter Dobkin Hall, *The Organization of American Culture, 1700–1900* (New York: New York University Press, 1982), p. 264; Gunther, *Inside U.S.A.,* p. 519; "In Investing, It's the Prudent Bostonian," *Business Week,* June 6, 1959, p. 57.

4. Holbrook, *Boston Trustee,* pp. 12–18.

5. James G. Smith, *The Development of Trust Companies in the United States* (New York: Henry Holt, 1928), p. 6 n. 2; Dalzell, *Enterprising Elite,* pp. 100, 103–104.

6. Wolbach, *Boston Safe Deposit,* p. 14; Diary, June 22, 1945.

7. Wolbach, *Boston Safe Deposit,* pp. 16–18; Boston Safe Deposit and Trust Company, Seventy-fifth Annual Report.

8. "Staid Boston Trustee Tries a New Venture," *Business Week,* October 17, 1964, p. 72; Wolbach, *Boston Safe Deposit,* pp. 18–19, 20.

9. Wolbach, *Boston Safe Deposit,* pp. 19–20; *Boston Globe,* May 7, 1953; William W. Wolbach, interview by author, June 27, 1991.

10. Diary, January 26, June 15, July 10, August 21, September 28, November 20, December 15, 1942; January 15, 20, 21, February 5, March 2, 3, 4, 8, 9, 11, 12, 1943; June 9, 1974; Wolbach, interview.

11. Diary, May 3, 1943.

12. Ibid., May 7, 14, 25, 26, June 9, 30, July 15, 20, 29, September 22, October 5, 1943; Wolbach, interview.

13. Diary, May 1, 4, June 1, 29, August 10, September 10, 14, 1943; March 24, April 7, 11, May 18, 23, June 27, July 19, September 6, October 16, November 2, 24, December 28, 1944; January 2, March 21, October 2, 5, November 27, December 11, 1945; January 3, 8, 1946.

14. Ibid., February 24, April 7, July 20, 26, 29, November 15, 1944; April 17, 27, September 18, 25, October 29, 1945.

15. Ibid., June 2, 7, 11, 18, August 10, 1943; June 5, 9, July 26, October 18, 1944; September 9, 1947; June 21, July 8, 1948.

16. Ibid., December 31, 1943; April 12, August 7, 1944; September 21, 1945; February 26, April 10, May 16, June 25, July 1, 2, 8, 17, October 25, 1946; April 2, 9, September 9, December 4, 1947; January 27, 1950; June 28, 1951; December 3, 1952.

17. Ibid., January 4, August 28, November 9, 13, 27, 1945; June 11, 1946; December 30, 1947; December 15, 1948; January 4, 1949.

18. Cleveland Amory, *The Proper Bostonians* (New York: Dodd, Mead, 1947), p. 179; Diary, September 21, 1945; *Christian Science Monitor,* January 24, 28, 1957; Pete Martin, "The George Apleys Banked Here," *Saturday Evening Post,* March 15, 1947, pp. 36–37.

19. Diary, April 6, 1949.

20. Ibid., August 10, 1944; July 2, 1943; *Lucy C. Farnsworth* (pamphlet printed by the William A. Farnsworth Museum); Charles Rawlings, "The Mystery of Lucy Farnsworth," *Saturday Evening Post,* May 2, 1953, pp. 32–33.

21. Diary, July 2, 8, 14, 1943; May 29, 30, 1947; August 15, 1948; July 11, 1969; July 16, 1970; *Boston Globe,* October 12, 1963.

22. Agreement and Declaration of Trust Executed by Boston Safe Deposit and Trust Company, 2d ed. (1921); Charles M. Rogerson, "Successful Operation of the Permanent Charity Fund in Boston," *Trust Companies* 32 (January 1921), pp. 47–49; Diary, August 29, 1952; January 13, 1955; July 31, 1961.

23. Diary, January 4, 1945, July 18, 1949; *Boston Globe,* October 6, 11, 1959; Richard Norton Smith, *The Harvard Century* (New York: Simon & Schuster, 1986), pp. 170, 214–216; *Toward A Deepening Sense of Community: The History of the Boston Foundation, 1915–1990* (Boston: Boston Foundation, 1990), p. 12.

24. Diary, September 20, November 13, 1961; June 25, 1962; J. Anthony Lukas, *Common Ground* (New York: Vintage, 1986), pp. 343–344 (on the advisory committee, see chapter 21).

25. Diary, January 21, 1963.

26. Ibid., May 15, 1943; September 12, 1947; April 22, 1949; April 30, 1952; Godfrey M. Hyams Trust, 1971 Annual Report; Lukas, *Common Ground,* pp. 339–341, 347–349.

27. Diary, December 22, 1943; August 11, 1953; January 23, 1963; Ralph Lowell, *Reminiscences* (New York: Columbia University Oral History Collection, 1964), p. 22.

28. Diary, January 25, 1956; February 16, 1950; June 29, December 12, 1951; September 9, 1953; *Christian Science Monitor*, January 24, 1957.

29. Diary, January 6, September 29, 1947; June 22, 1951; "Big Money in Boston," *Fortune*, December 1949, pp. 117–119.

30. Diary, April 12, 20, 26, May 4, 11, October 26, 1949; October 29, 1952; *New England T&T Company v. Department of Public Utilities* (1951), 327 Mass. 81.

31. Diary, January 26, October 2, 1959; *United States v. E. I. du Pont DeNemours & Co.*, 177 F. Supp. 32 (Northern District of Illinois, 1959).

32. Diary, February 21, 1952.

33. Ibid., January 15, 1945; January 9, July 26, 1946; November 9, 1950; Robert Cutler, *No Time for Rest* (Boston: Little, Brown, 1966).

34. Diary, January 19, October 27, 1949; January 12, May 10, 1950; January 26, 1951.

35. "In Investing. It's the Prudent Bostonian," *Business Week*, June 6, 1959, pp. 56–74.

36. Diary, January 24, February 3, 1947; November 30, 1949; June 5, 9, December 29, 1944; January 16, 1945; September 3, November 3, 1959.

37. Ibid., May 16, 1956; Freeman Lincoln, "After the Cabots–Jerry Blakeley," *Fortune*, November 1960, 171–184.

38. Diary, February 8, 1949; January 17, February 8, 1950; August 21, 1956; Wolbach, interview.

39. Diary, October 17, 1945; September 11, 1946; March 19, September 2, 1948.

40. Wolbach, interview; *Boston Herald*, January 6, 1966; Diary, May 21, 1943; December 17, 1945; July 17, 1946; October 4, 1948; January 22, 1952.

41. Diary, November 3, 24, December 15, 1954.

42. Ibid., August 25, 1955; April 25, May 2, June 29, July 31, 1956; May 29, December 6, 9, 11, 19, 26, 1957; March 26, May 1, October 22, 1958; January 28, 1959.

CHAPTER 7

1. Ferris Greenslet, *The Lowells and Their Seven Worlds* (Boston: Houghton Mifflin, 1946), pp. 196–214; Edward Weeks, *The Lowells and Their Institute* (Boston: Little, Brown, 1966), chaps. 1–6.

2. Weeks, *Lowells and Their Institute*, pp. 72, 82, 85–86, 109–111, 125.

3. Ibid., pp. 12–13; Greenslet, *Lowells*, p. 211.

4. Diary, January 11, 1943.

5. Ibid.; Ralph Lowell, *Reminiscences* (New York: Columbia University Oral History Collection, 1964), pp. 1, 26; Ninety-eighth Annual Report of the Trustee of the Lowell Institute, August 1, 1938, Lowell Institute MSS, Boston Athenaeum (hereafter cited as AR/LI); Ralph Lowell MSS, Harvard Correspondence box, A. Lawrence Lowell folders.

6. Lowell, *Reminiscences*, p. 2.

7. Eric Barnouw, *The Golden Web: A History of Broadcasting in the United States, 1933–1953* (New York: Oxford University Press, 1968), pp. 40–42, 129–30, 242–43.

8. Diary, June 20, 1939; James Bryant Conant to Edward Weeks, January 25, 1966, Edward

Weeks MSS, Massachusetts Historical Society, 1966/January–June box 1, Correspondence folder; Ralph Barton Perry MSS, HUA, UA I.10.522.3, Radio Board folder.

9. Report of the Ad Hoc Committee Appointed to Consider the Desirability of Applying for an FM Noncommercial Radio Station, [October 1945], President's Records, HUA, UA I.5.168, box 13 (1945–1946).

10. Ralph Barton Perry MSS, UA I.10.522.3, Radio Board folder; Eric Underwood, "The Radio University in Peace and War," *American Scholar* 14 (winter 1944–1945), pp. 86–96.

11. Diary, October 31, November 3, 1945; cf. Weeks, *Lowells and Their Institute,* p. 166.

12. Weeks, *Lowells and Their Institute,* p. 125; Diary, March 27, April 8, 1940; January 20, February 4, March 6, 1941; 108th AR/LI, August 1, 1948.

13. Lowell to Ralph Barton Perry, November 1, 1945, Ralph Barton Perry MSS, UA I.10.522.3, Radio Board folder; Diary, November 15, 1945; February 25, March 1, 5, 1946; Lowell to Harold D. Hodgkinson, January 26, 1946; Lowell to James Bryant Conant, March 6, 1946; Conant to Lowell, March 18, 1946; Lowell to John Cowles, April 3, 1946, WGBH Educational Foundation Historical Papers, box 3, Ralph Lowell–1946 folder (hereafter cited as WGBH Archives); Edward Weeks to Conant, December 28, 1965 Edward Weeks MSS, box 1, 1964–1965 Correspondence folder.

14. Diary, April 2, 17, 1946; unsigned and untitled memorandum, April 3, 1946; Lowell to Conant, April 18, 1946, WGBH Archives, box 3, Ralph Lowell–1946 folder; Barnouw, *Golden Web,* pp. 227–231.

15. Diary, April 17, 1946; Conant to Karl J. Compton et al., May 1, 1946, President's Records, HUA, box 13 (1945–1946).

16. Diary, May 24, 1946; Lowell to Conant, May 27, 1946; Conant to Lowell, June 13, 1946, WGBH Archives, box 3, Ralph Lowell–1946 folder, James R. Killian, memorandum, "Cooperative Radio Program in Boston," May 25, 1946, President's Records, AC 4, Massachusetts Institute of Technology Archives, box 149 (Compton-Killian) (hereafter cited as MITA).

17. Diary, July 25, 1946; Conant to Lowell, June 13, 1946; Lowell to Lyman Bryson, June 19, 1946; Bryson to Lowell, July 12, 1946; Lowell to Conant, August 1, 1946, WGBH Archives, box 3, Ralph Lowell–1946 folder.

18. Parker Wheatley, Oral History, "Public Television's Roots" Oral History Project MSS, State Historical Society of Wisconsin, box 4, folder 6, pp. 1–22; Lowell to Wheatley, July 29, 1946, in possession of Parker Wheatley.

19. Wheatley, Oral History, pp. 22–24; Wheatley, letter to author, October 28, 1989; Diary, August 6, September 3, 1946; Lowell to James Bryant Conant et al., August 27, 1946, WGBH Archives, box 3, Ralph Lowell–1946 folder.

20. Wheatley, Oral History, pp. 27–28; Diary, October 24, 1946; John E. Burchard, memorandum to James R. Killian, October 28, 1946, President's Records, MITA, box 149 (Compton-Killian).

21. Diary, September 3, 5, October 24, November 6, 1946; Lowell to William L. Keleher, SJ, May 27, 1946; Keleher to Lowell, May 31, 1946; Keleher to Lowell, September 3, 1946; Lowell to Keleher, September 4, 1946; Lowell to Parker Wheatley, September 4, 1946; Keleher to Lowell, October 16, 1946; Keleher to Lowell, November 5, 1946, WGBH Archives, box 3, Ralph Lowell–1946 folder.

22. David W. Bailey to James Bryant Conant, November 6, 1946, President's Records, HUA, box 10 (1946–1947); Diary, November 13, 15, 1946.

23. "Radio: Old School Tie-Up," *Time*, November 25, 1946, p. 85; *New York Times*, November 17, 1946; Diary, November 14, 1946.

24. Diary, February 3, July 2, August 11, 1947; Lowell Institute Cooperative Broadcasting Council (hereafter cited as LICBC), First Annual Report (1946–1947).

25. William Benton to Robert G. Caldwell, July 2, 1946, President's Records, MITA, box 149 (Compton-Killian).

26. Diary, May 6, 1947; Parker Wheatley, memorandum to Lowell, January 21, 1947; William L. Keleher, SJ, to Lowell, January 25, 1947; Lowell to Keleher, January 28, 1947, WGBH Archives, box 3, Ralph Lowell–1947 folder; Wheatley, telephone conversation with author, September 26, 1989; Thomas Fleming, SJ, interview by author, November 9, 1989; Lowell, *Reminiscences*, p. 11.

27. Minutes of LICBC, October 24, 1946, President's Records, HUA, box 10 (1946–1947); Diary, October 18, 1946; September 11, 1947.

28. Diary, March 29, July 9, 31, August 3, 14, October 8, November 6, 15, 1951.

29. 108th AR/LI, August 1, 1948; Diary, March 19, July 2, 1948; Lowell to James Bryant Conant, May 20, 1948; Conant to Lowell, May 22, 1948; Lowell to Conant, June 1, 1948, President's Records, HUA, box 12 (1947–1948).

30. LICBC, Third Annual Report (1948–1949), Fourth Annual Report (1949–1950); 110th AR/LI, August 1, 1950; Diary, September 23, 1949; April 25, 1950; John E. Burchard, memorandum to Karl T. Compton, February 21, 1951, Dean of Humanities Records, AC 20, MITA, box 3.

31. James Bryant Conant to James R. Killian, October 5, 1950, President's Records, MITA, box 150 (Compton-Killian); 111th AR/LI, August 1, 1951; Diary, December 21, 1950; David W. Bailey, interview by author, July 19, 1989.

32. Diary, October 18, 1950; March 16, May 10, 1951; Bailey to James R. Killian, October 27, 1950, President's Records, MITA, box 150 (Compton-Killian); Wheatley, Oral History, p. 31.

33. 111th AR/LI, August 1, 1951; Wheatley, Oral History, p. 30.

34. Ernest W. Jennes, letter to author, May 6, 1991.

35. Diary, October 6, 8, 1951.

36. LICBC, Sixth Annual Report (1951–1952).

37. Diary, January 15, February 13, 14, April 4, 1952; Parker Wheatley to Ralph Lowell, April 11, 1952, WGBH Archives box 3, Ralph Lowell–1952 (January–June) folder; Wheatley to G. H. Griffiths, October 14, 1954, Fund for Adult Education Records, Ford Foundation Archives, reel B1078, frames #2689–2690.

38. Robert J. Blakely, *To Serve the Public Interest* (Syracuse, N.Y.: Syracuse University Press, 1979), pp. 83–84, 86–87; John Walker Powell, *Channels of Learning* (Washington, D.C.: Public Affairs Press, 1962), pp. 55–64, 69–71; Diary, April 25, 1951; C. Scott Fletcher to Lowell, April 24, 1951, WGBH Archives, box 3, Ralph Lowell–1951 folder; G. H. Griffiths, letter to author, April 2, 1990.

39. Parker Wheatley to C. Scott Fletcher, February 28, 1952, frames #0033–0035; Wheatley to Fletcher, April 21, 1952, reel B1078, frames #2793–2795; Martha C. Howard to Lowell, May 29, 1952, reel B1078, frame #2790; dockets and minutes, Board of Directors' meetings, May 6, 1952, Fund for Adult Education Records, Ford Foundation Archives, box 1 (Administrative Series); Wheatley, Oral History, pp. 34–35; Wheatley to Lowell, April 14, 1951; Wheatley to Fletcher, April 17, 1951; Lowell to James Bryant Conant, June 5, 1952, WGBH Archives, box 3, Ralph Lowell–1952 (January–June) folder; Diary, May 6, 1952.

CHAPTER 8

1. Diary, January 31, February 6, July 20, August 9, 11, 1949; July 10, December 23, 28, 1952.

2. Eric Barnouw, *The Golden Web: A History of Broadcasting in the United States, 1933–1953* (New York: Oxford University Press, 1968), pp. 22–27, 293–295; Robert J. Blakely, *To Serve the Public Interest* (Syracuse, N.Y.: Syracuse University Press, 1979), pp. 1–25, 65–70, 74–75.

3. James Bryant Conant to Wayne Coy, November 18, 1950, President's Records, HUA, box 17 (1950–1951).

4. Lowell to Leverett Saltonstall, November 13, 1950; Saltonstall to Lowell, December 6, 1950, WGBH Archives, box 3, Ralph Lowell–1950 folder; transcripts of FCC hearings, docket nos. 8736, 8975, 9175, 8976, December 6, 1950, pp. 16601–16611.

5. Diary, March 23, 1951.

6. Lowell to James Bryant Conant, February 20, 1950; Conant to Lowell, February 24, 1950, President's Records, HUA, box 17 (1949–1950); Diary, January 31, 1949; December 12, 1950; Parker Wheatley to Richard B. Hull, July 9, 1949, WGBH Archives, box 3, Ralph Lowell–1949 folder.

7. Wheatley, memorandum to LICBC, December 13, 1950, Dean of Humanities Records, AC 20, MITA, box 3; Diary, March 23, 26, 1951; Lowell to John Lord O'Brian, April 10, 1951; Lowell to James Webb Young, May 4, 1951, WGBH Archives, box 3, Ralph Lowell–1951 folder; Lowell to C. Scott Fletcher, May 9, 1951, Fund for Adult Education Records, Ford Foundation Archives, reel F744, frame #1659.

8. Diary, May 4, June 13, July 31, 1951; John Walker Powell, *Channels of Learning* (Washington, D.C.: Public Affairs Press, 1962), pp. 60–62.

9. Parker Wheatley, Oral History, "Public Television's Roots" Oral History Project MSS, State Historical Society of Wisconsin, box 4, folder 6, p. 39; Lowell to James R. Killian, April 10, 1951, President's Records, AC 4, MITA, box 150 (Compton-Killian); Lowell to Leverett Saltonstall, April 11, 1951, Leverett Saltonstall MSS, Massachusetts Historical Society; Lowell to G. Harold Edgell, April 17, 1951, Directors' Correspondence (1901–1954), Museum of Fine Arts Archives, LICBC folder; LICBC, Fifth Annual Report (1951–1952).

10. U.S. Federal Communications Commission, "Sixth Report and Order," 17 *Federal Register* 3940 (May 2, 1952); John Lord O'Brian to Lowell, April 18, 1952, WGBH Archives, box 3, Ralph Lowell–1952 (January–June) folder.

11. Diary, July 21, 22, 1952; Lowell, memorandum to LICBC, July 22, 1952, WGBH Archives, box 3, Ralph Lowell–1952 (July–December) folder; David W. Bailey, memorandum to Paul Buck, April 5, 1953, President's Records, HUA, box 15 (1952–1953); 112th AR / LI, August 1, 1952.

12. Diary, June 13, 1951; June 23, 1952; February 5, May 5, 1953; Parker Wheatley, Oral History, p. 36; C. Scott Fletcher, Oral History, "Public Television's Roots" Oral History Project MSS, State Historical Society of Wisconsin, box 2, folder 1, p. 50.

13. *Christian Science Monitor*, April 15, 21, May 14, 1952; Diary, May 12, 1952; Commonwealth of Massachusetts, Acts and Resolves of 1952, chapter 96.

14. Ralph Lowell, *Reminiscences* (New York: Columbia University Oral History Collection, 1964), pp. 6, 9, 10; Diary, July 21, October 3, November 10, 25, 1952; Lowell, memorandum to LICBC, July 22, 1952, WGBH Archives, box 3, Ralph Lowell–1952 (July–December) folder; *Boston Globe*, January 15, 1967; Powell, *Channels of Learning*, p. 148; Ernest W. Jennes, letter to author, May 20, 1991.

15. Commonwealth of Massachusetts, Special Commission on Educational Television, *Preliminary Report* (December 3, 1952), Senate Document 513 (Boston: Commonwealth of Massachusetts, 1953), pp. 7–8, 11.

16. Christian Herter to Wayne Coy, April 13, 1951, Ralph Lowell–1951 folder; Lowell to Herter, November 19, 1952, Ralph Lowell–1952 (July–December) folder; Lowell to Harold D. Hodgkinson, February 18, 1953, Ralph Lowell–1953 folder, WGBH Archives, box 3; Diary, January 26, February 1, 5, 13, 1953; *Boston Herald,* January 30, February 25, 1953.

17. Diary, May 20, 1952; Lowell to Hodgkinson, June 13, 1952; June 16, 1952; June 26, 1952; Hodgkinson to Lowell, June 16, 1952, WGBH Archives, box 3, Ralph Lowell–1952 (January–June) folder; Evans Clark, memorandum to the Executive Committee, February 24, 1953, Twentieth Century Fund files, New York City.

18. Diary, July 10, 21, August 6, 1952; Lowell to C. Scott Fletcher, December 9, 1952, Educational Television and Radio Center (1952) folder; Lowell to Fletcher, January 23, 1953, National Association of Educational Broadcasters (1953–1955) folder, WGBH Archives, box 4.

19. Erwin D. Canham to Evans Clark, February 5, 1953; minutes of Executive Committee meeting, March 4, 1953, Twentieth Century Fund files; Diary, March 31, April 6, 14, 27, 30, 1953; Commonwealth of Massachusetts, Special Commission on Educational Television, *Second Report* (May 1953), S. Doc. 704 (Boston: Commonwealth of Massachusetts, 1953), p. 15; *Christian Science Monitor,* April 14, May 7, 28, 1953.

20. Diary, May 5, 6, June 1, July 16, 1953; Parker Wheatley, letter to author, January 11, 1990.

21. Diary, June 22, July 14, 15, 24, August 5, 31, September 9, 14, 19, October 16, November 17, 1953; May 3, 1954; 114th AR/LI, August 1, 1954.

22. Diary, April 7, May 8, December 2, 1953; March 16, 25, April 20, May 19, September 30, 1954; LICBC, Eighth Annual Report (1954–1955); Ninth Annual Report (1955–1956).

23. Diary, May 22, 1953, April 20, June 7, 8, December 9, 1954; 114th AR/LI, August 1, 1954; 116th AR/LI, August 1, 1956; 117th AR/LI, August 1, 1957.

24. Diary, May 1, December 3, 1957; May 27, June 2, 1959; April 25, September 7, 1960; 118th AR/LI, August 1, 1958.

25. "Boston Beacon," *Time,* March 18, 1957, p. 61.

26. Ibid.; *New York Times,* January 3, 4, 1957.

27. Powell, *Channels of Learning,* pp. 77–80; Blakely, *To Serve the Public Interest,* pp. 101–104; Diary, October 15, December 4, 1952.

28. Lowell, *Reminiscences,* pp. 87; Kenneth Oberholtzer, Oral History, "Public Television's Roots" Oral History Project MSS, State Historical Society of Wisconsin, box 3, folder 12, p. 37.

29. Blakely, *To Serve the Public Interest,* p. 104; Robert Hudson, Oral History, "Public Television's Roots" Oral History Project MSS, State Historical Society of Wisconsin, box 2, folder 8, p. 19; Hartford Gunn, Oral History, ibid., box 2, folder 6, pp. 28–29.

30. Blakely, *To Serve the Public Interest,* pp. 110–112; William Yandell Elliott, ed., *Television's Impact on American Culture* (East Lansing: Michigan State University Press, 1956), p. 6; James Day, *The Vanishing Vision: The Inside Story of Public Television* (Berkeley: University of California Press, 1995), pp. 63–69; Diary, December 1, 16, 1955; October 13, 1956; September 20, 1957; February 8, March 13, 1958; Hartford Gunn and Paul Rader, memorandum to Lowell, November 2, 1954, box 3, Ralph Lowell–1954 folder; Lowell to Harry K. Newburn, December 28, 1955, box 4, Ralph Lowell–1955 folder, WGBH Archives; Lowell, *Reminiscences,* p. 86.

31. Diary, October 30, 1955; January 27, September 20, November 11, 1957; June 17, September 6, 1958; January 23, 1959; Henry T. Heald to Lowell, July 18, 1958, WGBH Archives, box 4, Ralph Lowell–1958 folder; Lowell, *Reminiscences,* p. 85.

32. John White, Oral History, "Public Television's Roots" Oral History Project MSS, State Historical Society of Wisconsin, box 4, folder 7, pp. 1–26, 55; Lowell, *Reminiscences,* p. 86.

33. Diary, February 8, March 19, May 3, 1958; January 14, May 6, 1961; Powell, *Channels of Learning,* pp. 160–161; Day, *Vanishing Vision,* pp. 69–81.

34. Blakely, *To Serve the Public Interest,* pp. 133–143; John E. Burke, *An Historical-Analytical Study of the Legislative and Political Origins of the Public Broadcasting Act of 1967* (New York: Arno Press, 1979), pp. 68–74.

35. Fletcher, Oral History, pp. 75–85; Gunn, Oral History, p. 37.

36. Gunn, Oral History, pp. 37–43; Fletcher, Oral History, pp. 85–86; Diary, November 16, December 6, 7, 8, 1964; Frederick Breitenfeld Jr., *The Report of a Study on the Long-Range Financing of Educational Television Stations* (Washington, D.C.: ETS-NAEB, [1965]), pp. 38–40, 91–92; Burke, *Public Broadcasting Act of 1967,* pp. 91–93.

37. Burke, *Public Broadcasting Act of 1967,* p. 95; Fletcher, Oral History, p. 86; Gunn, Oral History, pp. 43–44; Diary, January 29, February 19, March 12, 1965.

38. Burke, *Public Broadcasting Act of 1967,* pp. 100–101; Douglas Cater, memorandum to the president, May 19, 1965, box 1 (Legislative Background, Public Broadcasting Corporation), Lyndon B. Johnson Library; Douglas Cater, Oral History, Lyndon B. Johnson Library, pp. 2–3; Douglas Cater to Lowell, June 9, 1965, Charlotte Loring Lowell MSS, March–December 1965 box M–Z, folder S–V; Fletcher, Oral History, pp. 92–93; Gunn, Oral History, pp. 45–48; Ellen Condliffe Lagemann, *The Politics of Knowledge: The Carnegie Corporation, Philanthropy, and Public Policy* (Middletown, Conn.: Wesleyan University Press, 1989), p. 224.

39. Gunn, Oral History, pp. 48–51; James R. Killian, Oral History, "Public Television's Roots" Oral History Project MSS, State Historical Society of Wisconsin, box 3, folder 1, pp. 12–13.

40. Files on the Carnegie Commission on Educational Television, James R. Killian MSS, Acquisition 80–8, MITA, box 1.

41. Diary, February 17, April 26, 1967; U.S. House, Committee on Interstate and Foreign Commerce, *Hearings on Public Television Act of 1967,* 90th Cong.; 1st sess., July 1967, pp. 485–489.

42. Diary, October 16, November 20, 22, 1968.

43. Ibid., October 22, 1946; April 25, 1950; April 16, 1951; April 22, 1955; April 10, 1957; Lowell to Parker Wheatley, May 7, 1957, in possession of Parker Wheatley.

44. Lowell, *Reminiscences,* p. 20; David O. Ives, interview by author, July 12, 1989.

45. Diary, September 26, 1946; January 21, 1947; August 30, 1948; June 7, 1949; April 16, 1951; January 16, 1952.

46. Ibid., July 24, 27, 1953; June 28, October 13, 15, 16, 20, 22, November 6, December 13, 16, 17, 21, 22, 28, 1954; May 2, 1957; Lowell, *Reminiscences,* pp. 20–21, 70; Wheatley, Oral History, pp. 41–42; Parker Wheatley, letter to author, June 4, 1990.

47. *St. Louis Post-Dispatch,* November 6, 1983; Wheatley, Oral History, pp. 42, 44; E. G. Sherburne Jr. to Lowell, May 6, 1957, WGBH Archives, box 4, Ralph Lowell–1957 folder.

48. Wheatley, Oral History, pp. 31–32, 42–43; Diary, April 22, December 19, 1951; October 17, 1952; Gunn, Oral History, pp. 1–4, 10–12; *St. Louis Post-Dispatch,* November 6, 1983; David M.

Davis, Oral History, "Public Television's Roots" Oral History Project MSS, State Historical Society of Wisconsin, box 1, folder 15, p. 8.

49. Lawrence Creshkoff, interview by author, June 3, 1991; Wheatley to Lowell, July 22, 1975, Charlotte Loring Lowell MSS, October 1974–April 1976 (L–Z) box, folder W; Wheatley, Oral History, p. 42; Davis, Oral History, p. 9; Lowell, *Reminiscences*, p. 70; Diary, April 15, 1957.

50. Lowell, *Reminiscences*, pp. 71–72; Diary, October 14, 1961; Ives interview, July 12, 1989.

51. Diary, October 18, 1961; Edward Weeks, "The Peripatetic Reviewer," *Atlantic*, January 1962, p. 94.

52. Diary, October 18, 1961; March 5, April 10, 29, May 28, 29, 31, August 13, 29, 1962; 122d AR / LI, August 1, 1962.

53. Diary, October 23, November 1, 6, 9, December 28, 1961; April 25, July 2, 30, November 23, December 21, 1962; Hartford Gunn, memorandum to Lowell, December 8, 1961, and other materials, administrative files of Hartford Gunn, WGBH Archives; box cg 9, Facilities (New Building) 1961 folder; Lowell, *Reminiscences*, pp. 74–75.

54. *Boston Globe*, May 2, 1965; Diary, May 1, 1965.

CHAPTER 9

1. Cleveland Amory, *The Proper Bostonians* (New York: Dodd, Mead, 1947), p. 292; Twenty-fifth Anniversary Report of the Harvard Class of 1912 (1937), p. 468.

2. Diary, June 19, 1946.

3. Materials on fiftieth reunion dinner, June 12, 1962, Charlotte Loring Lowell MSS, 1962 A–L box, folder G–H.

4. *Boston Herald*, January 9, 1937; *Boston Globe*, January 9, 1937.

5. Diary, February 7, 1948; October 29, 1923; December 8, 10, 18, 19, 1956; *The A.D. Club of Harvard University, 1836–1968* (A.D. Club, 1968).

6. Mal Barter to John Lowell, May 19, 1978, Ralph Lowell MSS, 1970–1979 Correspondence box, Letters of Condolence folder.

7. Diary, November 12, 1941; February 7, April 6, August 12, 1942; John L. Thorndike to Charlotte Loring Lowell, April 23, 1980, Charlotte Loring Lowell MSS, October 1, 1979–January 1, 1981 box, folder T.

8. Diary, August 11, 1942; March 20, 1946; February 20, March 5, 1947; Harvard Club of Boston, annual reports, 1940–1947.

9. William Bentinck-Smith, "Aid and Light in Great Objects," *Harvard Magazine* 93 (September–October 1990), p. 77; Diary, June 4, 11, 1946; February, 19, 27, 28, March 6, 10, May 14–18, 1947; Rudolph Altrocchi to Lowell, February 13, 1947; Lowell to Altrocchi, February 28, 1947; Altrocchi to Lowell, March 4, 1947; Lowell to Altrocchi, March 10, 1947, Ralph Lowell MSS, Scrapbooks (1944–1948); Lowell, undated typescript, Ralph Lowell MSS, Diary Transcript 1946–1949 box, Miscellaneous Transcripts 1946–1947 folder.

10. Diary, April 9, 1928.

11. Ibid., September 30, 1946; March 27, 1947; November 8, 1974.

12. David McCord, *In Sight of Sever* (Cambridge: Harvard University Press, 1963), pp. 154–167; Diary, June 3, 1924.

13. Diary, July 18, 1949; September 24, 1952; May 14, 1953; June 3, July 30, 1959; Harvard Univer-

sity, press release, July 7, 1959; "How $238,000 Grew to $2 Million," *U.S. News & World Report*, July 27, 1959, pp. 66–68.

14. "Big Business on the Campus," *Business Week*, June 3, 1950, p. 73; Ferris Greenslet, *The Lowells and Their Seven Worlds* (Boston: Houghton Mifflin, 1946), pp. 312–313; Samuel Eliot Morison, ed., *The Development of Harvard University since the Inauguration of President Eliot, 1869–1929* (Cambridge: Harvard University Press, 1929), p. xxx; Diary, May 8, 1944.

15. Diary, January 19, 1943.

16. Ibid., May 27, 1943.

17. Ibid., September 6, 1943; Henry K. Beecher and Mark D. Altschule, *Medicine at Harvard: The First Three Hundred Years* (Hanover, N.H.: University Press of New England, 1977), pp. 461–473; James Bryant Conant, *My Several Lives* (New York: Harper & Row, 1970), pp. 380–382.

18. Diary, June 29, 1944.

19. Ibid., August 9, September 25, 1944; Conant, *My Several Lives*, pp. 382–383.

20. Henry B. Cabot to Grenville Clark, November 14, 1946, Grenville Clark MSS, Dartmouth College Library, box 1 (Harvard Corporation Series).

21. Henry James to James Bryant Conant, December 3, 1946, President's Records, HUA, box 9 (1946–1947); James to Clark, December 3, 1946, Grenville Clark MSS, box 5 (Harvard Corporation Series), Henry James folder.

22. Clark, memorandum to the Harvard Corporation, December 13, 1946, Grenville Clark MSS, box 2 (Harvard Corporation Series), J. B. Conant folder; Diary, December 5, 1946.

23. Clark, memorandum to the Harvard Corporation, December 13, 1946.

24. Henry James to Clark, December 17, 1946, Grenville Clark MSS, box 5 (Harvard Corporation Series), Henry James folder.

25. James Bryant Conant to Clark, December 20, 1946, President's Records, HUA, box 5 (1946–1947).

26. Clark to Conant, December 20, 1946, Grenville Clark MSS, box 2 (Harvard Corporation Series), J. B. Conant folder.

27. Clark to Conant, December 27, December 30, 1946, box 5; Henry James to Clark, October 29, 1946, box 5; James to Conant, December 31, 1946, President's Records, HUA, box 9 (1946–1947); Clark to Conant, January 2, 1947, Grenville Clark MSS, box 2 (Harvard Corporation Series), J. B. Conant folder.

28. Conant, *My Several Lives*, pp. 495–496; William L. Marbury, *In the Catbird Seat* (Baltimore: Maryland Historical Society, 1988), pp. 243–246, 255; William L. Marbury to Conant, February 5, 1947; Conant to Marbury, March 3, 1947, President's Records, HUA, box 303 (1946–1947).

29. Henry James to Conant, April 16, 1947, President's Records, HUA, box 9 (1946–1947).

30. Clark to Conant, March 4, 1947, President's Records, HUA, box 5 (1946–1947); Clark to James, March 28, 1947, Grenville Clark MSS, box 5 (Harvard Corporation Series), Henry James folder; Gerald T. Dunne, *Grenville Clark: Public Citizen* (New York: Farrar, Straus, Giroux, 1986), pp. 199, 141–165.

31. Clark to James, March 28, 1947; James to Clark, May 15, 22, 1947, box 5, Henry James folder; Clark to Robert A. Lovett, April 28, 1947; Lovett to Clark, April 29, 1947, box 5, folder L; Clark to William L. Marbury, April 4, 1947; Clark memorandum, April 10, 1947, box 6, William Marbury folder; Clark to James Bryant Conant, May 9, 1947, box 2, J. B. Conant folder; Clark to George Whitney, December 4, 1947, Grenville Clark MSS, box 7 (Harvard Corpo-

ration Series), folder W; James to Conant, March 14, April 16, 1947, President's Records, HUA, box 9 (1946–1947).

32. Clark to Whitney, December 4, 1947, box 7, folder W; Conant to Clark, September 4, October 1, 1947, Grenville Clark MSS, box 2, J. B. Conant folder (Harvard Corporation Series); Diary, October 17, 1947.

33. Diary, October 17, 1947.

CHAPTER 10

1. Cleveland Amory, *The Proper Bostonians* (New York: Dodd, Mead, 1947), p. 27.

2. Diary, October 20, October 9–12, 1947.

3. Ibid., October 31, November 8, 1947; Lowell, memorandum, November 3, 1947; Lowell to Thomas S. Lamont, November 4, 1947, Ralph Lowell MSS, box 2 (Harvard University Files).

4. Lamont to Lowell, November 13, 1947; Lowell to Lamont, November 17, 1947, Ralph Lowell MSS, box 2 (Harvard University Files).

5. Diary, November 3, 1943; November 19, 1945; November 18, 1947.

6. Ibid., November 18, 20, 21, 22, 1947.

7. Ibid., November 24, 1947; Grenville Clark, memorandum to Henry Lee Shattuck and Roger Lee, December 3, 1947, Grenville Clark MSS, Dartmouth College Library, box 5 (Harvard Corporation Series), Roger Lee folder; Hanford MacNider to Lowell, December 10, 1947, Ralph Lowell MSS, box 2 (Harvard University Files).

8. Diary, November 24, 1947; David Bailey to Lowell, November 26, 1947; Lowell to Richard C. Curtis, December 12, 1947, Ralph Lowell MSS, box 2 (Harvard University Files).

9. Jerome D. Greene to Lowell, December 15, 1947; Lowell to Greene, December 22, 1947, Ralph Lowell MSS, box 2 (Harvard University Files).

10. Grenville Clark, memorandum to Shattuck and Lee, December 3, 1947; Clark to Laurence Coolidge, December 5, 1947, box 3, folder C; Lowell to Clark, December 3, 1947; Clark to Lowell, December 5, 1947; Lowell to Clark, December 8, 1947, Grenville Clark MSS, box 5, Ralph Lowell folder (Harvard Corporation Series).

11. Diary, December 18, 1947; Clark to George Rublee, January 2, 1948, Grenville Clark MSS, box 6 (Harvard Corporation Series), folder R.

12. Diary, December 24, 1947; Henry L. Shattuck to Conant, December 22, 1947, President's Records, HUA, box 324 (1947–1948).

13. Diary, December 24, 1947; Lowell to Hanford MacNider, December 30, 1947, Ralph Lowell MSS, box 2 (Harvard University Files).

14. Diary, December 24, 1947.

15. Grenville Clark to Clarence Little, December 9, 1947, President's Records, HUA, box 324 (1947–1948); Clark, memorandum, December 29, 1947, box 2; Clark, memorandum, January 2, 1948, Grenville Clark MSS, box 6 (Harvard Corporation Series); Gerald T. Dunne, *Grenville Clark: Public Citizen* (New York: Farrar, Straus, Giroux, 1986), pp. 167–168.

16. Diary, January 5, 1948; Hanford MacNider to Lowell, January 1, 1948, Ralph Lowell MSS, box 2 (Harvard University Files).

17. Diary, January 5, 1948.

18. Ibid.

19. Ibid., January 6, 1948; James Bryant Conant, statement, January 6, 1948, Grenville Clark MSS, box 2 (Harvard Corporation Series), J. B. Conant folder.

20. Diary, January 8, 1948.

21. Ibid., January 8, 9, 10, 11, 1948; *Boston Globe,* September 21, 1986; Paul H. Buck, interview by William Bentinck-Smith, 1974, HUA, HUG(B) B857.50, pp. 1–2.

22. Diary, January 12, 1948; draft of minutes of Board of Overseers meeting, January 12, 1948 (prepared by David Bailey), Ralph Lowell MSS, box 2 (Harvard University Files).

23. Letters regarding Marbury in President's Records, HUA, box 324 (1947–1948); Diary, January 12, 1948; draft of minutes of Board of Overseers meeting, January 12, 1948 (prepared by David Bailey), Ralph Lowell MSS, box 2 (Harvard University Files).

24. Diary, January 13, March 3, October 16, December 3, 1948.

25. Ibid., January 17, April 30, May 6, September 21, 1948; May 31, 1949; November 28, 1950; March 26, 1951.

26. Ibid., April 21, May 11, September 15, 1948; May 9, 1949; Lowell to Grenville Clark, November 28, 1950, Grenville Clark MSS, box 5 (Harvard Corporation Series), Ralph Lowell folder; Dunne, *Grenville Clark,* pp. 177–193.

27. Clark to George Whitney, January 8, 1948, box 7, folder W; Clark, Harvard memorandum, May 10, 1948, box 2 (Harvard Corporation Series), Grenville Clark MSS; Diary, April 16, 1948.

28. Diary, June 11, 12, October 1, 11, 21, 1948; William L. Marbury to James Bryant Conant, May 24, 1948, President's Records, HUA, box 324 (1947–1948); Charles C. Burlingham to Lowell, June 5, 1948; Lowell to Burlingham, June 18, 1948, Charles C. Burlingham MSS, Harvard Law School, box 6, folder 6–15.

29. John Kenneth Galbraith, *A Life in Our Times* (Boston: Houghton Mifflin, 1981), pp. 96–97; 269, 272–273.

30. Ibid., pp. 197, 199, 225–227.

31. Paul H. Buck to James Bryant Conant, April 15, 1949, Grenville Clark MSS, box 1 (Harvard Corporation Series), folder B.

32. Diary, May 9, June 8, 1949; Lowell to Clarence Randall, June 10, 1949, Sinclair Weeks MSS, Dartmouth College Library, box 6.

33. Diary, June 23, 1949; Galbraith, *Life,* p. 275; James Bryant Conant, *My Several Lives* (New York: Harper & Row, 1970), pp. 433–445.

34. Diary, June 23, 1949; Galbraith, *Life,* p. 274; Richard Norton Smith, *The Harvard Century* (New York: Simon & Schuster, 1986), pp. 174–175.

35. James G. Hershberg, *James Bryant Conant* (New York: Knopf, 1993), pp. 638–649; Diary, January 12, 13, April 4, May 9, 26, 1953; Felix Frankfurter to Charles C. Burlingham, January 23, 1953, box 5, folder 5–12; Burlingham to Grenville Clark, January 24, 1953, box 7, folder 7–6, Charles C. Burlingham MSS.

36. Diary, June 1, 1953; Smith, *Harvard Century,* pp. 197–201.

37. Diary, June 10, 1953; January 11, 1954; May 9, 1955.

38. Ellen W. Schrecker, *No Ivory Tower: McCarthyism and the Universities* (New York: Oxford University Press, 1986), pp. 87–88; *Milwaukee Journal,* May 28, 1947; *Boston Herald,* January 9, 1954.

39. *New York Herald-Tribune,* January 20, 1951; Diary, December 15, 1953; January 11, April 14, 1954.

40. Diary, March 15, 1952; James Bryant Conant to Lowell, March 10, 1952, Ralph Lowell MSS, box 3 (Harvard University Files).
41. Diary, January 13, June 16–19, 1952; Charles Cabot to Lowell, June 24, 1952, Ralph Lowell MSS, box 3 (Harvard University Files).

CHAPTER II

1. S. Huntington Wolcott to Lowell, December 18, 1912, Ralph Lowell MSS, 1909–1912 Correspondence box, 1912 folder; Ralph Lowell to Mary Emlen Hale Lowell, January 11, 1913, Ralph Lowell MSS, 1913–1917 Correspondence box, World Tour 1912–1913 folder; Walter Muir Whitehill, *The Provident Institution for Savings in the Town of Boston* (Boston: The Provident, 1966), pp. 6–15.
2. Diary, January 30, 1960. For a complete list of Lowell's trusteeships, see his Harvard class reports or his *Who's Who in America* entries.
3. *Boston Globe*, July 17, 1965; Ralph Lowell, *Reminiscences* (New York: Columbia University Oral History Collection, 1964), pp. 21–23.
4. Walter Muir Whitehill, *Museum of Fine Arts Boston* (Cambridge: Belknap Press of Harvard University Press, 1970), vol. 1, pp. 1–10, 14, 32–33, 210, 218–233, 246–287, 336, 358; vol. 2, p. 444.
5. Ibid., vol. 2, pp. 443–444; A. Lawrence Lowell to G. Harold Edgell, December 19, 1934; Edgell, minute on A. Lawrence Lowell, April 1943, Director's Correspondence (1901–1954), Museum of Fine Arts Archives (hereafter cited as MFA Archives), A. Lawrence Lowell folder.
6. Diary, October 21, 26, 1943.
7. Whitehill, *Museum of Fine Arts*, vol. 1, pp. 131–132, 356–358, 372–373, 408–409, 429, 611–612; Edward Jackson Holmes to A. Lawrence Lowell, October 22, 1934, Directors' Correspondence (1901–1954), MFA Archives, A. Lawrence Lowell folder; Museum of Fine Arts, *Annual Report for 1951*, p. 3.
8. Whitehill, *Museum of Fine Arts*, vol. 1, p. 132; vol. 2, p. 612; Diary, May 11, 1944.
9. Lowell, *Reminiscences*, p. 24; Diary, November 2, 8, 1950; January 18, 1951.
10. *Boston Herald*, February 2, 1951.
11. Diary, April 17, October 6, 1952; April 16, 1954; Whitehill, *Museum of Fine Arts*, vol. 2, p. 620.
12. Diary, April 17, May 15, 1952; January 6, 1953; Museum of Fine Arts, Annual Report for 1952, pp. 5–6; Annual Report for 1953, p. 5.
13. Museum of Fine Arts, Annual Report for 1950, p. 6; Annual Report for 1951, p. 10; Annual Report for 1954, p. 3; G. Harold Edgell to Lowell, April 18, 1951, Director's Correspondence (1901–1954), MFA Archives, LICBC folder.
14. Diary, December 11, 1952; January 8, 1953; Museum of Fine Arts, Annual Report for 1952, pp. 2, 4.
15. Diary, June 18, September 16, 1953; May 3, 6, 1954; Whitehill, *Museum of Fine Arts*, vol. 2, pp. 620–621; Edward W. Forbes and John H. Finley Jr., eds., *The Saturday Club: A Century Completed, 1920–1956* (Boston: Houghton Mifflin, 1958), p. 332.
16. Diary, September 16, 1953; June 30, July 28, 1954.
17. *Christian Science Monitor*, November 29, 1954; Karl E. Meyer, *The Plundered Past* (New York:

Atheneum, 1973), pp. 102–103; Nathaniel Burt, *Palaces for the People: A Social History of the American Art Museum* (Boston: Little, Brown, 1977), pp. 193–195, 311; Nelson W. Aldrich Jr., *Old Money: The Mythology of America's Upper Class* (New York: Knopf, 1988), p. 60.

18. *Christian Science Monitor*, November 29, 1954; Whitehill, *Museum of Fine Arts*, vol. 2, pp. 626–627.

19. Fiftieth Anniversary Report of the Harvard Class of 1933 (1983), p. 435; Whitehill, *Museum of Fine Arts*, vol. 2, pp. 629–639, 814–815.

20. Diary, November 15, 1955; April 29, 1958.

21. Whitehill, *Museum of Fine Arts*, vol. 2, p. 840; Diary, May 12, 1955; October 15, 1958.

22. Diary, October 9, 1957; January 9, October 9, 1958; May 11, 18, 1960; November 8, 1961; September 18, 1963; *New York Times*, June 1, 1965.

23. Diary, October 29, November 19, 1959; September 30, 1965; October 11, 1966; May 16, 1968.

24. Whitehill, *Museum of Fine Arts*, vol. 1, pp. 281–283; Museum of Fine Arts, Annual Report for 1964, p. 8.

25. Whitehill, *Museum of Fine Arts*, vol. 1, pp. 14–15, 382–383; vol. 2, pp. 598–600; Museum of Fine Arts, Annual Report for 1966, pp. 5–6.

26. Diary, July 5, 1966; *Boston Globe*, July 6, 11, 1966; Museum of Fine Arts, Annual Report for 1966, p. 6; Annual Report for 1967, p. 9.

27. Whitehill, *Museum of Fine Arts*, vol. 1, pp. 15–16, 27, 68–69, 83–86, 381–384; vol. 2, pp. 826–827; Museum of Fine Arts, *The Museum Year 1971–1972*, p. 8.

28. Museum of Fine Arts, Annual Report for 1961, p. 35.

29. Diary, September 29, October 29, December 7, 1965; January 3, February 10, 1966.

30. Ibid., September 7, 1966; January 4, February 21, April 25, 1967; February 7, November 13, December 19, 1968; George C. Seybolt to Ralph Lowell, March 13, 1967, Director's Papers (1955–1972), MFA Archives, box 3; Whitehill, *Museum of Fine Arts*, vol. 2, pp. 838–842.

31. Diary, March 28, April 11, 25, May 8, July 26, September 15, 21, 1967; January 30, 1968.

32. *Boston Globe*, February 16, 1968; Museum of Fine Arts, Annual Report for 1968, pp. 4, 8; Perry T. Rathbone to Lowell, February 28, 1968, Charlotte Loring Lowell MSS, box 1968 (M–Z), folder M–O.

33. Thirty-fifth Anniversary Report of the Harvard Class of 1933 (1968), pp. 256–257; Fiftieth Anniversary Report of the Harvard Class of 1933 (1983), p. 435.

34. Diary, March 19, 1970; Dana C. Chandler Jr., "A Proposal to Eradicate Institutional Racism at the Boston Museum of Fine Arts," January 15, 1970; Perry T. Rathbone to Chandler, January 27, 1970, Director's Papers (1955–1972), MFA Archives, box 1.

35. Whitehill, *Museum of Fine Arts*, vol. 2, p. 813.

36. Ad Hoc Policy Review Committee, Report to the Trustees, November 1970, Director's Papers (1955–1972), MFA Archives, box 3; Museum of Fine Arts, *The Museum Year 1970–1971*, p. 8; *Christian Science Monitor*, March 23, 1972; Charles Giuliano, "Good-bye, Perry Rathbone," *Boston Magazine*, August 1972, p. 46.

37. Jane Holtz Kay, "Modern Times at Boston's Art Museum," *Boston Sunday Globe Magazine*, February 13, 1972, pp. 8, 11–12; Diary, February 17, 1972.

38. Diary, November 15, 1940; November 28, 1941.

39. "'Mass General,'" *Newsweek*, February 6, 1961, p. 81.

40. Benjamin Castleman, David C. Crockett, and S. B. Sutton, eds., *The Massachusetts General Hospital, 1955–1980* (Boston: Little, Brown, 1983), pp. 3–5.

41. Diary, May 16, November 25, 29, December 2, 26, 1941; June 4, 10, 11, 14, 30, 1943; January 12, 1944; August 7, 24, 1945; August 9, November 18, 1946; July 6, 1948; June 3, 7, 24, 29, December 30, 1949; June 20, September 8, 1950; April 30, 1951; Nathaniel W. Faxon, *The Massachusetts General Hospital, 1935–1955* (Cambridge: Harvard University Press, 1959), pp. 59, 73–74, 76, 195–196, 204–206; Castleman, Crockett, and Sutton, eds., *Massachusetts General Hospital, 1955–1980*, pp. 3, 32–34, 54; David C. Crockett, interview by author, January 3, 1994.

42. Diary, April 27, May 24, 1949; August 17, 21, 1953; May 17, 1955; May 29, 1959; August 4, November 18, December 1, 2, 1960; July 16, December 20, 1963; June 19, 1964; April 28, 1967; Crockett, interview.

43. Castleman, Crockett, and Sutton, eds., *Massachusetts General Hospital, 1955–1980*, pp. 138–145, 8–10, 12–13; Faxon, *Massachusetts General Hospital, 1935–1955*, pp. 165–171; Diary, February 5, 1947; October 4, 1949; June 7, September 8, 1950; October 2, November 14, 17, December 2, 1952; February 5, 16, May 15, 1953; May 17, 27, 1955.

44. Diary, January 4, 6, 1950; Crockett, interview.

45. S. B. Sutton, *Crossroads in Psychiatry: A History of the McLean Hospital* (Washington, D.C.: American Psychiatric Press, 1986), pp. 238–239; Diary, October 26, 28, 29, 1948; November 22, 1949; January 8, August 11, 1954; November 21, 1956; March 13, April 9, 18, 21, May 15, June 20, 1970; Francis de Marneffe, interview by author, April 11, 1994; George Putnam, interview by author, May 24, 1994.

46. Diary, December 4, 10, 1940; May 23, 1941; December 23, 1943; March 23, June 15, July 13, December 14, 1944; April 5, 1945; Sutton, *Crossroads in Psychiatry*, pp. 237–242; Crockett, interview.

47. Diary, September 10, November 1, 1945; November 30, December 6, 1946; March 6, 20, May 1, June 12, August 21, November 14, December 8, 1947; Sutton, *Crossroads in Psychiatry*, pp. 242–246.

48. Sutton, *Crossroads in Psychiatry*, pp. 205–206, 210–212, 223–229, 246–257, 264–285; Diary, July 11, November 12, 1941; February 19, October 13, December 9, 1942; December 18, 1947; January 22, 30, October 8, 11, 13, 14, 15, 26, 28, 29, 1948; May 6, November 22, 1949; April 7, 1950; January 8, 1954; January 12, 13, 1961.

49. De Marneffe, interview; Putnam, interview; Diary, October 3, 1965.

CHAPTER 12

1. "New Champ," *Newsweek,* July 26, 1965, p. 71; *New York Herald-Tribune,* July 15, 1965; *Boston Globe,* July 17, 1965; May 17, 1967.

2. Diary, January 17, February 3, 1950; April 13, 1951; June 28, 1955; January 8, 22, 1960.

3. "Texmass Mess?" *Time,* April 24, 1950, p. 100; "In Investing, It's the Prudent Bostonian," *Business Week,* June 6, 1959, p. 60; Diary, November 5, 1948.

4. "Texmass Mess?" p. 100; Andrew J. Dunar, *The Truman Scandals and the Politics of Morality* (Columbia: University of Missouri Press, 1984), pp. 83–84.

5. Diary, May 5, 1950

6. Ibid., September 22, 1950; January 17, 22, February 12, November 27, 29, 1951; *New York Times*, February 13, 1951; *Boston Herald*, November 30, 1951.

7. "John Hancock Life," *Fortune*, April 1948, pp. 160, 168, 170; "How John Hancock Invests Its Money," *Business Week*, November 6, 1954, pp. 102–106.

8. Diary, November 16, December 28, 1948; January 28, June 28, 1949; January 10, March 31, June 6, 23, August 15, 1950; January 19, 22, February 6, 1951; January 8, May 27, 1952.

9. "Capture of the New Haven," *Fortune*, April 1949, p. 87; Tamara K. Hareven and Randolph Langenbach, *Amoskeag* (New York: Pantheon, 1978), pp. 10, 13, 18–25, 78–84, 295–304, 333–344; "The Waltham Mess," *Fortune*, April 1949, pp. 84–85, 198; Diary, October 6, 1943; January 16, 17, 1947; *Boston Globe*, September 18, 1976.

10. Diary, March 24, August 11, December 26, 1947; March 18, 1948; January 24, March 8, July 25, 1949; "Capture of the New Haven," p. 184.

11. Diary, December 18, 1950; January 29, May 27, 1951.

12. "Capture of the New Haven," p. 87; *New York Times*, March 14, 1954; "Legman Up," *Time*, June 18, 1951, p. 98.

13. Diary, April 28, June 8, 1953; June 2, 1954.

14. Stephen Mahoney, "It's Hertz Itself in the Driver's Seat," *Fortune*, October 1961, pp. 122–123; Martin Mayer, "Avis vs. Hertz: Madison Avenue's Favorite Feud," *Harper's*, January 1968, pp. 42–43; Diary, September 7, 17, 18, October 11, 23, 1956; January 8, 21, April 12, 24, October 3, 1957; June 19, August 18, 19, 20, 28, September 2, 16, 19, 23, 25, October 3, 8, 20, 31, November 5, 6, 12, December 5, 1958; January 22, June 22, August 24, December 16, 1959; May 5, July 25, December 8, 21, 1960; June 19, July 7, 13, August 2, October 6, November 20, December 11, 1961; January 5, 31, February 19, 1962; *New York Times*, January 3, March 22, 23, 1962; *Wall Street Journal*, July 30, 1962.

15. Diary, August 2, 1962; September 6, 9, November 4, December 23, 1963; October 5, November 15, 1965; February 7, March 31, April 4, December 5, 1966; January 12, March 8, 22, May 13, 20, September 13, December 10, 1968; May 2, November 3, 1969; February 5, April 13, December 7, 1970; September 29, 1971.

16. *Boston Globe*, June 23, 1921; Louis Lyons, *Newspaper Story: One Hundred Years of the Boston Globe* (Cambridge: Belknap Press of Harvard University Press, 1971), pp. 31–39; James Morgan, *Charles H. Taylor: Builder of the Boston Globe* (n.p., 1923), p. 91; Peter Braestrup, "What the Press Has Done to Boston and Vice-Versa," *Harper's*, October 1960, pp. 85, 90; Oswald Garrison Villard, *The Disappearing Daily* (New York: Knopf, 1944), p. 178.

17. Lyons, *Newspaper Story*, pp. 26–27, 226, 265–266; Eben D. Jordan, Last Will and Testament, May 22, 1895, Suffolk County Registry of Probate, Boston, Mass., Docket No. 100234.

18. *New York Times*, June 23, 1921.

19. "The Last Puritan," *Time*, May 5, 1941, p. 61; Villard, *Disappearing Daily*, pp. 176–177; Lyons, *Newspaper Story*, p. 268, 272; Doris Kearns Goodwin, *The Fitzgeralds and the Kennedys* (New York: Simon & Schuster, 1987), p. 503; Diary, October 24, 1950.

20. Lyons, *Newspaper Story*, pp. 135–137, 268–269; "The Herald's Century," *Time*, September 2, 1946, p. 50; Braestrup, "Press," p. 84.

21. *WHDH, Inc., et al.*, 22 Federal Communications Commission (FCC) Reports, 774–775 (1957); "Herald's Century," p. 50; Sterling Quinlan, *The Hundred Million Dollar Lunch* (Chicago: J. Philip O'Hara, 1974), p. 127.

22. *Boston Herald,* December 22, 1963; *Boston Globe,* December 22, 1963.

23. "Herald's Century," p. 50; "Up from Newspaper Row," *Time,* June 2, 1958, p. 39; Braestrup, "Press," p. 85; Lyons, *Newspaper Story,* p. 226.

24. Lyons, *Newspaper Story,* pp. 225, 271.

25. Diary, March 27, April 13, 1950.

26. Ibid., May 11, 1950; Davis Taylor, interview by author, October 17, 1988.

27. Lyons, *Newspaper Story,* pp. 265–266; Diary, October 20, December 13, 1950.

28. Diary, February 15, May 11, December 13, 1950; January 22, May 17, October 18, 24, November 15, December 11, 1951; January 28, 1952.

29. Ibid., January 25, June 5, 1952; May 27, June 19, August 13, September 14, 1953; March 17, May 17, 1954; Taylor, interview.

30. Diary, July 24, August 13, September 23, 1953; May 17, 20, 1954.

31. Ibid., July 10, 1953; Robert T. H. Davidson, interview by author, November 9, 1988.

32. Diary, July 21, September 23, 1953; April 26, 1954; Sidney Davidson, memorandum to Lowell, July 17, 1953; Davidson, memorandum to Lowell, April 23, 1954, Sidney W. Davidson MSS, American Heritage Center, University of Wyoming, box 13, 1953–1954 Correspondence file.

33. Diary, August 3, December 1, 1953; April 26, May 20, 28, 1954.

34. Ibid., July 26, August 2, 30, 1954; Sidney Davidson, memorandum to Lowell, April 27, 1954, Sidney W. Davidson MSS, box 13, 1953–1954 Correspondence file; William Bentinck-Smith, interview by author, October 19, 1988.

35. Diary, August 23, 25, 1954.

36. Ibid., August 25, September 10, October 21, 1954.

37. Ibid., January 24, 26, March 17, 1955.

38. *Boston Globe,* July 16, 1955.

39. Diary, August 15, December 28, 1949; June 5, 1952; August 3, 1953; April 21, July 20, August 8, September 15, October 7, 1955.

40. Taylor, interview; Diary, October 7, November 17, 1955.

41. Diary, October 20, November 17, December 9, 14, 1955.

42. Ibid., January 23, February 15, April 13, 19, May 9, 1956; Taylor, interview.

43. Taylor, interview.

44. *Boston Post,* April 6, 1956; *Boston Globe,* April 11, 1956; Diary, April 24, May 9, 11, 17, 1956.

45. Braestrup, "Press," p. 84; *Boston Globe,* February 21, 1959; December 22, 1963.

46. Diary, June 1, 1956; Taylor, interview.

47. Boston Herald-Traveler Corporation, Annual Reports, 1947–1949, 1955; *WHDH, Inc., et al.,* 22 FCC 767ff.; *WHDH, Inc., et al.,* 29 FCC 204ff (1960); U.S. House Committee on Interstate and Foreign Commerce, *Hearings on Communications Act Amendments,* 84th Cong., 2d sess., 1956, pp. 35–39, 345–348; Pre-Presidential Papers of John F. Kennedy, John F. Kennedy Library, box 666, Federal Communications Act folder; box 682 Television folder; James MacGregor Burns, *John Kennedy: A Political Profile* (New York: Harcourt, Brace & World, 1959), p. 219.

48. Diary, January 17, April 26, 1957; April 10, 15, 29, May 15, 16, August 22, September 5, 18, October 16, 1958; July 27, August 6, September 17, October 2, 14, 15, 1959; October 21, 1963.

49. Ibid., September 23, 27, November 5, December 2, 12, 1959; January 11, 1960.

50. Ibid., December 12, 1959; January 14, 21, April 21, May 13, 1960; Taylor, interview; Davidson, interview; Robert Haydock, interview by author, January 24, 1989.

51. Robert Healy, *The Taylors and the Boston Globe* (n.p.: Globe Newspaper Company, 1981), pp. 39–40; *Boston Globe*, January 13, 1982.

52. Taylor, interview; Davidson, interview.

CHAPTER 13

1. Walter Lippmann and Louis Brandeis quoted in Cleveland Amory, *The Proper Bostonians* (New York: Dodd, Mead, 1947), p. 324.

2. Ralph Lowell, *Reminiscences* (New York: Columbia University Oral History Collection, 1964), pp. 26, 29.

3. John Gunther, *Inside U.S.A.* (New York: Harper Bros., 1947), p. 512.

4. Diary, June 5, 9, December 19, 29, 1944; November 30, 1949.

5. Ibid., March 16, 1946; May 13, 1950; September 15, October 19, 1951; January 23, 1952; *Boston Globe*, November 1, 1958.

6. Diary, November 22, 1943; April 22, 1944; March 8, 1945; William V. Shannon, *The American Irish* (New York: Macmillan, 1966), pp. 191–196; James M. O'Toole, *Militant and Triumphant: William Henry O'Connell and the Catholic Church in Boston, 1859–1944* (Notre Dame, Ind.: University of Notre Dame Press, 1992).

7. *Dictionary of American Biography*, supplement 8, s.v. "Cushing, Richard."

8. Perkins Institution and Massachusetts School for the Blind, Annual Reports; Diary, January 10, 1927.

9. Perkins Institution officials, telephone interviews by author, April 1994; Perkins Institution, Annual Report, 1926, pp. 12–13.

10. Diary, January 28, 1946.

11. Ibid., March 6, 12, 1946.

12. Diary, November 14, 1941; April 17, July 24, December 15, 1947; November 1, 1949; C. Thomas Dienes, *Law, Politics, and Birth Control* (Urbana: University of Illinois Press, 1972), pp. 44–46, 123–137; James M. O'Toole, "Prelates and Politicos: Catholics and Politics in Massachusetts, 1900–1970," in *Catholic Boston: Studies in Religion and Community, 1870–1970*, ed. Robert E. Sullivan and James M. O'Toole (Boston: Roman Catholic Archbishop of Boston, 1985), pp. 49–57.

13. Diary, March 5, 1950; *Boston Herald*, March 6, 7, 1950; *Boston Globe*, March 6, 1950.

14. Diary, June 12, 1950; *Boston Globe*, June 12, 1950; *Pilot* (Boston), June 17, 1950.

15. Donald J. White, interview by author, February 25, 1988; Richard M. Freeland, *Academia's Golden Age* (New York: Oxford University Press, 1992), pp. 255–256; Michael P. Walsh, SJ, to Lowell, November 22, 1961, Charlotte Loring Lowell MSS, 1961 A–J box, folder A–B; Diary, March 20, 1958; June 11, 1962; April 20, 1963.

16. Diary, June 1, 22, August 13, 1967; Nathan Pusey to Lowell, May 24, 1967; Pusey to Richard Cardinal Cushing, June 20, 1967, Charlotte Loring Lowell MSS, 1967 A–L box, folder A–C.

17. James Michael Curley, *I'd Do It Again* (Englewood Cliffs, N.J.: Prentice-Hall, 1957), pp. 69, 229, 350, 359; Diary, July 24, 1957.

18. Diary, April 2, 1951; November 14, 1956; Peter Schrag, *Village School Downtown* (Boston: Beacon Press, 1967), pp. 49–50.

19. Barbara Miller Solomon, *Ancestors and Immigrants* (Cambridge: Harvard University Press, 1956); Allon Gal, *Brandeis of Boston* (Cambridge: Harvard University Press, 1980).

20. Diary, November 5, 1907; May 30, 1908; July 9, 15, 1911; April 22, 1912; December 23, 1912; January 5, June 18, June 27, 1913; March 3, 1946; June 28, 1947; August 2, 1954; April 7, 1959; March 18, 1960; Ralph Lowell to John Lowell, January 1, 1912 (actually 1913), Ralph Lowell MSS, 1909–1912 Correspondence box, 1912 folder.

21. Diary, March 25, 1965; February 16, 1950; September 12, 1956; May 17, 1954; April 22, 1963, Ralph Lowell Jr., interview by author, September 10, 1997.

22. Diary, October 7, 1949; May 11, October 13, 1953.

23. Ibid., April 14, 17, 1958; Leonard Silk and Mark Silk, *The American Establishment* (New York: Basic Books, 1980), pp. 42–47.

24. Diary, November 2, 1942; March 9, 1943; February 2, 1945; October 14, 1958.

25. Ibid., January 25, 1949; January 31, 1950; January 30, 1951; Bruce A. Phillips, *Brookline: The Evolution of a Jewish Community* (New York: Garland, 1990), pp. 104–109.

26. *What is the Massachusetts Committee of Catholics, Protestants, and Jews?* (pamphlet), 1957, Massachusetts State House Library; 105th AR/LI, August 1, 1945; Diary, May 15, 25, 1950; *Boston Globe*, April 27, May 19, 1967.

27. *Jewish Advocate*, December 19, 1957; Diary, December 20, 1957.

28. W. E. Burghardt Du Bois, *The Black North in 1901* (New York: Arno Press, 1969), pp. 31–33, 37; Diary, July 2, August 22, 1911; January 4, April 20, November 28, 1912; July 30, 1940.

29. Greater Boston Soldiers and Sailors Committee, a Record and Annual Report, 1946.

30. Diary, May 21, January 5, August 16, 1943.

31. Ibid., May 10, 1943; *Guardian* (Boston), May 15, 1943.

32. Diary, May 12, June 21, July 14, 26, 1943.

33. Ibid., August 2, 16, November 1, December 6, 1943; *Guardian* (Boston), December 18, 24, 1943.

34. *Dictionary of American Biography*, supplement 4, s.v. "Lewis, William H."; J. Clay Smith Jr., *Emancipation: The Making of the Black Lawyer, 1844–1944* (Philadelphia: University of Pennsylvania Press, 1993), pp. 541–544; Kelly Miller, "The Negro in New England," *Harvard Graduates' Magazine* 34 (June 1926), p. 547; *Boston Herald*, January 2, 1949.

35. Diary, August 17, 1943.

36. Lowell to William Henry Lewis, September 16, 1943; Charles H. Watkins to Lowell, September 13, 1943; Norman W. Bingham to Lowell, September 2, 1943; Lowell to Lewis, October 7, 1943, Ralph Lowell MSS, box 3 (Harvard University Files), Harvard Club folder; Diary, October 6, 1943.

37. Diary, December 5, 1945; May 10, July 26, 1946.

38. Ibid., October 21, 1946; E. Digby Baltzell, *The Protestant Establishment* (New York: Vintage, 1966), p. 370.

39. Diary, February 12, 1948.

40. Ibid., February 4, March 4, 1965; Massachusetts State Board of Education, *Because It Is Right— Educationally: Report of the Advisory Committee on Racial Imbalance and Education* (Boston, April 1965).

41. Ronald P. Formisano, *Boston Against Busing* (Chapel Hill: University of North Carolina Press, 1991), p. 36; Diary, September 22, November 14, 1965; June 20, November 7, 8, 1967.

42. See J. Anthony Lukas, *Common Ground* (New York: Vintage, 1986).

CHAPTER 14

1. *Dedham Transcript,* April 4, 1925.

2. Ibid.; Diary, April 4, 1925.

3. *Dedham Transcript,* May 2, 1925; March 19, April 2, May 28, 1926; Frank Smith, *A History of Dedham, Massachusetts* (Dedham, Mass: Transcript Press, 1936), pp. 508–509.

4. Diary, April 4, 1925; *Dedham Transcript,* November 5, 1926; March 11, 1927.

5. Robert Coles, "A Candidate for '72 or So: Mayor Kevin White of Boston," *New Republic,* October 26, 1968, p. 18.

6. John Gunther, *Inside U.S.A.* (New York: Harper Bros., 1947), pp. 510–512.

7. Ibid.; Walter McQuade, "Boston: What Can a Sick City Do?" *Fortune,* June 1964, pp. 134–135.

8. Diary, July 6, September 11, 1944; February 26, 1945; June 28, 30, 1947; October 27, 1959; 108th AR/LI, August 1, 1948; Report of Robert F. Bradford, Guardian *ad litem,* December 28, 1949, Eben D. Jordan Estate, Docket No. 100234, Suffolk County Registry of Probate, Boston, Mass.

9. Gunther, *Inside U.S.A.,* p. 520; Louis M. Lyons, "Boston: A Study in Inertia," in *Our Fair City,* ed. Robert S. Allen (New York: Vanguard Press, 1947), p. 29; Thomas H. O'Connor, *Building a New Boston: Politics and Urban Renewal, 1950–1970* (Boston: Northeastern University Press, 1993), pp. 15–17.

10. Diary, April 6, 1944; June 10, September 11, 1947; November 1, December 6, 1948; July 13, 1949; January 8, 1951; August 30, 1962; *Greater Boston Business,* January 1957, p. 7.

11. Diary, May 22, 1952; August 30, 1962.

12. Ibid., November 10, 1949; O'Connor, *Building a New Boston,* pp. 24–32.

13. Diary, October 8, 1947; March 21, 1950; November 7, 1951; October 25, 1954; "Boston: Building in History's Attic," *Business Week,* July 10, 1954, pp. 78–94.

14. Diary, May 23, 1951; *New York Times,* February 13, 1953.

15. *Christian Science Monitor,* October 11, November 4, 1954; "Court Trims City's Plans," *Business Week,* May 28, 1955, p. 86; Diary, July 22, 1953; October 25, 1954; O'Connor, *Building a New Boston,* p. 98.

16. Diary, October 14, 1954; August 11, November 9, 1955; *Boston Herald,* October 18, 1955.

17. *Christian Science Monitor,* January 3, May 16, 1956; January 10, August 6, 14, September 7, 1957; George Sternlieb, "Is Business Abandoning the Big City?" *Harvard Business Review* 39 (January/February 1961), pp. 6–12.

18. O'Connor, *Building a New Boston,* pp. 96–98, 102–111; Diary, October 26, 1954.

19. Peter Braestrup, "What the Press Has Done to Boston and Vice-Versa," *Harper's,* October 1960, p. 80; "Rainbow?" *Greater Boston Business,* April 1955, p. 12; Diary, February 14, 1956.

20. O'Connor, *Building a New Boston,* pp. 107–108; Proceedings, Boston College Citizen Seminar, January 15, 1957, p. 66; Diary, January 15, 1957.

21. Proceedings, Boston College Citizen Seminar, January 26, 1960, pp. 61–64; Lorin Peterson, *The Day of the Mugwump* (New York: Random House, 1961), p. 265; Diary, July 12, August 22, September 27, 1957.

22. "Is Boston 'Beginning to Boil'?" *Fortune,* June 1957, pp. 286, 288.

23. *New York Times,* June 12, 16, 1957; *Boston Globe,* June 16, 1957; Diary, July 22, 1953; January 23, 28, July 18, 1957.

24. Diary, June 26, July 24, August 22, 1957.

25. Ibid., August 9, 1954; May 4, October 19, 1955; September 27, 1957; August 30, 1962.

26. O'Connor, *Building a New Boston*, pp. 122–123, 136–143.

27. Diary, November 19, 1958; January 19, 29, February 6, 1959; Richard Chapman, in Proceedings, Boston College Citizen Seminar, January 27, 1959, pp. 7–9; *New York Times*, February 24, 1946; "Boston Bonds' Rating Slips a Notch," *Business Week*, December 12, 1959, pp. 90–94.

28. O'Connor, *Building a New Boston*, p. 150; Diary, March 6, 1958; *Christian Science Monitor*, October 30, 1959.

29. Diary, April 22, 1959.

30. Ibid., May 26, July 27, 1959.

31. O'Connor, *Building a New Boston*, pp. 151–160.

32. McQuade, "Boston: What Can a Sick City Do?" p. 136; Gerald W. Blakeley, interview by author, November 4, 1993.

33. Diary, August 18, 20, September 30, 1954.

34. *Boston Herald*, February 22, 1957; Diary, July 12, 1957; October 13, 1959; Blakeley, interview.

35. Diary, October 13, 1959; John F. Collins, interview by author, May 26, 1994.

36. Blakeley, interview; Diary, October 13, 1959.

37. Blakeley, interview; Diary, October 22, 1959.

38. Diary, November 3, 1959.

39. Ibid., November 4, 1959.

40. Ibid., November 25, 1959; Collins, interview.

41. Diary, December 17, 1959.

42. Ibid., April 24, 1958; December 17, 1959.

43. Ibid., December 21, 1959; *Boston Herald*, December 25, 1959; *Christian Science Monitor*, February 5, 1960; *Boston Globe*, April 29, 1970.

44. Diary, December 21–25, 1959; *Boston Herald*, December 25, 1959; *Boston Globe*, December 25, 1959; Blakeley, interview.

45. Blakeley, interview; Collins, interview.

46. Diary, December 29, 1959; January 7, 8, 12, 18, 22, 28, 29, April 22, 28, 29, May 12, 27, June 2, 15, July 6, August 10, September 22, 26, October 3, 27, November 2, 7, 30, December 9, 21, 1960; January 21, 23, 24, 25, June 20, July 7, 24, September 19, 26, 1961; January 27, July 17, September 18, 19, 28, October 16, November 17, 20, 1962; March 18, June 18, August 14, September 12, November 6, 26, 1963; January 6, March 17, April 22, June 16, November 17, December 15, 1964; March 16, 30, June 29, July 20, September 21, 1965; January 18, February 26, 1966; O'Connor, *Building a New Boston*, pp. 173–209.

47. Diary, May 25, 1966; January 9, 1967; November 24, 1970; *Boston Globe*, May 16, 1978.

CHAPTER 15

1. William W. Wolbach, interview by author, June 27, 1991; Diary, August 5, December 22, 1959; January 13, April 27, July 13, October 26, November 15, 1960; January 4, 11, 25, July 1, 11, 1961; January 2, February 6, March 22, 1962; April 17, July 15, 17, 24, September 4, 5, October 8, November 5, 8, 1963; February 5, March 31, April 10, 14, June 9, July 8, 29, September 14, 23, December 16, 31, 1964; January 4, April 2, May 19, October 13, 1965; January 5, February 8, 10,

March 21, 23, May 4, 1966; March 26, September 20, October 13, December 23, 1968; March 6, April 28, May 28, October 22, 31, 1969; January 27, February 17, April 6, June 21, 29, December 26, 1970; February 20, 24, 26, March 1, 3, 15, 17, 24, 26, April 12, 15, 1971; Boston Safe Deposit and Trust Company, 1965 Annual Report; Gerald W. Blakeley, interview by author, November 4, 1993; George Putnam, interview by author, May 24, 1994; "Staid Boston Trustee Tries a New Venture," *Business Week,* October 17, 1964, pp. 72–76; *Wall Street Journal,* January 5, April 14, 1965; August 28, 1978; February 13, July 27, 1981; "Boston Co.: A String of Matched Pearls," *Business Week,* February 6, 1971, pp. 36–40; *Boston Globe,* August 1, 1972; Beth McGoldrick, "The Boston Co.'s New Lease on Life," *Institutional Investor,* 21 (July 1987), pp. 129–134.

2. Diary, May 25, 27, November 1, 1965; April 27, 1966; 122d AR/LI, August 1, 1962; 123d AR/LI, August 1, 1963; 125th AR/LI, August 1, 1965; 126th AR/LI, August 1, 1966.

3. For information about WGBH's development during the 1960s, see the annual reports of the Trustee of the Lowell Institute and of the WGBH Educational Foundation, Inc.

4. Fiftieth Anniversary Report of the Harvard Class of 1912 (1962), p. 351; *New York Times,* June 1, 1965; Hartford Gunn, Oral History, "Public Television's Roots" Oral History Project MSS, State Historical Society of Wisconsin, box 2, folder 6, p. 26; Diary, October 25, 1965; June 3, 4, 7, 1966; David O. Ives to Charlotte Loring Lowell, June 6, 1978, Ralph Lowell MSS, 1970–1979 Correspondence box, Letters of Condolence folder.

5. Fiftieth Anniversary Report of the Harvard Class of 1912 (1962), p. 351; *Boston Globe,* May 16, 1978; Ralph Lowell, *Reminiscences* (New York: Columbia University Oral History Collection, 1964), p. 96.

6. "Boston," *Fortune,* February 1933, p. 29.

7. Hartford Gunn to E. Arthur Hungerford Jr., December 27, 1955, Records of Hartford Gunn, WGBH Archives, Correspondence, Metropolitan Educational Television Association, box cg 96, 1955–1956 folder.

8. *Boston Herald,* July 10, 1983.

9. Diary, August 9, 1964.

10. *Boston Herald American,* May 1, 1973; *Boston Globe,* May 1, 1973.

11. Lowell, *Reminiscences,* p. 23.

INDEX